CW01301594

Malimbus ibadanensis from an original painting by Martin Woodcock.

THE BIRDS OF NIGERIA

An annotated check-list

by

J. H. ELGOOD
AND
J. B. HEIGHAM
AMBERLEY M. MOORE
ANNE M. NASON
R. E. SHARLAND
N. J. SKINNER

B.O.U. Check-list No.4 (Second Edition)

British Ornithologists' Union, 1994
c/o The Natural History Museum, Tring, Herts HP23 6AP, UK

© British Ornithologists' Union 1981, 1994
Registered Charity No. 249877

Photographs: © I.G. Nason, A.P. Leventis, M.E. Gartshore, M. Dyer.

First Edition 1981
Second Edition 1994

ISBN 0-907446-16-7

Printed in Great Britain by Henry Ling Ltd., at the Dorset Press, Dorchester, Dorset

CONTENTS

Editor's Foreword	5
Preface	7
List of Figures and Colour Plates	12

Introduction
Review of previous work and literature	15
The Nigerian Environment	20
Migration	39
Breeding	45
General Points	57
Conservation in Nigeria	60
Acknowledgements	64

Systematic List
Non-passerines	71
Passerines	171

Appendix 1 – Analysis of Avian Families recorded in Nigeria	266
Appendix 2 – Published recoveries of birds ringed elsewhere and recovered within Nigeria up to the end of 1993	268
Appendix 3 – Recoveries of birds ringed in Nigeria and recovered elsewhere up to the end of 1993	270
Appendix 4 – Palaearctic migrants ringed in Nigeria (Sharland 1983)	271
Appendix 5 – New scientific names used in the Second Edition and the corresponding names used in the First Edition	273
Appendix 6 – New English names used in the Second Edition and the corresponding names used in the First Edition	275
Appendix 7 – Additional species not in the First Edition	277
Appendix 8 – The Conservation Strategy of the Nigerian Government	278
Gazetteer	279
References	282
Index of species	292
Index of genera	300
Index of English names	303

EDITOR'S FOREWORD

First Edition

This is the fourth in the series of check-lists being published by the British Ornithologists' Union and contains the largest number of species covered as yet for any one country. The same pattern has been followed as for its predecessors and the systematic treatment has been agreed between author and editor to follow Morony, Bock & Farrand (1975), the only exception being to divide the Accipitridae into more manageable subdivisions. The alphabetic treatment of genera and species used in the other check-lists of this series has again been followed.

Nigeria has a great potential to succeed in becoming in due course an industrialised nation, a success which inevitably brings with it a rapid change in huge areas of the environment, as the author points out. This check-list owes almost its whole compilation to the work by British ornithologists, most especially to the expatriates of recent years building on the firm foundations laid half a century or more ago by British naturalists. If Nigeria's total avifauna is to be maintained intact, it will be essential for the Nigerian himself to acquire an interest in the ornithology of his country, a point that the author, in his past capacity as a former Professor of Zoology at Ibadan, has been emphasizing for many years. The author's introduction and data presented here are the result of a long experience of Nigerian ornithology and should form a sound basis on which to assess changes in the bird populations of an important West African ornithological region, more especially for the Nigerian himself.

J.F. Monk.

Second Edition

This is the third of the successful check-list series to be revised and published by the British Ornithologists' Union. Its timing coincides with John Elgood's 85th year and he is to be congratulated on both accounts: so are the band of ornithologists who have compiled much of the new material. Special among these is Anne Nason who has been at the hub of its creation. The new edition contains information on many new species, particularly montane, that have been added to the Nigerian list within the last decade. New data on the status, breeding and migration of many species in the first edition have been included. Extra introductory chapters on co-operative and parasitic breeding, new maps and figures add much to the usefulness of the new edition. The inclusion of colour plates reflects the variety and richness of Nigerian habitats and will enable future workers to assess the inevitable changes that will occur to the environment as Nigeria continues to expand its industrial base. The colour plates of birds complement those of M.E.J. Gore illustrated in the 2nd Edition of the Gambian Check-list (No.3), include Elgood's *Malimbus ibadanensis* and beautifully illustrate other Nigerian avifauna. Welcome news is the formation of the Nigerian Conservation Foundation in 1982. If their conservation policy is effectively implemented, the Nigerian avifauna will be safeguarded for future generations to enjoy. The new edition highlights the importance of their work and it is hoped that it also will stimulate Nigerian ornithologists to study and conserve their avifauna and encourage long and short-term visitors to do the same; it will continue to be their authoritative source of information.

L.G. Grimes.

PREFACE

First Edition

For this check-list the over-riding circumstance has been the large number of species involved, approaching 850. For reasons of economy this number has necessitated a very condensed statement on each species, which it is hoped, nevertheless, gives a clear indication of numerical strength, habitat, distribution within the country, migration and breeding.

For numerical strength, only 5 terms have been employed: abundant, common, not uncommon, uncommon and rare. Such terms are subjective and another observer might disagree with the status assigned, though probably by a shift of not more than one point on the scale. The term rare implies less than 10 records (usually less than 5), while abundant implies either that the species is often met in large flocks or that in its preferred habitat it is met, without effort on the observer's part, in considerable profusion.

The statement on habitat has been difficult to compress, especially where widespread species may have somewhat different requirements in different areas. Most species can be designated as belonging to aquatic habitats, to forest or to savanna, while a few are montane. The vegetation belts first proposed by Keay (1949) have been much employed, not only in defining habitat, but also in describing the area of occurrence. Natural vegetation is seldom undisturbed, even in Reserves, so that the terms secondary forest, farmland and degraded savanna are used, as well as reference being made to urban and suburban habitats. Some species such as those associated with bare granitic hills (inselbergs) show strong preference for one habitat (stenotopic), while others are catholic in their choice (eurytopic).

In describing the area of a species' distribution, frequent use has been made of the division of the country by its Y-shaped river system, formed by the junction of the Benue with the Niger. This central junction, at Lokoja, divides the Niger into the Lower Niger from Lokoja south to the Delta, and the Middle Niger running northwest from Lokoja to Nigeria's western border. The Middle Niger and the Benue thus divide the country into northern and southern areas and the phrase 'north of the great rivers' has often been employed. Similarly the area enclosed by the Niger, Benin (formerly Dahomey) and the Atlantic has been denoted as the 'southwest' while that enclosed by the Benue, Lower Niger, Cameroon and the Atlantic has been called the 'southeast'. The name 'Tivland' (Gray 1965a) has sometimes been used for an area south of the Benue but north of the former Eastern Region, whose avifauna was discussed by Serle (1957). But the apparent distribution of many species is really only a reflection of the localities where serious ornithologists have worked and have published or sent me their findings.

A high proportion of the birds of Nigeria are migrant. About 150 species breed within the Palaearctic and 'winter' in Nigeria (PM). Their period of occurrence, whether on passage or overwintering is easily presented, and capture or recapture gives special extra information (Appendices 2 and 3). Intra-African migrants have been much more difficult to present briefly and adequately, and recourse to some of the terms used by Elgood, Fry & Dowsett (1973) has been employed where the migration pattern is clear. The distinction has been drawn between migrants within the country (Afm) as opposed to those that move at some season to outside the country (AfM). Some of this second category breed in Nigeria (AfM/B); others breed elsewhere (AfM/NB).

With regard to breeding it has emerged that relatively little is known about breeding seasons and behaviour even for some of the not uncommon species. Many of the resident breeding species – RB – have had to be classed as unproven breeders – R(B). Where only scant breeding data are available, these are presented in some detail, but where more is known the known breeding period has been indicated or said to be protracted or even continuous. For widespread species the latitudinal spread of the breeding localities has been shown by naming northernmost and most southerly places, but in the case of the latter, because the Atlantic coast is far from due west to east, distance from the coast is often given precedence over latitude.

Although care has been taken to accept only records that can be regarded as virtually certain it has not been necessary to exclude all but records of museum specimens. For one thing there are large tracts of the country in which almost no collecting has ever taken place and for another the mist-net and the camera have largely taken over from the gun in the last 25 years. The mist-net bird carefully examined and released, whether ringed or not, is regarded as certainly identified to species level, though unfortunately few have been placed in a subspecies. A satisfactory field photograph especially of larger species such as most predators, storks and the like has also been accepted for identification, for it is surprising how many large, easily identified pan-African species seem never to have been collected within Nigeria. On the other hand, species which could have been confused in the field, through small size or similarity to related species, and are unconfirmed by collected or netted birds, are shown in square brackets, and have not been assigned a reference number in the list. A very few species have been rejected (though previously included in the Nigerian avifauna) for the reasons given and also placed in square brackets and un-numbered.

Finally it may be remarked that the author spent almost 16 years (from 1949-1965) at Ibadan University and has revisited the country a number of times since, usually to places other than Ibadan and for periods up to 6 months. While at Ibadan, during University vacations, he was able to travel to most areas at least once and personally encountered nearly two-thirds of the species mentioned. These encounters have perhaps coloured, but hopefully not biased, his opinions on numerical strength and habitat preference.

Any check-list is almost certain to be out of date before it appears, so that a line has had to be drawn at the end of 1980; but a Postscript for important additional data has been added at the end of the systematic list.

Second Edition

Early in 1992 Dr Llewellyn Grimes informed me that the 1981 edition of *The Birds of Nigeria* had sold out and that, in consequence, a second updated Edition was being contemplated. He asked whether I would be prepared to undertake this task. My reply was that I would certainly want to be involved but that at my age I could not do it alone. Dr Grimes also said that it would be essential to illustrate this second edition with quality colour photographs comparable to those in Gore's Second Edition of *Birds of The Gambia*.

Shortly afterwards the opportunity arose to discuss the concept of a revised Nigerian checklist at a meeting of the West African Ornithological Society in Felixstowe in May 1992 with the result that a Working Group was set up, and later expanded, to comprise myself (Chairman), Anne Nason (Secretary), Bob Sharland (Treasurer), Jo Heigham, Neville Skinner and Amberley Moore. Later Neville became my deputy and did much of the final checking. Anne Nason had recently published an educational book (*Discovering Birds – An Introduction to the Birds of Nigeria*: Nature Conservation Bureau Ltd, 1992) illustrated with excellent photographs of birds taken in Nigeria by her husband Colonel Ian Nason. It was discovered that more of Col. Nason's photographs would be available to illustrate the second edition of the Check-list and later we were also able to select some from the fine collection of Tasso Leventis. Furthermore, Anne Nason with her experience in the use of computer technology in book production, was able to visit the printers Henry Ling of Dorchester with me to discuss how 'computer ready' copy could be best presented after Editorial revision. Anne subsequently took on the major role of word-processing and liaison between the various contributors, which has led to the production of this work.

The most important decision the Working Group took was to adopt the Sequence and Nomenclature of the *Birds of Africa* for the new Check-list. In 1981 there was no single pre-eminent authority to follow. The major works of both Bannerman and Mackworth-Praed & Grant were recognised. In addition the views of C.M.N. White (a great 'lumper', whereas the other two works were those of 'splitters') had also to be considered, especially in nomenclature. But the most important factor in determining the sequence was the Editor's (Dr. J.F. Monk) insistence that genera within a family and species within a genus be arranged alphabetically. Since this would have led to quite unacceptable arrangements in such groups as the Raptors and Ducks it was decided to subdivide these Families into Sub-Families and even Tribes to keep together such clearly related groups as Vultures within the Raptors and Geese within the Anatidae. With these problems in mind, it was decided for this edition to follow a single authority – *Birds of Africa* (BoA) – likely to be the standard work for African Birds for many years to come. Despite the difficulties that have arisen because BoA is not yet complete, we have had much help from those compiling the volumes still to appear, on the nomenclature and sequence of much of the Passerines – roughly our third and fourth 'quartiles'. The adoption of BoA sequence and nomenclature has necessitated a complete re-ordering and re-numbering of the birds and the loss of some familiar names, both scientific and English. To compensate, Appendices 5 and 6 contain respectively the list of new and old scientific and English names and the corresponding numbering of the species in both editions. All new species to the Nigerian List since the First Edition are given in Appendix 7.

The Systematic List of the the first edition has been revised by four contributors:

John Elgood	Quartile 1	Struthionidae-Scolopacidae
Amberley Moore	Quartile 2	Stercorariidae-Picidae
Neville Skinner	Quartile 3	Eurylaimidae-Sylviidae
Jo Heigham	Quartile 4	Muscicapidae-Corvidae

The total number of birds now treated is 883 numbered species, an increase of more than 50. Most of this increase represents new discoveries during the last decade but a few result from changes in taxonomy (i.e. 'splitting') and some from the substantiation of species formerly given square bracket status in the first edition. About a fifth are Palaearctic migrants.

Clearly the 'species by species' treatment occupies the bulk of any avian Check-list but the 1981 edition carried also a substantial Introduction featuring a Review of previous work and literature, the Nigerian Environment, Migration and Breeding, before the species treatment and ended with a series of appendices and indexes and also a Gazetteer and an extensive Reference List. Both these sections have been scrutinised to bring them up to date and a new index of specific trivial names has been added. I think it worth quoting from the concluding paragraph of the 1981 discussion of Previous Work and Literature:

"There are still, unhappily, no Nigerians to have made a contribution to the ornithology of their country other than in field support capacities and in museums". Also "the days of long staying expatriates is over". Both statements now need some qualification. The first ornithological articles by Nigerian scientists have appeared in *Malimbus* and elsewhere during the past decade and much more active participation must be encouraged. The formation and success of the Nigerian Conservation Foundation (NCF) has been largely due to its Founder and inspiration Chief S.L.Edu, who has been supported in this work by Tasso Leventis, a Trustee and Founder Member of the Organisation. Philip Hall, Technical Adviser to NCF and a British ornithologist resident in Nigeria, has played an important role in conservation, ornithology and training in Nigeria.

In another development, the former Nigerian Ornithological Society (NOS), started in 1964 by Hilary Fry (now heading the team producing *Birds of Africa*), Bob Sharland and myself, metamorphosed in 1979 to become the West African Ornithological Society. There is no doubt that West African ornithology, as a whole, benefited from this change with the publication in *Malimbus* of checklists of some West African territories for which no such treatment had existed previously. But the comparatively few (though very important) contributions made from within Nigeria reflect the 'low ebb' of Nigerian ornithology. It may be noted that the more exciting finds, like the discovery of *Picathartes* within Nigeria by John Ash, might not have happened but for the co-operation of former expatriate ornithologists on the one hand with, more importantly, the help of NCF on the ground.

The Section on the Nigerian Environment has been changed only a little, perhaps less than it should have been. The topography of Nigeria has not changed nor has its Geology but I did recruit the services of a geologist friend to ensure that the phraseology used had not fossilised unduly! When I asked Prof. Ronald Keay, whose opinions on African vegetation I had viewed as sacrosanct in 1981, his first comment, following a recent visit to Nigeria, was "There is no vegetation left in Nigeria"! Obviously I accepted that changes brought about by human factors had accelerated acutely. Not only had the Rain Forest Zone virtually ceased to exist except in the far east of the country, but also the various savanna zones had been so modified by extensive farming that their distinctiveness had largely disappeared. In the end, however, Prof. Keay very kindly revised this section and greatly helped by correcting the scientific names of the plant species mentioned where these had changed. There has been endless discussion on climatic change, not only in West Africa, and such phrases as global warming, cyclical change, Sahel drought are on everybody's lips.

The Section on Migration, together with Appendices on recoveries of ringed birds, was early entrusted to Bob Sharland. Sadly, Bob's leaving Nigeria more or less coincided with the appearance of the first edition in 1981, so that there has been relatively little updating to record. There are still no recoveries of Nigerian resident species a significant distance from their point of original capture. I did recapture a Village Weaver on the campus of Ahmadu Bello University, Zaria, where it had been ringed by Hilary Fry 10 years earlier, thus throwing a little light on the longevity of this species! Recently Dowsett (1993) has re-trapped a Bulbul after almost 19 years.

With regard to the Breeding Section, in addition to updating the statistics of the summary Tables, we have been fortunate to be able to strengthen this part by the addition of two essays by recognised experts on aspects of breeding which are of local significance in Nigera. The first of these is a contribution from Roger Wilkinson on Co-operative Breeding. This phenomenon, now recognised as occurring in many tropical birds, owes not a little to studies initiated within

Nigeria by Hilary Fry on colonies of the Red-throated Bee-eater *Merops bullocki*. The second essay on Parasitic Breeding, with particular reference to the Indigo Finches and their Waxbill hosts, is from Bob Payne. There are still a number of species presumed to breed in Nigeria that have yet to be proved to do so: workers still visiting Nigeria should note.

The section on Conservation has been completely re-written by Tasso Leventis and includes a new map showing the main National Parks, Game Reserves and surviving Forest Reserves (some partially converted to monocultural plantations). Due to the efforts of the Nigerian Conservation Foundation the framework of a sound conservation policy has been set up in co-operation with the Government of Nigeria, but the utmost vigilance and continuing effort will be required to implement it effectively.

Ornithology continues to offer a rich field for further study in Nigeria. One aspect is the importance of voice in field studies exemplified by the recognition of *C. dorsti* as a new and distinctive *Cisticola*. This could well lead the way to the discovery of yet more new species for Nigeria once the splendid tape recordings of Chappuis become more widely available to ornithologists. One thing is certain, this Check-list, like its predecessor, will be out of date almost as soon as it appears.

John H. Elgood
Flat 16
The Anchorage
157 Mudeford
Christchurch
Dorset
BH23 4AG
UK

LIST OF FIGURES

Figure 1. The main towns, topography and rivers of Nigeria.
Figure 2. The total annual rainfall distribution in Nigeria.
Figure 3. The length of the dry season: the number of months with negligible average rainfall in Nigeria.
Figure 4. The vegetation zones in Nigeria.
Figure 5. Patterns of migration within Nigeria (Motograms).
Figure 6. Diagram to show the difference between the number of migrant species wintering in the various vegetation zones of Nigeria.
Figure 7. The National Parks, Game Reserves, Forest Reserves and other conservation areas in Nigeria.

Cover: Red-throated Bee-eater. (M.E. Gartshore)

Frontispiece: Ibadan (Elgood's) Malimbe from an original painting by Martin Woodcock.

LIST OF COLOUR PLATES

Habitat

1. Mangrove swamp, Lekki Peninsula, near Lagos. (A.P. Leventis)
2. Sand dunes in the Sahel area, northern Yobe State. These plates illustrate the extreme range of habitats in Nigeria. (I.G. Nason)
3. Rainforest at the Kwa Falls, Oban Hills, southeastern Nigeria. (I.G. Nason)
4. Soil erosion following forest removal at Awka, near Onitsha in southern Nigeria. (I.G. Nason)
5. Montane grassland, the Obudu Plateau, southeast Nigeria. (A.P. Leventis)
6. Grassland meadow with montane forest in the valleys, the Obudu Plateau. (A.P. Leventis)
7. Gallery forest, Ogun River at Olokemeji; the habitat of Rock Pratincoles. (I.G. Nason)
8. Farmland in the Guinea Savanna belt near Jebba, central Nigeria. (I.G. Nason)
9. Riverbed in the dry season at the foot of the Jos Plateau, near Shendam. (I.G. Nason)
10. The escarpment of the Jos Plateau near Kagoro during the Harmattan season, with *Borassus* palms in the foreground. (I.G. Nason)
11. Inselberg and reservoir at Abuja, the Federal Capital, in central Nigeria. (I.G. Nason)
12. Guinea Savanna at Yankari National Park, with male waterbuck. (I.G. Nason)
13. River in the dry season near Serti, approaching the Mambilla Plateau. (I.G. Nason)
14. Degraded Sudan Savanna near Kano, with a Fulani cattle-herd on the move. (I.G. Nason)
15. The Hadejia Wetlands near Nguru with a flock of White-faced Whistling-Ducks in flight. (I.G. Nason)
16. The Hadejia Wetlands near Nguru at sunset; one of the most important wintering areas for Palaearctic migrants. (I.G. Nason)

Bird Plates

1. Great White Pelicans in the Hadejia Wetlands near Gorgoram with domestic cattle and Acacia forest in the background. (A.P. Leventis)
2. Cattle Egrets in full breeding plumage. (M.E. Gartshore)
3. Hadada on the floodplain of the Gaji River, Yankari National Park. (A.P. Leventis)
4. White-faced Whistling-Duck and Garganey, IITA. (I.G. Nason)
5. Male Pygmy Goose on the lake at IITA. (I.G. Nason)
6. White-backed Vulture above its nest in a *Borassus* palm at Yankari National Park. (I.G. Nason)
7. Bateleurs at Yankari National Park, showing both light and dark colour phases. (I.G. Nason)
8. Grasshopper Buzzard taking flight, Gorgoram, northeast Nigeria. (A.P. Leventis)
9. Fox Kestrel near Wase Rock, central Nigeria. (I.G. Nason)
10. Clapperton's Francolin, Sambisa G.R. (A.P.Leventis)
11. African Crake, Agenebode. (A.P. Leventis)
12. Allen's Gallinule, IITA, Ibadan. (A.P. Leventis)
13. Arabian Bustard near Bama. (A.P. Leventis)
14. & 15. Spotted Thick-knee in Acacia forest, Sahel-savanna zone, near Maiduguri (A.P. Leventis) and chicks near Zaria. (M.E. Gartshore)
16. Greater Painted-Snipe in rice paddies, IITA. (I.G. Nason)
17. White-crowned Plover, IITA, Ibadan. (I.G. Nason)
18. & 19. Egyptian Plover (left) and Grey Pratincole at IITA, Ibadan, where they appear as 'occasionals' when the Great Rivers are in flood. (I.G. Nason)
20. Rock Pratincoles on the Osse River, Ifon Forest Reserve. (A.P. Leventis)
21. Forbes' Plover in a fallow rice paddy at IITA, Ibadan. (I.G. Nason)
21. Cream-coloured Courser between Yusufari and the Bulatura oases. (A.P. Leventis)
23. & 24. Four-banded Sandgrouse, male (right) and female at Kainji Lake National Park. (I.G. Nason)
25. Female Namaqua Dove near Kano. (I.G. Nason)
26. Spotted Eagle Owl, the dark-eyed race *B. a. cinerascens*, near the Hadejia Wetlands Project Headquarters at Nguru. (I.G. Nason)
27. Standard-winged Nightjar on a laterite road near Idah, central Nigeria. (A.P. Leventis)
28. Grey-headed Kingfisher near Agenebode. (A.P.Leventis)
29. & 30. Adult Malachite Kingfisher (left) in the Hadejia Wetlands, and a black-billed juvenile on the Lekki Peninsula. (I.G. Nason)
31. Rosy Bee-eaters near nesting grounds, Kaduna River. (I.G. Nason)
32. Carmine Bee-eaters near Zaria. (M. Dyer)
33. Abyssinian Roller, Hadejia Wetlands. (I.G. Nason)
34. Vieillot's Barbet, northern Nigeria. (I.G. Nason)
35. White-crested Hornbill in degraded forest, Lekki Peninsula. (A.P. Leventis)
36. Gabon Woodpecker excavating nesthole, Lekki Peninsula, near Lagos. (I.G. Nason)
37. Plain-backed Pipit, Lekki Peninsula. (I.G. Nason)
38. Yellow-throated Longclaw, IITA, Ibadan. (I.G. Nason)
39. Northern Ant-eater Chat near Dagona. (I.G. Nason)
40. Rufous Scrub-Robin at its nest. (M.E. Gartshore)

41. Rufous-crowned Eremomela in the forest canopy, Okomu F.R. (A.P. Leventis)
42. Brown-throated Wattle-eye in a Lagos garden. (A.P. Leventis)
43. Red-headed Rockfowl on the nest in high forest near Bashu village, Kanyang/Sonkwala Mountains, S.E. Nigeria. (A.P. Leventis)
44. Beautiful Sunbird in a Kano garden. (A.P. Leventis)
45. Blue-eared Glossy Starling, Nguru. (I.G. Nason)
46. Yellow-billed Shrike in farmland, IITA, Ibadan. (I.G. Nason)
47. Red Bishop on farmland at Agenebode, south-central Nigeria. (A.P. Leventis)
48. Red-billed Fire-finch on the Jos Plateau. (A.P. Leventis)

INTRODUCTION

Review of Previous Work and Literature

Despite the size and importance of Nigeria, and excepting many papers in scientific journals, this check-list is the first work to be devoted exclusively and comprehensively to the birds of Nigeria. All previous books have dealt with the avifauna of West Africa as a whole, of which the most important have been: Swainson (2 Vols) 1837; Bates 1930; Bannerman (8 Vols) 1930-51, later presented in condensed form (2 Vols) 1953; Mackworth-Praed & Grant (Series III, 2 Vols) 1966 and 1973; Serle, Morel & Hartwig 1977, the only Field Guide and dealing with only about half of the species known to occur. At a more popular level, and of very limited scope, there have been Fairbairn (1952) on Game Birds and Elgood (1960) on Town and Garden Birds.

Bannerman's major work is somewhat discursive and it is therefore difficult sometimes to extract information on specific detail; but, nevertheless, it is both thorough and reliable to a very high degree, and it has therefore been taken as the base-line for this check-list. In only one or two cases has it been necessary to query his statements, which have in any case been largely derived from data supplied by others working in the field. Bannerman has given a brief summary of the ornithological work done prior to 1930 in each of the former British Colonies including Nigeria, and my own summary, below, is based on that section: but it has been necessary to omit the numerous workers that were exclusively concerned with the former British administered Cameroons which, until Nigeria's Independence in 1960, had formed an integral part of Nigeria. Although state political boundaries have no meaning in bio-geography, taking the present boundaries of Nigeria has the merit of setting limits for both inclusions and exclusions.

Bannerman's summary of work in Nigeria (Vol.I,1930) begins with a reference to the earliest ornithological expedition to the country, that of Denham and Clapperton (1822-24), whose names have been perpetuated in species of bustard and francolin respectively. Next Lewis Fraser, naturalist to the ill-fated Niger Expedition of 1841, is remembered in the generic name *Fraseria* of two species of forest flycatchers as well as in trivial names of a sunbird and a thrush. In 1882-3 W.A. Forbes was to journey up the Niger encountering every kind of difficulty and with an increasing health problem that was to end his life at Shonga; but we find his name attached to those of a plover and a bunting. At the turn of the century Dr. Ansorge collected over a thousand specimens from the area of the Lower Niger and has been remembered in a greenbul, a colourful estrildine and about a dozen subspecies. Robin Kemp working in the Niger Delta in 1905 had his name perpetuated in Kemp's Longbill *Macrosphenus kempi*. At the same period Boyd Alexander was making his celebrated journey 'from the Niger to the Nile' and contributed much to our knowledge of the birds of the Chad Basin, with local races of the Crested Lark and an Eremomela warbler named after him. While waiting for transport back to Britain at the end of the First World War W.P. Lowe made a noteworthy collection of birds of high forest at the Iju Waterworks outside Lagos. For several rare species Lowe's specimens remain almost the only records, though other more recent workers have had sightings or have netted individuals in the same area or in other forest enclaves. In the early 1920s G.L. Bates was travelling along the eastern (Cameroon) border to Lake Chad and beyond and incorporated his results in his most valuable *Handbook of the Birds of West Africa*, for 20 years until the completion of Bannerman, the only comprehensive work.

The years 1930-1951, during which the 8 Volumes of Bannerman were appearing (the second World War caused a break of 9 years between Vols V and VI), were very productive for Nigerian ornithology. Dr. W. Serle started collecting systematically in the north of the country, gaining field information and breeding data for many species. After the War a number of important workers came to the country. L.H. Brown worked for a while as an Agricultural Officer at Ilorin; S. Marchant was oil-prospecting in the southeast based at Owerri and P.I.R. Maclaren, who first introduced me to the Nigerian avifauna and who was to lose his life so tragically in Zambia, was able to get valuable information on shore birds while serving as a Fisheries Officer. Meanwhile Serle was persuading the Medical Authorities to send him to different areas to continue his ornithological observations; to Abeokuta in the southwest, next (unhappily from our present point of view) to Cameroon, and then to Enugu in the southeast. His data and papers have been freely quoted in the check-list. Surprisingly, in Bannerman's Preface to Vol VIII, devoted to additional information from the previous 2 decades, he only mentions Marchant and Serle, though in comments on the individual species he frequently quotes also not only Brown and Maclaren but also Ffoulkes-Roberts and R. Shuel. The latter, a Police Officer whose duties took him to Lokoja and Zaria, was one of the country's most important egg-collectors and providers of breeding data.

A noteworthy event was the formation in 1930 of the Nigerian Field Society and its quarterly journal has carried a number of important ornithological articles, such as F. Sander's papers on the birds of the Lagos area and several contributions from Sir Hugo Marshall and R.E. Sharland. The first two were at work before the completion of Bannerman, who quotes some of their findings, but I have found it necessary here to quote extensively from Sander's main contributions to the *Nigerian Field* in 1956 and 1957.

In quoting Bannerman I have not, as a rule, mentioned his source of information since Bannerman himself has given the necessary credit. For all work since the completion of Bannerman I have indicated the source of information either by direct reference to the quoted publication or, more often, by giving the initials of my informant, the latter mainly because the data has often been generously provided prior to its publication and not infrequently the information has been sent by more than one person and has subsequently appeared in more than one article.

The last 35 years have seen two major events of ornithological importance. First, in 1957 the then Federal Department of Agriculture became concerned that the Red-billed Quelea *Quelea quelea* might be a significant pest of grain crops, both of local farmers and of large scale rice and wheat schemes, along the northern border of Nigeria. I was asked to investigate, and went first to the Lake Chad basin northeastward from Maiduguri and subsequently to the extreme northwest corner beyond Sokoto. The problem was found to be formidable in the Chad area, but of little consequence in the northwest. The 2 main recommendations of my report were both implemented: a Control team based on Maiduguri was initiated, and a Research Fellowship was established for a postgraduate student in the Zoology Department of the University of Ibadan. This fellowship was awarded to the late Peter Ward, whose important and imaginative studies had repercussions well beyond the immediate *Quelea* problem. With breaks in Singapore and Britain, Ward was to continue work in this field until his sad death in Khartoum at the end of 1979. Quite apart from his *Quelea* work, Ward furnished field data for many birds and from many places within Nigeria as well as making a major contribution to an understanding of Palaearctic migrants in Nigeria.

The second major event was the inauguration of the Nigerian Ornithologists' Society in 1964, with myself, R.E. Sharland and C.H. Fry as the initiators. Despite sundry difficulties of editorship and production, the N.O.S. Bulletin appeared regularly until the Society metamorphosed in 1978 into the West African Ornithologists' Society with the Bulletin renamed *Malimbus*. In the early years, the Bulletin largely contained local avifaunal lists, with data on migration and breeding, just the material needed for the compilation of a check-list. The number of its contributors has been too great for full reference but their initials appear throughout the notes on the individual species and their identities are shown in the introduction to the Systematic List. Where the contribution has been regarded as of major importance, such as a first record for the country, formal reference has been given, but otherwise location, date and initials will make it posssible to trace the source from the N.O.S. Bulletin or *Malimbus*, if further details are sought.

For the first issue of the N.O.S. Bulletin (May 1964) I produced a provisional check-list of 814 species. In tabular form it showed habitat, whether sedentary or migratory, and gave an indication of abundance. Its chief merit was that it stimulated the Society's membership into adding to the faunal list and to produce new records of species listed as rare. This provisional list was superceded, with a somewhat confusing change to White's nomenclature, by a new list from R.H. Parker in 1968 (private circulation) with over 20 additions, largely Palaearctic migrants taken in mist-nets along the northern areas by R.E. Sharland in Kano and R.J. Dowsett and A.J. Hopson at Malamfatori. With the appearance of the West African volumes of Mackworth-Praed & Grant (1970,1973), yet further names were introduced for a number of species and a high proportion of English names were different from those used by Bannerman. In 1975 J.B. Heigham produced his *Comparative Nomenclature of Nigerian Birds for the Amateur* which not only greatly helped resolve the difficulties in both scientific and English names used by the 3 authorities but also added a few new species.

The N.O.S. Bulletin has been so important in the compilation of the present check-list as a successor to the above lists that some tribute needs to be paid to its succession of editors, all of whom have done far more for Nigerian ornithology than edit the journal. The first editor, based at Ahmadu Bello University, Zaria, was C.H. Fry. It was his willingness to undertake this task that made the launching of N.O.S. feasible and he retained editorship until his return to Britain in 1967. Fry's doctoral thesis on bee-eaters (Meropidae) has been the basis for much of the data on the members of this family. In addition his more general studies, first at Abeokuta, then at Zaria and while travelling widely in search of bee-eaters, have provided data for many more individual species. The next editor was J.A. Button, who, with only the facilities of a small grammar school at Ilaro, kept the journal going for the next 2 years until he too returned to Britain. An early mist-netter, Button made a special study of forest bulbuls and he has the special distinction of being the only person to date to have taken the nest and eggs of *Malimbus ibadanensis*, the only known bird endemic to Nigeria. The next editor was R.H. Parker, mentioned above, then Curator of the Zoology Museum at Ibadan University. At one time I had hoped to produce this check-list jointly with Parker, but its long gestation made this impossible and he too has now left Nigeria, after editing the Bulletin from 1969-1974. I am greatly indebted to Parker for access to the Museum's skin collection in 1972 and for keeping me informed about important accessions. In 1974 the editorship reverted to C.H. Fry, who at Aberdeen University kept the Bulletin going until its transformation into *Malimbus* in 1978. This, with the last 4 years of the Bulletin in a greatly improved format, has produced a steady flow of data suitable for the check-list. As a bonus to Nigerian ornithology, Fry has been able to send a succession of post-graduate students of Aberdeen University to work on various bird projects while based at Ahmadu Bello. B. Wood worked on *flava* wagtails and Dr. M. Dyer, and later Dr. H.Q.P. Crick, have extended Fry's own work on Bee-eaters.

Shortly before the establishment of the Nigerian Ornithologists' Society, F.C. Sibley had an all too temporary appointment to a lectureship in Zoology at Ibadan University. Between November 1959 and July 1961 he collected over 1000 bird skins, mainly in the Ibadan area and at the nearby Gambari Forest Reserve, but during vacation travel, often in my company, obtained specimens from such remote areas as Sokoto, the Chad Basin and the Obudu Plateau. At the last locality several new records for Nigeria were obtained despite the fact that Serle had collected extensively there nearly 20 years earlier. When through pressure of current work it became apparent that this collection was unlikely to be written up for publication Sibley very generously gave me his Field Journal, from which I have been able to extract collection dates and data on breeding condition.

The development of the mist-net has been a major factor in furthering ornithological research throughout the world, and in Nigeria, free from any restrictive need to hold a licence, many workers have been able to secure specimens quite literally in their own back gardens without recourse to the elaborate apparatus of earlier trapping stations. Quite apart from the mist-net's importance in migration studies it has revealed the presence of hitherto unsuspected shy species in forest areas, notably at Kagoro on the southern escarpment of the Jos Plateau, where a steadily growing number of small passerines are still being found 500 km north of the forest zone. Amongst many who have employed mist-nets, 3 deserve special mention: J.A. Broadbent at Ibadan, V.W. Smith at Vom and particularly R.E. Sharland at Kano. All concentrated on Palaearctic migrants, particularly the abundant *Motacilla flava* wagtails roosting in reed beds. Sharland's main roost in a midden just outside the old city walls at Kano was so unpleasant from the sheer quantity of ordure that only an enthusiastic amateur would ever have persisted over a succession of years. In addition Sharland has compiled an Annual Ringing Report, successively in the *Nigerian Field*, in the N.O.S. Bulletin and in *Malimbus*. The 21st Report, in the first issue of *Malimbus* (May 1979), shows almost 40,000 *flava* wagtails ringed, with enough retraps for the main passage routes and breeding areas to be clarified. Sedge Warbler, Garden Warbler, and Whitethroat all exceed the 2000 mark; non-passerines with significant numbers ringed are Ruff (600+), Wood Sandpiper (550+), Little Stint (350+) and Garganey (150+). For the Garganey there has been a remarkable recovery within Nigeria of a bird ringed in India (see Appendix 2).

Although ringers have tended to set mist-nets for Palaearctic migrants, over 15,000 intra-African birds have been ringed, but so far not a single bird has been recovered away from the original place of ringing.

Subsequent work and literature after 1981
Since the 1981 Check-List, some very important additions have been made to the Pan-African and to the West African rather than the Nigerian literature.

First and foremost is the major work, *Birds of Africa* in 8 volumes, still incomplete, very fully illustrated and which must remain the standard work on the region for the foreseeable future. It is perhaps inevitable that such a thorough work must take years to complete and in this case the untimely death of its first 'top' Editor, Leslie Brown, was a very severe blow to the project. But despite the fact that only 4 Volumes have so far been published it was decided that this work would follow *Birds of Africa* with regard to both Sequence and Nomenclature.

Very recently, in late 1993, two complementary works have appeared, both with R.J. Dowsett as first author, dealing with the birds of the Afrotropical and Malagasy Regions. The first volume, with A. Forbes-Watson as co-author, and entitled *Checklist of birds of the Afrotropical and Malagasy regions*; the second with F. Dowsett-Lemaire as co-author entitled *A Contribution to the distribution and taxonomy of Afrotropical and Malagasy birds*. Included in the second are 53 annotated checklists for each of the afrotropical countries from Aldabra to Zimbabwe, with Nigeria near the middle! How useful would this Nigeria checklist have been had it appeared near the start of this project instead of near its completion. But the disparities between the two lists would seem to be few!

From the West-African viewpoint the Journal *Malimbus*, between 1981 and 1994, has produced a steady stream of articles though, unhappily, few have had a Nigerian context, but data from adjacent countries, particularly with regard to records of migrants from the Palaearctic, have been noted and incorporated. Local lists, particularly from Conservation and Reserve areas such as Yankari, Gashaka-Gumti and the Oban Hills have provided much important data and not a few new species for Nigeria. The expeditions headed by John Ash, the Dowsetts and others, particularly to the areas near the Cameroon border, have all been reported in *Malimbus*.

Last, but not least, with a Nigerian context, mention must be made of Anne Nason's *Discovering Birds, An Introduction to the Birds of Nigeria*. The importance of this book is twofold. First it is written for 'the beginner', whether young or not so young, as it is from these recruits that the future of Nigerian Ornithology depends. In the second place it is in the quality of Ian Nason's photographs, of birds and their habitats, that the appeal of this book will largely lie. Most of the photographs in this revised Checklist are by Ian Nason and Tasso Leventis. They have set a standard to be emulated by other would-be bird photographers of Nigerian birds.

THE NIGERIAN ENVIRONMENT

For a proper understanding of the avifauna of Nigeria an outline of the country, its topography, geology and soils, climate and vegetation is necessary. The relationships of the various bird species with their habitats are complex and for the most part little understood, but a broad presentation of the environment follows.

The country has an area of about three-quarters of a million sq.km, about equal to that of France with the Benelux countries, or rather larger than Texas. It is bounded on 3 sides by the francophone countries of Benin (formerly Dahomey) to the west, Niger to the north and Cameroon to the east, while the extreme northeast borders Lake Chad, with Tchad on its further shores; and to the south is the Atlantic Ocean's Gulf of Guinea. The most southerly point, in the Niger Delta, lies at about 4°15′N, though the western coast near Lagos lies at about 6°30′N, while all the northern border lies close to 13°30′N. The southern half of the western border lies just west of 3°E, the northern half just west of 4°E. The eastern border, however, distorts the otherwise squarish shape by running nearly northeast from the coast near Calabar at 8°15′E to almost 15°E a little south of Lake Chad, and has a sharp kink due to the division of former British Cameroons, part of Nigeria prior to Independence in 1960, with the northern half of Cameroon remaining within Nigeria, while the southern half became incorporated in present day Cameroun. Modern Nigeria now comprises 30 States, each with its own capital.

TOPOGRAPHY

The country (Fig.1) as a whole slopes gently upward from the low coastal zone so that much of the northern half lies above 620 m (2000 ft), though the valleys of the great rivers, the Niger and the Benue, interrupt the ascent. In the northeast the land slopes down to the Chad basin and is traversed by the Komodugu-Gana river system. Similarly the Sokoto River and its tributaries dominate the northwest and these two northern river systems produce considerable wetlands of great ornithological importance to local birds and as reception areas for migrants from the Palaearctic. All the large rivers have extensive flood plains and the seasonal changes of water level expose sand banks of great importance to birds for both feeding and breeding, notably amongst the Charadriiformes.

There are no major mountain ranges within the confines of Nigeria, though in adjacent Cameroon there are extensive highlands along two thirds of the eastern border. Spurs from this mountain chain extend into Nigeria, notably at the Obudu and Mambilla Plateaux which are above 1540 m (5000 ft) and provide important montane mist forest and grassland avian habitats. In the centre of the country lies the Jos Plateau, most of which lies below the critical 1500 m (Moreau 1966) necessary for the formation of montane habitats and none of its more elevated peaks show montane vegetation or have any montane bird species. Nevertheless, the Jos Plateau has an important effect on the distribution of rainfall; its steep western and southern escarpments face the rain-bearing winds and carry a forest vegetation, locally not met with again southward for several hundred kilometres, that support a range of forest bird species so well separated from other populations that some may be expected to differentiate at least as subspecies. The Jos Plateau forms a watershed separating 3 river systems: the Kaduna River leading to the Niger, the Gongola leading to the Benue, and the Jemaare, a tributary of the Komodugu-Gana flowing to Lake Chad. All 3 flow in different directions from a small elevated area near Jos.

Between the rivers the land carries a vegetation depending on rainfall and soil conditions but broadly changing progressively from lush tropical forest in the south to arid thorn scrub in the north. The natural vegetation has been much altered by human influences, particularly in the north and south, while central areas, largely through tsetse infestation, are less heavily populated and have more natural areas.

GEOLOGY AND SOILS

The chief feature of the geology of Nigeria is the great gap between the Pre-Cambrian and Late-Mesozoic. The oldest rocks, the Pre-Cambrian granites, gneisses and schists – collectively known as the Basement Complex – form the surface of about half the total area, including all the more elevated parts. Rocks from the early and late Cretaceous are found in the valleys of the Niger, Benue and Sokoto Rivers. Tertiary rocks are found only in 3 well-separated main areas: Eocene deposits in the extreme northwest and also across the south; Pleistocene sands in the northeast from near Kano across to Lake Chad; while the whole of the coastal zone, but especially the Niger Delta, has recent (Quaternary) deposits. Quaternary sands are again found in much of the extreme north due to the current southward advance of the Sahara.

Areas where Basement Complex occurs are often obvious even to the layman by the fact that inselbergs may rise sharply several hundred feet above the general level. Inselbergs are typically rounded bare granite hills that through periodic splitting away of large surface sheets of rock maintain their bare surfaces, while pediments of rough rock pile up round the bases, frequently carrying a number of large trees. These inselbergs, particularly their bare rock surfaces, form the habitat for a number of highly stenotopic bird species such as *Caprimulgus tristigma*, *Tachymarptis aequatorialis*, *Hirundo fuligula*, *Myrmecocichla cinnamomeiventris* and *Cisticola aberrans*.

The nature of the soil is mainly determined by the character of the underlying rock, except where recent deposits are superimposed. Pedology has made rapid advance in recent years and soil classification in Nigeria has still not stabilised, but Vine (1949) distinguished 5 main types. The most important type, covering much of the country, is a reddish laterite soil with low humus content and fertility and subject to moderate to strong leaching. Locally, particularly on the lower slopes of hills, such soils give rise to concretionary ironstone deposits. The other types are much more local: the well drained, moderately leached soils with high humus content of montane areas; the yellow, excessively leached acid soils of the forest zone; the dark swamp soils of the mangroves and swamp forest, the former being markedly saline; and lastly the poorly drained clays alternating with dry sands in the Chad basin.

Though soil character is a major factor in determining the vegetation, its influence on the avifauna is usually only indirect, though some species such as *Emberiza tahapisi*, *Pterocles quadricinctus* and *Ptilopachus petrosus* favour concretionary ironstone areas.

CLIMATE

The climate of Nigeria depends on the seasonal movement of the Intertropical Front (Intertropical Convergence Zone), which runs approximately west to east, separating the Equatorial Maritime air mass from the Tropical Continental air

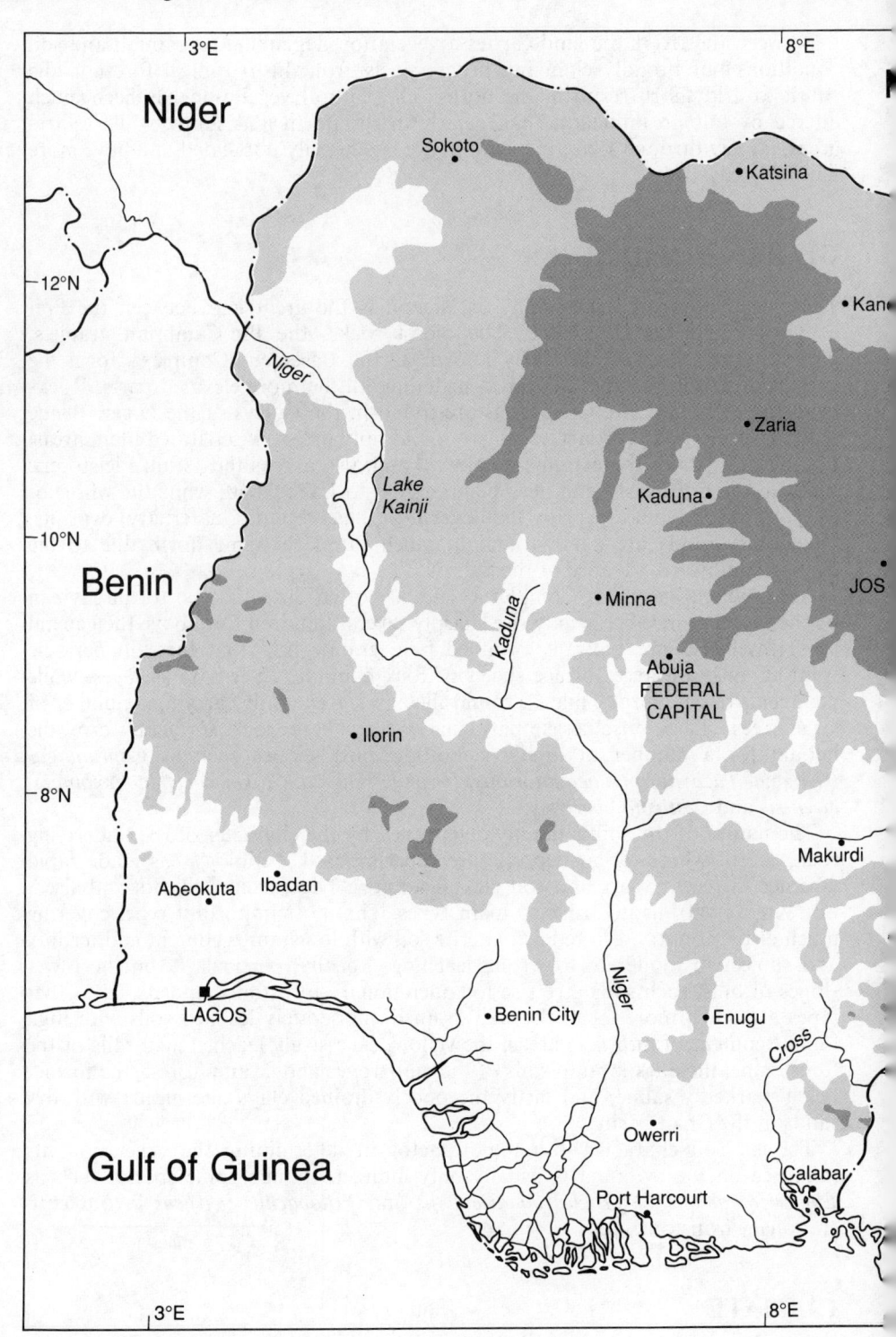

Figure 1. The main towns, topography and rivers of Nigeria.

The Nigerian Environment

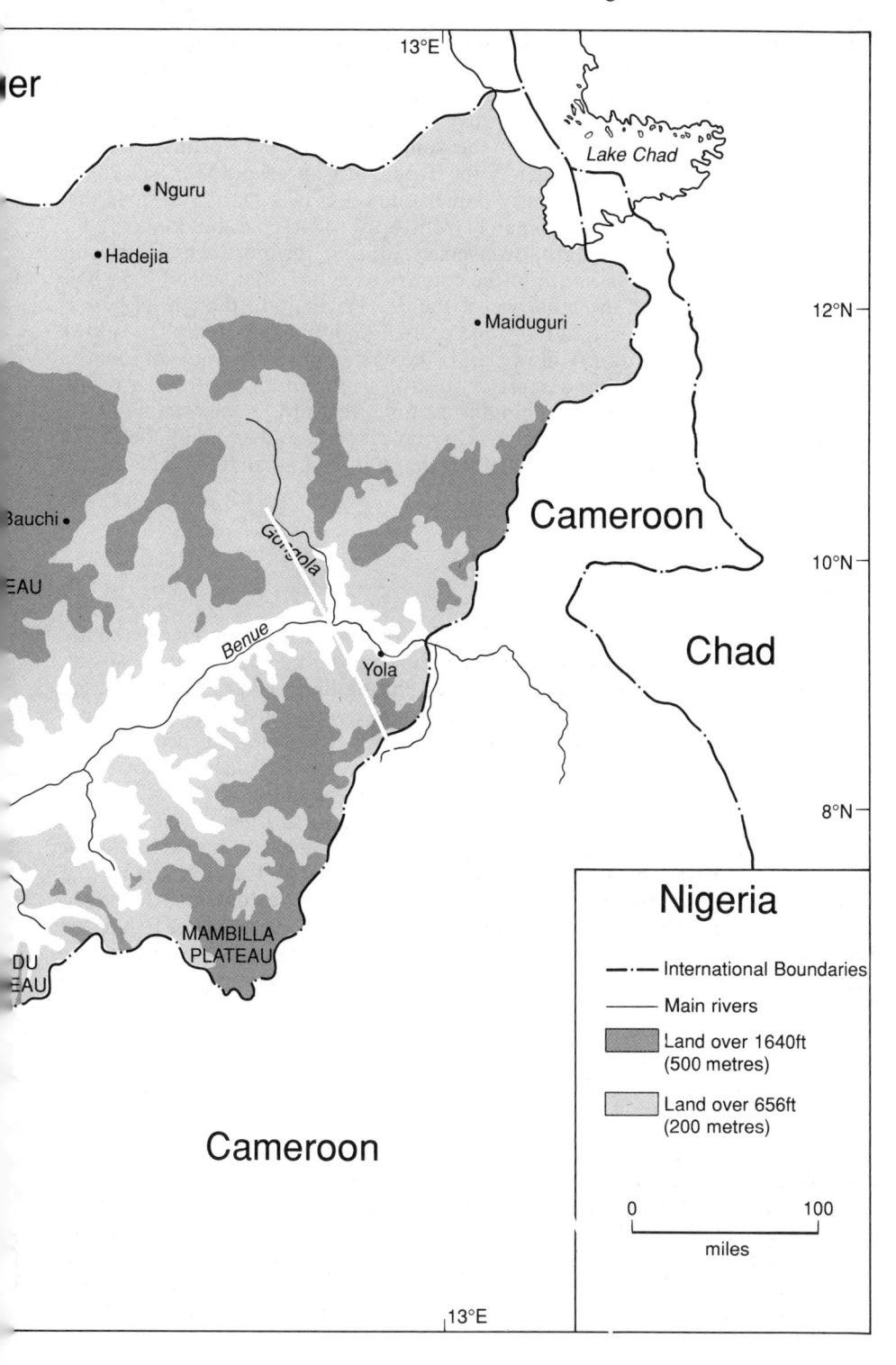

Nigeria

- ·—·— International Boundaries
- ——— Main rivers
- ▓ Land over 1640ft (500 metres)
- ░ Land over 656ft (200 metres)

0 — 100 miles

mass. The former is characterised by moist southwesterly winds coming from the Atlantic Ocean, while the latter produces the arid and dusty northeasterly wind blowing from the Sahara and known as the Harmattan.

The Intertropical Front moves approximately (but with a lag of 1-2 months) with the overhead noon position of the sun, so that at the northern summer solstice it lies, at ground level, near to the Tropic of Cancer and thus well to the north of Nigeria. The whole country is then subject to wet maritime winds that produce the rainy season, approximately from April to October, but longer in the south and shorter in the north. Conversely, during the northern winter, the Intertropical Front may lie south of the country over the Atlantic and the whole of Nigeria comes under the influence of the dry Harmattan, though its flow is very short lived at the coast and in some years does not occur at all. The overall climatic pattern of the country, however, is the changing length of the dry season with distance from the coast: a short dry season in the south lengthening northward to over 7 essentially rainless months, October to April, in the extreme north. The length of the dry season is a more important factor in determining the nature of the vegetational cover, and therefore the avifauna, than the total annual precipitation.

Winds

In general winds are light, Force 1-2 (Beaufort Scale) throughout the south, except briefly during the passage of line squalls bearing local thunderstorms, when gusts may reach Force 10. In the north, during the height of the Harmattan period, steady light winds of Force 3-4 may blow continuously for several days, but with little force at night, while in the wet season squalls may be accompanied by gusts often reaching Force 12. Line squalls are most frequent, and accompanied by the most severe gusts, at the beginning of the rains.

The effect of winds on birds in Nigeria are not great. The general lack of strong winds facilitates the diurnal build up of thermals, which are important to the flight of many predators, storks and some other large birds. It is noteworthy that in the south the Common Kestrel *Falco tinnunculus* is seldom able to hover, though it does so in the north when a steady Harmattan breeze blows. Exhausted Sooty Terns *Sterna fuscata* have been picked up as far inland as 100 km from the coast, though large-scale 'wrecks' as the result of on-shore storm winds, have not been reported.

Rainfall

As noted above, rainfall is the most important climatic factor, the year being divided into wet and dry seasons, the dry season becoming longer and more severe northward. Such a pattern has a high degree of predictability, but there is, nevertheless, much variability. Most of the rain falls during the passage of very local line squall storms, which are quite irregular and sudden. At Ibadan, for example (Smithies 1941), within a period of only 10 years, the highest monthly rainfall in one year occurred in every one of the 8 months from March to October. Similarly at Kano a heavy rain in April or October (or both) can obscure the normal picture of a 7-month dry season which usually includes both these months. It is noteworthy that since the total precipitation decreases from south to north so the variation from year to year becomes more marked.

Table 1. Rainfall regimes in Nigeria

STATION	Lat.	Alt. m asl	Jan	Feb	Mar	Apr	May	Jun	Jul	Aug	Sep	Oct	Nov	Dec	Total mm	Months Dry
BONNY	04°27'N	2 m	85	123	198	253	420	748	650	418	555	445	298	95	4288	0
CALABAR	04°58'N	55 m	40	75	153	213	313	400	442	398	420	308	185	45	2992	0
LAGOS	06°27'N	3 m	28	40	98	138	270	453	278	68	138	203	68	25	1807	0
ENUGU	06°27'N	240 m	**18**	25	65	148	258	280	193	168	315	243	53	**13**	1779	2
IBADAN	07°26'N	240 m	**10**	**23**	85	135	148	185	158	85	175	153	43	**10**	1210	3
ILORIN	08°26'N	370 m	**5**	**18**	60	98	168	188	135	135	238	153	30	**8**	1236	3
MINNA	09°37'N	275 m	**0**	**5**	18	60	148	183	210	283	308	150	**5**	**0**	1370	5
JOS	09°52'N	1300 m	**3**	**3**	25	85	198	225	323	293	210	40	**3**	**3**	1411	4
KADUNA	10°36'N	680 m	**0**	**3**	**13**	65	148	175	218	313	275	80	**5**	**0**	1295	5
ZARIA	11°06'N	670 m	**0**	**3**	**3**	45	115	160	218	315	218	33	**3**	**0**	1113	5
KANO	12°02'N	500 m	**0**	**0**	**3**	**10**	63	115	200	308	128	**13**	**0**	**0**	840	7
SOKOTO	13°01'N	360 m	**0**	**0**	**0**	**10**	50	88	145	233	143	**13**	**0**	**0**	682	7

Calculated from data in 'The Nigerian Handbook' (1953)

Months with less than 25 mm (= 1 in) have rainfall figures in bold type. Such months constitute the dry season.

Table 1 shows the monthly rainfall at 12 selected stations based on means over a period in excess of 30 years (except Zaria – 24 years). The data show that total precipitation decreases and length of the dry season increases with the distance from the coast. Both this Table and the rainfall maps (Fig. 2, Fig. 3) show the general picture of clear wet and dry seasons, the latter becoming progressively developed northward (see Fig. 3), with the elevated Jos Plateau interrupting the northward trend. For more recent climatic data see Griffiths (1972).

Fig. 2 shows the annual rainfall in the conventional manner, with the wettest areas on the southeast coast, the country becoming progressively more dry northward until at the northeast corner (with Sahel type vegetation) there is the lowest rainfall. A more meaningful demonstration of the increasing length of the dry season northward is provided (Fig. 3) by delimiting the areas where the number of months having less than 25 mm of rain are shown: the coastal southeast has no such month, while across the northern border the dry season is of 7 months, from October to April.

There is some evidence that rainfall has been diminishing over recent years, probably throughout the country. Hopkins (1962) remarked on this tendency in the south, though he could not be sure whether the trend was cyclical or a steady change due to human environmental influences. On the other hand the Sahel drought of the early 70s was thought not to have been cyclical but rather the result of long term climatic change associated with a southward march of the Sahara (incidentally accompanied by a southward expansion of some bird species). Some authorities challenge both views, believing that unpredictable fluctuation is responsible.

Table 1 also shows that the monthly rainfall at the first 6 listed stations, those south of the great rivers, has 2 peaks, typically in June and September, with an intervening period of reduced rainfall often called the 'little dry season'. This phenomenon is most marked at Lagos where September is, on average, less wet than October. By contrast north of the great rivers the stations show a single peak, typically in August, though again the effect of the elevated central Jos Plateau is to be noted, with Minna and Jos having peaks in September and July respectively.

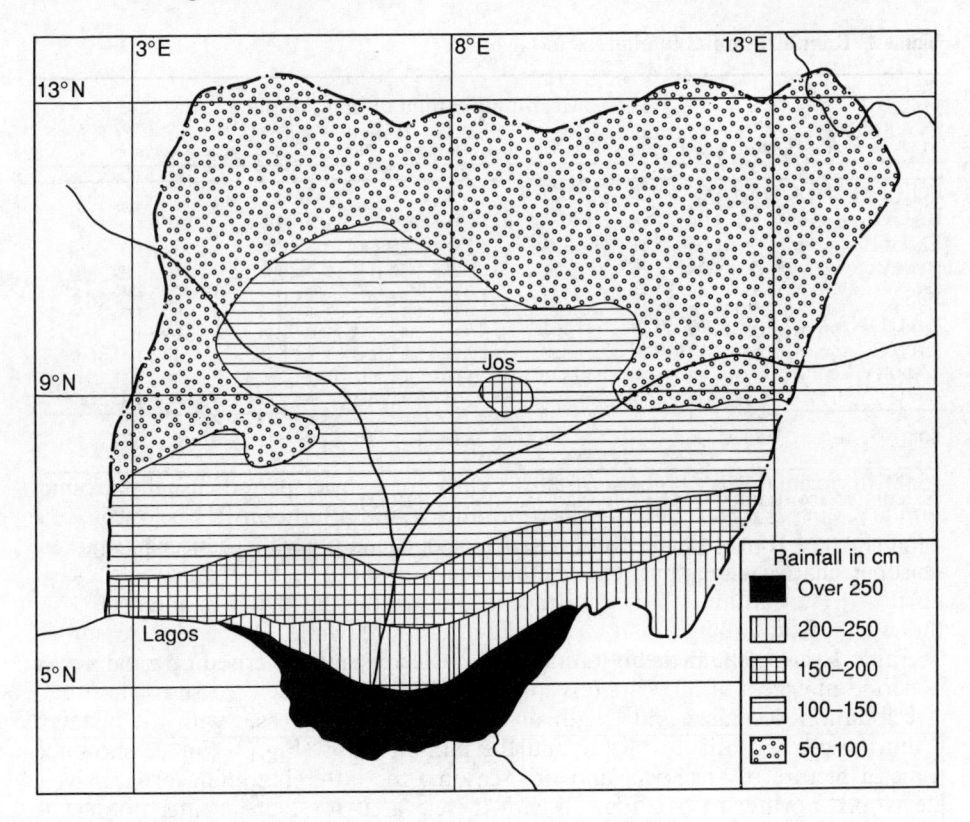

Figure 2. The total annual rainfall distribution in Nigeria.

Temperature

Temperature seems much less important than rainfall in determining the seasonality to which birds respond by breeding and migration. There are 2 broad generalisations that may be made with regard to temperature regimes: maximum temperatures, both mean and absolute, increase northward from the coast; and temperature range, again both diurnal mean and absolute, also increases from the coast northward.

Table 2 shows the temperature regime at some of the stations used in the rainfall analysis (Table 1). Data are not available for the others and Port Harcourt has been added to give a second coastal station – it lies near Bonny, though it is much less wet since it is situated on an estuary further from the ocean than Bonny.

In summary, temperature is subject to relatively little annual or diurnal variation on the coast, but progressively northward the temperature ranges become greater, though nowhere are they of a magnitude to have a major effect on the energy requirements of birds and thus on their seasonal behaviour patterns.

Humidity and cloud cover

Near the coast the maximum relative humidity (RH) is 95-100% from dusk to mid-morning throughout the year and the minimum in mid-afternoon (14.00-

Table 2. Temperature (°C) variations in Nigeria

STATION	Latitude	Mean Max	Mean Min	Range	Absolute Max	Absolute Min	Range
PORT HARCOURT	04°51'N	30.5	22.9	7.6	35.0	16.7	18.3
LAGOS	06°27'N	30.7	21.8	8.9	35.0	15.6	19.4
ENUGU	06°27'N	31.0	22.4	8.6	37.2	16.7	20.5
IBADAN	07°26'N	31.4	21.4	10.0	38.9	10.0	28.9
JOS	09°52'N	27.9	16.6	11.3	35.0	8.9	26.1
KADUNA	10°36'N	31.3	17.4	13.9	38.9	8.9	30.0
KANO	12°02'N	33.1	19.2	13.9	42.8	7.8	35.0
SOKOTO	13°01'N	35.3	20.9	14.4	43.3	8.3	35.0

15.00 hrs) remains as high as 70-80%. Only for a brief period, usually around January, does the Harmattan airflow produce a mid-afternoon RH below 50%.

Northward from the coast the RH decreases steadily and is subject to marked seasonal change depending on whether the wet southwesterly wind or the dry northeast Harmattan is blowing. In central areas the dawn RH is about 90% in the wet season falling to 70% in mid-afternoon, while in the dry season it averages about 45% at dawn to fall to near 30% by mid-afternoon. In the north

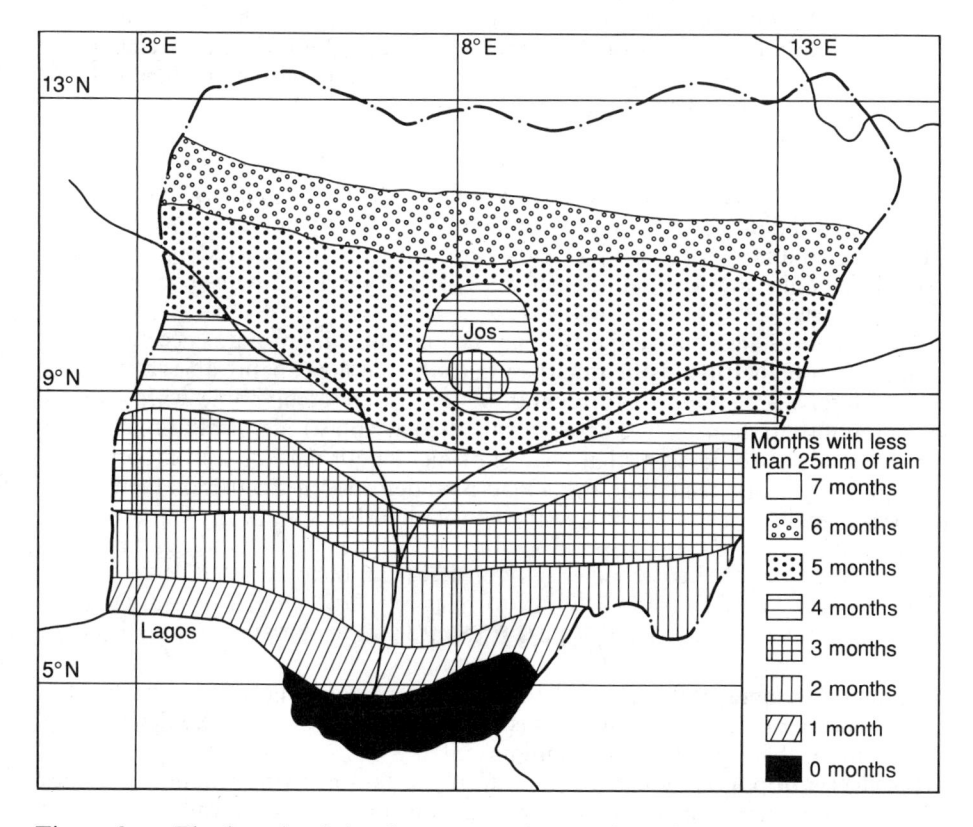

Figure 3. The length of the dry season: the number of months with negligible average rainfall in Nigeria.

the wet season RH values are similar to those of central areas but in the dry season the dawn RH averages about 35% to drop to as low as 12% in mid-afternoon.

For birds, the lower RH obtaining when temperatures are highest in mid-afternoon provides them with the necessary respiratory evaporational cooling. Nevertheless their activity tends to be reduced during the hottest part of the day and birds with open bills and rapid panting movements are then commonly observed. A further consequence of the RH regime is that early morning dew, an important source of drinking water for temperate zone birds, is a rare phenomenon, except in elevated areas.

In the south, cloud cover is high, almost continuous during the wetter months from April to October; while in the drier months cloud cover may be low in the afternoon, but tends to be total at night and for the earlier part of the morning. This blankets the ground against temperature change. In the north, even in the wet months from June to September, cloud is quite broken and in the other months there is little or no cloud cover so that the diurnal temperature range may be over 30°C. (See Table 2).

Day Length

A major feature of any tropical environment is the relatively constant length of day throughout the year, contrasting sharply with the long and short days of summer and winter in the temperate zone, where day length is an important factor determining the seasonal rhythms of birds. Both the total change of daylength and its rate of change are functions of latitude, but within Nigeria lying between about 4°N and 13°N these changes are quite small.

At 10°N, roughly the central latitude in Nigeria, the longest June day is 12 hours 43 minutes from sunrise to sunset, the shortest December day is 11 hours 33 minutes. The maximum difference in day length in one year is thus only 70 minutes and the rate of change (not quite uniform) is only about 2 mins per week. At 5°N, in southern Nigeria, these values are approximately halved at 35 minutes overall difference and c. 1 minute per week; at 13°N c. 90 minutes overall at c. 3 minutes per week.

These small changes, nevertheless, may well be quite important, since an animal with a much higher metabolic rate than that of Man is probably able to measure shorter intervals of time more accurately – an ability comparable with a bird's greater ability to discriminate between sounds that appear identical to the human ear. Even so, it would seem that change of day length may be less important in initiating migratory behaviour and gonad recrudescence in the tropics than in the temperate zone.

VEGETATION ZONES

Although environmental factors of topography, geology and climate have some direct bearing on bird distribution, it is their indirect effect in largely determining the nature of the vegetation that is important.

In Nigeria, topography has little effect on vegetation. Lying within the tropics there is no difference in insolation on opposite sides of hill or valley, and only along parts of the Cameroon border is altitude sufficient to produce montane types of vegetation, the Jos Plateau not being sufficiently elevated to do so. Soil differences, basically due to geology but leading to differences in texture and water retention and also changes in atmospheric humidities, are certainly of great importance in determining the nature of the vegetation; but the paramount primary factor, resulting in a progressive change from the lush forest of the south to the sparse thorn scrub of the north, is the diminishing total rainfall and the accompanying increasing length of the dry season. A comparison of the map of the vegetation zones (Fig 4.) with that of the length of the dry season (Fig 3.) shows a high degree of similarity.

The classification of the vegetation used below is based on that proposed by Keay (1949 and later editions in 1953, 1959 and 1965). Although modified in details in subsequent reviews, the classification and the delimitation of the various zones has remained substantially unchanged and has now been widely accepted. Only when Keay's classification is extrapolated into other parts of Africa are difficulties encountered, but that does not concern us here.

Broadly, Keay recognised Forest, Savanna and Montane vegetation as the 3 major types with subdivisions as shown below:

Forest	Mangrove Forest and Coastal Vegetation
	Freshwater Swamp Forest
	Lowland Rain Forest
	Derived Savanna (with relict forest)
Savanna	Southern Guinea Zone
	Northern Guinea Zone
	Sudan Zone
	The Sahel
Montane	Montane Forest
	Montane Grassland

Between the forest and the true savanna an area known as 'Derived Savanna' has been recognised. It is a mosaic of forest, farm, fallow and open savanna. The mainly savanna-like vegetation is due to human influences such as farming and regular burning; forest would quickly regenerate following removal of human influence. Understandably, it is not possible to draw a clearly defined boundary between Derived Savanna and that of the Southern Guinea zone. It is, however, a sufficiently distinct avian habitat for separate description below. Throughout all the vegetation zones there has been much destruction of forest and modification, especially in the past 50 years.

Aquatic vegetation has also been described separately and could be added to Keay's list.

Forest Vegetation

Mangrove Forest and Coastal Vegetation

The Nigerian coast is dominated by the Niger Delta, a maze of tidal, mainly brackish creeks and lagoons reaching up to 50 km inland. This system of waterways spreads along the entire coastline from Badagri to Calabar but in the

30 Vegetation Zones

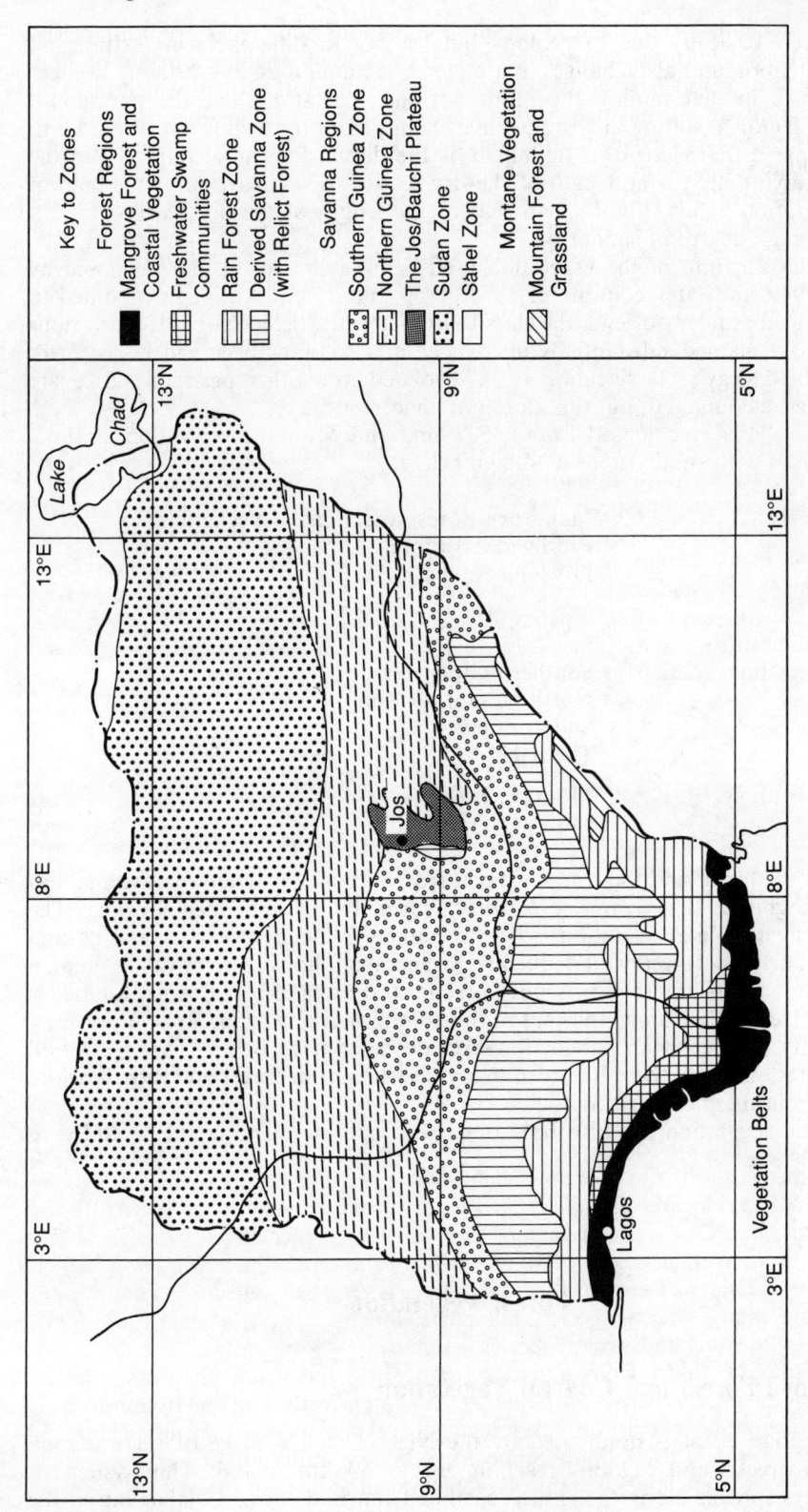

Figure 4. The vegetation zones in Nigeria.

west it extends less far inland. Typically the lagoons and creeks are bordered by Red Mangrove *Rhizophora racemosa*, a tree capable of reaching a height of 40 m and a girth of 2.5 m, and developing a mass of stilt roots around which blackish mud accumulates so that penetration on foot is almost impossible. Behind this, away from the creek edge, the predominant plant is White Mangrove *Avicennia germinans*, which seldom reaches 30 m and has finger-like aerial roots protruding vertically from the mud. Noteworthy also is the only fern to withstand brackish soil, *Acrostichum aureum*, often forming dense tangles. Larger birds, especially aquatics, are readily seen from a boat but too little is known of the small passerines since little mist-netting is possible. Conspicuous by voice or by a preference for the margins are African Blue Flycatcher *Elminia longicauda*, Brown-throated Wattle-Eye *Platysteira cyanea* and Oriole Warbler (Moho) *Hypergerus atriceps*. Conspicuous aquatics are Green-backed Heron *Butorides striatus*, the southern race of Hamerkop *Scopus umbretta minor* and seasonally a number of migrant waders from the Palaearctic.

Along sandy shores, which face the open ocean along much of the coast, is a strand vegetation with dominant shrubs such as *Conocarpus erectus* and *Hibiscus tiliaceus* and the trailing herb *Ipomaea pes-caprae*, while near fishing villages are plantations of the Coconut *Cocos nucifera*. Because of a very small tidal range (only c. 1 m at springs) combined with severe wave action, sandy shores are mostly steep, erosive and sterile and therefore avoided by birds. But where shallow shelving deposition beaches occur, as at the west of the harbour mouth at Lagos, they attract many marine birds, notably terns, some migrants from the Palaearctic and others from southern Africa.

Freshwater Swamp Forest

Inland from the coastal mangroves lies a belt of freshwater swamp forest. The zone is narrow, just recognisable in the west, widening towards the Niger Delta, where it reaches its maximum development, penetrating between the main channels of the river up to 100 km inland from the edges of the mangroves, which in that area also have a maximum width of zone. East of Port Harcourt there is no such continuous swamp forest, though patches occur locally. Because of flooded ground and water channels such terrain is very difficult to traverse on the ground; exploration is only possible by boat, where the water-edge communities of plants, and probably of birds also, are not typical of the swamp forest proper. On the open water are such floating plants as *Pistia*, *Salvinia*, *Azolla* and *Lemna* spp. Swards of the grass *Vossia cuspidata*, over 1 m high, form floating rafts at the channel edges but are rooted on the landward side. Sedges and *Pandanus* spp are also characteristic of the shoreline. Behind this is a deep zone of *Raphia* palms, notably *R. vinifera* and *R. hookeri*, 10-15 m in height. The main swamp forest composed largely of dicotyledonous trees is still further away from the open water, with an average height of 30 m. Many of these trees have stilt roots, which add to the difficulty of ground traverse. This is a very rich vegetation community, comprising many woody species, but characteristic are *Symphonia globulifera*, *Millettia griffoniana* and several species of *Ficus*.

The avifauna, apart from aquatics frequenting the water channels such as Hartlaub's Duck *Pteronetta hartlaubi*, is very imperfectly known. It comprises a mixture of aquatic and forest species but also some species that are seldom, if ever, met outside this habitat. Some little known rails and ibises, for which Nigerian records are sparse, are probably confined to swamp forest.

Lowland Rain Forest

Tropical rain forest is both the most complex and the most vulnerable of all plant communities; once destroyed it can never be fully restored, since some species become at least locally extinct.

In Nigeria, where the forest zone has long had a fairly dense human population, it is thought that no area carries true primary forest. Artefacts, such as remains of habitations, pottery and middens, together with the presence of the widely planted Oil-palm *Elaeis guineensis* and other species characteristic of secondary forest, afford evidence of former human occupation, though the degree of secondary modification is impossible to estimate. Where the forest has been long enough undisturbed for the restoration of the stratification typical of primary forest in equatorial Africa, the term 'high forest' has been used, avoiding the issue as to whether the vegetation is primary or secondary. In the last 30 years there has been a great reduction in high forest, partly through timber extraction, partly through clearance for plantations of such cash crops as banana, cocoa, rubber and oil-palm and also for the cultivation of exotic trees that, like teak, grow more swiftly than local timber trees. To a varying degree such areas of monoculture are 'biological deserts', almost devoid of birds. Teak in Nigeria, for example, is almost free from insect attack and at Ibadan less than 10 species of birds were encountered in teak plantations in 15 years.

It is possible to recognise moister types of forest in the south and drier types further north but the change is progressive, deciduous species occurring throughout, increasingly so northward, while the forest as a whole remains heavily foliaged at all seasons. Other differences are a gradual decrease in the continuity of the upper stratum, resulting from a change in the proportions of evergreen and deciduous trees, leading to various seasonal changes such as the time and duration of leaf fall. Since forest bird species are quite distinct from those of savanna, and since no distinction has been drawn by ornithologists between rain forest and dry forest species, this habitat differentiation has not been used here.

The somewhat idealised stratified structure of high forest is not always apparent. In many areas the vegetation seems to be a "chaotic muddle of trees of all sizes and shapes" (Keay 1949), but where high forest has been long undisturbed, 3 distinct tree strata can be discerned. The tallest stratum, comprised of the emergents which attain a height of over 40 m, include prominently most of the valuable timber trees such as *Khaya ivorensis* (African mahogany), *Milicia excelsa* (iroko), *Triplochiton scleroxylon* (obeche) and *Entandrophragma cylindricum* (Sapele). The crowns of these emergents tower above the general forest canopy and the bases of many develop strong buttresses. Trees of Sapele may reach a height of 60 m and present a girth measurement, above the buttresses, of 17 m.

The middle stratum of trees, with heights between 15 and 35 m, forms the continuous forest canopy. The number of species in this layer runs into hundreds and although locally some occur frequently enough to be regarded as characteristic, none shows the dominance of a few trees typical of temperate forests. Richards (1952) found 70 species with a girth of over 0.3 m in a plot of 1.5 hectares. This diversity is more pronounced in the moister rain forest than in the drier deciduous areas. Because of this diversity, typical species are difficult to select but include *Dialium guineense*, *Monodora tenuifolia*, *Cola* spp, *Sterculia* spp, *Hildegardia barteri* and *Terminalia* spp.

The third stratum, or understorey, comprises small trees with heights of 2-8 m. Again there is a wide variety of species present, but the families Anonaceae, Rubiaceae and Apocynaceae are prominent. What may be regarded as a fourth stratum consists of undershrubs and herbs; this is poorly developed in areas of

Plate 1. Mangrove swamp, Lekki Peninsula, near Lagos. (A. P. Leventis)

Plate 2. Sand dunes in the Sahel area, northern Yobe State. These plates illustrate the extreme range of habitats in Nigeria. (I. G. Nason)

Plate 3. Rainforest at the Kwa Falls, Oban Hills, southeastern Nigeria. (I. G. Nason)

Plate 4. Soil erosion following forest removal at Awka, near Onitsha in southern Nigeria. (I. G. Nason)

Plate 5. Montane grassland, the Obudu Plateau, southeast Nigeria. (A. P. Leventis)

Plate 6. Grassland meadow with montane forest in the valleys, the Obudu Plateau. (A. P. Leventis)

Plate 7. Gallery forest, Ogun River at Olokemeji; the habitat of Rock Pratincoles. (I. G. Nason)

Plate 8. Farmland in the Guinea Savanna belt south of Jebba, central Nigeria. (I. G. Nason)

Plate 9. Riverbed in the dry season at the foot of the Jos Plateau, near Shendam. (I. G. Nason)

Plate 10. The escarpment of the Jos Plateau near Kagoro during the Harmattan season, with *Borassus* palms in the foreground. (I. G. Nason)

Plate 11. Inselberg and reservoir at Abuja, the Federal Capital, in central Nigeria. (I. G. Nason)

Plate 12. Guinea Savanna at Yankari National Park, with male waterbuck. (I. G. Nason)

Plate 13. River in the dry season near Serti, approaching the Mambilla Plateau. (I. G. Nason)

Plate 14. Degraded Sudan Savanna near Kano, with a Fulani cattle-herd on the move. (I. G. Nason)

Plate 15. The Hadejia Wetlands near Nguru with a flock of White-faced Whistling-Ducks in flight. (I. G. Nason)

Plate 16. The Hadejia Wetlands near Nguru at sunset; one of the most important wintering areas for Palaearctic migrants. (I. G. Nason)

least disturbance because of the low light intensity at ground level and grasses are virtually absent from the forest.

All the tree strata carry an array of epiphytes (ferns and orchids) and lianas which, with the trees, present an extremely complex plant community and enough ecological niches for an avifauna of some 200 species (Elgood 1977), the majority showing preference for one or other of the vegetational strata. Non-passerine families with 10 or more species present are Capitonidae (barbets), Cuculidae (cuckoos) and Accipitridae (diurnal birds of prey), while important passerine taxa are Pycnonotidae (bulbuls) with over 20 species, Muscicapidae (*sensu latu*) (flycatchers) with over 15 species, Nectariniidae (sunbirds) and Sylviidae (warblers) each with over 10 species (Elgood 1977). This rich forest avifauna is gravely threatened by the rapid erosion of forest for the various reasons mentioned above. The so-called forest reserves such as Gambari (Elgood 1977) are regrettably used more for experimental purposes than for maintaining areas sacrosanct for the conservation of forest plants and animals.

Derived Savanna

Between the forest and true savanna lies a broad belt of country known as derived savanna and intrusive savanna. Although its north and south limits are far from closely defined, its greatest area is just east of the Lower Niger, where it is usually estimated to be 300 km wide from south to north. This zone owes its existence to farming and to fire and would revert to forest if protected from these agents. It is an area of shifting farming, a mosaic of plots of food crops such as yams, cassava and maize, leading, where farming has been abandoned, to all stages in forest regeneration from a light scrub to dense secondary forest which could come to approach high forest in time. There are also patches of relict high forest in areas which have been considered unsuitable for farming. When the forest is cleared, oil palms are left standing and are a feature of the derived savanna, their range more or less deciding that of the Palm-nut Vulture *Gypohierax angolensis*. Other trees with valuable fruits or of religious significance, such as *Bombax* spp and *Ceiba pentandra*, are also left and may reach immense size to form a significant feature of the landscape. This mixture of forest patches, relict and secondary, with open savanna-like country subject to regular (usually annual) burning, supports a mixed avifauna of forest and savanna forms, though only a few of the genuine forest species are found outside the relict or mature secondary forest patches, and of these it is chiefly the small, mainly passerine, forms that occur (Elgood & Sibley 1964). Larger species like hornbills, turacos and the Grey Parrot *Psittacus erithacus*, require larger tracts of continuous forest. As might be expected of a man-induced environment, of recent origin, there are no bird species peculiar to derived savanna.

Savanna

Ecologists are not agreed where the boundary should be drawn between the true or natural savanna and the derived savanna resulting from human influences. Some maintain there is little if any true savanna south of the great rivers, while others place the boundary much further south. The ecotone between grass-less forest and grassy savanna is sharp enough and some birds seem to prefer living at this interface, though not confined to it; but no such separation occurs between the derived and natural savannas, nor is there any clear demarcation between the

Guinea, Sudan and Sahel zones, still less between the Southern and Northern Guinea zones. Again many ecologists believe that at least the Southern Guinea zone is partly shaped by human factors. There is, however, clearly a gradual diminution of tree cover and tree height with the successive zones northward, leaves of woody plants tending to become smaller and the plants generally more xeromorphic and spiny. The true savanna presents not only a general picture of progressive change but also each zone has some plants, mainly trees, that are characteristic of that zone.

Through the savannas run the gallery or fringing forests. Even in the Sahel, provided some water continues for much of the year merely to pass through the sands of the river bed (rather than flow as surface water), river valleys always have a sufficiently lush vegetation to earn the title of gallery forest (*kurimi* in Hausa). The character of the gallery forest is different in each savanna zone, but an approximation could describe it as having many of the plants that occur in the wooded parts of the zone next further south, plus a great many peculiar to gallery forest, the deep moist soil of a river valley producing a more forest-like type of vegetation.

The converse is also true; where the soil is shallow (and particularly where it has an ironstone content) it will tend to be drier than average for its latitude and the character of the vegetation will take on that of the zone further north.

Southern Guinea Savanna

Much of the Southern Guinea zone has been degraded by farming, but in undisturbed areas its climax vegetation is a woodland of 13-17 m high trees comprising a mixture of mainly fire-tolerant trees with a few fire-tender species and with a compact grass cover between the trees usually about 2 m high, but locally up to 4 m. Three tree species are conspicuous: the useful timber tree *Daniellia oliveri*, Shea-butter *Vitellaria paradoxa* and the African Locust-bean *Parkia biglobosa*. Because of their economic importance, these are left undisturbed when the land is cleared for farming and the locust-bean may grow to a large tree, greatly liked by the Senegal Parrot *Poicephalus senegalus*. Where the water table is high the Fan-palm *Borassus aethiopum* becomes abundant and in the gallery forest are *Berlinia grandiflora*, *Terminalia* spp, *Pterocarpus santalinoides* and *Brachystegia eurycoma*. The tall grasses are mainly *Andropogon* spp, and *Hyparrhenia* spp. On stony hills and ironstone ridges the vegetation is of the type that characterises the next zone northward.

As can be seen from the map of the vegetation zones much of the Southern Guinea Savanna lies across the valleys of the great rivers.

Northern Guinea Savanna

The broad leaved woodland that forms the climax vegetation of the Northern Guinea zone is very like the 'miombo' or *Brachystegia* woodlands of much of eastern and southern Africa, though paradoxically, all species of *Brachystegia* are replaced by the closely related *Isoberlinia* spp, of which far and away the most important is *Isoberlinia doka*, so characteristic that these Northern Guinea woodlands are often called Doka or Doka Woodlands. Although *Vitellaria paradoxa* and *Parkia biglobosa* occur commonly, particularly near villages, *Daniellia oliveri* is quite uncommon, while *Isoberlinia doka*, virtually absent from the Southern Guinea zone, not only dominates the scene but also quickly regenerates over abandoned farmland. Also highly characteristic are *Uapaca somon* and *Combretum* spp, while gallery forest is characterised by the mahogany *Khaya senegalensis*, the palm *Raphia sudanica* and the large bamboo *Oxytenanthera abyssinica*. The grass seldom exceeds 1.7 m, but comprises species of the same genera as in the Southern Guinea zone. In both Guinea savannas tsetse have kept the human population relatively low, with less farming and more natural vegetation and the two zones are not so very different either in floristic composition or in the avifauna they support.

The Northern Guinea zone lies mainly well north of the great rivers and to the north of the Jos Plateau, though it comes well south of the middle Niger, southwest from Kainji Lake into the Borgu sector of the Kainji Lake National Park.

Sudan Savanna

The Sudan zone occupying all the northernmost areas except the extreme northeast, is heavily populated and farmed, at least in the more central areas, despite a 7-month dry season. Natural vegetation is characterised by thorny species with finely divided leaves such as *Acacia* spp, and *Ziziphus* spp, often spoken of as thorn scrub. The trees are seldom over 9 m and the grass cover just over 1 m, dominated by *Cenchrus* spp, grasses with long-awned fruits. In many areas the Dum-palm *Hyphaene thebaica*, recognised by its branching stems, is abundant. Although by no means confined to this zone the Baobab *Adansonia digitata* is common and around villages, through constant lopping for firewood, grows very much narrower and taller (up to 35 m) than it ever does when left alone. Until a programme of river dam construction was started about 20 years ago, few rivers in this area held surface water for more than half the year, usually June to December; nevertheless, their courses are marked by large trees notably of *Khaya senegalensis* and *Mitragyna inermis*, the latter sometimes forming thickets. On the dry shallow soils of the northwest a low shrubby vegetation occurs comprising *Combretum* spp, and *Gueira senegalensis*, with many other low bushes but few trees.

Sahel Savanna

There is only a very small area of the Sahel, in the extreme northeast along the western shore of Lake Chad and westward along the northern border for about 100 km, though it is generally held that this area is not typical Sahel because of the proximity of the Lake. During the dry season the prevalent Harmattan wind blows essentially from Lake Chad into this corner of Nigeria and the moisture it picks up at least ameliorates the very low humidity of the Harmattan winds with their drying effect, and at the same time appreciably lowers the temperature. During a brief visit to Malamfatori in mid March 1963, the maximum temperature each day did not exceed 35°C compared with over 40°C in Maiduguri 200 km south, the opposite of the general trend for maximum temperatures to increase northward.

In the Sahel, trees are quite patchily distributed and not much over 7 m in height, often flat topped. The most prevalent are *Acacia tortilis*, *A. senegal* and *A. seyal*, together with *Salvadora persica* and *Commiphora africana*. The most important shrubs are *Salvadora persica* (the fruits of which are important to Palaearctic migrants prior to northward migration in spring) and *Grewia* spp, while the grasses, chiefly *Cenchrus* spp, and *Aristidia stipoides*, form only a loose covering even at the height of the rains and reach a height of less than 1 m. Some areas have a much closer cover of the much taller wild *Sorghum* spp, up to 2 m high, cultivated types of which are an important local cereal crop, the grain of both the wild and cultivated types forming a major item in the diet of *Quelea quelea*, most of whose nesting colonies occur in this area. The Komodugu-Gana River, traversing the Sahel zone to flow into Lake Chad, has quite a dense tree cover along its banks, including *Hyphaene thebaica* and even *Mitragyna inermis*.

Much of the Nigerian Sahel is undulating, with wind blown sand dunes, locally stabilised by the *Acacia*, alternating with poorly draining clay pans, where the grasses predominate.

Although each savanna zone has some birds that are characteristic, seasonal movements of many savanna birds are such that the numbers limited to any single zone are very small. Nevertheless each zone has a few indicator species and also highly characteristic species of broadly occurring taxa such as Columbidae and *Lamprotornis* starlings.

Montane Vegetation

Montane areas only occur as spurs from the Cameroon Highlands that jut into Nigeria, notably the Obudu and Mambilla Plateaux, the only montane areas to have been explored ornithologically. Although parts of the Jos Plateau lie above 1650 m, which may be the minimum altitude for montane conditions, this area shows no signs of montane vegetation. It has been very largely denuded of any woody plants, since the local demand for timber for fire wood, pit props and for building has been massive as a result of a high population exploiting the mineral wealth of the plateau, especially its tin. It is doubtful, however, if there ever was any montane vegetation on the Jos Plateau.

At both Obudu and Mambilla Plateaux there are two main types of upland vegetation: forest and grassland with low shrubs. During the last 15 years the Mambilla Plateau has become more accessible and better known ornithologically. The Obudu Plateau has also yielded new species for Nigeria.

Montane Forest

Montane forest, forest above 1650 m, is very different from lowland forest. Because of high humidity and lower temperature, for much of the year there are many whole days on which the forest is shrouded in mist, giving it its appropriate other name of mist forest. The trees are 15-25 m high, and their canopies do not meet to exclude light at ground level, so that a lush low vegetation is found, in which the tree fern *Cyathea manniana* is the most noteworthy, as generally they do not occur in lowland forest in Africa. The tree species are numerous but those most commonly occurring are *Polyscias fulva*, *Entandrophragma angolense*, *Schefflera* spp, and *Ficus* spp. The tree trunks are covered in epiphytic plants such as orchids and begonias and, most obviously, quite large mosses; but lianas are much less evident than in lowland forest. Today most of the forest lies in valleys, the grassland occurring on the rolling hills between, separated by a well defined ecotone favoured by several small birds such as *Nesocharis shelleyi* and montane sunbirds. There is evidence, however, that formerly the hill tops were also forested and the savanna-like grassland owes its existence to human influences, fire and grazing of livestock, in much the same way as in lowland derived savanna.

Montane Grassland

Nowhere in Nigeria is there any primary montane grassland, to be found elsewhere in Africa at a much higher altitude above the tree line. In the secondary vegetation of the plateaux hill tops the grasses grow in tussocks for the most part and seldom exceed 0.6 m, one of the most common being *Andropogon distachyus*. The grasslands also carry many herbaceous or low shrubby plants, many with temperate zone affinities, such as brackens *Pteridium* spp, brambles *Rubus* spp, and such Compositae as *Helichrysum* spp, ('everlasting' plants), *Coreopsis monticola* and a blue-flowered lettuce *Lactuca capensis*. Conspicuous also are giant lobelias, up to 2 m high (*Lobelia columnaris*), found also in montane areas of eastern Africa.

Aquatic Environments

Mention has already been made of marine environments in discussing coastal vegetation. The absence of rocky shores and cliffs limits the number of marine bird species. On the other hand freshwater environments are found throughout the country, with major and minor rivers, natural lakes varying from the small up to Lake Chad in size, and recently man-made lakes from the small village fish pond to the huge Lake Kainji.

The major rivers for the most part flow through broad valleys which usually have seasonal flooding, producing large areas of wetlands of great importance to aquatic and other birds. Although the major rivers are perennial, the water levels and flow rates can be very different at different seasons. At the season of low water level, usually January to June, large sand banks appear that afford feeding facilities for many aquatic birds and also breeding grounds not only for shore birds such as pratincoles and skimmers but also for more terrestrial birds like the bee-eaters *Merops malimbicus* and *M. nubicus*. Major tributary rivers such as the Sokoto, Kaduna and Gongola are only perennial in their lower reaches, flowing through rocky gorges in the middle reaches and in some places continuing to flow only through sand deposits in their beds, entirely lacking surface flow. All the smaller rivers, except for some in the wetter parts of the south, become a series of isolated pools for many of the dry months, with not even hidden flow through sand. Such changes in the rivers lead inevitably to local seasonal movement not only of aquatic birds but also of terrestrial species that require drinking water.

Special mention must be made of Lake Chad. Not only did it greatly diminish during the Quaternary Period, shrinking considerably compared with 'Mega Chad' of the Pleistocene, but in addition, during the last 30 years it has rapidly contracted still further. It has altered its character by division into two basins through extension of the Baga Peninsula, a sand spit on the Nigerian west shore.

The southern basin, receiving water from the Shari River, still provides a large area of open water, but the northern basin, fed by the Komodugu-Gana, may now lack any open water in some years. There are two possible reasons for this: a decrease in total precipitation in the area – the 'Sahel Drought'; or the effect of dam construction on the Kano and Jemaare Rivers, major tributaries of the Komodugu-Gana.

Lake Chad seems to be a focal point for Palaearctic migrants, with major concentrations in spring prior to trans-Sahara migration of such birds as Sand Martin *Riparia riparia* and several *Acrocephalus* warblers. Similarly in autumn it is a target for innumerable immigrants, notably waders and ducks, but also for many small passerines. Despite its present contraction and change of general character it will probably long remain a focus for migrant birds as well as a major breeding area for African species of herons, cormorants, ibises and smaller aquatic birds.

Man-made lakes have become increasingly important during the last 35 years. The outstanding achievement has been the damming of the Niger to form Lake Kainji, which has already attracted numerous terns and gulls, including the Palaearctic migrant Black-headed Gull *Larus ridibundus* and the generally similar African breeding Grey-headed Gull *L. cirrocephalus* and even the usually strictly marine Pomarine Skua *Stercorarius pomarinus*. Similar large dams have been made to meet the needs of the large towns for drinking water, such as Lake Asijere on the Oshun River for Ibadan and on the Kano River, Lake Tiga, which also furnishes irrigation water for large areas of dry season wheat production. The seasonal drop in water level, to uncover progressively rich muddy shores, in innumerable reservoirs throughout the country, almost exactly coincides with the season during which waders migrant from the Palaearctic are present.

Aquatic Vegetation

In general, aquatic vegetation is very similar to the temperate zone equivalent. The dominant peripheral plants on natural and man-made lakes are grasses, including *Phragmites* (reed), sedges, with *Cyperus papyrus* (papyrus) noteworthy, though uncommon away from Lake Chad, and *Typha* spp (reed mace). Similar plants occur at the margins of the rivers, often backed by tangles of shrubs, such as *Mimosa pigra*, used to support the nests of *Euplectes* spp. As the dry season advances and muddy lake shores become exposed, they become overgrown with massive knot-grasses (*Polygonum* spp) and other herbaceous plants, but the shores are often used by local people for vegetable crops. In shallow water plants are rooted in the mud below, the most conspicuous being water-lilies *Nymphae* spp, and pond weeds *Potamogeton* spp, such areas being inhabited by Jacanidae and the African Pygmy Goose *Nettapus auritus*. Further out from the shore line are free-floating plants, though they do not reach far into open water in the centres of lakes and reservoirs. These floating plants, *Pistia*, *Salvinia*, etc. have already been mentioned in the section on fresh-water swamp vegetation.

MIGRATION

The geographical position of Nigeria is important in that it lies south of western Europe, bounded on the south by the Atlantic Ocean, an insuperable barrier to terrestrial birds, and to the north by the Sahara Desert, an effective barrier to movement for many birds. Despite the inhospitable Sahara, about 170 of Nigeria's 883 species (19%) cross it southward after breeding in Palaearctic Europe or Asia and having 'wintered' in Africa, return to their breeding grounds the following spring. Of the African breeding populations, many savanna species will move seasonally north or south, between the barriers of ocean and desert, as the result of the alternation of wet and dry seasons, perhaps in very wet years rather more individuals than usual moving north and in very dry years more moving south. This may well account for some of the conflicting data and in future a closer watch for correlation between extreme movements and weather conditions could be rewarding. Similarly aquatic species will be forced to move, particularly in years of less than average rainfall, from drying wetlands, but their movements may be less orientated than those of terrestrial birds and directed merely to the nearest suitable habitat. Of the 720 species breeding within Africa, about 115 (16%) show dramatic annual migration patterns and at least as many again show local movements. On the other hand forest species are more or less stationary, the forest zone having a much less pronounced alternation of wet and dry seasons than the savannas, resulting in environmental conditions productive of a relatively constant food supply. Similarly, montane species find conditions in surrounding lowlands hostile enough to isolate them permanently on their upland physiological islands.

A further sedentary group, from the savanna, needs mentioning. Within the savannas, apart from those of the far northeast, the granitic outcrops known as inselbergs, often rising several hundred metres above the plain, are closely associated with about 10 savanna species at all seasons, though some, like the Fox Kestrel *Falco alopex*, may range well away from the inselberg to secure prey. Inselbergs are also important breeding areas for Great White Pelican *Pelecanus onocrotalus* and Ruppell's Griffon *Gyps rueppellii*.

Ringing in Nigeria was initiated about 35 years ago by R.E. Sharland and has proved of great importance. Although there has been a tendency to concentrate on Palaearctic migrants (over 55,000 birds of over 80 species), over 15,000 of about 250 Afrotropical species have also been ringed, but to date no African bird has been re-trapped away from its place of original ringing (R.E. Sharland). Although no light has thus been thrown on intra-African migration, some recaptures have given useful information on longevity: Laughing Dove *Streptopelia senegalensis* 2444 days, Little Greenbul *Andropadus virens* 3079 days, White-throated Greenbul *Phyllastrephus albigularis* 2402 days, Common Bulbul *Pycnonotus barbatus* 19 years, Grey-headed Bristlebill *Bleda canicapilla* 3078 days, Forest Robin *Stiphrornis erythrothorax* 1408 days, Olive Green Camaroptera *Camaroptera chloronata* 1519 days, Moloney's Illadopsis *Illadopsis fulvescens* 1134 days, Village Weaver *Ploceus cucullatus* 8 years and Blue-bill *Spermophaga haematina* 2792 days.

The whole problem of intra-African migration in Nigeria was reviewed by Elgood, Fry & Dowsett (1973), and since then many local observers have produced data which will prompt some revision of their conclusions, but the general picture remains unchanged. Some new data and a reconsideration of former information have led to a more conservative assessment of migratory status of some species. Elgood *et al.* (1973) attempted to clarify the various patterns of intra-African migration by producing diagrams showing the seasonal presence or absence of birds from the various vegetation zones, which they called 'motograms'. They also used the terms 'hump-back(ed) bridge' (which is what one

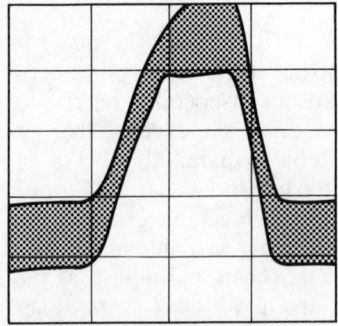

Full migration: breeding and non-breeding ranges exclusive.

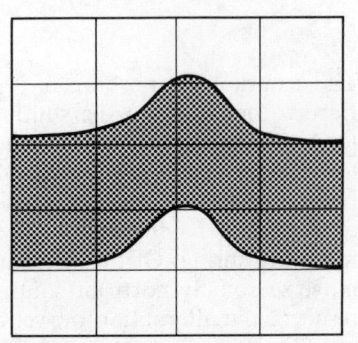

Shift to north during rains: 'hump-back bridge' pattern.

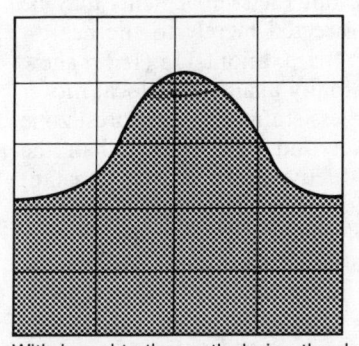

Withdrawal to the south during the dry season: 'southern concertina' pattern.

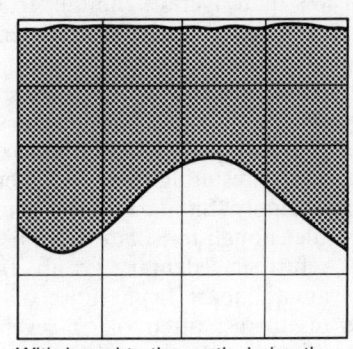

Withdrawal to the north during the rains: 'northern concertina' pattern.

Figure 5. Patterns of migration within Nigeria (Motograms).

> Vertical divisions represent latitude intervals corresponding approximately with Forest, Derived savanna, Guinea, Sudan and Sahel zones.
> Horizontal divisions represent seasonal intervals: Jan-Mar, Apr-Jun, Jul-Sep, Oct-Dec.

type of migration pattern resembled on the motogram) and either northern or southern 'concertina' movement for species whose populations were centred respectively in the north or the south, but expanded seasonally to occupy the whole country. Fig. 5 illustrates idealised motograms (though individual species always show some minor variations) and these terms have been used to describe succinctly the migration patterns of individual species in the systematic list.

Palaearctic Migrants

Of Nigeria's 880 or so bird species about 170 (19%) move to the Palaearctic to breed. Of these migrants, about one third are aquatics, mainly waders and ducks, about another third are small passerines, while the rest are marine birds (gulls, terns and skuas), predators (accipiters, falcons and owls), and a group of other non-passerines (swifts, nightjars, cuckoos, etc.), in nearly equal proportions. Palaearctic migrants to Nigeria were reviewed by Elgood, Sharland & Ward (1966) and little change in their status and duration of stay in Africa has been noted since, though much else has been learned and nearly 40 extra species have been recorded since then, mostly marine birds (Wallace 1973) and small passerines taken in mist-nests. The general migratory behaviour of these Palaearctic species, their provenance, their migratory routes and general ecology while in Africa have become much better known as a result of the two major pan-African treatments of Moreau (1966, 1972); while the extensive ringing programme within Nigeria has resulted in sufficient recaptures at least to suggest the routes or the breeding destinations of several species. R.E. Sharland found a huge roost of *Motacilla flava* in reed beds bordering a large midden just outside the old city walls at Kano. With workers mist-netting in other localities, notably V.W. Smith at Vom and J.A. Broadbent at Ibadan, almost 40,000 *flava* wagtails have now been netted for ringing. Of these many have been trapped again north of the Sahara from Morocco to Libya in north Africa, in Mediterranean Islands from Malta to Crete and in most countries of central and eastern Europe; but almost 30% of all recaptures are from Italy, surely due more to indiscriminate shooting there of all small birds than to Italy being a major breeding area for Nigerian Palaearctic visitors (see Appendix 3). There is also a growing number of birds ringed on their Palaearctic breeding grounds that have been retaken in Nigeria. Often, however, the more interesting birds retrapped in Nigeria are those taken again in subsequent years. These show conclusively that an individual may be as faithful to its African wintering grounds as to its Palaearctic breeding area. Data on retrapped *flava* wagtails to illustrate this are presented in Table 3.

Appendix 2 lists the places of ringing and recapture of selected Palaearctic species and summarises the data for species, like *Motacilla flava*, for which a full tabulation would be too cumbersome. Sharland has produced Annual Ringing Reports which not only show the full details of all recaptures but also the numbers of each species ringed, both Palaearctic and African. In addition Appendix 4 shows the numbers of the 80 or more Palaearctic species ringed and throws an interesting light on the relative abundance of related species-for example of *Phylloscopus* warblers, with *P. trochilus* 1,009 ringed, *P. sibilatrix* 188, *P. collybita* 6 and *P. bonelli* 27.

Table 3. Live recoveries of *Motacilla flava* ringed in Nigeria and retrapped at their place of ringing up to the time work at Vom ceased in 1969

		Data from Kano (RES)	Data from Vom (VWS)
Retrapped after	1 year	360	126
	2 years	148	51
	3	44	16
	4	14	4
	5	4	1
	6	—	—
	7	1	—
Total retrapped		571	198
Total ringed		12,580	12,086

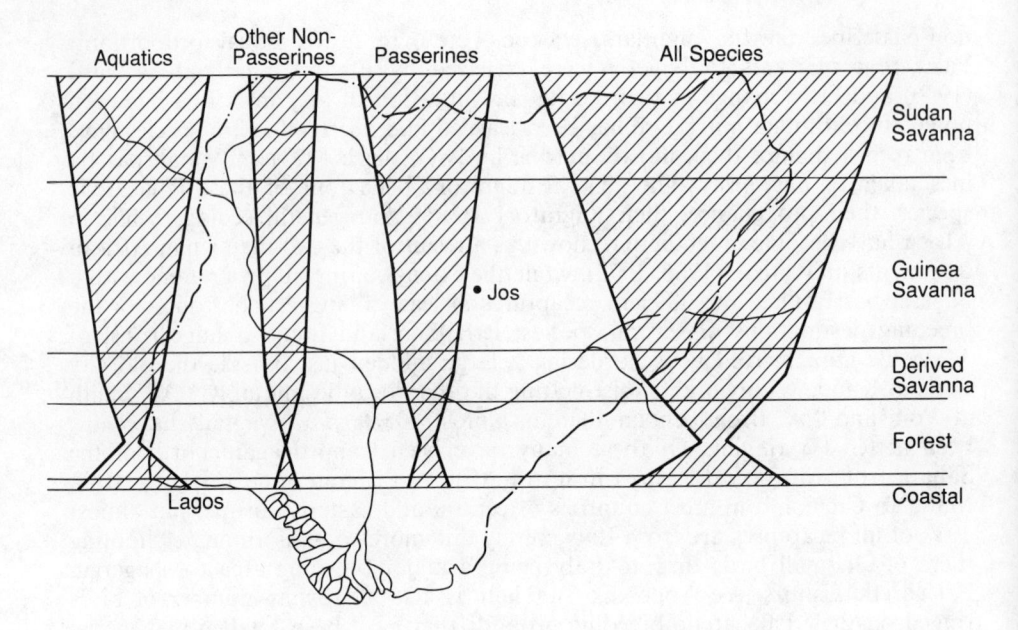

Figure 6. Diagram to show the difference between the number of migrant species wintering in the various vegetation zones of Nigeria.

Fig. 6 (taken from Elgood *et al*. 1966) shows the relative number of Palaearctic migrant species met in the various main vegetation zones. The migrants have been separated as passerines, aquatics and other non-passerines, while a summation of these groups is also shown. Two important facts emerge. First, with the exception of the narrow coastal belt, the maximum number of species of each group is found in the relatively arid Sudan savanna of the far north, the numbers diminishing progressively southward to reach a minimum in the lush rain forest. R.E. Moreau involved himself sufficiently with this phenomenon for it to become known as Moreau's Paradox, viz. that the Sahel dries out continuously for the 6 months during which Palaearctic species winter in West Africa and yet supports the largest migrant bird population of any of the sub-Saharan vegetation zones. The crux of Moreau's Paradox is how the migrants ever manage to build up sufficient fat reserves for the northward trans-Sahara migration from such a 'clapped-out' environment.

The second fact to emerge, now taken for granted, is that there are more aquatic bird species wintering in the arid north than are present even on the coast. This is definitely true of the ducks and most of the waders (perhaps only the Eurasian Oyster Catcher *Haematopus ostralegus* comes exclusively via the coasts), though gulls and skuas, but certainly not all terns, apparently travel mainly round the bulge of West Africa.

Intra-African Migrants

Nigeria is singularly well placed for the study of intra-African migration for 3 reasons. In the first place it lies between the Atlantic Ocean and the Sahara, both acting as barriers to further north/south movement. Secondly, because of the rainfall pattern, the vegetation becomes progressively more sparse in steps northward in the successive vegetation zones which run east to west across the country, in harmony with the change of day length. Although this change of day length is minimal within the tropics it is, nevertheless, a factor in orienting intra-African bird movements in a north/south direction. Thirdly, Nigeria is essentially a flat country; there are no mountain ranges to alter the rainfall or impede the migration flight paths, in sharp contrast to the mountainous areas and plateaux of eastern Africa, which has a much more complex seasonal rainfall pattern at the corresponding latitudes.

African breeding species can be broadly classed as Forest, Savanna, Montane and Aquatic, the last including a few that might be better described as Marine. Only the Savanna and Aquatic species are subject to seasonal movement, amounting to true migration in a significant proportion (Table 4).

Forest species are essentially sedentary; they are only exceptionally met outside forest, but will undoubtedly move around within their habitat seeking food and in the case of large hornbills the distance travelled may be many miles. That other movements occur, especially at night, is evidenced by early morning corpses of *Francolinus lathami* and *Bleda canicapilla*, both normally confined to forest, being found near university buildings at Ibadan. Of possible significance is the fact that a former forest area was cleared for the university campus. *Pitta angolensis* is too rare a bird of the Nigerian forest floor to tell whether it behaves in the way Moreau (1966) found the eastern African race did, namely being attracted to lights at night.

Montane birds similarly are essentially stationary, though some may move seasonally to higher or lower levels, a phenomenon well known in the Himalayas and other major mountain ranges. In Nigeria the only possible case of altitudinal movement is that *Motacilla clara*, apparently normally a mountain stream wagtail, has several times been encountered at lower levels, once almost at sea level at Calabar, though G.D. Field has found this species often at low altitudes in Sierra Leone.

Savanna birds have a well defined migration pattern. Data are available for 20% and a further 10% may well do so. Allowing for the considerable number of uncommon species for which there is too little data from which to attribute regular seasonal movements, something approaching half of the savanna birds may well migrate. These movements must be mainly in response to seasonally changing food supplies. With the increasing severity of the northern dry season, food for most species will become more scarce tending to lead to a southward movement. Northward movement in the rains from the southern areas is less easy to understand, but Lynes (1925) made the striking comparison that the wet season can bury

Table 4. Proportions of sedentary and migratory African bird species in different habitat groups in Nigeria

	Total spp.	Sedentary spp.	Migratory spp. Definite	Possible
Forest	197	196 = 99.5%	0	1 = 0.5%
Montane	47	46 = 98%	0	1 = 2%
Savanna	417	291 = 70%	78 = 19%	48 = 11.5%
Aquatic	67	51 = 76%	9 = 13%	7 = 11%

small terrestrial prey animals beneath a lush vegetation cover as effectively as snow can conceal them from birds in the Palaearctic winter. Since the grass cover becomes less and less complete northward in the successive vegetation zones a move to the north may become necessary for many savanna birds.

Movements of many species may vary considerably from year to year. Exceptionally dry years, like those associated with the 'Sahel Drought' of the early seventies, are likely to induce a larger scale southward movement than normal, with some species also moving further south than usual, such as the Swallow-tailed Kite *Chelictinia riocourii* which reached as far south as Ilorin. Conversely years of higher than average rainfall may lead to an increased northward passage during the wet season or a reduced southward passage with the ensuing dry season.

African aquatic birds have about one species in eight that are clearly migrant and almost as many again that are probably so. One of the most dramatic is the trans-equatorial migrant Abdim's Stork *Ciconia abdimii*, which breeds during the rains in the northern tropics, including much of Nigeria north of the great rivers, and spends its off season in southern Africa, again in the wet season, so that it is present when the wetlands of both hemispheres offer maximal food sources. But almost all aquatics of the savanna wetlands will move, at least locally, as the result of the complex rise and fall of the major rivers. The Niger, because of its great length produces peak floods that occur typically twice in each annual cycle, out of phase with peak floods on its tributaries. For example a back flow up the lower Kaduna River, north from Pategi, with the May/June first peak of the Niger, is a regular phenomenon than can lead to wetland flooding locally that birds are quick to exploit. Similarly the Shari River (outside Nigeria) flowing into Lake Chad usually causes the Lake level to rise until well into the New Year, some three months after the rains have ceased, in some years giving ideal conditions for opportunist breeding for such aquatic birds as cormorants and herons (Hopson 1966). Consequently the movement of many aquatic birds may vary greatly in time from year to year and are random in direction, usually to the closest standing water or wet marsh. Clearly such movements do not constitute true migration.

Migrations of Marine Birds

The movements of marine birds to and along the coast of Nigeria are very imperfectly known. The Systematic List includes c.30 marine species, mostly Laridae; but the number occurring on the Nigerian coast may well be greater, since Wallace (1973) has shown that careful observation by a competent discriminator between similar species can produce some remarkable additions to the marine avifauna.

The maps of sea-bird distribution and migration by Tuck & Heinzel (1978) indicate that not only do few sea-birds breed in Nigeria but that its waters are also largely avoided by most of the long-distance pelagic species such as shearwaters, petrels and phalaropes. There are, indeed, only 6 rare vagrants from these families to Nigerian waters: Sooty Shearwater *Puffinus griseus*, Manx Shearwater *Puffinus puffinus*, Wilson's Storm-petrel *Oceanites oceanicus*, Madeiran Storm-petrel *Oceanodroma castro*, Grey Phalarope *Phalaropus fulicarius*, Red-necked Phalarope *Phalaropus lobatus*. On the other hand, the Nigerian list of Laridae (4 skuas, 5 marine gulls and 15 tern species) is surprisingly long, since almost all of them are migrant from the Palaearctic and most have recently been found further south along the coast of West Africa than previous records had shown (Wallace 1973).

BREEDING

While collating the data for this check-list, the very little that is known of the breeding of most species within Nigeria became even more apparent. Apart from *Quelea quelea*, which, because of its economic importance, has probably been better studied in all aspects of its biology (Ward 1965a,b) than any other bird, together with a few others that have been the subject of postgraduate studies, like bee-eaters and especially *Merops bullocki* (Fry 1966), really very little is known about the common basics of breeding biology such as seasonality, nest construction, the eggs and clutch size, incubation and fledging times. There are not a few quite common species, some even breeding colonially like the *Gymnobucco* barbets, of which virtually nothing is known, all of which would be admirable subjects for future work.

There has been no earlier review of breeding in Nigeria and in attempting a summary one is very aware that scanty information can be easily misinterpreted and incorrect conclusions reached.

Of the 720 or so African breeding species that occur in Nigeria only 14 (including only 3 passerines) almost certainly migrate beyond the borders of the country to breed. Where exactly they move to is unknown. Some, like *Caprimulgus rufigena*, *Macrodipteryx vexillaria* and probably *Riparia cincta* (one of the 3 passerines), move south across the equator to breed in southern Africa. Some, like *Passer luteus* and *Chelictinia riocourii*, move north into the sub-Sahara of Niger, while others, like *Vanellus crassirostris* and *Charadrius tricollaris*, are thought to move east to breed in eastern Africa.

A further group of about 30 species are rare, either vagrant, or at the very edge of their known range, so that the absence of breeding data is to be expected. Of the remaining 680 or so species thought to breed within Nigeria, only about 500 (73%) have known breeding data, data which too often is limited to dates for nest building or copulation only, or a reference to gonad condition of collected specimens. Copulation may be misleading, since it has been noted prior to migration, e.g. in the bee-eater *Merops albicollis* at Ibadan before it moves 1000 km to the Sahel to breed, while the Shikra *Accipiter badius* draws attention to its matings with a distinctive call which can be heard at Ibadan over a 6-month period. Collected females with yolking eggs in the ovary or with an oviducal egg certainly afford good evidence of time and place of breeding, but males with enlarged testes demonstrating to breeding seasonality is far less satisfactory. The sighting of juveniles, unless accompanied by an indication of probable age is not even indicative of local breeding. Nest building can be equally misleading. At Lagos, where significant rainfall can occur in every month, a heavy shower always triggers off frenzied building activity by the commonest weavers there, *Ploceus cucullatus* and *P. nigerrimus castaneofuscus*, but egg laying does not necessarily follow.

Perhaps for a tropical environment, with nearly constant day length and no inhospitable season, such as the temperate zone winter, the most interesting aspect is the breeding seasonality of the various species. One might have supposed that all members of one family would have similarities of breeding season, but this is not so (see Tables 5 and 6); so that one is led to conjecture that one of the factors in species differentiation may well have been a separation of breeding seasons, particularly when a single ancestral form may have originally occupied a wide habitat embracing differing climatic seasonalities.

Since in any month of the year there will be some species found breeding, it follows that some will time their peak activity to coincide with either the start of the rains or with the beginning of the dry season. Nevertheless, it is thought that bird species may most conveniently be distinguished as those breeding in the rains or those breeding in the dry season. Although these seasons are of differing length in the various vegetational zones, in the main those that breed in the rains do not have to compete with related migrants from the Palaearctic for food while rearing young. On the other hand, dry season breeders may well come into close competition with nearly related forms overwintering from the Palaearctic. It has therefore been thought not unreasonable to regard wet season and dry season breeders as the 2 main categories of seasonal breeders rather than to complicate matters by adding categories of 'between season' breeders.

Accordingly, despite the paucity of the data, it has been found convenient to assign each breeding species to one of 4 main categories:-

> **Dry Season Breeders**, which includes, especially, ground nesting species and predators.
> **Wet Season Breeders** including many insectivorous passerines.
> **Species with protracted breeding seasons**, in some cases seeming to breed throughout the year and certainly in both wet and dry months. Many pigeons are noteworthy examples.
> **An ill-defined group**, some of which may be opportunist breeders, while the rest are species for which the scanty data are conflicting, suggesting both wet and dry season breeding.

In very few species indeed has double brooding been proven, though it is possible in many others, and in most cases where breeding seasons seem to be protracted it is not known whether individual pairs are nesting at different months or whether some or all pairs are multibrooded. An interesting exception is the Scarlet-chested Sunbird *Nectarinia senegalensis*, which at Ilorin has produced 3 broods between March and October (Brown 1948) and at Jos has raised 3 successive broods at 6 month intervals, embracing wet and dry seasons, in the same nest (R.Kemp).

Table 5 summarises the data by families for the non-passerines with African breeding species and similarly Table 6 deals with the passerine families. For each family these Tables show the total number of species occurring in Nigeria compared with both the number presumed to breed (i.e. excluding Palaearctic and African non-breeding migrants) and with the number for which actual breeding data exists.

The right hand columns show the numbers in each family of those known or expected to breed in each of the 4 seasonal breeding categories mentioned above.

There are about equal numbers of families that show a bias towards the dry season or the wet season, though this excludes the aquatic families that mostly breed when the water levels are lowest, equivalent to dry season breeding. There are slightly more species which breed in the dry season than in the wet (207:185); but of these there are 117 passerine species which breed in the wet season compared with 93 in the dry. An interesting feature is that all the larger families have some species breeding in each of the main seasons, dry and wet, while some show a remarkable balance of species between these two halves of the year.

Two further points of interest are the relationship between breeding seasonality and food and breeding seasonality and general habitat. The major families can be assigned to one of 7 feeding groups (shown in the first column after the family name in Tables 5 and 6). These are, with examples:

1. Aquatic feeders – Ardeidae, Anatidae, Rallidae
2. Predators – Accipitridae, Strigidae

Table 5. Non-Passerine Families with Breeding Records In Nigeria

FAMILY	Feeding Categ.	Total spp.	B+(B)	B	Breeding season Dry	Wet	Protr.	?	Remarks
Struthionidae	6	1	1	1	1				
Podicipedidae	1	2	1	1			1		
Phalacrocoracidae	1	2	2	2	2				
Pelecanidae	1	2	2	2	2				
Anhingidae	1	1	1	1	1				
Ardeidae	1	19	16	14	8	5	0	1	most breed dry season
Scopidae	1	1	1	1		1			*S.u. minor* breeds dry season
Ciconiidae	1	8	6	4	3	1			
Threskiornithidae	1	6	4	3	1	2			
Anatidae	1	24	11	7	3	3	1		
Accipitridae	2	49	40	28	22	3	2	1	most breed dry season
Sagittariidae	2	1	1	1	1				
Falconidae	2	10	6	6	3	1		2	
Phasianidae	6	14	12	10	4	3	3		seasonal balance
Turnicidae	6	3	3	2	1			1	
Rallidae	1	17	8	8	1	5	2		most breed wet season
Gruidae	6	3	1	1		1			
Heliornithidae	1	1	1	1				1	
Otididae	6	6	4	3		2	1		
Jacanidae	1	2	2	1			1		
Rostratulidae	1	1	1	1	1				
Burhinidae	6	4	3	2		1	1		
Glareolidae	1	8	6	6	3	3			
Charadriidae	1	19	9	9	5	2	2		low water
Laridae	1	7	1	—					
Sternidae	1	17	2	2	2				low water
Rynchopidae	1	1	1	1	1				low water
Pteroclididae	6	2	2	2	2				dry season
Columbidae	4,6	19	17	13	4	1	7	1	most protracted
Psittacidae	4	5	4	4	2	1		1	
Musophagidae	4	6	6	4	2	1		1	
Cuculidae	3	19	16	12	1	11			brood parasites
Tytonidae	2	1	1	1	1				most breed dry season
Strigidae	2	13	12	9	7			2	most breed dry season
Caprimulgidae	3	10	6	5	2	1		2	
Apodidae	3	14	8	5		3	2		
Coliidae	4	2	2	2		2			wet season
Trogonidae	3	3	2	—					
Alcedinidae	1,3	12	12	9	3	4		2	seasonal balance
Meropidae	3	13	12	12	5	3		4	seasonal balance
Coraciidae	3	6	5	4	1	1	1	1	seasonal balance
Phoeniculidae	3	4	4	3	1		1	1	
Upupidae	3	1	1	1	1				
Bucerotidae	3	12	12	8		4		4	
Capitonidae	4	16	16	15	7	1	4	3	most avoid wet season
Indicatoridae	3	9	9	6	4	2			brood parasites
Picidae	3	16	15	8	7		1		most breed dry season

B = proven breeder   (B) = should breed but unproven

48   Breeding

Table 6. Passerine Families with Breeding Records in Nigeria

FAMILY	Feeding Categ.	Total spp	B+(B)	B	Dry	Wet	Protr.	?	Remarks
Alaudidae	6	13	7	6	4		1	1	mostly dry season
Hirundinidae	3	22	18	13	4	6	2	1	seasonal balance
Motacillidae	3	11	6	3	1	1	1		
Campephagidae	3	7	6	1		1			poorly recorded
Pycnonotidae	4	29	29	18	8	8	2		seasonal balance
Turdidae	3,6	40	27	19	8	10		1	seasonal balance
Sylviidae	3	81	57	34	7	21	4	2	mostly wet season
Muscicapidae	3	21	18	13	9	4			
Platysteiridae	3	10	10	8	2	3		3	
Monarchidae	3	7	7	4	2	2			
Timaliidae	3,6	11	11	8	1	4	2	1	
Paridae	3	2	2	1	1				
Remizidae	3	3	3	1		1			
Zosteropidae	4	1	1	1	1				
Nectariniidae	7	26	25	21	7	5	6	3	
Laniidae	3	11	6	4	1	1	2		protracted
Malaconotidae	3	21	21	10	3	3	3	1	protracted
Prionopidae	3	2	2	2	1	1			
Dicruridae	3	3	3	3	2	1			
Corvidae	6	3	2	2		2			
Oriolidae	4	4	3	3	2	1			
Sturnidae	4	14	14	12	7	5			
Passeridae	5	5	4	4	2	1	1		
Ploceidae	5	39	38	30	5	16	6	3	mostly wet season
Estrildidae	5	36	36	31	14	16	1		seasonal balance
Viduidae	5	7	7	3		2		1	brood parasites
Fringillidae	5	5	5	4	1	1	2		
Emberizidae	5	5	4	3		2		1	

B = proven breeder   (B) = should breed but unproven

3. Insectivores – Apodidae, Meropidae, Muscicapidae
4. Fruit feeders – Musophagidae, Capitonidae, Pycnonotidae
5. Seed eaters – Fringillidae, Estrildidae
6. Ground feeders – Columbidae, Corvidae, Alaudidae
7. Flower feeders (nectar & small arthropods) – Nectariniidae

However the feeding pattern may differ widely between the members of a family and allowance has to be made in, for example, the Alcedinidae where Cerylinae and Alcedininae have been regarded as aquatic fish eaters and Dacelonidae as insectiverous though even this does not do justice to the range of feeding stratagems in the kingfisher family (Fry 1980). Furthermore many seed eaters (e.g. in the Ploceidae) feed their small nestlings on insects during the fledging period. Some of the above feeding groups are widely recognised; others like general ground feeders and even aquatic feeders are rather more contrived.

Table 7 shows that feeding groups (1), (2) and (6), involving mainly live prey or carrion, but also (4), the fruit eaters and (7), the Nectariniidae, have more dry than wet season breeders. On the other hand, groups (3) and (5), the insectivores and seed eaters, have more wet season breeders than dry. Only for the predators is there a very marked disparity between the main seasons, the reasons for which are mainly conjectural. A contributory factor for predators being dry season breeders may be that their long incubation and fledging periods cause their young

Table 7. The relationship of avian feeding habits to breeding patterns in Nigeria

Feeding group	Spp with breeding records B	Dry	Breeding Season Wet	Protracted	Ill defined
1 Aquatic	68	34	25	6	3
2 Predators	45	34	4	2	5
3 Insectivores	182	61	78	20	23
4 Fruit feeders	61	29	19	8	5
5 Seed eaters	75	22	38	10	5
6 Ground feeders	51	20	16	12	3
7 Flower feeders	21	7	5	6	3

to become first independent well into the ensuing wet season, the season at which plant growth is obviously maximal. It would seem that this maximal activity, in the rains, must apply to all the intervening trophic levels within the community, herbivores and smaller carnivores, so that feeding for the larger carnivores, such as bird predators, should then be rather easier with reduced competition between adults and juveniles for the same food supply.

The relationship between habitat and breeding season (Table 8) can be obtained from the information in Appendix 1 in combination with the raw data used in the compilation of Table 7 showing the relation between feeding ecology and breeding season. The most striking feature of Table 8 is that the ecological habitat groupings all tend to reflect a rather even balance between dry and wet season breeding as already noted above. Only for aquatic and montane species are there distinct seasonal preferences, in each case the dry season being somewhat favoured.

Table 8. Relationship between habitat and breeding seasons of birds in Nigeria

Habitat	Spp with breeding records B	Dry	Breeding Season Wet	Protracted	Ill defined
Savanna	288	110	109	43	26
Forest	124	49	45	17	13
Montane	27	15	10	1	1
Aquatic	64	33	21	3	7

Comparatively little has been published on the breeding seasonality of West African birds. The clear preference noted above for dry season breeding by raptors has also been found by Grimes (1987) for the coastal region of Ghana. Similarly there is broad agreement that when all species are considered there is a very even distribution of breeding throughout the year in the forest regions of the two countries. However, in Ghana in the northern savannas, although breeding occurs in all months, there is a wet season maximum. A rather detailed study has been made by Serle (1981) for forest species in west Cameroon. He also found that lowland forest species show a remarkably even distribution of breeding throughout the year with only a slight peak in activity in May at the beginning of the rainy season. On the other hand, montane forest birds nearly all nest in the dry season and avoid the period of heavy rains and mist. A further complication is that many forest species which favour wet season breeding in lowland areas of West Africa are found to nest in the dry season at higher altitudes in west Cameroon (Tye 1992).

Colonial breeding

Of colonial nesting species, there have been few well documented cases of mixed colonies. One of the most important has been the mixed cormorant and heron colony in riparian woodland near Lake Chad (Hopson 1966). The colony was in an area of thickets and isolated trees which was maximally flooded in January by the rising waters of Lake Chad, but which had dried out by June.

In the period December 1963 to March 1965 the maximum counts of nests and peak activity were as follows:

Phalacrocorax africanus	1322	(Jan '64)
Phalacrocorax carbo	22	(Feb '64)
Anhinga melanogaster	207	(Jan '64)
Egretta alba	200	(Feb '64)
Egretta intermedia	c.60	(Feb '64)
Egretta garzetta	17	(Feb '64) but more were hidden
Egretta ardesiaca	c.60	(end of Feb '64)
Threskiornis aethiopica	130	(Mar '65)
Platalea alba	28	(Feb '65)

There are 3 interesting features. First, for 3 species – *Phalacrocorax carbo*, *Egretta garzetta* and *Platalea alba* – these are still the only breeding records for Nigeria. Of particular interest is the proof that *E. garzetta* populations are not exclusively migrant to the Palaearctic to breed. Secondly, some of the remaining species were found breeding at times differing from records elsewhere, which strongly suggests opportunism. Most other records for *Phalacrocorax africanus* are consonant with this Lake Chad data, but Mundy & Cook (1972) found it breeding at Sokoto in September. Most *Egretta alba* records have been for September, though 2 are more consonant, being at least in the dry season. Similarly the only other record for *Threskiornis aethiopica* was for Sokoto in June (Bannerman 1951). *Anhinga melanogaster* has been found breeding at a number of widespread localities but always between December and April, fully consonant with Hopson's observations. The third feature of note is that the time of peak breeding activity is slightly different for the different species, *Threskiornis* and *Platalea* reaching peak activity a year later having had much smaller numbers the previous year when the others were maximal. In the late 1965-early 1966 season, the floods were much less extensive and no nest of any species was found; whether the birds miss breeding altogether in locally unfavourable years or seek and find suitable conditions elsewhere, perhaps in quite another area away from Lake Chad, is unknown, but the observations clearly illustrate a high degree of opportunism.

Mixed colonies are not confined to the larger water birds but commonly occur amongst *Ploceus* and *Euplectes* weavers and have been seen also in *Gymnobucco* barbets. Throughout the forest zone, in large towns as well as villages, Village Weavers *Ploceus cucullatus* and Vieillot's Masked Weaver *P. nigerrimus castaneo-*

fuscus almost always nest together, particularly in Oil-Palms *Elaeis guineensis*. Local residents regard them as bringers of good luck and do not molest them despite the damage they do to the trees by stripping the palm fronds and greatly reducing the output of fruit. In sub-coastal areas these colonies, which may number several hundred nests, are often joined, though in much smaller numbers, by the Orange Weaver *P. aurantius*. Mixed colonies of the Bishops, *Euplectes orix*, *E. hordaceus* and *E. afer* sometimes occur (for example at fish ponds north of Zaria in August 1968, N.J.S.). More remarkable are the mixed colonies of the Naked-faced Barbet *Gymnobucco calvus* and the very similar Bristle-nosed Barbet *G. peli*. Several hundred pairs, but with *calvus* predominant, may excavate their nest holes in a 20-foot length of the upper main trunk of a large dead forest tree, their tunnelling hastening the fall of the tree. The egg chambers being almost a foot below the entrance hole, it will be appreciated how honeycombed the interior becomes with so many chambers so close together.

Single species colonies occur too often for more than a brief allusion, and are found in many groups. Noteworthy examples include the White Pelican *Pelecanus onocrotalus* colony of formerly 1000 pairs on Wase Rock, a high inselberg between the Benue and the Jos Plateau (Dunger 1965); Ruppell's Griffon *Gyps rueppellii*, formerly 50 pairs (Bannerman 1951) on Kotorkoshi (or Kwatarkwashi, an inselberg near Gusau), but now greatly reduced in numbers (Cook & Mundy 1980) and the huge separate colonies of bee-eaters, *Merops nubicus* and *M. malimbicus* on Niger sandbanks at Eggan (Bannerman 1951, Brown 1940) with similar colonies still in the same general area 25 years later (Fry 1966).

Co-operative Breeding (Essay by Dr Roger Wilkinson)

Co-operative (or communal) breeding occurs when birds other than the parents help care for the youngsters. Helpers at the nest normally provide food for the chicks but can take other roles including nest-building, the sharing of incubation, sentinel duties and nest-defence.

Skutch (1961) reviewed instances of helping behaviour for about 50 bird species. By 1980 increasing interest in this area of social behaviour had raised the number of co-operatively breeding species three-fold and it is now thought that the behaviour may occur in 200-300 species worldwide (Emlen 1984, Brown 1987).

Although there are many variations in the social organisation of co-operatively breeding birds, a 'typical' co-operative breeder resides in the tropics or subtropics, is sedentary, lives in communities with fairly constant population sizes, has low reproductive rates, deferred maturity and high adult survival. Helpers are usually related to the breeding pair even if not their progeny (Skutch 1987).

Nearly 60 years ago the *Nigerian Field* published behavioural observations of co-operative breeding in Straight-crested Helmet Shrikes. Clarke (1936) watched a group of 4 shrikes involved in building a nest and saw 6 birds perch near this nest. At Kano, Gill (1939) observed a group of 7 shrikes and noted 3 different birds bringing food, one after the other, to the nest and realised the whole flock were spending most of their day visiting the nest with food. He referred to group members, other than the breeding pair, as 'Uncles and Aunts' but was unable to determine whether only the parents incubated or if this duty was shared by other group members. As only one nest was being attended by this group of birds, Gill suggested they "might all be cocks except the mother bird" and noted their chief function was to guard the nest from enemies. Such questions as the functions of helping behaviour and the relationship between flock members initially raised by

Gill over 50 years ago, are central to all studies of co-operative breeding in birds.

Bee-eaters as a group have been extremely well studied compared to many other bird familes. Hilary Fry pioneered a study on Red-throated Bee-eaters and his seminal research in the 1960s was followed up by his students Michael Dyer and Humphrey Crick in the 1970s and 1980s (Fry 1966, 1967, 1973, 1984; Dyer 1979, 1983, Dyer & Crick 1983, Dyer & Fry 1980, Crick 1984, 1987, 1992, Crick and Fry 1986). Red-throated Bee-eaters have complicated societies nesting in colonies with breeding units of normally monogamous pairs often assisted by a small number of helpers. These helpers are usually the elder brothers of the chicks they help to rear. Several units often associate closely as a 'clan' which defends a territorial feeding area sometimes up to 2 km from the nest site (Fry *et al.* 1992).

Wilkinson's (1978a) observations of co-operative breeding in the Chestnut-bellied Starling led to an intensive five year study of this species at Kano (Wilkinson 1982, 1983, Wilkinson & Brown 1984). Chestnut-bellied Starlings live in social groups, generally of 10-30 individuals, comprising 2-6 breeding pairs, non-breeding adults of both sexes and juveniles. Nestlings are fed by both parents assisted by up to 12 helpers. Individual helpers may successively or simultaneously attend the nest of different breeders, the pattern of helping differing with the sex and age of the helper (Wilkinson 1982).

Grimes (1976) reviewed instances of co-operative breeding in African birds. Of 52 species in which co-operative breeding was then recorded, 31 occur in Nigeria as resident breeders. A number of these have been well-studied outside Nigeria and include the Ostrich (Bertram 1980), the Pied Kingfisher (Reyer 1980a), the Green Wood-Hoopoe (Kakelaar) (Ligon and Ligon 1978) and the Yellow-billed Shrike (Long-tailed Shrike) (Grimes 1980). Since the 1976 review, the following species, all resident in Nigeria, have been shown to be co-operative breeders: Striped Kingfisher (Reyer 1980b); Black-headed Bee-eater (Dyer *et al.* 1981); Swallow-tailed Bee-eater (Fry 1984); Black-and-white-casqued Hornbill (Grey-cheeked Hornbill) (Kilham 1956); Grey-backed Fiscal (Zack and Ligon 1985); Violet-backed (Amethyst) Starling (Ginn 1986); Chestnut-bellied Starling (Wilkinson, *op. cit.*) and Velvet-mantled Drongo (Thangamani *et al.* 1981)

The occurrence of co-operative breeding is known to occur, or suspected to occur, in many other species found in Nigeria but none have been investigated thoroughly. It is known to occur in captive Long-tailed Glossy Starlings (for details see Wilkinson 1988) and may well occur in closely related starlings, e.g. Lesser Blue-eared (Swainson's) Glossy Starling, in which 4 adults have been seen close to an active nest (R. Wilkinson, unpublished). Co-operative breeding is likely to occur in the Grey-headed Bush Shrike for at a nest in Kano a bird brooded chicks on the nest whilst two other individuals chased off a Pied Crow (Wilkinson, 1978b). Widespread birds known to be co-operative breeders include the Piapiac and Brown and Black-cap Babblers (Grimes 1976). Many other African babblers are suspected of being co-operative breeders and in West Africa this family begs further research. Other species which may reward further study include the White-winged Black Tit (co-operative breeding occurs in the related Black Tit – see Tarboton (1981) for details), and the Chestnut-crowned Sparrow Weaver (co-operative breeding occurs in the related White-headed Sparrow Weaver – see Collias & Collias (1978) for details). The breeding system of the colonially nesting Buffalo Weaver remains unknown and may well be co-operative.

This review has highlighted the occurrence of co-operative breeding in Nigerian birds and indicated those species which need in-depth studies before the details of their life-histories are known. Such studies offer rich rewards and will furnish more fuel for the continuing debate on the evolution and ecological significance of co-operative breeding. I hope it will encourage Nigerian ornithologists to enter this intellectually stimulating and enjoyable area of avian behavioural ecology.

Brood Parasitism in Nigerian Birds (Essay by Dr Robert Payne)

Brood parasites lay their eggs in the nests of other species, their foster species. The foster pair rears the young brood parasites, either at a cost to their own young or along with them. Their effect on their foster species varies with the group, the honey-guides and most cuckoos killing the foster eggs or young but the viduine finches growing up with little effect on their foster young. Their effect also varies with the frequency with which the foster species is parasitized. The proportion of bird species that are brood parasites is high in the Old World tropics. In Nigeria, 12 cuckoos, 9 honey-guides, a weaver and 10 species of parasitic finches make up about 5% of the breeding species. The high proportion of brood parasites in tropical regions may be related to the high incidence of nest predation. By laying their eggs in different nests rather than all in one, the brood parasites decrease the variability of their success and this spreading of the risk may increase the chance that some of the young will escape predation (Payne 1977a,b).

Although about half of the world's cuckoo species rear their own young, most African cuckoos are brood parasites. Some have more than one kind of egg, with the colour and pattern of spots matching that of their foster species. This variation has not been studied in detail in Nigeria. Elsewhere, Didric Cuckoos have unmarked blue eggs which the female lays in the nests of bishops, and spotted eggs in the nests of weaver finches with spotted eggs. Each female lays a single kind of egg, and she may restrict her parasitism to the single foster species that raised her, but learning whom to parasitize from early experience has not been shown for any species. Cuckoo eggs have a short incubation period and they hatch before the foster eggs. Cuckoo nestlings usually evict the eggs or small nestlings of their foster species by lifting them onto their back and pushing them out of the nest. After evicting their competition, they receive all the care of the parent. However, the Great Spotted Cuckoo is smaller than its foster species the Pied Crow, and the young grow up together with their foster nest-mates. The non-evicting cuckoos may lay more than one egg in a nest, but the evicting species lay a single egg, as the first to hatch would evict the other cuckoo eggs along with the foster eggs. None of the African cuckoos are known to mimic the calls of their foster species in the way that the parasitic viduine finches do.

The honey-guides are all brood parasites as far as known. They parasitize mainly hole-nesters such as bee-eaters, barbets, woodpeckers and swallows, though the slender-billed honey-guides *Prodotiscus* are known elsewhere to use the open nests of small warblers and white-eyes. Honey-guide eggs are white like the eggs of many hole-nesting birds, and the colour is the result of their common ancestry with woodpeckers and barbets which also have white eggs (Payne 1977a, 1989). The young nestlings have a sharp hook at the end of the bill and use this to kill the nestlings of their foster species. The honey-guides gain all the parental care of their foster species for themselves. Their foster species are unknown for several species of honey-guides.

There are two groups of finches with parasitic species. The Parasitic Weaver lays in the nest of *Cisticola* and *Prinia* grass warblers. The young are large and crowd out the foster young and the foster parents then succeed in rearing only the young parasites. The other parasitic finches are the viduines *Vidua* spp, which parasitize the estrildid finches. Most use a single species to foster its young.

However, the Pin-tailed Whydah uses several species including Black-crowned Waxbill, Common Waxbill, Black-rumped Waxbill and Orange-cheeked Waxbill. The young of these waxbills have similar mouth patterns, and the whydah has a mouth pattern that is a match close enough for them. Also, in Nigeria there is one kind of paradise whydah *Vidua interjecta* that is associated with two species of fosterers, the Red-winged Pytilia and Yellow-winged Pytilia, both with a similar mouth pattern. The others are species-specific in their foster associations as far as is known. The Paradise Whydah *V. orientalis* parasitizes the Melba Finch. Although the two live together in the drier northern region, there are no definite records of parasitism in Nigeria. There are several species of indigobirds. In some cases the association of an indigobird species with a foster species in brood parasitism is inferred from its song mimicry, as each male mimics the songs of a single foster species. Males that mimic the same foster species look alike, and they differ in plumage colour from males that mimic the songs of other species. The females of all the indigobirds in Nigeria look alike, though in southern Africa they are distinct and can readily be identified in the field.

The viduine finches are genetically adapted to their foster species. The mouth pattern of the young matches the pattern of the begging young of the foster. This may secure the parental care of their foster adults, which otherwise might give more food to their own young. They are also behaviourally adapted to their foster species. The male learns and mimics the songs of his foster species. The female chooses a male with the same songs as her own fosterer. In this way she mates with a male with the same upbringing, and she secures for her own young a mouth pattern that resembles the mouth of the foster species.

The common foster in the north, the Red-billed Firefinch, is the foster of the Village Indigobird *Vidua chalybeata* (Payne 1973). The adult male indigobirds sing the song and calls of the firefinch. The mouth of the nestling firefinch is marked by four white papillae at the gape, the papillae have a dark blue base, and the roof of the mouth is yellow with a ring of black spots. The mouth of the nestling indigobird has the same four white gape papillae with a dark blue base, and the roof is yellow with the ring of black spots. In the nest the gape signals the parent to feed, and the match of parasite young to the foster young may increase its chances of being fed along with them. In a mixed brood the foster parents often raise young of both their own and indigobirds, which do not interfere with their nest-mates. When the firefinches fledge, they beg and show the mouth pattern for 3 weeks after leaving the nest. The young Village Indigobirds are streaked brown on the head in contrast to the young firefinches, and they have a brown rather than red rump, but they retain the same mouth pattern while they are in the care of their foster parents.

The indigobirds can be identified mainly by their song, though some species are sufficiently distinct in plumage to be distinct in the field by sight as well. The Village Indigobird *Vidua chalybeata* is bright blue in male breeding plumage, with black wings and orange feet unlike other Nigerian species, and lives in the dry northern areas. Where it has been tape-recorded in Nigeria (Sokoto, Gusau, Kano, Zaria, Numan, Kiri), it mimics the 'chick-pea-pea' songs of Red-billed Firefinch. The other indigobirds in west Africa have brown wings and pale pinkish or whitish feet. *V. wilsoni* is widespread in Nigeria and it mimics the chattery staccato songs of the Bar-breasted Firefinch (tape recordings from Yankari and Zaria, and specimens from Agoulierie and Yendi). *V. raricola*, which mimics and parasitizes the Zebra Waxbill or Goldbreast, is known at Kogum and Enugu (BMNH, Payne and Payne 1994). In Cameroon and Sierra Leone it mimics the songs and parasitizes this waxbill. It has a bright green gloss in male breeding plumage. *V. nigeriae* has a dull green gloss in breeding plumage and is known in Nigeria from the type specimen on the Gongola River. There it occurs with Quail-finch, which it mimics in song in northern Cameroon. *V. maryae*, which has bright green plumage and longer wings than the other green birds, occurs on the Jos Plateau. It has been tape recorded at Panshanu and Kagoro and mimics songs of the African Firefinch (Payne 1982). *V. larvaticola* is blue to green in gloss and it mimics the songs of Black-faced Firefinch at Zaria, Panshanu, and Bauchi. Two other indigobirds are known elsewhere in West Africa and may appear in Nigeria where their foster species occur, but they have not yet been tape recorded or otherwise identified. The males are blue in breeding plumage and mimic the songs of Black-bellied Firefinch in Ghana and Brown Twinspot in Cameroon and African Firefinch and Dybowski's Twinspot in Sierra Leone (Payne and Payne 1994). The species status of these blue indigobirds is not yet known with certainty, and one or all of them may prove to be *V. camerunensis* (Table 9).

The only indigobirds that have been directly observed to parasitize their song-mimic species in Nigeria are *V. chalybeata*, *V. larvaticola* and *V. wilsoni*

Table 9. Brood parasitic finches *Vidua* and their foster species in Nigeria.

Parasitic finches	Foster species
Vidua macroura (Pin-tailed Whydah)	*Estrilda astrild* (Common Waxbill)
	E. melpoda (Orange-cheeked Waxbill)
	other *Estrilda* Waxbills?
V. orientalis (Broad-tailed Paradise Whydah)	*Pytilia melba* (Green-winged Pytilia)
V. interjecta (Exclamatory Paradise Whydah)	*P. phoenicoptera* (Red-winged Pytilia)
	P. hypogrammica (Yellow-winged Pytilia)
V. chalybeata (Village Indigobird)	*Lagonosticta senegala* (Red-billed Firefinch)
V. wilsoni (Bar-breasted Firefinch Indigobird)	*L. rufopicta* (Bar-breasted Firefinch)
V. larvaticola (Black-faced Firefinch Indigobird)	*L. larvata* (Black-faced Firefinch)
V. maryae (*funerea*) (Jos Plateau Indigobird)	*L. rubricata* (African Firefinch)
**V. camerunensis* (Cameroon Indigobird)	*L. rara* (Black-bellied Firefinch)
	L. rubricata (African Firefinch)
	Clytospiza monteiri (Brown Twinspot)
	C. dybowskii (Dybowski's Dusky Twinspot)
V. nigeriae (Quail-finch Indigobird)	*Ortygospiza atricollis* (Quail-finch)
V. raricola (Goldbreast Indigobird)	*Amandava subflava* (Goldbreast)

* indicate indigobirds not known in Nigeria, but known in northern Cameroon and likely to occur in Nigeria.

(Payne 1982). The foster-species associations of the others are known from song and in some cases from observations of brood parasitism elsewhere in West Africa. In most of them the young indigobirds are known to have mouth patterns that match the species-distinctive mouth patterns of their foster-species as nestlings and fledglings. Field observations on the life histories are needed in Nigeria.

CONCLUSION

Although it has been possible to make some tentative statements about the breeding patterns of birds in Nigeria, for most species there is a need to obtain very much more basic information on breeding. In East and southern Africa this is being achieved by Nest Record Card Schemes, operated by local ornithological or natural history societies, and modelled on the long-running scheme in the United Kingdom. It would be highly desirable to operate a similar scheme within West Africa.

In addition to gathering basic breeding information there is ample scope for more detailed investigations of, for example, the breeding biology of individual species, brood parasitism, co-operative breeding, and the association of some bird species with other animals, particularly hymenopterous insects. Such projects offer a challenge to the scientific community in Nigeria and afford a rich field for post-graduate work in the biological departments of Nigerian universities.

GENERAL POINTS

Clines, subspecies and barriers

Biologists today generally favour the lumping or mergence of species and of genera, thus reducing the numbers of both these taxa and simplifying nomenclature. With the recognition that populations of a species from different areas will usually differ in certain details, subspecies too are also being lost through mergence. In the absence of natural barriers, such as the sea or a mountain range, inhibiting gene flow, closer investigation often reveals clines with a gradual change in such characters as body and limb measurements and colour intensity that were formerly much used in racial differentiation. For wide-ranging (mainly larger) species it is often possible to separate quite well-defined races from say western, eastern and southern Africa, though indeterminate intermediates also occur in boundary areas. Similarly forest birds, including passerines, ranging through West Africa from Sierra Leone to Zaïre show distinct races from west and east of the Dahomey Gap, which is an ecological barrier to forest forms.

When dealing with such cases as those just mentioned, White (1960-65) used a laudable degree of subspecific differentiation, in keeping with his general lumping philosophy. He has, nevertheless, retained a high degree of subspecific differentiation amongst many smaller birds such as barbets, woodpeckers and nightjars amongst non-passerines and pipits, bulbuls and cisticolas amongst passerines and there are not a few species within Nigeria in which he recognises 2 or more races. There are thus a number of species, notably forest bulbuls, where White recognises separate races usually east and west of the Lower Niger. This problem as related to forest birds was reviewed by Marchant (1954), who noted that the separation of races from 'Upper' and 'Lower Guinea' was sometimes provided by the Dahomey Gap, but also often occurred within Nigeria at the Lower Niger. A river, even a mile wide, is apparently an adequate barrier for small forest birds, which may well turn back into forest cover on reaching the river margin. Unfortunately problems of racial discrimination and geographical separation can only be resolved by intensive collection and such collection has been avoided during the last 35 years.

Two cases of east/west subspecific differentiation warrant mention. East of the Niger is found the flycatcher *Terpsiphone rufiventer tricolor* with slate-grey back and to the west *T. r. fagani* with rufous back; but intermediacy has been reported both east (Serle 1957) and just west (Heigham 1976) of the Lower Niger.

In a few areas of the extreme east (and in adjacent Cameroon) is an entirely black male weaver *Ploceus n. nigerrimus*, whereas throughout the rest of southern Nigeria, the male of the same species, racially *P. nigerrimus castaneofuscus*, has striking chestnut and black plumage. Intermediacy has been reported as far west as Enugu (Serle 1957), but there is in fact no obvious barrier to limit gene flow.

The absence of a clear barrier running east to west separating northern and southern populations suggests that intensive collection would show most differentiation to be clinal. Nevertheless White recognises a number of species as having distinct north and south races, though none have the clear cut differentiation mentioned above for east to west racial separations. A typical case is that of the abundant small warbler *Camaroptera brevicaudata* with northern populations attributed to *C. b. brevicaudata* and southern to the more intensively coloured *C. b. tincta*, though seasonal plumage change obscures the distinction. It is thought that a cline with gradual change is likely to be involved. On the other hand the drongo *Dicrurus adsimilis* is an interesting case, warranting further investigation.

Its 3 races, *divaricatus*, *coracinus* and *atactus* are placed by White within Nigeria; though he says *atactus* is "apparently a hybrid form . . . due to inter-gradation of *coracinus* and *adsimilis*", yet he places the nominate race only in southern Africa, with little, if any, contact with *coracinus*. In the field, birds from Ilorin northward, presumably *divaricatus*, have a silvery appearance in the open wing not seen in birds of the Derived Savanna, which are said to be *atactus* in the southwest and *coracinus* further east. Furthermore their voices seem to be distinctive and need to be recorded and subjected to sonographic analysis.

Population changes

In a country developing as rapidly as Nigeria, the whole environment is changing dramatically in ways that directly or indirectly affect the avifauna.

Probably the most important change is created by the continued destruction of the rain forest, thus diminishing the populations of the largely stenotopic forest species, some, like the large hornbills, to near extinction, with others likely to disappear before the end of the century. The gradual replacement of 'slash and burn' farming in savanna by modern, largely mechanised, techniques, while favouring such graminivores as weavers and doves, has adversely affected most savanna species, as indicated by diminished numbers of birds of prey at the apex of the pyramid of numbers. Formerly no road journey of any length north of the Niger would fail to give sightings of Bateleur *Terathopius ecaudatus*, which was not infrequently met also south to near Ilorin; 25 were sighted between Ilorin, Kano and Jos in Dec 1963/Jan 1964. Pettet (1975) reporting on a journey only 4 years later from Ibadan to Lake Chad (via Kano but not Jos) had only 2 sightings south of Kano and only a further 9 between Potiskum and Lake Chad. During 2 visits to Kano State in Oct 1976 and Apr 1977, involving daily travel averaging about 150 miles, J.H.E. had but a single sighting. Possibly the much heavier road traffic of today has driven these magnificent birds to more remote areas, or else, and more likely, the large increase of the human population has been the major factor; but their decline in numbers seems undoubted.

The wetlands of the northernmost areas, associated with the Sokoto River in the northwest and the Kano/Hadejia/Nguru/Komodugu-Gana River leading to Lake Chad across the central and northeast northern border, have always been a major wintering area for large numbers of aquatics migrant from the Palaearctic. The development of river dams to supply water and hydro-electric power, notably at Kainji on the Niger and at Tiga on the Kano, has greatly supplemented the natural wetlands, and more southerly records of some gulls and terns have resulted. An interesting example is afforded by the Avocet *Recurvirostra avosetta*, which had not been met within Nigeria until 1955 (although numbers had been reported on the coast in Cameroon), but is now regular in small numbers at many of the northern bore holes and dams and even found as far south as the Lekki Peninsula near Lagos. Such a change in this species' status may be partly due to local environmental change but possibly recent breeding success within the Palaearctic may also be responsible.

The most important overall data on population changes can be inferred from comparing the statements on the Lagos avifauna of Alexander-Marrack *et.al* (1985) with Gee & Heigham (1977) and Sander (1956-7). Gee and Heigham comment on environmental changes in the 20 years since Sander's time and record the addition of 104 species to the local avifauna and the loss of 38 species. On the other hand Alexander-Marrack *et.al* find that in the 8 years since the report of Gee and Heigham, there were only 9 further additions to the Lagos list,

8 species appeared to have increased in number but 53 species had decreased in abundance, most of these being aquatic or marsh birds. Cowper (1977), present in Enugu through the dry season of 1975/6, recorded only 13 Palaearctic migrants there compared with 52 noted 20 years earlier by Serle (1957), but the time available to him for field work was insufficient for more than an impression of reduced numbers. At Ibadan, as an example of a changing avifauna, the area cleared for the establishment of the University was left with so little vegetation that from 1950-55 the common kingfisher was the savanna species *Halcyon chelicuti*. Its numbers declined with the development of suburban gardens and there followed a period in which the dominant species became the widely ranging *H. senegalensis*, itself to be replaced in the early sixties largely by the forest and gallery forest bird *H. malimbica*, as the gardens became somewhat overgrown with shrubs and trees. During this same period there were of course many other changes in numbers of different species, with the more or less complete disappearance of the larger forest species such as *Turaco persa*, hornbills (apart from *Tockus fasciatus*), *Phoeniculus bollei* and *Dendropicos pyrrhogaster*.

Normal and abnormal ranges of species

Although forest and montane species remain stationary, savanna and aquatic birds are subject to seasonal movement to a greater or lesser extent, movements that are probably influenced by the severity or otherwise of each particular season. It is therefore seldom possible to know the range of these more mobile savanna and aquatic species and to say when a record is beyond the normal range.

A small number of competent observers, usually expatriate, and only temporarily resident, spread over a large country means it is often impossible to know which records should be regarded as normal and which refer to vagrants beyond their normal range. The hope is that more Nigerians will in time become concerned about the welfare of their wildlife in general and of their avifauna in particular for a future revision of regular ranges to be possible. It must be a rare occurrence in Nigeria for a bird at or just beyond its normal range limit to coincide in time and space with a competent ornithologist. But Lagos has had a succession of competent observers and a surprising number of northern savanna species have been sighted there, notably by D.I.M. Wallace. R. Farmer reported yet another case, a pair of Chanting Goshawks *Melierax metabates* seen so regularly at one locality as to suggest they were "probably resident". The species had not been met before and has hardly been reported south of the Northern Guinea zone. Is the species extending its range? Was the presence of this pair only temporary? Could they have been escapes from captivity? There was no doubt of identity. A similar case is afforded by J.H.E's unconfirmed sighting of *Cossypha heuglini* near Lake Chad. He has little doubt personally about the identification, but possible confusion with the smaller *C. polioptera* cannot be dismissed entirely. Does this species' normal range extend into extreme northeast Nigeria? Had some climatic extreme caused it to be vagrant beyond the normal range? The answers to all such questions are unhappily unlikely in the near future.

CONSERVATION IN NIGERIA

(by A.P. Leventis)

In physical terms, the last two decades have witnessed an acceleration in the rate of habitat destruction. This results principally from a combination of population expansion (the continuous erosion of forests for relatively inefficient and frequently unsustainable food production and firewood collection) and direct Government or quasi-Government action (large-scale clearing by River-Basin Authorities as well as forest clear-felling for the establishment of mono-cultural plantations). Much of this destruction has taken place in Forest Reserves which have been de-reserved by Government or which have disappeared in all but name.

Bird populations and distribution have been affected by this unprecedented rate of habitat destruction but also, to a lesser extent, by direct hunting and trapping pressures.

Habitat destruction

Specialised species with a restricted geographical spread have been put at risk and numbers/distribution patterns in more disseminated species have altered. It is significant that birds with a desert or semi-desert habitat have recently been added to the Nigerian Check-list and this almost certainly results from habitat degradation and the destruction of the Sahelian Acacia forests. It is also notable that birds of the forest edges and clearings, and those which inhabit mixed farm/scrubland, in a relative sense, have prospered – with the puzzling exception of the Ibadan Malimbe (*Malimbus ibadanensis*). Birds are clearly important indicators of ecological change.

The construction of water impoundment schemes, with associated large-scale artificial irrigation, has restricted or even eliminated annual flooding in river basins (in dry years) and this has had a drastic effect on resident and migratory bird populations in northern Nigeria. This reduction in flood plains has also constricted dry-season pasture which has resulted in widespread grazing pressure and the destruction of tree-cover in Guinea-savanna areas. Sand-filling and land reclamation, as well as the silting-up of estuaries through forest degradation on sensitive watersheds, has led to the elimination of much important fresh-water and Mangrove swamp habitat and this problem has been exacerbated by the spread of exotic parasite species such as the Nipa Palm.

Hunting and Trapping Pressures

These affect mainly larger birds in Sahel, Sudan and Guinea Savanna areas and has resulted in the virtual elimination – within Nigeria's borders – of the Black Crowned Crane (*Balearica pavonina*) and the notable fall in numbers of the large Bustards *Neotis denhami* and *Ardeotis arabs*. Pressure on many wading species also occurs but these also have to contend with loss of water habitat, resulting from lack of flooding and the fall in ground-water levels.

A positive reaction to the threats and actualities outlined above is gathering pace. The Nigerian Government has adopted a conservation strategy and Nigerians are becoming more conscious of their natural heritage. The important milestones in this process are listed in Appendix 8.

Table 10. Habitats and Parks in Nigeria

Habitat/Ecological Zone	Name of Park
Mangrove/Swamp Forest	Stubbs Creek/Taylor Creek Reserves.
Moist lowland Rainforest	Okomu Reserve (West); Omo Forest; Cross River National Park (East).
Drier lowland Forest	Ifon Reserve (West); Cross River National Park (Oboshi-Okwango) (East).
Moist Montane Forest	Cross River National Park.
Derived/Southern Guinea Savanna	Gashaka-Gumti National Park; Upper Ogun/ Old Oyo National Park, Ifon Reserve.
Northern Guinea Savanna	Yankari National Park; Kainji Lake National Park; Kamuku/Kwiambana Reserves; Gashaka-Gumti National Park.
Sudan/Sahel Savanna	Chad Basin National Park.
Sahelian Wetlands	Chad Basin National Park (includes oases at Bulatura and parts of the threatened Hadejia/ Nguru Wetlands).
Drier Montane Forest and Grassland	Gashaka-Gumti

Some of these Parks are still in their formative stages, with boundaries not yet defined or in process of definition (see Fig. 7).

Active support-zone projects are being developed in the Cross River Park area and are in preparation near Gashaka-Gumti and at Okomu. Other areas in which there are active conservation projects include the Omo Forest (West).

In addition to the parks set up by the Nigerian Government (see Appendix 8 and Fig. 7) representations are being made, with the support of appropriate State Governments, to create National Parks or special conservation areas covering the following: Okomu Forest and Ifon Reserves; Omo Forest; Stubbs Creek Reserve; Taylor Creek Reserve; Kamuku/Kwiambana Reserves; parts of the Afi River Reserve and the Mbe Mountains. If these conservation areas are added to established parks, then a comprehensive range of Nigeria's habitats/ecological zones will have received total protection (see Table 10, Fig. 7 and Appendix 8).

The urgent need now is to translate into action the formal and institutional measures proposed by various bodies, supported as they are by emerging changes in Government policy and thinking. More important, the public must be made aware of the dangers inherent in uncontrolled, short-term exploitation of natural resources, with its concomitants of soil degradation, loss of habitat and loss of genetic diversity.

62   Conservation in Nigeria

NATIONAL PARKS
- 6 Kainji Lake
- 7 Kainji Lake (Zugurma sector)
- 9 Old Oyo
- 24 Cross River (Oban Hills sector)
- 26 Cross River (Boshi-Okwango sector)
- 37 Yankari
- 28 Gashaka-Gumti
- 29 Chad Basin (Chingurma-Duguma sector)
- 33 Chad Basin (Bulatura Oasis sector)

GAME RESERVES
- 1 Kwiambana
- 3 Kamuku
- 4 Alawa
- 5 Dagida
- 19 Ifon
- 22 Taylor's Creek
- 23 Stubbs Creek
- 30 Sambisa
- 35 Kogin Kano/Falgore
- 36 Lame-Burra
- 38 Pai River
- 39 Kambari
- 40 Wase Rock
- 41 Pandam

FOREST RESERVES
- 2 Birnin Gwari*
- 8 Teshi;
- 10 Gambari*
- 11 Ilaro*
- 13 Omo*
- 14 Oluwa*
- 15 Ejigbobini
- 16 Okomu (includes Okomu Wildlife Sanctuary)*
- 17 Ebba Kampe
- 18 Shokoshoko
- 19 Ifon
- 20 Orle River*
- 21 Sapoba*
- 25 Afi River
- 27 Bissaula
- 31 Gombole
- 32 Gujba*
- 42 Doma

CONSERVATION AREAS
- 12 Lekki Conservation Centre
- 34 Hadejia-Nguru Wetlands Conservation Area

* Reserves partially converted into Monocultural Plantations.

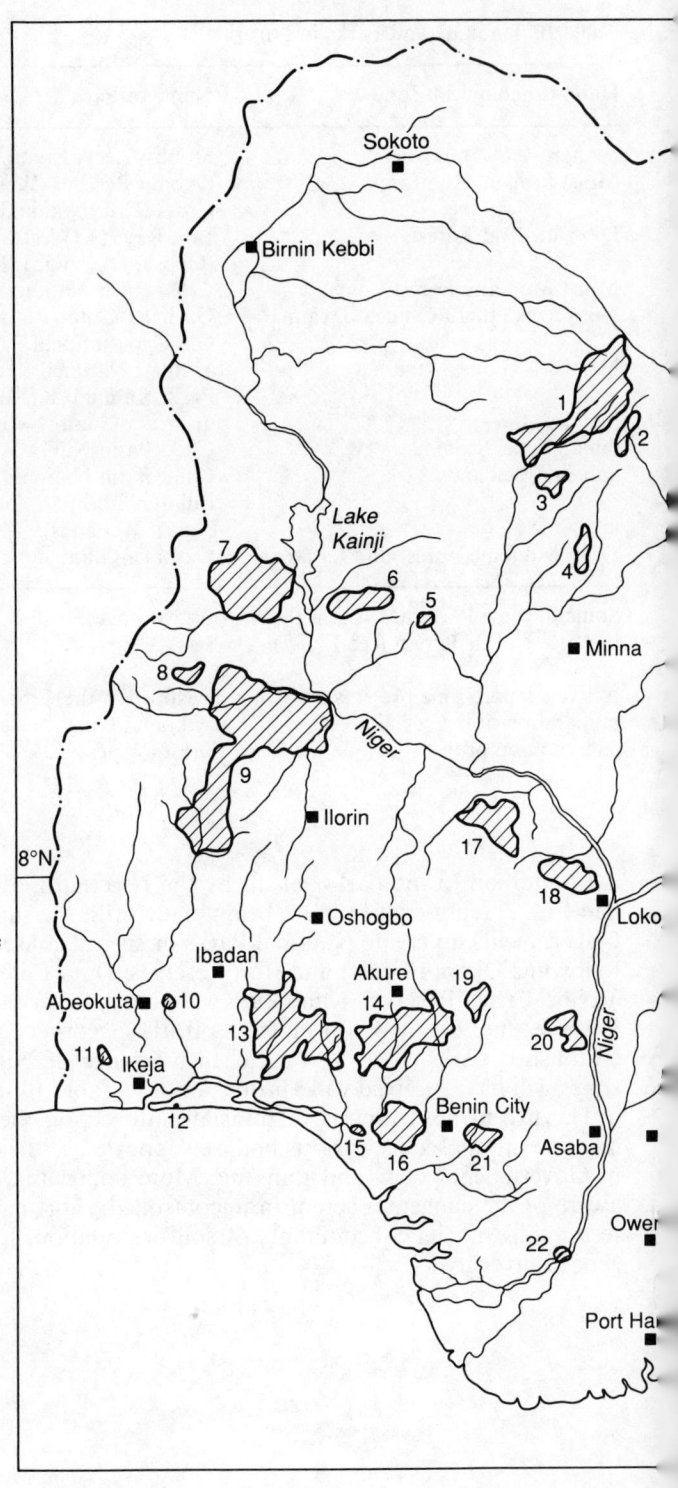

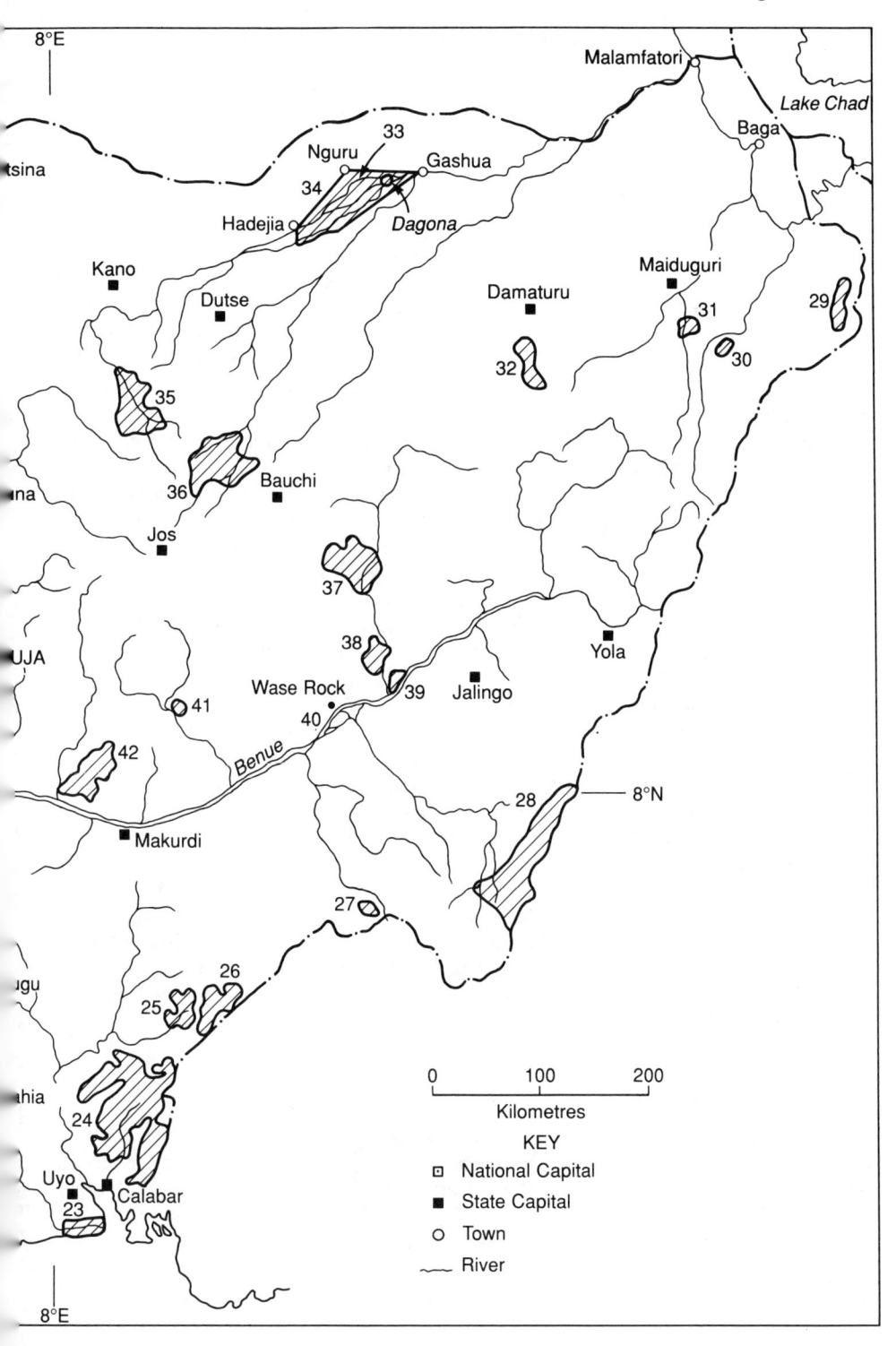

Figure 7. The National Parks, Game Reserves, Forest Reserves and other conservation areas in Nigeria.

ACKNOWLEDGEMENTS

First Edition

Without the help of the many correspondents resident in Nigeria, currently or in the recent past, to supplement my own observations, this check-list could never have been compiled. Almost all these correspondents are members of the West African Ornithologists' Society (formerly the Nigerian Ornithologists' Society) and I am therefore indebted to the officers of these Societies, especially the editors of their publications, currently Dr. C.H. Fry editor of *Malimbus*. The names of these people appear in the introduction to the systematic list and I trust they will accept that the omission of their names at this point does not lessen the level of my gratitude for their help. It may seem invidious to select any for special mention, but I must make an exception for Dr. & Mrs Dyer and Fr. Farmer who have been such regular correspondents, with a keen sense of what might be of special importance.

I am indebted to Dr. S.G. Cowper, currently cataloguing the African bird skins in the Merseyside Museum, for sending data in advance of publication; to F.C. Sibley for so generously passing over to me his catalogue of specimens collected in Nigeria and the accompanying journal of field notes; to R.E. Sharland, whose compilation of the Annual Ringing Reports in Nigeria has yielded data of great interest and importance on all relevant recoveries; to Dr. D.W. Snow and his colleagues at the BMNH (Tring) for access to the collections; to Dr. B. Hopkins for valuable criticism of earlier drafts of the section on the Nigerian Environment; and to Dr. G.D. Field for similar help with the sections on Breeding and Migration.

My very special thanks are due to my daughter Shirley Duggan, who for token reward, prepared the illustrations either from original work on maps and diagrams or by modification of illustrations I have previously used in *Ibis*, to whose editor I am grateful for permission to use them again. My wife deserves thanks, not only for patience and forbearance during the long gestation of this list, but also for vital help in assembling the notes on the individual species into meaningful sequence, a task involving careful attention to detail, boring repetitive mechanical skill and a great deal of time.

Finally my greatest debt is to the General Editor of this series of check-lists, Dr. J.F. Monk. We have argued about sequences, about methods of presentation and details of content, but have remained, I trust, good friends. If the style seems over telegraphic blame the editor, but if the veracity of a statement is in doubt, the blame is entirely mine.

Second Edition

As made clear in the Foreword and Preface, this second edition of the *Birds of Nigeria* is a team effort. The work has been supported financially by a generous Research Grant from the British Ornithologists' Union, for which we are most grateful. The contribution of each of the four 'Quartilers' has been made clear in the Preface (p. 7) and so has the up-dating, where necessary, of the sections on Geology by Vera Copp, Vegetation by Ronald Keay, and Conservation by Tasso Leventis. Similarly, the special articles on Co-operative Breeding by Roger Wilkinson and on Parasitic Breeding by Robert Payne (pp. 51 & 53) have been credited elsewhere.

We have been greatly helped by new information from the few ornithologists still working in Nigeria: chiefly Tasso Leventis, Philip Hall, Mark Hopkins and, until recently, John Barker. Mike Dyer, the Project Officer of the Hadejia Wetlands from 1989-1991, gave us useful details on the breeding and wintering bird-populations in the wetlands and also supplied one of the photographs. Captain Sharffetter, skipper of a seismic ship working in inshore Nigerian waters, and a distinguished German ornithologist, sent us many valuable sightings of seabirds, including 2 new to the Nigeria list and several additional records of marine 'vagrants'. Perhaps the birds are less vagrant than the ornithologists! For the new map, showing the present National Parks and Reserves, we are indebted to Philip Hall, and our thanks to our printers, Henry Ling for having the topographical map and Figures redrawn.

We realise that the chief feature of this new edition is the inclusion of colour plates of both habitats and a range of bird species. A very high standard for these has been set by Ian Nason and Tasso Leventis. On a recent trip to Nigeria Tasso specifically took some excellent habitat pictures for us. Our thanks also to Mary Gartshore who kindly sent some of her best photographs for inclusion, but the care and skill of Henry Ling's in translating the quality photographs into quality plates must also be acknowledged.

We are grateful to Martin Woodcock for allowing his beautiful painting of what may well be Nigeria's only endemic species, *Malimbus ibadanensis*, to be reproduced here as the Frontispiece. (Our Editor, Llew Grimes, lists *M. cassini* in his Check-list for Ghana but knows also that we think it more likely to have been *M. ibadanensis* even though, if we are right, it costs Nigeria the endemic status for this endangered bird). We are also grateful to Martin Woodcock, Emil Urban and Andrew Nye (of Academic Press) for information on Nomenclature and Sequence for Vols. V, VI and VII of *Birds of Africa*, planned, but not yet published.

Next we would like to thank James Monk, the Editor of the first edition, for his interest in the second edition, and in particular for suggesting we include an index of species, rightly pointing out that trivial names are much more stable than generic names.

Finally we are very grateful to Llewellyn Grimes, as General Editor for the BOU Check-lists, for his great help and encouragement, for his prompt dealing with our various queries and textual submissions and for the many useful suggestions which have helped to improve both the ornithology and the text.

SYSTEMATIC LIST

The most important change to this section from the First Edition is that the sequence of Families and Species, and the Scientific and English Nomenclature, now follow that used in *Birds of Africa* (Brown *et.al* 1985, Urban *et.al* 1986, Fry *et.al* 1988, Keith *et.al* 1992). The rationale for this decision is explained in the Author's Preface to this edition. At the time this volume went to press only the first 4 volumes of *Birds of Africa* had been published but the Editors kindly made available the detailed lists of species and nomenclature being used in Vol.V and the planning lists for Vols. VI and VII. For the last two volumes no proposed English names were given so that a best judgement has had to be made for these. It should be mentioned that during the course of the production of the *Birds of Africa* series, avian systematics has undergone something of a revolution with the work of Sibley and Ahlquist (1990) and Sibley and Monroe (1990). It remains to be seen whether their taxonomy will receive final acceptance by the scientific community however. Whilst doing the revision of the Systematic List for this edition we have been aware that an important Pan-African Checklist was in preparation elsewhere and this has recently been published (Dowsett & Forbes-Watson 1993), together with a complementary work giving individual country check-lists and comments on taxonomy (ed. Dowsett & Dowsett-Lemaire 1993). This has proved useful in the final checking, especially of the Passerines.

In the Systematic List the status of each species is abbreviated as follows:

RB	Resident breeder
R(B)	Resident, but breeding unproved
PM	Palaearctic migrant
Afm	Migrates within Nigeria
AfM/B	Migrates to and from Nigeria to breed in Nigeria
AfM/NB	Migrates to and from Nigeria to spend off-season in Nigeria
V	Vagrant
?	Indicates a doubt over status but not of occurrence

Those species which have a dual status have the more important stated first. Species whose occurrence is open to doubt appear in square brackets and are un-numbered and a very few, previously regarded as occurring in Nigeria, have also been labelled as 'Rejected' but are included in the systematic list with the reasons for their rejection stated.

The reference numbers in parentheses in front of the English names (e.g. I.212, II.935) are those of Mackworth-Praed & Grant (1970 & 1973, Vols I & II).

Many of the Scientific and English names differ from those used in the First Edition. Tables showing the main changes are given in Appendices 5 and 6 respectively.

The paragraph on each species gives a statement of abundance, status, habitat, area of distribution within Nigeria and for intra-African migrants some indication of the pattern of migration employed. Five categories of abundance have been used: abundant, common, not uncommon, uncommon and rare (see p. 7 for definition and comment on subjectivity). Habitat has been difficult to quote tersely, especially for wide ranging species and those subject to seasonal movement, but broad distinctions are aquatic, marine, forest, savanna and montane. Recoveries of ringed birds are included when of importance. Details of these can be found in Appendices 2,3 and 4. For species which breed within Nigeria a brief statement is made on place and timing if known.

Systematic List

A number of important changes in place names have taken place since the publication of the First Edition. These include:
'Bioko' for 'Fernando Po'
'Pagalu' for 'Annobon Is.'

Kainji Lake Nat. Park now includes the former Borgu Game Reserve and Old Oyo Nat. Park was formerly described as Upper Ogun G.R. We have followed BoA in using the spelling Cameroon, rather than Cameroun, except in direct quotations from other works, especially MP&G.

The following abbreviations are also commonly used:

F.R.	Forest Reserve
G.R.	Game Reserve
IITA	International Institute of Tropical Agriculture (Ibadan)
BoA	*Birds of Africa*
MP&G	Mackworth-Praed and Grant
BMNH	British Museum of Natural History

With regard to references, to save space, only the initials of various workers are shown (except where first records for Nigeria or first breeding records are involved); their identities and the main localities in which they have worked are listed below. We are greatly indebted to all who appear in this list for the data they have supplied so generously, often long before ultimate publication. They may not all have been actually mentioned in the text but all have given us data at some time or another that has been incorporated, and we hope they will regard their appearance in the list as due acknowledgement for their help. In the interest of brevity even initials have not always been appended if no other worker has ever supplied data from a particular locality.

RECORDERS OF NIGERIAN BIRDS

Initials	*Identities*	*Localities Worked*
J.S.A.	J.S. Ash	Mambilla & Obudu Plateaux, Oban Hills etc.
R.W.A.	R.W. Ashford	Ibadan, Oyo, etc.
J.B.	John Barker	Jos Plateau
H.G.M.B.	H.G.M. Bass	Ibadan
J.R.B.	J.R. Best	Kano
P.B.	P. Blasdale	Potiskum, etc.
H.B.	H. Boulter	Mambilla Plateau
J.A.Br.	J.A. Broadbent	Ibadan
L.H.B.	L.H. Brown	Ilorin, Kabba, etc.
J.A.B.	J.A. Button	Ilaro, Ipake F.R., Badagri, Mubi
H.C.	H. Caswell	Zaria
C.C.	Claude Chappuis	Expeditions to make recordings
A.W.C.	A.W. Cook	Sokoto
I.D.	I. Debski	Hadejia-Nguru Wetlands, Katsina
K.D.	Miss K. Dobbs	Sokoto
R.J.D.	R.J. Dowsett	Malamfatori, Mambilla & Obudu Plateaux, Oban Hills etc.
F.D-L.	F. Dowsett-Lemaire	Mambilla & Obudu Plateaux, Oban Hills, etc.
M.D.	Dr. M. Dyer	Zaria, Kagoro, Oban Hills, Obudu Plateau, Yankari, Hadejia-Nguru Wetlands etc.
D.& G.	Dyer & Gartshore	Zaria, Kagoro etc.
D.P.E.	D.P. Ebbutt	Jos Plateau
E.H.S.& S.	Ebbutt, Horwood, Sharland & Smith	Jos Plateau
J.H.E.	J.H. Elgood	Ibadan, Gambari, Obudu Plateau, etc.
A.U.E.	Dr. A.U. Ezealor	Hadejia-Nguru Wetlands
B.N.F.	B.N. Forrester	Lagos
R.F.	Fr. R. Farmer	Ife, Lagos, etc.
C.H.F.	C.H. Fry	Zaria, Abeokuta, Malamfatori, etc.
M.G.	M. Gartshore	Zaria, Kagoro, etc.
J.P.G.	J.P. Gee	Lagos, etc.
C.G.	C. Geerling	Yankari & Kainji Lake Nat. Parks
N.G.	Rev. N. Gower	Zaria, etc.
H.H.G.	Dr. H.H. Grey	Mbaakon, Obudu Plateau,
P.H.	P. Hall	Maiduguri, Serti, Mambilla Plateau, Hadejia, Lekki etc.
D.C.H.	D.C. Happold	Abuja, etc.
J.B.H.	J.B. Heigham	Lagos, Sapele, etc.
M.Ho.	Mark Hopkins	Jos Plateau
A.J.H.	A.J. Hopson	Malamfatori, Maiduguri, etc.
J.H.	Mrs Jane Hopson	Malamfatori, etc.
H.& H.	Hopson & Hopson	Malamfatori, etc.
M.H.	M. Horwood	Jos Plateau, Minna, etc.
P.J.	Peter Jenkins	Cross River State
D.N.J.	D.N. Johnson	Benin

Recorders of Nigerian Birds

Initials	Identities	Localities Worked
P.N.J.	P.N. Joshi	Oron
M.K.	Fr. Maurice Kelly	Obudu
R.K.	R. Kemp	Jos, Old Oyo Nat. Park
K.& Co.	Koeman, Rijksen & Smies	Aliya
J.R.L.	J.R. Lang	Jos Plateau etc.
A.P.L.	Tasso Leventis	Lagos, Hadejia wetlands etc.
T.L.	T. Ludlow	Imesi-Ile
E.M.	Dr. E. Macgregor	Northern Nigeria
J.M.	J. Mackenzie	Ibadan, Old Oyo Nat. Park
P.M.	P. Mackenzie	Calabar, Obudu Plateau, etc.
P.I.R.M.	P.I.R. Maclaren	Lagos, Niger Delta, Nigeria coasts
S.M.	S. Marchant	Owerri, etc.
H.F.M.	Sir Hugo Marshall	Lagos, Ibadan, etc
P.F.M.	P.F. Mason	Benin district
P.J.M.	P.J. Mundy	Sokoto
M.& C.	Mundy & Cook	Sokoto
A.M.N.	Anne Nason	Kaduna, Lagos, etc.
I.G.N.	Col. I.G. Nason	Kaduna, Lagos, etc.
R.H.P.	R.H. Parker	Ibadan, etc.
A.P.	A. Pettet	Ibadan, Zaria, etc.
G.P.	G. Pettitt	Lagos
C.S.P.	C.S Porteous	Sapele
R.& R.	Robinson & Robinson	Ilesha
T.R-S.	T. Russell-Smith	Ibadan
F.S.	F. Sander	Lagos
Capt.F.S.	Capt. F. Scharffetter	Seismic ship, Niger Delta
R.E.S.	R.E. Sharland	Kano, Calabar, Burutu, etc.
R.S.	R. Shuel	Lokoja, Zaria, etc.
F.C.S.	F.C. Sibley	Ibadan, Gambari, Sapoba, Obudu Plateau, Logomani, etc.
M.S.	M. Skilleter	Kaduna, etc.
N.J.S.	Dr. N.J. Skinner	Zaria, etc.
C.S.	C. Smeenk	Pandam Wildlife Park
P.A.S.	P.A. Smith	Niger Delta
V.S.	V. Smith	Jos Plateau
H.V.	H. Volsoe	General
D.I.M.W.	D.I.M. Wallace	Lagos, etc.
F.W.	F. Walsh	Kainji Lake Nat. Park, etc.
P.W.	P. Ward	Ibadan, Zaria, Maiduguri, Malamfatori etc.
F.E.W.	Mrs. F.E. Warr	Sapele, etc.
D.R.W.	D.R. Wells	Kainji Lake Nat. Park, etc.
W.& W.	Wells & Walsh	Kainji Lake Nat. Park, etc.
R.W.	Dr. R. Wilkinson	Kano
B.W.	B. Wood	Zaria, Vom
P.J.E.W.	P.J.E. Woods	Jos Plateau

NON-PASSERINES
STRUTHIONIDAE

1. STRUTHIO CAMELUS   RB

    (I.1)   Ostrich

Uncommon resident. All recent records of wild Ostriches (*S. c. camelus*) are from dry grass savanna of the extreme northeast, south to Biu (P.H.). Formerly extended as far west as Azare (Bannerman 1951) and possibly further south, as the BMNH has an egg from Jebba (1899), though no proof it was local in origin.

Breeding. A healthy breeding population survives at Sambisa G.R. where crèches with up to 40 juvs. have been seen (P.H.).

PROCELLARIIDAE

2. PUFFINUS GRISEUS   V

    (I.17) Sooty Shearwater

Coastal vagrant. Previously, a single sight record from the Niger Delta at Burutu, undated (R.E.S.). Well documented for waters of the Gulf of Guinea; there is a BMNH skin from Santa Isabel, Bioko (Fernando Po). Recent sighting, same area, Jul 1992 (Capt F.S.).

3. PUFFINUS PUFFINUS   V

    (I.15) Manx Shearwater

Coastal vagrant, a new species for Nigeria. Recorded from a seismic observation vessel patrolling off the Niger Delta, 14 Jul 92; noon fix 5°15'N, 4°42.5'E (Capt. F.S.).

HYDROBATIDAE

4. OCEANITES OCEANICUS   V

    (I.7)   Wilson's Storm-petrel

Coastal vagrant, migrant from Antarctica. Previously, 2 sight records only: Calabar undated (Jardine 1846-quoted by Serle 1957); Lagos, "isolated birds seen by Mr Maclaren", Jun (Sander 1956). (There is a BMNH skin from Ghana). Recent probable sighting from vessel patrolling off Niger Delta, 2 Jul 1992 (Capt.F.S.).

5. OCEANODROMA CASTRO   V

    (I.5)   Madeiran Storm-Petrel

Coastal vagrant; a new species for Nigeria. Only 3 sightings, all in the Niger Delta area: 17 Jul 1992, noon fix 5°54.3'N, 4°37.6'E (forked tail noted); 19 Jul 1992, noon fix 5°34.9'N, 4°37.6'E; 26 Jul 1992, noon fix 5°27'N, 4°44'E (Capt.F.S.).

PODICIPEDIDAE

6.   TACHYBAPTUS RUFICOLLIS   RB

   (I.3)   Little Grebe

Resident, (*T. r. capensis*), not uncommon on still freshwater lakes, natural and man-made, throughout, becoming common in northern wetlands. Probably mainly sedentary but new man-made lakes are quickly colonised and numbers may fluctuate dramatically, e.g. 100+ only on one day Apr at Jakara Dam, near Kano (J.H.E.)

Breeding. Throughout, season extensive, May-Feb, peaking Aug and Sep.

7.   PODICEPS NIGRICOLLIS   PM

   (Not in MP&G)   Black-necked Grebe

New species for Nigeria, but mentioned in Postscript of 1981 edition. Recent records from Hadejia Wetlands: 2 at Bulatura Oases on 5 Nov 1985 (P.H.), single sightings Jan 1988, and Feb 1989 (M.D.); 3 Kurra, near Jos on 3 Aug 91 (M.Ho.& J.B.).

SULIDAE

8.   SULA CAPENSIS   V

   (I.24)   Cape Gannet

No unequivocal records of (N. Atlantic) *S. bassana* from the coast, but 2 Cape Gannets *S. capensis*, ringed in southern Africa, have been recovered at Bori and Brass, both Jul (Serle 1957).

9.   SULA LEUCOGASTER   V

   (I.20)   Brown Booby

Occasional visitor (*S. l. leucogaster*) to the coast. Several sight records (all from Lagos), Jul (Maclaren 1953, D.I.M.W.). One, probably a juv. in the Niger Delta, 13 Jul 92 (Capt.F.S.).

Breeding. Breeds on islands of the Gulf of Guinea, but no records for Nigeria.

PHALACROCORACIDAE

10.   PHALACROCORAX CARBO   RB

   (I.25)   White-breasted Cormorant

Uncommon (*P. c. lucidus*), both coastal and on inland waters, from Lagos to Lake Chad. Most records are for the northeast, but max. number seen away from nests, 12 near Shendam (M.H.), is central.

Breeding. Reported only from Malamfatori, Dec-Jan, 3 separate years in the early 60s, max. 11 nests (J.H.)

11. PHALACROCORAX AFRICANUS   RB
    (I.26)   Long-tailed Cormorant

Common (*P. a. africanus*) on inland freshwaters and in coastal mangrove creeks. Resident throughout, but changes in water level cause movements, when large numbers may appear and disappear locally. Non-breeding birds (max. 28) regular Rayfield, Jos, Apr-Jun (J.B.).

Breeding. Probably opportunist; nesting recorded Sep-Feb and Jun, mostly in north but there was a coastal creek colony near Opobo-20+ pairs 15 Jan 1953 (Serle 1957). Largest known colony, 1300 nests, Malamfatori, Jan (J.H.). Breeding population in Hadejia Wetlands (1989-1991) c. 100 pairs (M.D.).

ANHINGIDAE

12. ANHINGA MELANOGASTER   RB
    (I.28)   Darter

Previously recorded as not uncommon (*A. m. rufa*) on inland waters throughout, when fluctuations in numbers mainly resulted from changes in water levels causing local movements. However, numbers may have significantly reduced in recent years. No sightings in the last 20 years (P.H.).

Breeding. Previously, Dec-Apr, in a few well dispersed localities from Atan to Malamfatori; largest known colony, 200 nests at Malamfatori (J.H.)

PELECANIDAE

13. PELECANUS ONOCROTALUS   RB, PM
    (I.31)   Great White Pelican

Locally common, mostly in the northeast between Lake Chad and the Benue, but flocks up to 150 have been met through to the southwest at Lagos (J.P.G.). Probably post-breeding dispersal accounts for most records. Max. 160+ seen in Hadejia Wetlands, Jan (M.D.).

Breeding. Up to 1000 pairs at Wase Rock, near the Benue, Dec-Feb; 15 Dec 1963 "eggs were abundant" (Dunger 1965). BoA suggest this was abandoned in 1980 but a few birds were still breeding there, Jun 1991 (A.M.N.) and an estimated min. of 75 pairs present 18 Dec 1993, similar to 1992-93 season (M.Ho.). No other colony known. Bannerman separated birds from the Palaearctic as nominate *onocrotalus* from African breeding *roseus* on size grounds; he accepted a bird shot by F.D. Golding, 4 Jun 1933, at Wulgo, (from a party of 5) as being nominate race (Bannerman 1951). Both White and BoA regard the species as monotypic.

14. PELECANUS RUFESCENS   RB
    (I.32)   Pink-backed (or Grey) Pelican

Locally still not uncommon, but numbers have diminished greatly in last 30 years and continue to do so. Confined to the coastal belt, the valleys of the great rivers, but mostly to the northern wetlands.

Breeding. Formerly in many northern towns including Kano and Sokoto,

Sep-Mar, eggs mainly Oct; probably breeds now in remote wooded wetlands. Breeding population in Hadejia Wetlands (1989-1991) estimated at 15 pairs (M.D.).

ARDEIDAE

Botaurinae

15. BOTAURUS STELLARIS   PM

    (I.52)   Eurasian Bittern

Rare Palaearctic migrant (*B. s. stellaris*), noted in 11 localities, once at Ibadan (R.H.P., T.R-S.) for over 2 months. Silent in Africa and may be overlooked. Recorded Oct-Mar from Ibadan to Lake Chad. One, Rockwater Fish Farm, Rayfield, 30 Oct 1993 (M.Ho.).

16. IXOBRYCHUS MINUTUS   RB, PM

    (I.50)   Little Bittern

Resident (*I. m. payesi*) not uncommon in reed beds and swamps throughout. Records of nominate *minutus*, migrant from the Palaearctic, on 20 Apr 1970 at Kano (R.E.S.), Dec-Apr at Malamfatori (A.J.H.) and 2 adult males at Bulatura wetlands (J.S.A. 1987). All Lagos records coincide with the rains (P.H.).

    Breeding. All records are for southwest, Lagos to Sapele, May-Oct, but probably nests much more widely. Egg-laying, Jun-Sep (BoA).

17. IXOBRYCHUS STURMII   RB

    (I.51)   Dwarf Bittern

Uncommon but widespread resident in swamps, marshes and areas subject to seasonal flooding. Recorded from southeast only at Owerri (Marchant 1942); there are more records from the southwest than the north, where it is an uncommon rains migrant to the Hadejia Wetlands (M.D.). A dry season sighting, Kaduna, when one flew out of a drainage ditch near the river, 5 Feb 1994 (A.M.N.). Local movements occur due to water level changes.

    Breeding. Bred regularly during 1970s and early 1980s in wet season in inundated acacia bush near Maiduguri; at one site there were 8 nests. This site was destroyed, but breeding confirmed in Lompanoru F.R. with 8 nests found in the early 1990s (P.H.). Breeds Ghana, Jul (Grimes 1987).

Ardeinae

18. TIGRIORNIS LEUCOLOPHUS   R(B)

    (I.49)   White-crested Tiger Heron

Uncommon to rare resident along streams in the forest zone from Lagos to Calabar; Ife is the most northerly locality (R.F.). Noteworthy new records from Emi River, Okwango F.R. and from near Oban (J.S.A.).

    Breeding. No records, but an immature, presumably of local origin, was brought to the Ibadan University Zoo, 17 Sep 1964 (J.H.E.).

19. GORSACHIUS LEUCONOTUS RB

(I.48) White-backed Night Heron

Uncommon resident in wetlands with thickets, possibly over-looked through confusion with juvenile *N. nycticorax*. The known localities, though few, range from Lagos to Potiskum; none in southeast.

Breeding. 2 well-grown young Ajeokuta, 30 Oct 1944 (Brown 1948); "nesting" Pandam, Oct (C.S.); Sep and Oct (MP&G).

20. NYCTICORAX NYCTICORAX PM, RB

(I.47) Black-crowned Night Heron

Mainly a Palaearctic migrant (*N. n. nycticorax*) Nov-Mar, as yet unreported from the southeast, not uncommon elsewhere, particularly where suitable roosting thickets occur in wetlands. Max number reported 300+, Dec, Nguru (R.E.S.). Birds ringed in Czechoslovakia, France, Hungary and Russia (one each) have been recovered (R.E.S.). Some present all year.

Breeding. 3 breeding populations reported: a small colony, Maiduguri, started nesting Sep (P.H.); c. 50 pairs Sambisa G.R. (P.H.); c. 200 pairs Hadejia Wetlands, 1989-1991 (M.D.).

21. ARDEOLA RALLOIDES PM, RB

(I.43) Squacco Heron

Common, mainly as Palaearctic migrant Oct-Mar, throughout the north; less common in southwest; surprisingly as yet unreported from southeast. Some present all year. 1000+ at Hadejia Wetlands, 6 Nov (Ash 1990). Birds ringed in Bulgaria and Yugoslavia (3) have been recovered.

Breeding. Bannerman (1951) quotes a 1913 nest on the Bauchi Plateau; more recently, a colony of 27 nests (with other herons) found Malamfatori, Feb (J.H.). Breeding population of Hadejia Wetlands (1989-1991) c. 500 pairs (M.D.).

22. ARDEOLA RUFIVENTRIS ?

(I.46) Rufous-bellied Heron

Vagrant from southern Africa. Not listed by Bannerman and named *Erythrocnus rufiventris* by MP&G. Sight records only: Lagos, 24 Feb 1969 (J.B.H.), 31 Aug 1969 (D.I.M.W.) and 1 Jan 1972 (J.B.H. with J.P.G.). Also probable sighting, pair, Old Oyo Nat. Park, 8 Feb 1969 (J.H.E.).

23. BUBULCUS IBIS Afm/B

(I.42) Cattle Egret

Abundant (*B. i. ibis*) all year north of c.10°N, but south of this is present only mid Oct to mid May; a "northern concertina" migrant (Elgood *et al.* 1973). Although reported from coast, is sparse in forest clearings but common in derived savanna and northward, associating with cattle.

Breeding. Throughout north, usually in village shade trees, Mar-Jul, peaking May and Jun in the rains. Breeding population in Hadejia Wetlands (1989-1991) estimated at c. 12,000 pairs (M.D.).

24.   BUTORIDES STRIATUS   RB, ?Afm

      (I.45)   Green-backed Heron

Common resident (*B. s. atricapillus*) in mangrove creeks, forest pools and streams throughout the south, rather less common in wetlands of the savanna zones, becoming uncommon in the far north, where wetland tends to be seasonal, and where it may be only a rains migrant.

Breeding. Throughout from the coast to Sokoto, May-Nov; nests singly, earlier in south than north. Many young are seen in the Hadejia Wetlands at the end of the rains, but proof of breeding there still required (M.D.).

25.   EGRETTA ARDESIACA   RB

      (I.39)   Black Heron

Resident, locally not uncommon in wetlands with clear shallow water. In small numbers in a few localities of southwest, but flock of c. 200 on Lekki Peninsula throughout Sep and Oct 1992 (P.H.); unrecorded in southeast; more numerous and at more localities in north. A flock of 100, Sokoto, Aug (Mundy & Cook 1972-73).

Breeding. Malamfatori, 47 nests (with other herons) Feb-Apr (J.H.). Hadejia Wetlands c. 20 breeding pairs (M.D.).

26.   EGRETTA GULARIS   RB

      (I.41)   Western Reef Heron

Not uncommon locally in mangrove creeks and occasionally on open sea beaches. Rare inland but one photographed on lake at IITA on 1 Apr 1989 (I.G.N.). Records are mostly from Niger Delta and Lagos. A roost of 500-1000, Bonny (Maclaren 1952).

Breeding. One record: Opobo, 12 pairs, Jan (Serle 1957).

27.   EGRETTA GARZETTA   PM, RB

      (I.40)   Little Egret

Common Palaearctic migrant throughout in all types of wetlands and along shores but tends to avoid brackish or salt water. Numbers diminished May-Sep, but many birds, perhaps immatures, present all areas throughout year and a few breed. Wintering population in the Hadejia Wetlands c. 1,200. Birds ringed in Russia (3) have been recovered.

Breeding. One record: 17 nests (with other herons) Malamfatori, Feb (J.H.).

28. EGRETTA INTERMEDIA   RB
   (I.38)   Yellow-billed Egret

Locally not uncommon (*E. i. brachyrhyncha*) on grassy banks of coastal lagoons, man-made reservoirs and lakes. May have previously been taken for *E. alba* but first record was a specimen collected at Ibadan, 29 Apr 1960 (F.C. Sibley). Now recognised in many localities throughout, from Lagos to Lake Chad.
   Breeding. 60 nests, Malamfatori, Feb (J.H.); "several nests" Potiskum, Mar (P.B.); c. 120 pairs bred in Hadejia Wetlands, 1989-1991 (M.D.).

29. EGRETTA ALBA   RB
   (I.37)   Great White Egret

Common (*E. a. melanorhynchos*) at brackish coastal lagoons, lake and river shores and wetlands throughout the country, with flocks of 50+ in several localities. No evidence of Palaearctic migrants.
   Breeding. Sep-Apr, mostly in north and valleys of great rivers. Largest colony reported, 200+ nests, Malamfatori, Feb (J.H.). Breeding population of c. 20 pairs in Hadejia Wetlands, 1989-1991 (M.D.).

30. ARDEA PURPUREA   PM
   (I.36)   Purple Heron

Not uncommon (*A. p. purpurea*) on lake and reservoir shores and wetlands throughout, mainly Sep-Mar, but a few, probably immatures, remain all year. No evidence of breeding. A bird ringed in Russia was recovered at Funtua and one ringed Germany was recovered in southern Nigeria.

31. ARDEA CINEREA   PM, RB
   (I.33)   Grey Heron

Common (*A. c. cinerea*) in mangrove creeks and all types of inland wetlands throughout, Oct-Mar, markedly less common Apr-Sep, indicating most are migrant from the Palaearctic, but there is a resident breeding population. Recoveries of ringed birds from Germany, Hungary and Russia range from Sokoto to Port Harcourt (R.E.S.). The max. dry season count in the Hadejia Wetlands (1989-1991) c. 2,500 (M.D.).
   Breeding. No recent records. Bannerman (1930) quotes "rains" breeding from Kano, Bauchi and Niger Provinces, but Serle (1957) found "not less than 12 nests", one "at least" with large young, Opobo, in Jan. Breeds Nigeria, Jan, May-Jun (BoA).

32. ARDEA MELANOCEPHALA   Afm/B
   (I.34)   Black-headed Heron

Common all months, usually near water but not confined to wetlands, from the great rivers northward. A dry season non-breeding migrant in southern areas, reaching the coast at Lagos where, surprisingly, Sander (1957) had a Jun record. 30+ birds in Kapok tree Shendam, Jun 1992 but no nests observed (J.B.).

Breeding. Many colonies in trees, up to 25 nests, sometimes with other herons, all north of c.11°N, from Argungu to Gajebo. Some activity occurs at nests Mar-Sep. Laying dates Nigeria, Jan-Feb, Apr-Dec (BoA).

33. ARDEA GOLIATH   R(B)

   (I.35) Goliath Heron

Uncommon, in mangrove creeks and marshes and on river banks and sand bars, in all localities, but mainly coastal and in valleys of the great rivers and wetlands of northern areas. Still not uncommon at Yankari. Usually solitary, pairs occasional, max. 5 together on Komadugu-Gana River (P.B.). No evidence of migration but wanders, birds seldom remaining long in one place.
Breeding. No records for Nigeria.

SCOPIDAE

34. SCOPUS UMBRETTA   RB

   (I.53) Hamerkop (Hammerkop)

Common (*S. u. minor*) in coastal creeks from Calabar to Warri, but uncommon from there westward to Lagos. Equally common (*S. u. umbretta*) in areas north from the great rivers, but uncommon in the Hadejia Wetlands. Very few sightings, racially undetermined, between these areas. One, Obudu Cattle Ranch, 23 Dec 91 (M.Ho.).
Breeding. Probably protracted, but *minor* reported only in Dec (Bannerman 1951); *umbretta* Mar-Sep, but mainly Mar-Jun. Laying dates in N. Nigeria, Jan-Apr (BoA).

CICONIIDAE

35. MYCTERIA IBIS   RB/Afm

   (I.62) Yellow-billed Stork

Uncommon resident throughout, along rivers and in marshes, and probably only a dry season migrant to coastal swamps; but from the great rivers northward occurs in all months. Max. 250 in Hadejia Wetlands during dry seasons, 1989-1991 (M.D.).
Breeding. Aug-Feb; mostly in the Sudan zone in small colonies, sometimes with other birds, sometimes in towns; also south to the Niger at Baro, Jan (Bannerman 1931). Laying dates in N. Nigeria, Aug-Sep (BoA).

36. ANASTOMUS LAMELLIGERUS   AfM/B

   (I.59) African Open-bill Stork

Not uncommon locally (*A. l. lamelligerus*) throughout, in or near wetlands. Formerly regarded only as a trans-equatorial migrant breeding south of the equator, but flocks of up to 100 have remained all year at Lagos (J.P.G.), although only 1 sighting in Lagos area between 1987-91 (P.H.). Elsewhere much smaller flocks occur, mostly Nov-Apr, but max. 200 in Hadejia Wetlands during dry seasons, 1989-1991 (M.D.). Unrecorded in southeast.

Breeding. Once, possibly opportunist only: well grown young in nest, Potiskum area, Jan (P.B.).

37. CICONIA NIGRA   PM

　　(I.56)　Black Stork

Uncommon Palaearctic migrant recorded Nov-Apr from Lake Chad south to the Benue in the east and as far south as the Oli River (Kainji Lake Nat. Park) in west. Several records at Yankari, max. 6, Dec-Jan (M.D.). Max. 30 recorded Hadejia Wetlands, 1989-1991 (M.D.). 4, Felak Farm (on edge of Lame-Burra G.R.), 7 Jan 1994 (M.Ho).
　　Breeding. Although nests in southern Africa there are no records for West Africa.

38. CICONIA ABDIMII   AfM/B

　　(I.58)　Abdim's Stork, White-bellied Stork

Locally common and well-documented trans-equatorial migrant, Apr-Oct, with early and late stragglers, in open savanna near water, mostly north of 11°N. Seldom recorded in southern areas, which it must overfly to and from its off-season quarters in southern Africa; but 13 at Ibadan after severe storm, 16 Apr 1963 (J.H.E.)
　　Breeding. Throughout north Apr-Jul, peaking Jun. Loko, on the Benue (8°N), is most southerly point recorded, almost all others are north of 11°N.

39. CICONIA EPISCOPUS   AfM/B

　　(I.57)　Woolly-necked Stork

Uncommon (*C. e. microscelis*) in wetlands south of the great rivers, Sep to mid May. Mainly on passage, Mar-May, in a central belt and recorded more numerously in north at all seasons. On balance, it seems to be an intra-African migrant though whether it only breeds in other parts of Africa is unclear.
　　Breeding. Laying date N. Nigeria, Jan (BoA); Jan and Feb in Sierra Leone (Bannerman 1953); Uganda Nov, Dec, Feb, Mar (BoA). Present all months in Yankari (Crick & Marshall 1981) strongly suggesting it must breed there.

40. CICONIA CICONIA   PM

　　(I.55)　White Stork

Palaearctic migrant, locally not uncommon (*C. c. ciconia*), usually on areas subject to seasonal flood in the Sudan and Sahel zones, Oct-Apr. Several flocks of 100+ noted in north and one of c. 2000 flying over Lake Alo on 6 Feb 1991 (P.H.). Max. dry season count of 500 in Hadejia Wetlands, 1989-1991 (M.D.). 11 at Calabar (R.E.S.). Some southern records of single birds (Ibadan, Ughelli) could refer to escapes. Birds ringed in Algeria, Morocco, Tunisia, France, Germany, Portugal, Greece, Estonia and Spain have been recovered (R.E.S).

41. EPHIPPIORHYNCHUS SENEGALENSIS R(B)

(I.60) Saddle-bill Stork

Uncommon, probably resident, in swamps and on watersides, mainly in valleys of great rivers northward to Lake Chad, but also on the Oli River and at Yankari. Subject to sporadic local short appearances; only two records in Hadejia Wetlands, 1989-91 (M.D.).

Breeding. Unproven, but adults with juvs. encountered twice in Potiskum area, Apr and May (P.B.). Similarly, small numbers at Yankari Nat. Park with "immatures seen regularly" (I.D.). Breeds Niger "inland" delta (Green & Sayer 1979). Laying date Ghana, Oct; well grown chicks Ivory Coast, Dec (Grimes 1987).

42. LEPTOPTILOS CRUMENIFERUS RB

(I.61) Marabou Stork

Not uncommon resident in Sudan zone, usually near or in towns, but numbers probably diminishing. Less common southward to the great rivers. Only southern record, Ibadan 23 Mar 1974 (T.R-S). Local seasonal movements possible.

Breeding. Dec-May, formerly in main streets of major towns such as Sokoto and Birnin Kudu, but now more suburban. A nest "in Bornu" late Aug "said to contain eggs" (Bannerman 1951) is probably an error. Breeding population of Hadejia Wetlands (1989-1991) was 8-11 pairs (M.D.). Laying dates W. Africa, Dec-Feb (BoA).

THRESKIORNITHIDAE

43. PLEGADIS FALCINELLUS PM

(I.68) Glossy Ibis

Common Palaearctic migrant (*P. f. falcinellus*) late Aug to early Apr to wetlands of the most northerly areas; flocks of 100+ at Nguru and Sokoto (R.E.S). Wintering population of up to 2000 in the Hadejia Wetlands (M.D.). Much smaller flocks straggle south to the coast, e.g. 10 at Lagos (D.I.M.W.). Some remain all year, notably at Lake Chad.

44. BOSTRYCHIA HAGEDASH RB

(I.65) Hadada

Not uncommon resident (*B. h. brevirostris*) in the Guinea savannas along wooded streams, but uncommon both south to the coast and northward.

Breeding. C/3 Kafanchan, Jun; C/2 Loko, Jun (Bannerman 1951); "nesting" Pandam, Apr (C.S.).

45. BOSTRYCHIA OLIVACEA R(B)

(I.67) Olive Ibis

Earlier single record – a pair by stream in forest at Oban Hills, 1 Aug 1980

(M.D.), presumably *B. o. eupreipennis*. More recent sightings from same general area in Feb 1987 (J.S.A. 1990) where 2 or 3 flew over calling. Because of the difficulty in distinguishing it from *B. rara*, which is much more common in adjacent Cameroon, Ash suggests the present records need confirming.

Breeding. No records within W. Africa.

46. THRESKIORNIS AETHIOPICA   RB

    (I.63)   Sacred Ibis

Not uncommon resident (*T. a. aethiopica*), mainly in wetlands from the valleys of the great rivers northward; max. count 90 in Hadejia Wetlands, 1989-1991 (M.D.). Only sporadic in dry season in south, though Serle (1957) recorded 100 at Bonny.

Breeding. Only records are: Sokoto, Jun and Jul (Serle 1943); 130 nests Malamfatori, Jan (J.H.). Dates suggest opportunist breeding. Laying dates, Dec-Feb and May-Jun (BoA).

47. PLATALEA LEUCORODIA   VPM

    (I.69)   Eurasian Spoonbill

Palaearctic migrant, probably only vagrant to the Chad basin in extreme northeast. Several sightings between Malamfatori and Lake Alau, the first in Feb 1961 at Lake Alau; max. 3 at Wulgo, Mar 1961 (both R.E.S.). Group of 18 birds Hadejia Wetlands, 2 Mar 1987 (J.S.A.).

48. PLATALEA ALBA   RB

    (I.70)   African Spoonbill

Not uncommon resident all year at Lake Chad, uncommon elsewhere, but seen on the Niger at Onitsha, 25 May 1953 (Serle 1957); Sapele, 18 Jan 1980 (C.S.P.); 1 Rayfield, Jos, 10 May 1991 (J.B.).

Breeding. 28 pairs Malamfatori, Jan-Apr (J.H.). Laying dates, Jan-Feb (BoA).

PHOENICOPTERIDAE

49. PHOENICONAIAS MINOR   V, AfM

    (I.72)   Lesser Flamingo

Formerly African migrant to mangrove swamps, sometimes in large numbers. Last record for this area, a flock of 30 Obe, Jul 1932 (H.F.M.) Although not recognised for southeast by Serle (1957), Bannerman (1951) mentions 2000 in the Calabar estuary. There are other old records west to Ipepe. In the north, there are one or 2 records for the Hadejia Wetlands and 45 were counted on an oasis near the Niger border, Feb 1988 (M.D.).

Breeding. No records, but Mauritania, Jun-Jul (BoA).

ANATIDAE

Dendrocygninae

50. DENDROCYGNA BICOLOR   RB

   (I.94) Fulvous Whistling-Duck

Common resident, in small numbers, locally on freshwater lakes of northern wetlands, with a max. of 800 in Hadejia Wetlands, 1989-1991 (M.D.). Previously flocks up to 5000 on Lake Chad. Mostly in the Sudan zone, but also south to Kainji and Agenebode on the lower Niger. Subject to local movement.
   Breeding. Previously only recorded at Gwadabawa, Aug-Sep (Serle 1943), but in early 1990s broods seen in Hadejia wetlands, Jan-Feb (M.D. and independently A.U.E.). Laying dates, Jul-Sep (BoA).

51. DENDROCYGNA VIDUATA   RB

   (I.93) White-faced Whistling-Duck

By far the most common resident duck, abundant from the great rivers northward, with up to 5000 in the Hadejia Wetlands, 1989-1991 (M.D.). Uncommon in the southwest, mostly in coastal swamps in dry season. Rare in southeast: 2 records Obubra and one Onitsha (Serle 1957).
   Breeding. Widespread in the north, Jul-Oct. Rayfield, Jos from Jun (J.B.).

52. THALASSORNIS LEUCONOTUS   RB

   (I.74) White-backed Duck

Previously not uncommon resident (*T. l. leuconotus*) in wetlands of the northernmost areas, from Sokoto to Potiskum, but no records in the last 20 years (P.H.). Local movements were dependent on water level changes.
   Breeding. Only recorded at Gwadabawa, Aug (Serle 1943).

Anserinae

53. ANSER ALBIFRONS   PM

   (Not in MP&G)   (Greater) White-fronted Goose

Several sightings, probably the same bird, in dry season of 1973/4 at Zaria by two observers (N.G. & H.C.) independently. An undoubted *Anser* sp, *A. albifrons* is the only species admitted by White ("vagrant in north Sudan"). Although this early record might have been an escape there is a more recent sighting of one at Dumbari in the Hadejia Wetlands, Jan 1989 (M.D.).

Tadorninae

54. ALOPOCHEN AEGYPTIACUS   RB

   (I.97) Egyptian Goose

Uncommon resident on lakes and rivers in diminishing numbers recently, mostly in wetlands of the northernmost areas, from Sokoto (flocks 30+) to Lake Chad; rather fewer recorded south to the great rivers and only 2 (Lagos and near Abeokuta) in southwest; none from southeast.

Breeding. Ajeokuta, Jan (Brown 1948); Malamfatori, Mar (A.J.H.); juvs. near Kano, Dec (R.E.S.). Laying dates Nigeria, Jan, Sep (BoA).

Anatinae

55. PLECTROPTERUS GAMBENSIS RB

(I.98) Spur-winged Goose

Common and widespread resident in wetlands from the great rivers northward; flocks 50-100 frequent. Max. count of 2000 in Hadejia Wetlands, 1989-1991 (M.D.). Uncommon in southwest but 80 near Lagos, 17 Feb 1969 (Gee & Heigham) and several at Ibeju, Lekki Peninsula, 24 Feb 91 (A.M.N.); in southeast only at Calabar and Onitsha.

Breeding. Aug-Nov, only in north.

56. PTERONETTA HARTLAUBII R(B)

(I.92) Hartlaub's Duck

A resident species formerly not uncommon and well distributed in creeks and rivers of coastal and forest zones, right across the country, but habitat destruction is leading to diminished numbers. A few records also in well wooded pools, north to Ilorin (Brown 1948).

Breeding. Unrecorded anywhere in the species' world range. Occurs in all months, except Feb and Nov, on forest pools near Calabar, with several pairs; breeding inferred (Mackenzie 1979).

57. SARKIDIORNIS MELANOTOS RB

(I.96) Knob-billed Duck

Common and widespread resident (*S. m. melanotos*) in wetlands, from the great rivers northward, with flocks of 100+ frequent. Max. of 2000+ in Hadejia Wetlands, 1989-1991 (M.D.). Very few records from the south: Lagos and Onitsha in the dry season, Okene and Obubra in the rains. Also north Bornu, Jul (Bannerman 1951), Borgu Game Reserve (now Kainji Lake Nat. Park) "in rains" (W.& W.).

Breeding. Well-grown young Wulgo, Jan 1957 (J.H.E.). Laying date, Sep (BoA).

58. NETTAPUS AURITUS RB

(I.95) African Pygmy Goose

Widespread and not uncommon resident on freshwater lakes with floating vegetation, from the great rivers northward; uncommon and more local in southwest to Lagos; only one record from southeast, Afikpo (Serle 1957).

Breeding. Oviducal egg Jul, young Jun, Lagos (Sander 1956); young in nest holes Birnin Kudu, mid Aug (R.E.S.): young Zaria, late Jun (A.P.); adult with 4 half-grown young Ibadan, 29 Oct 1987 (J.S.A).

59. ANAS PENELOPE   PM
    (I.84)   Eurasian Wigeon

Uncommon Palaearctic migrant, Nov-Mar, mainly in small parties in wetlands of northernmost areas, Sokoto to Lake Chad, but max. 80 Hadejia Wetlands (M.D.). Also south to Ibadan, but never in southeast.

60. ANAS STREPERA   VPM
    (I.83)   Gadwall

Vagrant from the Palaearctic (presumably *A. s. strepera*). Only 3 previous records: "Mongama" (probably Mongonu), Nov 1929 (Bannerman 1951); Nguru (R.E.S.); sighting near Kano (R.E.S.), but recorded as "rare" in Hadejia Wetlands (1989-91) with 20-30 sightings (M.D.).

61. ANAS CRECCA   PM
    (I.85)   Common Teal

Uncommon Palaearctic migrant (*A. c. crecca*) in small flocks to northernmost wetlands, Sep-Feb, from Sokoto to Lake Chad, south to Zaria and Jos. Max. count of 500 in Hadejia Wetlands, 1989-1991 (M.D.). Southwestern records: 1 male and 5 females Ibadan, 11 Jan 1942 (H.F.M.), 1 female Sapele, Dec (J.B.H.) and Lagos, 2 Jan 1971 (D.I.M.W.); none from southeast. A hundred years ago Dr. Hartert observed "hundreds" at Sokoto (Bannerman 1930).

62. ANAS CAPENSIS   R(B)
    (I.88)   Cape Wigeon

A small population is resident on Lake Chad and small flocks, max. 50, have been sighted (and some collected) on bore-hole lakes in the Chad basin; also at a soda lake north of Yusufari (P.H.). Regular in small numbers in oases near the Niger border, 1989-1991 (M.D.). 6 at Kazaure, Kano State, 6 Apr 1979 (S.& W.). One sighting at Zaria (M.D.).
    Breeding. No evidence of breeding within Nigeria.

[ANAS PLATYRHYNCHOS   PM
    (I.80)   Mallard

Occurrence unsubstantiated (presumably *A. p. platyrhynchos*). Bannerman (1953) felt sure it "must regularly visit the shallow lakes north of Sokoto and Kano" and mentions (1951) 2 reported shot. Fairbairn (1952) says "observed in the Ibadan area" but gives no details. Also a dubious sighting "after a severe dust storm" at Malamfatori (J.H.). Status remains dubious with no confirmed records from Nigeria. "Très rare" in Mali with 3 encounters between 1947 and 1976 (B. Lamarche 1980) – but see postscript.]

63. ANAS UNDULATA   V
     (I.81) Yellow-billed Duck

Vagrant probably from further east, presumably *A. u. undulata*, reported by White from Cameroon highlands. 5 photographed on stream on Mambilla Plateau, Dec 1979 (R.E.S.). See *Malimbus* 8:43, where the photograph is reproduced.

64. ANAS SPARSA   R(B)
     (I.82) African Black Duck

Range has been extended west into Nigeria (presumably *A. s. leucostigma*) by sightings of pairs and single birds, Sep, Oct and Dec 1974, at 3 separate highland streams on the Mambilla Plateau (P.H.). More recently seen several times on the Kam, Gashaka and Yim Rivers and elsewhere on the Mambilla Plateau (A.A.G).

65. ANAS ACUTA   PM
     (I.91) (Northern) Pintail

Common Palaearctic migrant (*A. a. acuta*), Nov to early Mar. Flocks up to 5000 throughout the northernmost wetlands, and up to 70 as far south as Zaria and Jos Plateau. 13,000+ present in the dry season in the Hadejia Wetlands, 1989-1991 (M.D.). Stragglers south to Ibadan, "8 on various occasions Nov-Jan 73/74" (R.H.P.), but not recorded in southeast.

66. ANAS HOTTENTOTA   RB
     (I.89) Hottentot Teal

Uncommon resident in pools with muddy shores from Sokoto to Lake Chad, south to Zaria and Kainji Lake Nat. Park. Numbers decreasing in Kano State by 1987 with no records since then (S.& W). About 100 on oases near Niger border (M.D.).
    Breeding. Yusufari, Mar (P.H.). 2 broods of "week-old" ducklings Kazaure, mid Feb (R.E.S.).

67. ANAS QUERQUEDULA   PM
     (I.86) Garganey

Abundant Palaearctic migrant, early Oct to Apr. Flocks of up to 10,000. Throughout northernmost wetlands from Sokoto to Lake Chad (where stragglers have remained till Jun), with small parties southward to Ibadan, Ife and Lagos. Serle (1957) is doubtful about the only record from the southeast. Birds ringed in Latvia and Russia (R. Volga) have been recovered and most remarkably one from India: birds ringed in Nigeria have been recovered in Greece, Poland and Russia (4).

Anatidae

68. ANAS CLYPEATA PM

(I.79) (Northern) Shoveler

Not uncommon Palaearctic migrant to the northernmost wetlands, from Sokoto to Lake Chad, late Oct to Mar, in flocks up to 100. Max. of 400 wintering in Hadejia wetlands, 1989-1991 (M.D.). Much less common southward to Zaria; isolated records from Ibadan and Lagos, but none from southeast.

69. MARMARONETTA ANGUSTIROSTRIS VPM

(I.87) Marbled Teal

Palaearctic vagrant, only 2 records: R.E.S. identified one (said to be "one of 50") shot by Mallam Yakubu at Nguru, 27 Dec 1977; one in Hadejia Wetlands, 11 Jan 1988 (P.H.).

70. AYTHYA FERINA PM

(I.76) Common Pochard

Not uncommon, but irregular, Palaearctic migrant, mainly to the northernmost wetlands, Dec-Feb. Flocks some years, e.g. 1961/2, are of 100+, and a max. of 350 wintering in the Hadejia Wetlands, 1989-1991 (M.D.). Only 2 more southerly records: female shot on the Benue at Bagaji, 7 Dec 1948 (Bannerman 1951) and a pair present Ibadan, Dec 1973-Feb 1974 (T.R-S.).

71. AYTHYA NYROCA PM

(I.75) Ferruginous Duck

Regular Palaearctic migrant, but in fluctuating numbers, mainly to the wetlands of the northernmost areas, from Sokoto to Lake Chad, Oct-Apr, a few till mid May. When common, flocks of up to 1000. Less common southward to Zaria and Jos, with southwest records from Ibadan (R.H.P.), Ife (R.F.) and coastal lagoons at Lekki (Bannerman 1951).

72. AYTHYA FULIGULA PM

(I.78) Tufted Duck

Uncommon Palaearctic migrant to the northernmost wetlands, from Sokoto to Lake Chad, Nov-Feb. Usually small groups, but 60 at Malamfatori (A.J.H.) and c. 150 wintering in Hadejia Wetlands, 1989-1991 (M.D.). Most southerly record is Samaru Lake, Zaria – pair on 29 Jan 1973 (J.H.E.).

ACCIPITRIDAE

Pandioninae

73. PANDION HALIAETUS   PM
(I.172) Osprey

Not uncommon Palaearctic migrant (*P. h. haliaetus*), regular and widespread to lakes and larger rivers throughout, Oct-Apr. Some records for "summer" and year round records from Kainji (F.W.) probably refer to immatures, but possibly indicate local breeding. Birds ringed Finland (12) Germany (1) and Sweden (11) have been recovered at widespread localities. Ash (1989) reported 22 on dead trees at Lake Kainji, 29 Oct 1987.

Accipitrinae

74. AVICEDA CUCULOIDES   Afm/B
(I.121) African Cuckoo Falcon

Not uncommon resident (presumably *A. c. batesi*) in the forest zone and seen all year at Lagos (J.P.G. & J.B.H.), though possibly numbers diminish in the rains. In savanna woodland is much less common (presumably *A. c. cuculoides*) and at Zaria and Kano only during the rains.

Breeding. From the coast at Calabar and Lagos north to Ilorin and Pandam; season ill-defined as most records refer to feeding young out of the nest, Jan-Sep. Ibadan (IITA), incubating 2 juvs. in nest to fledging Apr to May, (T.R-S). Laying date Nigeria, Jun (BoA).

75. PERNIS APIVORUS   PM
(I.126) Honey Buzzard

Uncommon Palaearctic migrant, widespread early Oct to early Apr. Mostly in the south: 10+ Lagos with 3 together (D.I.M.W.) and several Owerri (Marchant 1953). Only one sighting from far north, Kano, 8 Dec 1953 (R.E.S.). Recent records from Calabar (P.M.) and Nindam F.R. on the southern escarpment of the Jos Plateau (Dyer *et al.* 1986) indicate more widespread occurrence. Birds ringed in Sweden and Netherlands have been recovered in southern Nigeria.

76. MACHAERHAMPHUS ALCINUS   RB
(I.125) Bat Hawk

Uncommon resident (*M. a. anderssoni*), recorded from Lagos and Calabar north to Sokoto and the Jos Plateau. Habitat ill-defined, but most sightings are urban/suburban though this probably merely reflects restricted crepuscular activities of man. Recorded from Okomu F.R. where one was feeding on Naked-faced Barbets (P.H.). Several noted at Yankari Nat. Park in rains when bats are plentiful; also at Hadejia Wetlands, Dec and Jan (I.D.). Some evidence for northward shift during the rains.

Breeding. Virtually nothing known, but building and copulation Ibadan, 9 a.m. 19 Jul 1976 (J.H.E.). Immature present at Nguru Nov 1988 to Apr 1989 (M.D.).

88   Accipitridae

77.   ELANUS CAERULEUS   RB
   (I.124)   Black-shouldered Kite

Common resident (*E. c. caeruleus*) in wooded savanna from Derived Savanna to Sudan zones, much less common in forest clearings and Sahel. No evidence for seasonal movement.
   Breeding. Abeokuta to Sokoto, Sep-Apr. Laying dates Nigeria, Nov and Apr (BoA).

78.   CHELICTINIA RIOCOURII   AfM/NB
   (I.122)   African Swallow-tailed Kite

Uncommon intra-African migrant in arid savanna of the Sahel and elsewhere, always in the dry season except very occasionally. 1200 seen Sokoto, Dec 1953 (R.E.S.) otherwise small flocks, max. 20 Sokoto, Nov-Feb (M.& C.). Irregular records south of Sudan zone, probably only in very dry years; southward limit Ilorin, 10+ birds 17 Feb 1960 (J.H.E.).
   Breeding. No records. Breeds Niger, May-Jun.

79.   MILVUS MIGRANS   Afm/B, PM
   (I.123)   Black Kite

Abundant resident (*M. m. parasitus*) throughout, but almost absent in south, Jun-Sep (Elgood *et al.* 1973). Southward visible migration in Oct of flocks up to 1000; some at least are Palaearctic migrants (*M. m. migrans*), proved by recovery in Feb 1969 of one ringed Switzerland and later of one ringed Germany.
   Breeding. Throughout, in south Nov-Feb, later northward, e.g. Sokoto, Mar-May.

80.   HALIAEETUS VOCIFER   RB
   (I.147)   African Fish Eagle

Uncommon resident along wooded streams and at lakes with wooded shores throughout, but mostly north of the great rivers.
   Breeding. Noted in the Guinea zones, Old Oyo and Kainji Lake Nat. Parks and Pandam Wildlife Park, Nov-Feb. Laying dates Nigeria, Oct-Nov, perhaps Dec (BoA).

81.   GYPOHIERAX ANGOLENSIS   RB
   (I.148)   Vulturine Fish-Eagle, Palm-nut Vulture

Common resident in the coastal creeks, not uncommon and widespread in the forest zone, becoming more sparse northward in gallery forest and only where the oil-palm *Elais guineensis* occurs. Many records from the southern escarpment of the Jos Plateau; northernmost records Kari (P.B.) and Sokoto (K.D.).
   Breeding. Bida, Dec (J.H.E.); Kafanchan, Jan-Mar (Serle 1939); Bussa, "dry season" (F.W.); adult with 2 juvs. Ife, Dec (R.F.); incubating or brooding Ekang, 28 Jan 1987 (J.S.A.).

82. NEOPHRON PERCNOPTERUS   ?Afm/B, ?PM

(I.105)   Egyptian Vulture

Uncommon resident (*N. p. percnopterus*) mostly in arid savanna of northeast from Kazaure to Lake Chad but also southward at Yola, Numan, Wase Rock and Ibi, all in the Benue valley. Most records are dry season suggesting immigration from either the Palaearctic or northeast Africa. One record in the Hadejia wetlands of an immature, Dec 1989 (M.D.). Both African and Palaearctic populations said to occur in Chad (Newby 1979).
Breeding. Kazaure, undated (J.R.B.); "Nigeria, November to March" (MP&G). Juv. Yankari, suggests breeding there (S.& W.). Laying date, Nov (BoA).

83. NECROSYRTES MONACHUS   RB

(I.106)   Hooded Vulture

Abundant resident round towns and villages throughout all the savanna zones, but with an unexplained patchy distribution through the townships of the forest and derived savanna zones. Absent from Lagos and Ibadan, but present at Epe (P.H.); common at Enugu, Port Harcourt and Calabar. Numbers declining in Kano State (R.E.S. & R.W.) which may be partly due to species being used as human food (Thiollay 1985). Air pollution may be a further factor and account for long absence from Lagos and Ibadan.
Breeding. Oct-Mar, peaking Dec-Feb, in urban and suburban sites.

84. GYPS AFRICANUS   ?Afm/B

(I.102)   African White-backed Vulture

Not uncommon resident in northernmost areas from Sokoto to Lake Chad. Tendency to assemble at carcases, max. 40 at Minetti bore-hole (P.H.). All more southern records, "northern Oyo" and Kabba (Brown 1948), Mambilla Plateau, Old Oyo and Kainji Lake Nat. Parks, are for dry season, suggesting seasonal migration.
Breeding. 6 nests at Kari, Jan (P.B.); Sokoto, Feb (Fairbairn 1931); Malamfatori, Mar (J.H.E.); Falgore Game Reserve, Mar-Apr (Wilkinson & Beecroft 1985).

85. GYPS RUEPPELLII   ?Afm/B

(I.101)   Ruppell's Griffon

Not uncommon resident (*G. r. rueppellii*) in northernmost areas from Sokoto to Lake Chad. Conspicuous at Mambilla Plateau, Oct-Apr, and records, also in dry season, for "northern Oyo Province" and Kabba (Brown 1948) suggest seasonal migration. For further comment on the decline of this species see Cook & Mundy (1980). Although noted most months at Yankari, Green (1989) remarked on the species absence for nearly 3 years (Jun 1985 to Nov 1987) which is probably further evidence of decline in numbers.
Breeding. A colony on the inselberg at Kotorkoshi, known for over 40 years, is diminishing: Serle (1943) counted "over 100 birds"; 8-10 pairs 1972 (J.H.E.). Breeds Feb-Mar.

Accipitridae

86. AEGYPIUS TRACHELIOTUS RB
(I.103)   Lappet-faced Vulture

Uncommon resident in arid savanna, mainly of the Sahel and adjacent Sudan savanna of extreme northeast, from Lake Chad west to Potiskum. Usually singly or in pairs, but 10 together at Minetti bore hole, Feb (P.H.).
Breeding. One record: Maiduguri, Feb (P.H.).

87. AEGYPIUS OCCIPITALIS ?Afm/B
(I.104)   White-headed Vulture

Uncommon resident in northeast from Bauchi and Yankari to Lake Chad; much less numerous to west and south. Several records of 6 together. Southerly records, "northern Oyo Province" and Kabba (Brown 1948) and Serti (P.H.), are all in dry season, suggesting seasonal migration.
Breeding. Breeds Yankari, Dec-May (Green 1989).

88. CIRCAETUS GALLICUS PM
(I.140)   Short-toed Eagle

Uncommon Palaearctic migrant in dry season, Sep-Mar, mostly to northernmost areas with daily southward passage at Malamfatori from 7 Sep (R.J.D.). Southern limits probably Lake Kainji Nat. Park and Jos, but confusion with *C. beaudouini* (q.v.) makes limits and dates problematic.

Since White differentiates *Circaetus gallicus*, the Palaearctic migrant Short-toed Eagle, from *C. beaudouini* an African breeding species, the 2 have been accorded specific, rather than subspecific rank here, but Brown (1970), and others, e.g. BoA, regard the 2 forms as conspecific. They are virtually indistinguishable in the field with the result that differentiation inside Nigeria is unreliable, most observers tending to attribute dry season (winter) records to migrant *gallicus* and wet season (summer) or through the year records to resident *beaudouini*.

89. CIRCAETUS BEAUDOUINI RB
(I.143)   Beaudouin's Snake Eagle

Resident, status uncertain because indistinguishable in the field from *C. gallicus* (q.v.). Brown (1970) regarded this form as an African breeding race of *gallicus-C. gallicus beaudouini*. Collected at Bauchi, Apr and Zaria, Jan (Bannerman 1951). Dubious dry season sight records from Kainji Lake Nat. Park to Malamfatori.
Breeding. Zaria, Jan (Serle 1943); estimated laying date, Nov (BoA).

90. CIRCAETUS CINEREUS R(B)
(I.141)   Brown Snake Eagle

Uncommon resident widespread in all wooded savannas except the Sahel, from Sokoto to Maiduguri south to Old Oyo Nat. Park and Serti. Less uncommon

than *C. cinerascens*: "frequent" Yankari (C.G.) and "several records Jan-Jul" Potiskum (P.B.). Recently observed Obudu Plateau, Nov 1985 (J.S.A.), south of previous known range.
Breeding. No records.

91. CIRCAETUS CINERASCENS   R(B)

    (I.144) Smaller Banded Snake Eagle

Uncommon resident mainly in riparian woodland of the Guinea savannas, also north to Kano (R.E.S.) and south to Oyo (collected by H. Volsoe), Anambra Creek (Bannerman 1931) and Serti (P.H.)
Breeding. No records.

92. TERATHOPIUS ECAUDATUS   RB

    (I.146) Bateleur

Resident, formerly not uncommon in wooded savanna from the great rivers northward, but numbers are declining or the species is retreating into areas less frequently visited. Recorded as "uncommon" in oases north of Hadejia wetlands, 1989-1991 (M.D.), but "common" in Sambisa G.R. in 1992 (P.H.). Lissam (Bannerman 1951) is the only locality south of the Benue; but present Kainji Lake Nat. Park south to Old Oyo Nat. Park, with numerous intermediate localities south of the middle Niger.
   Breeding. Mongu, undated (Bannerman 1951); Yankari, Jan (C.&.M.); Sambisa (P.H.). Breeding probably widespread formerly, but populations have declined sharply since the 1950s.

93. DRYOTRIORCHIS SPECTABILIS   R(B)

    (I.139) Congo Serpent-Eagle

Rare resident (*D. s. spectabilis*) in high forest, known from Cross River to Gambari; specimens from Cross River (Bannerman 1951) and Ondo, 17 Jan 1938 (BMNH skin from Ffoulkes-Roberts). In the 1970s sightings at Sapoba (F.E.W.), Gambari (F.C.S.) and Ife, where it is said to be resident (R.F.).
   Breeding. Ash (1990) photographed a juv. (thought to be locally bred) at Bashu, 10 Oct 1987. Thiollay (1985) says this species "is a primary rainforest raptor rarely entering secondary growth".

94. POLYBOROIDES TYPUS   RB

    (I.171) African Harrier Hawk

Common resident (presumably *P. t. pectoralis*) in forest zone, becoming progressively less common northward (presumably *P. t. typus*) from at least 11°N. The population north of the forest undoubtedly shifts northward to the Sahel in the rains, greatly confusing racial limits.
   Breeding. In south (?*pectoralis*), Nov-Jul; in north (?*typus*), Mar-May.

Accipitridae

95. CIRCUS MACROURUS   PM
(I.169)   Pallid Harrier

Not uncommon Palaearctic migrant in open and degraded savanna, mid Oct to early Apr, but immatures recorded all months except Aug. In northern areas probably common locally, but much less common south of the great rivers to coast at Lagos, though regarded as common in derived savanna of southeast by Serle (1957).

96. CIRCUS PYGARGUS   PM
(I.168)   Montagu's Harrier

Not uncommon Palaearctic migrant to open and degraded savanna north of the great rivers, late Sep to Apr. Only southerly location is Enugu (S.G.C.), but field separation from *C. macrourus* is possible only for adult male, so may be more widespread in south. Sweden ringed bird recovered at Yola (Bannerman 1951).

97. CIRCUS AERUGINOSUS   PM, ?RB
(I.170)   Marsh Harrier

Not uncommon Palaearctic migrant (*C. a. aeruginosus*) in marshy areas mainly north of the great rivers, mid Nov to mid Mar. Described as "common" in Hadejia Wetlands, 1989-1991 (M.D.). Southwest records to coast at Lagos numerous; but only Awgu (Serle 1957) and Port Harcourt (Maclaren 1953) in southeast. Reported to be present at Rayfield (Jos) all months except Aug and Sep (J.B.), which might mean some remain all year, possibly *ranivorus* or nominate *aeruginosus*.

Breeding. One uncertain record from Zaria, Feb, could be possible breeding range extension of *C. a. ranivorus* from Angola, but no recent data to support this possibility.

98. MICRONISUS GABAR   RB
(I.165)   Gabar Goshawk

Not uncommon resident in Northern Guinea and Sudan zones, less common in Sahel and noted further south only in dry season to Lagos (A.P., J.P.G.), Auchi (J.B.H.) and Ife (R.F.). Melanics (c.25% at Sokoto-M.& C.) are encountered throughout the north.

Breeding. Sokoto, Apr-May (Serle in Bannerman 1951); "Nigeria April to July" (MP&G).

99. MELIERAX METABATES   RB, Afm/B
(I.166)   Dark Chanting Goshawk

Common resident (*M. m. metabates*), widespread through the Northern Guinea and Sudan zones, less common in Sahel to Lake Chad. Noted south to Kainji Lake Nat. Park (W.& W.) and Enugu (Serle 1957). Subject to southerly movement in the dry season causing increased numbers, Dec-Feb, in southern part of range.

Breeding. Eggs in 8 nests Sokoto and Zaria, Mar and Apr (Serle in Bannerman 1951); pulli Zaria, May (C.H.F.).

100. ACCIPITER TACHIRO   RB

(I.163)   African Goshawk

Common resident (*A. t. macroscelides*) in the forest zone right across the country, more in dense secondary growth than high forest, north to Ibadan, Auchi and Enugu; netted at Kagoro, 16 Sep 1979, and noted at Pandam Wildlife Park where it was "uncommon in and around kurimis" (C.S.).
Breeding. Owerri, Feb-Mar (Marchant 1953); fledglings Ibadan, Apr (A.P.).

101. ACCIPITER CASTANILIUS   Afm/(B)

(I.164)   Chestnut-flanked Sparrowhawk

Rare resident in lowland forest. Specimens from Benin (Bannerman 1951), Oban (BMNH skins from P.A. Talbot) and Ikom, a road kill (P.M.). May be more common, since difficult to recognise in field. A sight record from Ibadan (T.R-S.) suggests it could range even further west. One in dense forest Nindam F.R., 31 Oct 1985 (J.S.A.). Chappuis (1991) has not recorded voice, which may be distinctive.
Breeding. No records anywhere in Africa.

102. ACCIPITER BADIUS   Afm/B

(I.160)   Shikra,

Common resident (*A. b. sphenurus*), ubiquitous in all types of savanna, but in forest zone only in major clearings. Becomes much more sparse in coastal and derived savanna in the rains and only noted in the Sahel at that season; "a southern concertina" migrant (Elgood *et al.* 1973).
Breeding. From coast north to Kano, Jan-Apr, later in north.

103. ACCIPITER ERYTHROPUS   R(B)

(I.156)   African Little Sparrowhawk

Uncommon resident (*A. e. erythropus*) mainly at forest edges and clearings, from Lagos to Owerri. (*A. e. zenkeri* ranges east from southern Cameroon, so *erythropus* may well be absent from extreme southeast Nigeria). Only locality north of derived savanna is Yankari, a sighting in Feb (C.G.). Recorded Nindam F.R. on southern escarpment of Jos Plateau (Dyer, Gartshore & Sharland 1986) and several times at Isheri, Lagos (P.D.Alexander-Marrack *et al.* 1985). Since late 1980s Ishieri has been completely cleared of forest (P.H.).
Breeding. No records. Breeds Gambia, Senegal and Ivory Coast (Dowsett 1993a).

104. ACCIPITER OVAMPENSIS   AfM/NB

(I.157)   Ovampo Sparrowhawk

Uncommon intra-African migrant mainly in Guinea savannas, but south to Ibadan and north to Kano, mostly Jul-Nov. Resemblance to *A. badius* in the field may mean it is more common than records suggest. Almost certainly a non-breeding migrant from south of the equator. Most recent records (but not all) are for the wet season but regarded as resident in Togo and Ghana (BoA).

105. ACCIPITER MELANOLEUCUS RB

(I.159) Black Sparrowhawk

Not uncommon (*A. m. temminckii*) in lowland, montane and gallery forest from the coast north to the great rivers. The most northerly records are Kagoro, Pandam and Yankari.

Breeding. Several records Ibadan, Sapele and Lokoja, Jan-Feb; Owerri, Aug-Sep (Marchant 1953).

106. UROTRIORCHIS MACROURUS R(B)

(I.167) Long-tailed Hawk

Uncommon resident in high forest, but recorded from Lagos to Ikom, and at Kagoro (R.E.S.) on southern escarpment of Jos Plateau suggesting formerly more widespread and, since difficult to observe, less uncommon than sparse records indicate. Recent records from Okomu, 25 Oct 1987 (Ash 1990), and Calabar (P.M.) extend range to extreme southeast.

Breeding. No records. Breeds Sierra Leone, Liberia and Ivory Coast (Dowsett 1993a).

107. BUTASTUR RUFIPENNIS Afm/B

(I.145) Grasshopper Buzzard

Common resident, all months, in wooded savanna of Northern Guinea zone; in Southern Guinea zone rather less common in dry season only, entering Derived Savanna south to Ogbomosho in some years. Most records for Sudan zone and the few from Sahel are for the rains. Common in the Hadejia Wetlands, 1989-1991 (M.D.).

Breeding. C/3 Nasarawa, Mar (Serle in Bannerman 1951); juv. at Jos, Jun (V.S.).

108. KAUPIFALCO MONOGRAMMICUS RB, ?Afm

(I.138) Lizard Buzzard

Common resident widespread in Forest and Derived Savanna zones, less common in riparian woodland northward and not recorded in the Sahel. Most records in northernmost areas, Sokoto to Potiskum, are for the rains, suggesting some northward migration.

Breeding. Sapele to Zaria, Mar-Jun.

109. BUTEO BUTEO PM

(I.149) Steppe Buzzard

A new species for Nigeria. A buzzard, sighted several times 3-5 Jan 1966 near

Sokoto, was at first thought to be *rufinus*, definitely not *auguralis*; it was finally seen closely and attributed to *B. buteo vulpinus* (Fry 1966c), and similarly a further sighting near Lake Chad (C.H.Fry with J.S.Ash and I.J.Ferguson-Lees), Mar 1968. These Nigerian records are regarded as certain since there are records right across W. Africa from Senegal to Cameroon and ringing recoveries from Ghana and Togo (Holyoak & Seddon 1990), although it is noted that BoA does not recognise *B. buteo* as occurring in Nigeria despite this 1966 record by Fry.

110. BUTEO RUFINUS   PM
(I.151) Long-legged Buzzard

Uncommon migrant, first noted at Malamfatori, Dec 1964 (A.J.H.). Since recorded throughout from Sokoto (photographed by P.J.M.) to Lake Chad, south to Ibadan and Lagos (J.P.G.), mid Nov to Mar. No specimens obtained so at least some may belong to *B. r. cirtensis*, breeding Morocco to Tunis, but Palaearctic migrant *B. r. rufinus* is more likely.

111. BUTEO AUGURALIS   Afm/B
(I.153) Red-tailed Buzzard

Not uncommon resident seasonally throughout, including the high plateaux. In Northern Guinea Savanna present all months; southward to coast from Calabar to Lagos in dry season, Nov-Apr; northward from Sokoto to Lake Chad in rains, May-Oct. A clear "hump-backed bridge" African migrant (Elgood *et al.*1973).

Breeding. In dry season, Jan to early May, from Owerri (Marchant 1953) north to Vom (V.S.).

[AQUILA POMARINA   PM
(I.129) Lesser Spotted Eagle

"A bird tentatively identified as *A. pomarina* 6 km south of Maiduguri on 20 Nov 85" (J.S.Ash 1990). This record, if subsequently substantiated, would represent a considerable westward extension of the autumn passage of the Palaearctic migrant from Eastern Europe and the Middle East to Africa south of the equator.]

112. AQUILA RAPAX   RB
(I.128) Tawny Eagle

Not uncommon resident (*A. r. belisarius*), local but widespread throughout the area north of the great rivers. The few southerly records – Ibadan (R.H.P.), Lagos (several observers) and Serti (P.H.) – are all dry season, evidence for some seasonal southerly migration.

Breeding. Sokoto to Kano south to Zaria and Vom, Oct-Jan. Photographed on nest near Gashua, 27 Feb 1989 (I.G.N.). Evidence of breeding in 1992 in same area (P.H.).

113. AQUILA WAHLBERGI   RB

(I.130) Wahlberg's Eagle

Not uncommon resident in savanna woodland of the Guinea zones south to Ilorin and Old Oyo Nat. Park. Less common in the Sudan zone, rarely met in the Chad area. Probably no seasonal movement.

Breeding. Jun-Sep (MP&G); nest with eggs Zaria, early Sep (P.W.); nest with chicks Zaria, 2 Dec 1975 (M.D.).

114. HIERAAETUS SPILOGASTER   RB

(I.131) African Hawk-Eagle

Uncommon resident widespread in savanna woodlands north of the great rivers, mainly in Northern Guinea zone and south to Lake Kainji area and Gboko. Several records from Yankari and from Falgore (Kano State) in late 1980s.

Breeding. Nesting Pandam Wildlife Park, Dec and adult there with full grown juv., Jul (C.S.); juvs. twice at Potiskum, Jan (P.B.).

115. HIERAAETUS PENNATUS   PM

(I.133) Booted Eagle

Rare Palaearctic migrant, probably regular. Prior to 1970s recorded from 2 localities: Kano, 27 Jan 1962 (R.E.S) and 6 Jan 1970 (D.I.M.W.); Sokoto, 13 sightings Oct-Mar (M.& C.). Several sightings since 1981, mostly from the north-east, also Zaria and Oban. Regularly sighted Katsina in dry season 1993-4, also Yankari Nat. Park in 1994 (I.D.). Only light-phase noted but extra-limital dark-phase noted in Mauritania (J.P.G.).

116. HIERAAETUS DUBIUS   R(B)

(I.132) Ayres' Hawk-Eagle

Two unconfirmed sightings: near Kontagora, 3 Jan 1964 (J.H.E.), Ife University Campus, undated (R.F.). A clearer sighting Oban Hills, 24 Nov 1985 (J.S.A & R.E.S.), warrants full acceptance of species. Sighted also montane area, Mambilla Plateau, Mar (Green 1990). The species has been collected in both Togo and Cameroon (Bannerman 1931) and Ghana (Grimes 1987).

Breeding. No records anywhere in West Africa.

117. LOPHAETUS OCCIPITALIS   RB

(I.137) Long-crested Eagle

Not uncommon resident in well wooded areas throughout the country. Elgood *et al.* (1973) concluded it was essentially sedentary, but most Sahel records are rainy season.

Breeding. Zaria, Mar (Bannerman 1951); Sapele, Jul-Oct (Serle 1958); Pandam, Nov (C.S.). Such variation in breeding times supports a non-migratory status.

118. SPIZAETUS AFRICANUS R(B)

(I.136) Cassin's Hawk-Eagle

Rare in forest. Few records: BMNH skin collected by A.W.J. Pomeroy at Ife, undated and apparently overlooked by Bannerman; sightings "southern edge of Jos Plateau" (M.H.), Ipake Forest Reserve (J.P.G. and J.B.H.) and Sapele, 2 Mar 1975 (J.B.H.). Records since 1981 from Calabar (P.H.) and extra-limital Cameroon Mt. extend range southeast.
Breeding. No records. Nest with well grown young bird Ghana, 16 Dec (Macdonald & Taylor 1977).

119. STEPHANOAETUS CORONATUS RB

(I.135) Crowned Eagle

Rare resident, usually in forest but also in wooded patches in savanna. Probable sighting Omo Forest, 18 Sep 1988 (A.M.N.).
Breeding. B/1, nest in a wooded inselberg pediment in Southern Guinea Savanna in "northern Oyo Province", 26 Dec 1941 (Brown 1948); "a juvenile feeding on a squirrel" in relict forest near Lagos (J.P.G.); forest near Calabar, 4 Jul 1976 (P.M.): "uncommon, an old nest probably of this species" Pandam Wildlife Park (C.S.). Also well north of forest in Guinea zone. Laying date, Oct (BoA).

120. POLEMAETUS BELLICOSUS RB

(I.134) Martial Eagle

Uncommon resident, widespread in wooded savanna north of the great rivers and even more sparse southward to Kainji Lake Nat. Park, Kabba and Serti. Some evidence for southward movement in the dry season. Occasional at oasis north of Hadejia Wetlands, Dec (M.D.).
Breeding. Near Kabba, Aug-Jan (Brown 1948).

SAGITTARIIDAE

121. SAGITTARIUS SERPENTARIUS R(B)

(I.99) Secretary Bird

Uncommon resident, well distributed in open savanna north of the great rivers. Recorded in southwest only at Igbetti (H.S. Clausen) and in southeast at Mambilla and Obudu Plateaux. Almost all recent records are from Reserves – Yankari, Falgore, Gashaka-Gumti and Sambisa. The high density of the present human population and the more intensive farming methods used, probably prevent a wider distribution today.
Breeding. No records, but MP&G say "probably breeds in Nigeria" An immature in the Hadejia Wetlands, dry season 1988/89 (M.D.).

FALCONIDAE

Falconinae

122. FALCO NAUMANNI
PM

(I.117)   Lesser Kestrel

Uncommon Palaearctic migrant to savanna grasslands, almost entirely north of the great rivers, Oct-Mar. J. Dent Young (in Bannerman 1951) thought it "quite common on the Bauchi Plateau" but this is not so at present. Probably much more common north of the border in Niger (Elgood *et al.* 1966). Only 2 southern localities known: Lagos, May and Sep (D.I.M.W.); Ife, 1 Mar 1972 (R.F.).

123. FALCO TINNUNCULUS
PM, RB

(I.116)   Common Kestrel

Two poorly differentiated populations: *F. t. tinnunculus*, a common Palaearctic migrant north of the great rivers, not uncommon in savanna south to the coast; *F. t. rufescens* an uncommon and local resident, usually breeding at inselbergs but recently at city high-rise buildings. Flocks 60+ at Malamfatori, Oct-Apr (A.J.H.), indicate *F. t. tinnunculus* overwinters there. A bird ringed France has been recovered.

Breeding. Mostly south of middle Niger (Ibadan, Ilorin, Ife), Mar-May. Also young juv. netted Vom, Jul (V.S.).

124. FALCO ALOPEX
RB

(I.118)   Fox Kestrel

Not uncommon resident locally at inselbergs and steep cliffs north of the great rivers. Southerly records from Idanre and Igbetti in the west to Serti and Obudu Plateau in east.

Breeding. C/3, 31 Mar 1962 and C/4 (same nest), 19 Mar 1963 – nest site a rock ledge at Sir Gawain Falls, Yankari, which was then dry (J.H.E.). Kigom Hills, Apr-May (B.W.); "feeding young away from nest" Jos, May (J.R.L.).

125. FALCO ARDOSIACEUS
RB, Afm

(I.119)   Grey Kestrel

Not uncommon resident seasonally in farm and open land with trees north of the great rivers, less common in southwest, unrecorded in southeast south of Sankwala (M.K.), Mbaakon and Serti. Southerly records mainly dry season, the most northerly mainly in the rains. Recent data from within Nigeria, and elsewhere in West Africa, strongly uphold that this species is an intra-African migrant.

Breeding. From Zaria, Bauchi to the Mambilla Plateau, Dec-May, but mostly Mar-Apr. Laying date Nigeria, Apr (BoA).

126. FALCO CHICQUERA   RB, Afm/B

   (I.115)   Red-necked Falcon

Not uncommon resident (*F. c. ruficollis*) in wooded savanna with *Borassus* palms north of the great rivers, but very local. Apart from Pategi, 21 Jul 1956, (J.H.E.) on south bank of the middle Niger, other southerly records are dry season: Kainji Lake Nat. Park "total dry season migrant Nov-June" (W.& W.); Benin, Oct (D.N.J.); Mbaakon, Jan-Mar (H.G.). Described as uncommon, (breeding) in Hadejia Wetlands, 1989-1991 (M.D.).
   Breeding. "Certainly nests on the Bauchi Plateau" (no dates) (Bannerman 1951): Mbaakon, Jan-Mar (H.G.); twice Maiduguri, Feb-Mar (P.H.).

127. FALCO VESPERTINUS   PM

   (I.112)   Red-footed Falcon

Locally common Palaearctic spring-passage migrant, Mar-Apr, flocks frequently 500-1000, chiefly crossing Jos Plateau but also smaller numbers from Zaria to Lake Chad. Flocks tend to follow rain storms. Flock of 500+ Falgore G.R., April 1988 (J.B.). Not recorded in "mid-winter" and only twice in autumn, both small groups, at Ibadan (T.R-S.) and Malamfatori (Sir P. Pedler), both in Oct.

128. FALCO SUBBUTEO   PM

   (I.109)   Hobby

Palaearctic migrant, first reported Kainji Lake Nat. Park, Oct 1965 (W.& W.). Further sightings since suggest it is regular but rare. Seen mostly north of the great rivers, Oct-May, and once at Kano in Jun (R.E.S.). One southern location: Sapele, "five singles from 24 Nov 74 to 12 Mar 75" (J.B.H.).

129. FALCO CUVIERI   RB

   (I.110)   African Hobby

Uncommon resident, usually over wetlands, throughout, from the coast north to Kano, but not in the Chad basin. No evidence of seasonal movement, although a rains visitor in the Hadejia Wetlands (M.D.).
   Breeding. Ubiaja, May (Bannerman 1951); "breeding attempted" Pandam Wildlife Park, Apr (C.S.).

130. FALCO BIARMICUS   RB, Afm/B

   (I.108)   Lanner Falcon

Not uncommon resident (*F. b. abyssinicus*) throughout in open savanna and with Kites in urban skies. Mostly in dry season in south, but more records during the rains in extreme north, indicating some seasonal movement.
   Breeding. Almost confined to the Guinea zone, Ilorin and Lokoja north to Zaria and Pandam, Feb-Mar; also Sokoto in Sudan zone, Jan-Feb (Mundy & Cook 1972-3).

131. FALCO PEREGRINUS   PM, ?RB

   (I.107)   Peregrine Falcon

Uncommon, in open country, probably almost all migrant from the Palaearctic (*F. p. calidus*), though the African resident *F. p. minor* cannot be ruled out; all records between 21 Aug 1969 (R.J.D.) and mid Apr (A.J.H.), both extreme dates at Lake Chad. The only known specimen was *calidus* "mouth of the Escravos River" (Bannerman 1951). One Rayfield (Jos), Mar 1990, another Taboru, Sep 1992 (J.B.). Other recent records from West Africa are mostly extra limital and confirm a mainly Palaearctic provenance.
Breeding. No records.

PHASIANIDAE

Numidinae

132. AGELASTES NIGER   ?RB

   (I.196)   Black Guineafowl

A new species for Nigeria. Very local resident, recently located in relict forest of extreme southeast adjacent to Cameroon, where it is said to be "fairly common" in Korup Nat. Park (Thomas 1991). Ash (1990) mentions Ekonganaku (5°04'N 8°40'E) as site of a photographed bird. Possibly extended further west before forest destruction reduced habitat severely.

133. GUTTERA PUCHERANI   RB

   (I.198)   Crested Guineafowl

Uncommon resident in forest in the southeast (*G. p. sclateri*) and in the southwest (*G. p. verreauxi*), with the Niger probably the barrier. Mostly in the forest zone from around Ibadan to Calabar; also northward in gallery forest to the Niger at Pategi and in montane forest near Obudu Plateau.
   Breeding. C/7 in gallery forest in "N.W. Benin Province", Feb (Mason 1940).

134. NUMIDA MELEAGRIS   RB

   (I.197)   Helmeted Guineafowl

Locally not uncommon resident (*N. m. galeata*) in undisturbed savanna north of the great rivers, less common southward to Eruwa, Ilorin, Old Oyo Nat. Park and Kabba south of the middle Niger, but locally common south of the Benue to Awgu (Marchant 1953). Widespread domestication leading to feral populations makes status assessment difficult.
   Breeding. Surprisingly little recorded: small young Sokoto, Sep and C/12 Lokoja, Oct (Bannerman 1951); "young in rains" Pandam (C.S.). Egg-laying Jul-Aug, Kainji Lake Nat. Park (Ayeni 1983).

Gallinae

135. COTURNIX COTURNIX PM
(I.192)   Common Quail

Formerly regular and not uncommon Palaearctic migrant (*C. c. coturnix*) in savanna scrub and farmlands, Sep-Apr, right across the north from Birnin Kebbi to Lake Chad; also numerous on the Jos/Bauchi Plateau. Southward limits Ilorin (Bannerman 1951) and Orlu (Serle 1957), but no recent records south of the great rivers. Numbers have diminished and are still doing so generally.

136. COTURNIX CHINENSIS ? AfM/B
(I.194)   Blue Quail

Local and uncommon breeder (*C. c. adansonii*) in moist grassy areas. Widely reported in the south, Lagos to Umuahia, north to Ilorin and Enugu, with fewer north of the great rivers, mainly from the Jos Plateau, in the rains. At Lagos present only mid Mar to Jul, clearly a breeding migrant but migration direction is obscure – possibly east/west. Thiollay (1985) stated this is "the only common quail" in savannas from the coast to 10°N, mostly Nov-May. No recent Nigerian records.
   Breeding. Only known from "a pair of adults and a number of very small young" Lagos, 3 Jul (Sander 1956).

137. COTURNIX DELEGORGUEI AfM/NB
(I.193)   Harlequin Quail

Uncommon, African non-breeding migrant (*C. c. delegorguei*), usually in open grassy areas mostly from Lake Chad to Kano in the rains. Golding (1934) reported arrival near Lake Chad in mid May, numbers increasing thereafter to coveys of up to 10 through Jun. Rare wet season migrant, May-Aug, Kano State (R.E.S. & R.W.). Widespread on Jos Plateau, but no comment on seasonality (Ebbutt *et al.* 1964). Two caught in south – Ibadan, 1 Dec 1964 (J.H.E.) and Ilaro, 16 Dec 1964 (J.A.B.) – suggests southward migration at that time (mid dry season). Sightings near Sapele, twice May (C.S.P.) and twice Jun (J.B.H.), confuse the pattern.
   Breeding. No records.

138. PTILOPACHUS PETROSUS RB
(I.195)   Stone Partridge

Common resident (*P. p. petrosus*) locally on rocky ground, inselberg pediments and erosion gullies, mainly in the Guinea zones, extending to Eruwa, Ibadan and Abeokuta in southwest, but in southeast only around Serti. Uncommon in the Sudan zone from Sokoto to Kari; absent from the extreme northeast where rocky outcrops are absent but recorded from Sambisa G.R. and Maiduguri (P.H.).
   Breeding. C/4 Lokoja, 6 Aug 1932, C/4 Minna, 22 Jan 1936 (Bannerman 1951); breeding in the rains Borgu (Kainji Lake Nat.Park) (W.&W.); nesting Kari, Feb (P.B.); adults with very young chicks Falgore G.R., 12 Apr 1977 (J.H.E.).

139. FRANCOLINUS LATHAMI RB

(I.173) Latham's Forest Francolin

Uncommon resident (*F. l. lathami*), mainly in mature lowland forest, from Lagos to Oban. Probably numbers greatly reduced through forest clearance; said to have been common in high forest of northwest Benin prior to 1940 (Mason 1940). Bannerman (1931) has a record from "the Northern Provinces", Niaji, not now locatable. Ash 1989 encountered a freshly killed bird in Okomu F.R. and commented "said to be common in many parts of the forest", but only one other record there since (P.H.)

Breeding. Northwest Benin Province, Jan-Feb (Mason 1940). Eggs Ghana, Feb (Grimes 1987), and W. Cameroon, Feb, Dec (BoA).

140. FRANCOLINUS COQUI RB

(I.175) Coqui Francolin

Rare resident (*F. c. spinetorum*), perhaps less rare very locally, mainly between Kano and Lake Chad in grassy savanna on sandy soils in Sudan and Sahel zones where it replaces *F. albogularis* of the more southern ironstone soils. Not yet reported from the extreme northwest though it occurs west to Senegal. No records in the early 1990s (P.H.).

Breeding. Gadau, Jul (Bannerman 1951).

141. FRANCOLINUS ALBOGULARIS RB

(I.179) White-throated Francolin

Locally common resident (*F. a. buckleyi*) in grassy savanna on rolling ironstone hills in the Northern Guinea and Sudan zones, south to Ilorin and around Enugu.

Breeding. C/4 Kafanchan, 6 Jun 1937 (Bannerman 1951); Yankari, dry season (M.D. & M.G.).

142. FRANCOLINUS SQUAMATUS RB

(I.187) Scaly Francolin

Not uncommon resident (*F. s. squamatus*) in the southeast, mainly in the forest zone in dense secondary growth, north to Enugu, extending in gallery forest north of the great rivers to southern slopes of the Jos Plateau, west to Minna (BMNH skin). Replaces *F. ahantensis* (q.v.) to east and north of the lower and middle Niger.

Breeding. C/4 Kurmin Nunku, 4 Dec 1963 (M.H.).

143. FRANCOLINUS AHANTENSIS R(B)

(I.188) Ahanta Francolin

Uncommon resident (*F. a. ahantensis*) in tangled scrub between gallery forest and farmed savanna of the southwest only, the middle and lower Niger apparently forming a barrier, *F. squamatus* replacing it east and north. (A record from Minna, north of the middle Niger (Fairbairn 1952) is regarded as suspect). The absence of any recent records suggests it has become rare, possibly through more intense hunting. The voice is said to be distinctive.

Breeding. No records. Egg laying Ghana, Dec, Jan; half-grown broods, Feb-Apr (Grimes 1987).

144. FRANCOLINUS BICALCARATUS RB

(I.183)   Double-spurred Francolin (Bushfowl)

Common resident in all types of savanna except Sahel, locally abundant where not persecuted. In the Sahel and Sudan savanna of northeast is replaced by *F. clappertoni*. Clinal intergrading between nominate *bicalcaratus* of the west with *ogilvie-granti* of the southeast occurs through central areas, while *adamauae* (not recognised by White but distinguished by Hall 1963) also intergrades in part of the Bauchi area.

Breeding. Through the dry season, mainly Nov-Feb, but overall Sep-Mar. No obvious latitudinal difference in breeding season.

145. FRANCOLINUS CLAPPERTONI RB

(I.185)   Clapperton's Francolin

Common resident (*F. c. clappertoni*), in grassy savanna with some bush cover, in the extreme northeast only between Nguru and Katagum in the west and Lake Chad to east of Maiduguri in the east, replacing *F. bicalcaratus* as the common 'bushfowl'.

Breeding. Juvs. Lake Chad area, from late Mar (Bannerman 1951); "chick" Dikwa, Mar (D.A. Holmes); pair with 2 young at Sambisa G.R., 27 May 1986 (P.H.). Laying dates Nigeria, Feb-Mar (BoA).

TURNICIDAE

146. ORTYXELOS MEIFFRENII Afm/(B)

(I.330)   Quail-Plover

Status obscure. Uncommon and confined to thorn-scrub and grasslands of the extreme north from Sokoto to Lake Chad, mostly in the dry season, suggesting movement to beyond the northern border during the rains.

Breeding. No records; probably nests in dry season, i.e. when most common. Breeds in the Sudan Dec-Jan (MP&G). Probably breeds Jan in Chad (Newby 1979). Kano, pair remained several weeks from mid March in a study area visited regularly (S&W).

147. TURNIX SYLVATICA RB, ?Afm/B

(I.328)   Little Button-Quail

Not uncommon local resident (*T. s. lepurana*), widespread in savanna grasslands and farms. Common in all months at Lagos (Gee & Heigham 1977), but in most localities records indicate seasonal movement, or at least local migration (Elgood *et al.* 1973), notably of one that flew into a lighted room at night, Ibadan 1 Jun 1957, the only record there in 15 years.

Breeding. C/2 Sokoto, Jul (Bannerman 1951) and "Nigeria, August"

(MP&G) suggest rains breeding. However, data at Lagos suggest that it breeds in dry season: 3 chicks, Jan (J.P.G.); chick with adults, Apr (J.B.H.).

148. TURNIX HOTTENTOTTA ?

(I.329)   Black-rumped Button-Quail

Probably vagrant (*T. h. nana*), known only from Lagos, where it was collected by Sander (1956) from "a small community, estimated at between 6 and 10 pairs", present only Dec-Jun.

Breeding. From a half-grown young bird seen in Jan, Sander deduced that breeding occurs in Dec and Jan. No records since.

RALLIDAE

Himantornithinae

149. HIMANTORNIS HAEMATOPUS ?

(I.202)   Nkulengu Rail

Only one previous record, "an example collected by Ansorge at Degema" (undated) quoted by Serle (1957). Despite a loud distinct call (6 notes repeated) there are no subsequent records until 20 Sep 1992 when 2 were sighted in swamp forest near Lekki Conservation Centre (P.H.).

Rallinae

150. CANIRALLUS OCULEUS ?

(I.203)   Grey-throated Rail

May be locally extinct as its habitat, swamp forest, is rapidly disappearing. Only 2 old undated records: Igoriake, near Benin, (Bannerman 1951) and "N.W.Benin Province" "flushed twice near small streams in high forest", one shot (Mason 1940). No new records for Nigeria, although a possible sighting along a small stream in Omo Forest, 1987 (P.H.).

Breeding. No records. Laying dates Cameroon, Feb, Apr, Jul (BoA).

Flufftails, Pygmy Rails, Spotted Crakes

These tiny elusive birds have a remarkable story in Nigeria. Only *S. pulchra* is at all common and widespread. Two others, *S. boehmi* and *S. elegans* are known positively through single individuals being captured within houses at night. A fourth, *S. rufa* was known only from Nigeria from a handful of (quite unmistakable) feathers in the BMNH but has recently been observed near Serti in a part of the country virtually unexplored ornithologically until P. Hall worked there and others have continued his work. Finally, *S. lugens* was rejected in 1982 because Bannerman's (1955) record from Adamawa was extra-limital. Probably all these *Sarathrura* species have easily recognised voices; *pulchra* certainly has, *boehmi* and *elegans* have been said to have distinctive voices and most have now been tape-recorded (see BoA Vol. II).

151. SAROTHRURA PULCHRA RB

(I.216)   White-spotted Crake (Flufftail)

Locally not uncommon resident (*S. p. pulchra*) in swampy areas of the forest zone from Lagos to Opobo, even "abundant and widespread" in the southeast (Serle 1957) north to Enugu, where 34 were collected, and several other localities as far north as Zaria (C.H.F.) and the Jos Plateau (Bannerman 1931). Calling persistently, morning and evening on Lagos University Campus, Jan-Jun 1972, and would emerge from reeds and approach closely in response to human imitation of call (J.H.E.).

Breeding. No records, but "at Enugu two females obtained on 12 September had ovaries with large yolked eggs and two obtained on 22 December had just finished laying" (Serle 1957).

152. SAROTHRURA ELEGANS ?

(I.217)   Buff-spotted Crake (Flufftail)

Only one record, a bird taken by Sir Hugo Marshall at Ubiaja, 2 Apr 1935 (Bannerman 1951). Nocturnal and may escape detection, though said to have a distinctive voice.

153. SAROTHRURA RUFA RB

(I.124)   Red-chested Flufftail

Formerly only one tenuous inclusion, a bird collected by Boughton-Leigh at Ilorin, undated (in the 1920's). (A bunch of the very distinctive feathers remain at the BMNH, where they were identified by C.H.B.Grant). Recently a pair, Gashaka-Gumti Nat. Park near Serti, in low altitude wetlands, Mar 1988 (Green 1990 – quoting Ash *et al.* 1989).

Breeding. Laying date Nigeria, Dec (BoA) – source unknown.

154. SAROTHRURA BOEHMI ?

(I.212)   Böhm's Flufftail

Only one record, a bird captured at Ife University, Feb 1968, though a nocturnal call thought to be from this species was not infrequently heard there (R.F.).

155. CREX EGREGIA Afm/B

(I.206)   African Crake

Not uncommon resident in swamps, rice fields and seasonally flooded shallow valleys throughout, except the Sahel. Present uniformly all months at Lagos (J.P.G. & J.B.H.), but other southerly records are mostly dry season. From Ibadan and Enugu northward to Sokoto and Kano mostly recorded in the rains, May-Oct. Northward movement in the rains is clear (Elgood *et al.* 1973).

Breeding. Apr-Nov in south; Jun-Sep in central areas, (Rayfield, Jos, Jul-Aug, J.B.); northerly extreme, Sokoto, Aug to mid Sep (Serle 1943).

156. CREX CREX   PM

    (I.205)   Corncrake

Rare, possibly vagrant, Palaearctic migrant; "The Corncrake presents a great puzzle" (Moreau 1972). "Oyo Province", 5 Apr 1929 (Bannerman 1931); Ibadan, Apr 1923 (Golding 1936); Calabar, 8 Apr 1960 (R.E.S.) – all in southern areas of derived savanna. "Live bird handled and ringed" at Vom, 12 Apr 1973 caught by A. McCausland in degraded Guinea savanna (J.R.L.). All recorded on spring passage. A few recent extra limital records: none from Nigeria.

157. PORZANA PARVA   PM

    (I.211)   Little Crake

A new species for Nigeria. Rare Palaearctic migrant with only a few records south of the Sahara between Sudan and Senegal. First encountered at Jekara dam near Kano, Dec 1981. Up to 3 together seen with conclusive identification, 13 Dec but none netted (Wilkinson *et al.* 1982). The species was met on 5 consecutive visits to Jekara, Dec 1 to Dec 20. Several encounters at Adirjani fadama and Badam in the Hadejia Wetlands, up to 2 males and 2 females between 20 Feb and 5 Mar 1987 (Ash 1990).

158. PORZANA PORZANA   PM

    (I.209)   Spotted Crake

Rare Palaearctic migrant to swamps and reed beds of only 4 widely separated localities: 3 caught in mist nets set at *Motacilla flava* roosts in reed beds at Kano, 10 Nov 1956, 20 Mar 1958 and 12 Nov 75, also a sighting, Mar 75 (R.E.S.); Malamfatori, 15 Mar 1965 (A.J.H.); 3 sightings at Lagos, Jan-Feb 1971 (D.I.M.W.); several, including 3 netted, Badam in the Hadejia Wetlands (Ash 1990).

159. AENIGMATOLIMNAS MARGINALIS   RB

    (I.208)   Striped Crake

Uncommon resident in swamps from north to south. Recorded Ibadan (twice) and Sapele (2 Dec 1950) in dry season, but dated northerly breeding season records are in the rains, suggesting latitudinal movement within Nigeria.

    Breeding. C/5 Sokoto, Aug (Bannerman 1951); female with enlarged ovary near Maiduguri, late Jun (Bates 1930).

160. AMAURORNIS FLAVIROSTRIS   RB

    (I.207)   Black Crake

Common resident throughout in swamps at river banks and lake margins. Strictly stationary.

    Breeding. Extended season: 6 clutches Sapele, 24 Aug to 7 Nov (Serle 1958); juvs. Pategi, Feb (J.H.E.); chicks Lagos, Jun (J.B.H.); Abeokuta, Aug (Serle 1950).

161. PORPHYRIO ALLENI
RB, ?Afm

(I.219)   Allen's Gallinule

Subject to irregular local movement throughout much of Africa. Not uncommon seasonally in swampy localities in all areas, in some regarded as a rains migrant, present only May-Sep; but there are a few dry season records from the coastal zone (Lagos, Yenagoa) and it remains at Malamfatori till Dec (A.J.H.). It probably is migratory, but may become much more nocturnal in the dry season and escape detection.

Breeding. Throughout, May-Oct. Nest with 6 eggs, Kano, Aug (Sharland & Wilkinson 1981). Breeding density of 1-2 pairs/ha in rank vegetation around lakes in Hadejia wetlands, 1989-1991 (M.D.).

162. PORPHYRIO PORPHYRIO
RB

(I.218)   Purple Gallinule

Uncommon and very local resident (*P. p. madagascariensis*), formerly only recorded close to the northern border from Sokoto to Lake Chad, where numbers have since declined. Bannerman (1951) indicated it demanded "perennial lakes . . . where there were high reeds or coarse sedges growing out of the water". An adult with 1 juv. in dense reeds on the Lekki Peninsula, 20 Nov 1992 (P.H.).

Breeding. 14 nests Sokoto, Jul-Aug (Serle 1943); juvs. Kazaure, Nov (R.E.S.); pair with 2 juvs. at bore hole in Chad basin, Feb (P.H.). Laying dates Nigeria, Jan-Feb, Jul-Oct (BoA).

163. GALLINULA CHLOROPUS
RB, PM

(I.220)   Common Moorhen

Not uncommon resident (*G. c. meridionalis*) along marshy river banks, in fadamas and on lakes with floating vegetation, mostly in the far north from Sokoto to Lake Chad. No southerly records in the east except one from Enugu (S.G.C.); in the west south to Kainji Dam, Ibadan and Lagos. *G. c. chloropus*, migrant from the Palaearctic (distinguished by larger wing) has been trapped at Kazaure (R.E.S.).

Breeding. 10 nests Sokoto, Jul-Aug (Serle 1943); breeding in Hadejia wetlands, 1989-1991 (M.D.).

164. GALLINULA ANGULATA
AfM/B

(I.221)   Lesser Moorhen

Not uncommon in swamps and ricefields and at reservoirs, everywhere except southeast. Almost all records are Mar-Sep, so is doubtless a breeding rains migrant, but where it migrates to is not established, probably south of the equator. The only dry season records are Ife (R.F.) and Lagos, Jan (J.P.G.) and Ringim, 1 Nov 1976 (J.H.E.). Small numbers Hadejia Wetlands in dry season (I.D.).

Breeding. Well documented: 21 nests Sokoto, Jul-Sep (Serle 1943); 3 nests Vom, Aug-Sep (V.S.); C/4 Sapele, Sep (Serle 1958); "mating" Ife, Feb (R.F.). Breeding density 1-2 pairs/ha on lakes in Nguru area, 1989-1991, with flocks of up to 150 (M.D.).

165. FULICA ATRA PM

(I.222)   Eurasian Coot

Uncommon Palaearctic migrant, probably of increasing frequency to West Africa recently. Not mentioned by Bannerman (1951) though noted at Ibadan, 19 Nov 1944 (H.F.M.) and subsequently at Malamfatori "regular Jan-Mar" (A.J.H.). A flock of 500+ appeared at Kazaure, Dec 1978 (R.E.S.) on a temporary pool. Reported as common in the Hadejia wetlands, 1989-1991 (M.D.).

GRUIDAE

Gruinae

166. GRUS GRUS PM

(Not in MP&G)   Common Crane

New species for Nigeria. Palaearctic migrant, five recent sightings, between Dec and Mar, in the Hadejia Wetlands and oases near the border with Niger, 1989-1991 (M.D.).

167. ANTHROPOIDES VIRGO PM

(I.227)   Demoiselle Crane

Palaearctic migrant, formerly locally common, to Sahel of the Chad basin, usually mid Jan to mid May. Singly or in small groups, sometimes with *Balearica pavonina*, but once reported "common winter visitor to the clay plains" Dikwa area, with "possibly up to 900 birds" (D.Holmes). No records from this area since 1972 (P.H.), but 1 adult in the Hadejia Wetlands, Dec 1988-Feb 1989 (M.D.).

Balearicinae

168. BALEARICA PAVONINA RB

(I.225)   Black Crowned Crane

Formerly not uncommon resident (*B. p. pavonina*) in the valleys of the great rivers northward, usually in marshy areas or on sandy river banks or bars, with flocks up to 200. Subject to local movements with seasonal changes of water level, but those seen occasionally in the south are probably escapes from captivity. Numbers are decreasing probably in all areas, but definitely in Kano State (Sharland & Wilkinson 1981). May well be extinct as a wild bird in Nigeria (I.D. – pers. comm. 1994).

Breeding. Several records all from central north, Jul-Sep. Adults with fledged young in oases north of wetlands, Jan 1990 (M.D.).

HELIORNITHIDAE

169. PODICA SENEGALENSIS RB

(I.224)   African Finfoot

Not uncommon resident (*P. s. senegalensis*) on shaded streams of the forest and derived savanna zones, at several localities in the valleys of the great rivers and the Jos Plateau. Becomes progressively less common northwards but extends to Yankari, Potiskum, Gaya Reserve near Kano and Sambisa G.R. near Maiduguri (P.H.).

Breeding. Little known; in breeding condition, Jan-Feb (MP&G); downy young Anambara Creek, 6 Oct 1905 (Bannerman 1931); "displaying" Pandam Wildlife Park, Jun-Jul (C.S.); adults with young, Sambisa Oct (P.H.).

OTIDIDAE

All Bustards are diminishing in numbers through human activities such as shooting, farming and habitat destruction.

170. NEOTIS DENHAMI   Afm/B

(I.230)   Denham's Bustard

Status uncertain. Uncommon (*N. d. denhami*) in open savannas throughout the area north of the great rivers, but subject to seasonal movement. Visible migration frequently reported from central areas, northward in May, southward Oct-Dec. Most records south of the great rivers are for dry season, but Lagos May-Jun confuses the issue.

Breeding. C/1 near Kaduna, at same site twice, undated (Bannerman 1951); "the breeding season is apparently in January and February" (Bannerman 1953); Nigeria, May (MP&G). Data is scanty and confusing; one would have expected it to be a rainy season breeder in the north like other bustards. The few new data throw no light on migration or breeding.

171. NEOTIS NUBA   V?

(I.231)   Nubian Bustard

A single record: a pair seen between Udubo and Gadau, 20 May 1959 (P.B.). Probably *N. n. agaze* which White (1965) places in Niger northwest of Lake Chad. No new records for Nigeria but Lamarche (1980) states it occurs mainly north of 15°N in Mali, breeding Jul to Sep/Oct. Un-numbered in 1981 Checklist, but this now seems unjustified since it breeds in adjacent Niger (Dowsett 1993a).

172. ARDEOTIS ARABS   ?AfM/NB

(I.229)   Arabian Bustard

Intra-African migrant (*A. a. steiberi*), now uncommon on open sandy plains of the Sudan and Sahel zones, mostly from the Chad Basin, a few westward to Kano and Katsina; only noted Yankari (a new area), May (C.& M.). Moves to north of Nigeria, Jun-Oct, occasionally seen Aug. "Much decreased in last 20 years in West Africa" (Thiollay 1985).

173. EUPODOTIS RUFICRISTA   RB, ?AfM/NB

(I.234)   Crested Bustard

Uncommon resident (*E. r. savilei*) in dry open country in the northeast only, from

Kano to Lake Chad and north of about 12°N. Reported as "uncommon in woodland/grassland south of the wetlands", 1989-1991 (M.D.), and only 1 record from Sambisa G.R. since 1988; sighted Yankari Nat. Park, Jul 1991 (I.D.). No migratory movements known, but may move north of the border in the rains to breed. It is surprising that BoA has overlooked the very strong case for making *E. r. savilei* a full species in view of its allopatric distribution and distinctive voice (Chappuis *et al.*1979).

Breeding. No records in Nigeria. Jul-Sep in Darfur (MP&G). Young just able to fly Sep, Chad (Newby 1979). Laying dates Chad, Jun-Aug (BoA).

174. EUPODOTIS SENEGALENSIS   RB

(I.232)   White-bellied Bustard

Formerly not uncommon resident (*E. s. senegalensis*) in open savanna and on grassy plains of the Northern Guinea and Sudan zones, notably over much of the Jos/Bauchi Plateau; also on the shores of Lake Chad, Malamfatori to Ngala. No evidence of seasonal movement though there is an undated record from Arochuku in the southeast. Numbers now declining in areas where formerly common. "Rare" Yankari, Apr only (Green 1989).

Breeding. Laying dates Nigeria, Jun, Sep-Oct (BoA).

175. EUPODOTIS MELANOGASTER   Afm/B

(I.235)   Black-bellied Bustard

Resident and not uncommon in much of the Guinea zone, in all types of savanna including farmland. Partially migrant, occurring southward into derived savanna to Ibadan and Enugu and recently Obudu (Heaton & Heaton 1980) in the dry season, and northward to Malamfatori mainly in the rains. It is noteworthy that numbers seem to be well maintained in Reserves such as Yankari and Falgore.

Breeding. Eggs Zaria, Jul-Aug (Bannerman 1951), Vom, Jul-Sep, C/1 30 Aug (V.S.); display flight Upper Ogun Estate (? southerly breeding limit), 16 Jun 1961 (J.H.E.), also Pandam Wildlife Park, Jul (C.S.).

JACANIDAE

176. ACTOPHILORNIS AFRICANA   RB

(I.240)   Lily Trotter

Abundant resident throughout, in swamps and shallow pools with floating vegetation; much less common in brackish swamps near the coast. Only very local movements occur with change of water levels.

Breeding. Peaks Jul-Sep, but eggs or small young, Apr-Jan.

177. MICROPARRA CAPENSIS   R(B)

(I.241)   Lesser Lily-Trotter

Uncommon resident in pools with floating vegetation north of about 11°N, from Sokoto to Lake Chad, but occurs further south at Aliya and recently Pandam Wildlife Park; one, 8 Mar 1989 (A.M.N.) and several pairs, 29-30 Jan 1994

(M.Ho.). Occurs on the coast in Ivory Coast (Thiollay 1985) so should be looked for in southern Nigeria.
Breeding. No records anywhere in West Africa.

ROSTRATULIDAE

178. ROSTRATULA BENGHALENSIS ?Afm/B

(I.241)   Greater Painted-Snipe

Not uncommon resident (*R. b. benghalensis*) in marshes and at lake edges throughout the north and south to the coast in the west, but not yet recorded in the southeast. Some evidence of partial migration to the north in the rains, perhaps to breed and remain until the drying out of the habitat forces a return south (Elgood *et al.* 1973). Regarded as a common rains visitor to the Hadejia wetlands, 1989-1991 (M.D.).
Breeding. Few records, all from southwest: C/4 Iwo, 8 Apr 1961 and 16 Apr 1961 (Elgood and Donald 1962); very young chick Ibadan, 7 Apr 1961 (J.H.E.); chicks Lagos, Jun-Aug (Gee & Heigham 1977).

HAEMATOPODIDAE

179. HAEMATOPUS OSTRALEGUS PM

(I.262)   Eurasian Oystercatcher

Uncommon Palaearctic migrant (*H. o. ostralegus*) to coastal creeks only; not recorded before 1963. Numbers reaching lower latitudes appear to be increasing but only along the West African coast. First noted mouth of Bonny River, 31 Aug 1963 and 1 Sep 1963 and subsequently 5 together, 9 Oct 1963; also Andoni River, 17 Nov 1963 (Smith 1966), Lagos (D.I.M.W.) and Warri (F.E.W.). No new records for Nigeria but many coastal extra-limital records plus a few inland from Mali (Lamarche 1980).

RECURVIROSTRIDAE

180. HIMANTOPUS HIMANTOPUS R(B), PM

(I.264)   Black-winged Stilt

Status doubtful, but seasonal bias suggest most are of Palaearctic provenance. Common (*H. h. himantopus*) in wetlands and at reservoirs throughout the area north of the great rivers and not uncommon southward to Lagos; 100 on lagoon shore, Dec (Gee & Heigham 1977). Numbers increase Oct-Apr, but whether from Palaearctic or elsewhere in Africa has not been established.
Breeding. No records. Egg laying coastal Ghana, mainly Apr-Jul (Grimes 1987).

181. RECURVIROSTRA AVOSETTA PM

(I.263)   Eurasian Avocet

Probably mainly migrant from the Palaearctic (*R. a. avosetta*) to shallow lake margins and estuaries. Numbers have increased dramatically in last 30 years but there have been earlier extra-limital records from Rio del Ray in Cameroon – max. 100 birds in Feb (Maclaren 1953). First noted in Nigeria at Kano, 20 Feb 1955 (R.E.S.); now many records across north from Kano to Lake Chad and south to Zaria, with largest flock 180 near Yusufu (P.H.). Most records Oct-Mar suggest Palaearctic provenance, but 54 in Jun near Maiduguri (P.H.) suggest more local origin. Flock of 45 in Hadejia Wetlands (M.D.) and recently several records from the coast, including one seen Lekki Peninsula, Jun 1986 (M.K.), and 10 there Nov 1992 (P.H.).

BURHINIDAE

[BURHINUS OEDICNEMUS   PM

(I.236)   Stone Curlew

Palaearctic migrant. No unequivocal records, since only handled specimens can be distinguished certainly from *B. senegalensis*. Bannerman (1951) mentions a specimen collected by Bates (just extra-limital) "between Sokoto and Tawa" in Niger. Several unacceptable sightings, but one "on 12 Feb 1969 with 6 *senegalensis*, with which comparisons were made" at Lagos (J.B.H.), seems probable. Bannerman ascribed Bates's Niger specimen to the nominate race but *saharae* seems equally likely.]

182. BURHINUS SENEGALENSIS   RB

(I.237)   Senegal Thick-knee

Common resident locally in some types of open moist country and along sandy rivers throughout. Subject to local movement with water level changes but no true migration.

Breeding. Mostly south of the great rivers (also from the Bauchi Plateau), mostly Mar-Aug, but a fledgling reported Lagos, Dec.

183. BURHINUS VERMICULATUS   R(B)

(I.239)   Water Thick-knee

Probably uncommon resident (*B. v. buttikoferi*) at lakes and river banks with bushy cover. Status very difficult to assess, *vermiculatus* being almost impossible to distinguish from *B. senegalensis* except in the hand. Has been collected on the Quorra River (Serle 1957), "mouth of the Dodo River" (Bannerman 1951), and Lagos, 9 Feb 1954 (Sander 1956). Sightings reported from all parts north to Zaria and Maiduguri must be treated with caution but probably indicate the species is widespread. Positively identified Yankari Nat. Park, 2 on 30 Dec 1993 (I.D.).

Breeding. Unrecorded in West Africa.

184. BURHINUS CAPENSIS   RB

(I.238)   Spotted Thick-knee

Uncommon resident (*B. c. maculosus*) in open sandy savanna north of the great rivers south to around Bida; also seen in Kainji Lake Nat. Park just south of the middle Niger.

Breeding. Bida, Mar (Brown 1948); eggs Yankari, Apr (A.P.), Zaria, Apr (A.P.); downy young Zaria, May (M.G.).

GLAREOLIDAE

Cursoriinae

185. PLUVIANUS AEGYPTIUS   RB

(I.301)   Egyptian Plover (Crocodile-Bird)

Not uncommon resident on sandy river banks north of the forest zone, and irregular along rivers in the forest zone, but avoids saline coastal creeks. Water level changes cause local movements; when rivers are in spate birds appear in some unexpected habitats, e.g. the tarmac road beside the lake at IITA, 30 Sep 1989 (A.M.N.).
Breeding. Confined to banks of great rivers and major tributaries, Feb-May, when water levels are low.

186. CURSORIUS CURSOR   PM

(I.294)   Cream-coloured Courser

A new species for Nigeria. Palaearctic migrant, possibly becoming more common in West Africa, perhaps due to the southward march of the Sahel drought. Occurs at oases north of Hadejia wetlands, 1989-1991 (M.D.), with three separate flocks of 9,18 and 7 on the sand dunes between Yusufaria and the Bulatura Oases, Yobe State on 30 Jan 1988 (photographed by A.P.L.).

187. CURSORIUS TEMMINCKII   RB

(I.295)   Temminck's Courser

Not uncommon resident in farmland and areas of short grass (including man-made habitats such as airfields), mostly in the Guinea savanna zones, more sporadically northward to Sokoto and the Chad basin; also in coastal grassy areas at Calabar and regularly at Lagos (max. flock there 21-Gee & Heigham 1977). More recently sighted Obudu town (H.& H.), Obudu Cattle Ranch, 10 Mar 1989 (photographed by I.G.N.), and Mambilla Plateau (Green 1990). Some evidence of seasonal movement at least in Kano State (Sharland & Wilkinson 1981). Recently recorded regularly at Katsina (I.D.).
Breeding. Nest Bida, Mar (Brown 1948); chick Lagos (Apapa airfield), Jul (Sander 1956); non-flying chicks Jos Plateau, Jun and mid Aug (V.S.). Laying dates, Feb-Jun (BoA).

188. CURSORIUS CHALCOPTERUS   Afm/B

(I.296)   Bronze-winged Courser

Uncommon resident in savanna woodlands, favouring recently burned ground, but virtually unrecorded south of the great rivers. Mainly nocturnal, may be more common than records suggest, but records agree also with a regular "humped-back bridge" pattern of seasonal movement (Elgood *et al.* 1973). Rare rains

visitor to the Hadejia wetlands, 1989-1991 (M.D.). Sighted Katsina, 26 Nov 1993 (I.D.).
Breeding. Adults with young near Potiskum, 25 Mar (P.B.); pair with small young Zaria, Feb (A.P.). Laying dates, Jan-Feb (BoA).

Glareolinae

189. GLAREOLA PRATINCOLA   RB, ?PM

(297)   Common Pratincole

Locally common resident (*G. p. fulleborni=boweni*) on muddy lake and river shores. Probably a partial migrant, but evidence is inconclusive (Elgood *et al.* 1973). Flocks of 1000+ at Kainji (W.& W.) and on the Benue at Ibi (C.H.F.). Much smaller flocks north to Sokoto and Malamfatori. Not recorded in southeast, but met on coast at Lagos, Aug-Oct (max.8), possibly some being nominate *pratincola* from Palaearctic (Gee & Heigham 1977).
Breeding. 2 nests each C/2 and a chick Pategi, 22 May 1960 (J.H.E.). Suspected breeding Kainji, Apr (W.& W.) and Maiduguri, Jun (P.B.).

190. GLAREOLA NORDMANNI   PM

(I.298)   Black-winged Pratincole

Palaearctic migrant, probably not uncommon locally but status obscured by close similarity to common resident *G. pratincola*. Collected only at Calabar (Oct, twice), but reliably sighted elsewhere in numbers alongside *G. pratincola*, e.g. flocks up to 200 Kainji, Dec-Apr (W.& W.) and Malamfatori, Sep (R.J.D.). Also 2 sighted at Jos, 26 Oct 1952 and 20 at Kano, 3 Nov 1962 (R.E.S.).

191. GLAREOLA NUCHALIS   RB

(I.299)   Rock Pratincole

Not uncommon resident (*G. n. liberiae*, in which the collar is chestnut, not white) locally along rocky streams from near the coast north to about 11°N. Subject to seasonal movement due to water level changes and met on the coast at Lagos, Sep-Oct, when rivers are in spate.
Breeding. On rocks in mid-stream at low water, Apr-Jun, from Olokemeji and Ajeokuta north to Yelwa and Keffi.

192. GLAREOLA CINEREA   RB

(I.300)   Grey Pratincole

Locally common resident, Nov-Jun, on sandbanks of the larger rivers, where they breed (see below). Post-breeding dispersal occurs when rivers are in spate (Jul-Sep) to Lake Chad, Malamfatori where 500+, Sep (R.J.D.), and to the coast at Lagos, where up to 300, Jul-Nov; birds also briefly stay at local reservoirs, etc.
Breeding. Many loose colonies (too diffuse to estimate numbers) along Niger, Benue and Kaduna Rivers, Mar-May. Pair with downy young Kaduna River below Bida, 8 Jun 1991 (A.M.N.).

CHARADRIIDAE

Charadriinae

193. **CHARADRIUS DUBIUS**   PM

(I.243) Little Ringed Plover

Common Palaearctic migrant (*C. d. curonicus*) to inland shores and mown grass (air-fields, golf links, playing fields) throughout, mainly mid Oct to late Apr but recorded all months except Jul and Aug. Wintering population of up to 1000 recorded in Hadejia wetlands, 1989-1991 (M.D.). Uncommon coastal lagoons and marine shores. Mostly parties of 5-20, but 40 seen Lagos and 50 Malamfatori. A bird ringed Germany recovered at Nguru (R.E.S.).

194. **CHARADRIUS HIATICULA**   PM

(I.242) Ringed Plover

Common Palaearctic migrant (*C. h. tundrae*) to coastal mud flats and inland shores throughout, Sep to Apr or mid May. Flocks up to 50, but mostly small groups. Flock size and abundance greatest at passage, Sep-Oct and Mar-Apr. A bird ringed Kano was recovered in Malta.

195. **CHARADRIUS PECUARIUS**   RB

(I.246) Kittlitz's Sand-Plover

Not uncommon resident (*C. p. pecuarius*) on dry mud flats and sandy beaches, mostly coastal or near northern border from Sokoto to Lake Chad, or centrally only on Jos Plateau and on Niger and Benue Rivers. No evidence of seasonal movement.

Breeding. Several Lagos records Jun-Aug, and one in Nov; also Onitsha, May (Serle 1957), Malamfatori, undated (A.J.H.).

196. **CHARADRIUS TRICOLLARIS**   ?AfM/NB

(I.247) Three-banded Plover

Uncommon (*C. t. tricollaris*) on shingle beaches of rivers and along inland muddy shores in a limited area from Kano to Lake Chad south to the Jos and Mambilla Plateaux, Aug-Feb, and single records Mar, May and Jun. Status uncertain because of few records but is probably a non-breeding migrant from eastern Africa; unrecorded west of Ghana.

Breeding. Unrecorded anywhere in West Africa.

197. **CHARADRIUS FORBESI**   RB

(I.248) Forbes' Plover

Common resident, seasonally local, from the coast north to the great rivers and on the Jos Plateau. In the dry season it frequents short grass, bare ground and farms; in the rains it moves (not always locally) to areas with exposed rock, inselbergs, etc. to breed.

Breeding. First elucidated by Brown (1948) at several localities, Jun-Aug; later data advance season to late Mar.

198. CHARADRIUS ALEXANDRINUS   PM

    (I.245)   Kentish Plover

Uncommon Palaearctic migrant (*C. a. alexandrinus*) to coastal muddy shores and inland shores across north from Sokoto and Kano to Lake Chad, mid Aug to Mar. Unrecorded from most of central Nigeria, suggesting some birds cross the Sahara and others come via the West African coast. Usually small parties, max. 20 at Malamfatori, mid Oct (A.J.H.), but wintering population of up to 1000 estimated in Hadejia Wetlands, 1989-1991 (M.D.).

199. CHARADRIUS MARGINATUS   RB, ?Afm/B

    (I.244)   White-fronted Plover

Locally common resident (*C. m. hesperius*) on sandy shores, both coastal and inland, although not recorded recently in the Hadejia wetlands (M.D.). Seasonal movements may be due to water level changes but also suggest more regular migration in some localities.

    Breeding. Only along the great rivers from Kainji and Loko to Onitsha, Feb-May, when water levels low. Possibly birds leave both the coast and northern areas, such as Lake Chad, to breed centrally, not always in the same months.

200. CHARADRIUS LESCHENAULTII   VPM

    (Not in MP&G)   Greater Sand-Plover

Vagrant, only 2 records, both at Malamfatori: singletons 2 Aug 1968 and 21 Aug 1968 (R.J.D.). No new records for Nigeria but extra limital records from Senegal to Gabon.

201. CHARADRIUS ASIATICUS   VPM

    (I.250)   Caspian Plover

Vagrant from mid-Palaearctic (*C. a. asiaticus*). Only 3, well separated, records: Kano, 10 Nov 1953 (R.E.S); male in breeding plumage Calabar, 29 Mar 1960 (R.E.S.); male in breeding plumage Sokoto, 5 Feb 1972 (Mundy & Cook 1972-73).

202. PLUVIALIS DOMINICA/APRICARIA   VPM

    (I.251)   Golden Plover

Rare Palaearctic migrant (probably *P. d. fulva*) sighted only Lagos. First noted several times in "winter" 1962/3 by J.M.E. Took, and with J.H.E., 5 Mar 1963. Several subsequent sightings Nov-Mar. No specimen collected, but consensus opinion is *P. dominica*. MP&G quote *P. apricaria* as reaching West Africa (São Tomé) from the western Palaearctic; White only recognises the eastern Palaearctic race *P. d. fulva* as migrant to Africa. The few Golden Plovers encountered

203. PLUVIALIS SQUATAROLA PM

(I.252) Grey Plover

Not uncommon Palaearctic migrant, mainly Oct to late Apr, to muddy shores of coastal creeks, and occasionally inland; Malamfatori (twice), Kainji, Oct-Jan; Lake Tiga, Kano State, 2 in late Jan 83 (Sharland and Wilkinson); one record, May, for Hadejia wetlands, (M.D.); one Bukuru, 16 Dec 1990 (M.Ho.). Singly or small groups, but 60 at Bonny, 31 Aug 1963 and 100, 1 Sep 1963 (Smith 1966) are exceptional for being earliest and largest records.

Vanellinae

204. VANELLUS SENEGALLUS RB

(I.259) Wattled Plover

Not uncommon resident (*V. s. senegallus*) in swampy areas near water north of the great rivers and south to Ilorin and Nsukka. Records for the far north, Sokoto to Dikwa, are for the rains. Paradoxically, earlier Lagos records (Apr-Sep) are also for the rains (Sander 1956), so no clear pattern of seasonal movement is presented.

Breeding. Eggs, 31 Mar-19 Jun from area between the Benue, the Jos Plateau and Yankari Nat. Park, at which season the species seems most widely dispersed.

205. VANELLUS ALBICEPS Afm/B

(I.258) White-crowned Plover

Not uncommon seasonally on sandy river banks and sand bars from near the coast (but never on tidal shores) north to c.11°N. It leaves the south, Jun-Oct, where flooded rivers present no sand banks and may then occur northward to Sokoto and Yankari Nat. Park.

Breeding. Mainly along the great rivers, south to Onitsha, Feb-May; also small rivers of Benin area, Mar-May (J.B.H.).

206. VANELLUS TECTUS RB

(I.260) Blackhead Plover

Not uncommon resident (*V. t. tectus*) in dry grassy areas (including e.g. airfields and race courses) from Sokoto to Lake Chad south to Kaduna. Usually in small flocks, max. 40 at Malamfatori (A.J.H.). Bannerman (1931) suggested it was a dry season migrant at Kaduna, but it has since been found breeding there in the rains, 3 Jul 1958 (M.S.). Described as uncommon in Hadejia wetlands area, 1989-1991 (M.D.).

Breeding. Mostly Mar-May; but also Jul (above) and Maiduguri polo ground, 2 clutches in Nov (Bannerman 1931). C/3 Katsina, Nov (I.D.).

118 Charadriidae

207. VANELLUS SPINOSUS RB

(I.255) Spur-winged Plover

Common resident along all types of lake and river shores north of the great rivers, always regarded as "about the southward limit of its range" (Brown 1948) until sightings at Ife, 1 Mar 1972 (R.F.) and Sapele, 21 Mar 1976 (C.S.P.). Common resident around lake at IITA, Ibadan (A.M.N.).

Breeding. Sokoto to Lake Chad south to the great rivers, and Ibadan, Mar-May. Chick in Aug (BoA).

208. VANELLUS SUPERCILIOSUS AfM/B

(I.257) Brown-chested Wattled Plover

Uncommon intra-African migrant to dry grassy savanna, widespread from Lagos and Okigwi north to Zaria and Maiduguri, all late Nov to early Jun. Four on Golf Course at Oguta Lake, Imo State, 22 Dec 1989 (A.M.N.) and several there, Jan 1994 (A.P.L.). Transequatorial migrant breeding in low latitudes north of the equator.

Breeding. 8 nests Onitsha, 21 Jan-5 Feb (Serle 1957); C/4 Sanga River F.R.; nest C/4, 20 Feb 87 (Wilkinson et al. 1989). They also mention Ilorin and Enugu as known breeding areas.

209. VANELLUS LUGUBRIS RB

(I.254) Senegal Plover

Uncommon resident in dry open areas and farmland, mostly at the coast from Lagos to Badagri; also Malamfatori, mid Oct and once only Yankari Nat. Park, Jan (C.G.). At Lagos formerly not uncommon: "frequently to be met with in flocks up to about twenty birds" (Sander 1956) but very few recent records (Gee & Heigham 1977).

Breeding. Pair with chicks Lagos, 22 Sep (H.F.M.).

210. VANELLUS LEUCURUS VPM

(Not in MP&G) White-tailed Lapwing

Vagrant from the Palaearctic, only 3 sightings: 6 at Malamfatori, 29 Jan 1969 (J.H.), and 4 on 31 Jan 1969 (H.&H.); 3 sighted and photographed at Maguwa near Kirikisama, 19 Feb 1987 (Ash 1990).

211. VANELLUS CRASSIROSTRIS ?AfM/NB

(I.261) Long-toed Lapwing

Not uncommon (*V. c. crassirostris*) in short grass near water on the southern shores of Lake Chad from Malamfatori (where probably present all year-A.J.H.) to Wulgo. Sight records only by a number of observers, until a single bird photographed Pandam Wildlife Park, 8 Mar 1989 (I.G.N.). Further sightings in one area of Pandam, 29-30 Jan 1994 (M.Ho.).

Breeding. No records. Lake Chad is at the northwest edge of its range and even if birds remain all year they may not breed, or indeed anywhere north of the equator. Nearest known breeding locality southern Sudan (BoA).

SCOLOPACIDAE

Calidridinae

212. CALIDRIS CANUTUS PM

(I.274) (Red) Knot

Uncommon Palaearctic migrant (*C. c. canutus*), numbers probably increasing. Not noted east of Ghana by Bannerman (1951) but now numerous records on sandy shores and coastal mud flats, particularly Lagos, mid Aug to Feb, max. flock 25 (J.B.H.). 15 at Bururu, 23 Nov 1952 (R.E.S.) is the most easterly locality. A bird ringed Sweden recovered in southeast Nigeria.

213. CALIDRIS ALBA PM

(I.277) Sanderling

Not uncommon Palaearctic migrant to sandy shores, mainly on the coast, but also at Lake Chad and banks of major rivers and some reservoirs. Present all months, mainly Aug to early May. 100+ at several coastal localities with max. 250 Lagos, Nov (D.I.M.W.).

214. CALIDRIS MINUTA PM

(I.272) Little Stint

Palaearctic migrant to tidal and inland shores, common throughout the area north of the great rivers (100+ in several localities), much less common in the south and on the coast (max. 20 at Bonny – P.A.S.).

215. CALIDRIS TEMMINCKII PM

(I.273) Temminck's Stint

Not uncommon Palaearctic migrant to northern wetlands, Sokoto to Lake Chad, mid Aug to early Apr; flock of 100+ at Malamfatori built up during autumn of 1969 (R.J.D.). Regular at Zaria, reported at Kainji and recently near Jos: 2 Bukuru, 6 Apr 1991; one Rayfield, 2 Nov 1991 (M.Ho). The only coastal records come from Lagos: collected 15 Sep 1955 (Sander); up to 10, Nov-Dec (D.I.M.W.). Unrecorded in southeast. Much less common than *C. minuta* with which it often associates.

216. CALIDRIS FERRUGINEA PM

(I.270) Curlew Sandpiper

Regular and sometimes abundant Palaearctic migrant, mainly mid Aug to early Apr, to muddy shores both coastal and inland. Probably increasing in numbers: before 1960 no large numbers, up to 2000 at Bonny, Aug/Sep 1963 (Smith 1966), which suggests larger numbers on autumn passage. Similarly, previously only occasional at Lagos, Sep-Jan (Sander 1956), but in 1970s common, Aug-Mar

120   Scolopacidae

(Gee & Heigham 1977). Described as common in the Hadejia wetlands, 1989-1991 (M.D.). A bird ringed Austria recovered southwest Nigeria.

217. CALIDRIS ALPINA   PM, ?V
(I.271)   Dunlin

Uncommon Palaearctic migrant (*C. a. alpina*), possibly only vagrant. Sightings from only a few localities, all Sep-Dec: 10 at Lagos, 3 Sep 1949 (R.E.S.) and single 25 Dec 1970 (D.I.M.W.); single Sabon Gida (Jos Plateau), 30 Dec 1966 (D.P.E.); single Malamfatori, with *C. ferruginea* and *C. minuta*, 6 Sep 1968 (R.J.D.); 3 at confluence of Kaduna and Niger Rivers, with *C. alba*, 14 Nov 1969 (C.H.F.); max 3 birds Lake Tiga, Kano State, Jan-Feb 1983 (Beecroft & Wilkinson 1983). Small flock in Hadejia Wetlands, Jan/Feb 1989 (M.D.).

218. LIMICOLA FALCINELLUS   VPM
(I.276)   Broad-billed Sandpiper

Vagrant. One sight record: a single bird at Malamfatori which remained on the shore of Lake Chad for a few days in mid Aug 1968 (R.J.D.). Several new records of this "accidental" from elsewhere in West Africa but none from Nigeria.

219. PHILOMACHUS PUGNAX   PM
(I.278)   Ruff

Abundant Palaearctic migrant in extreme north from Sokoto to Lake Chad in wetlands and rice fields, where it is a pest with flocks of up to 10,000. In the Hadejia wetlands the wintering population, 1989-1991, estimated at 50,000+ (M.D.). Individuals present all months, large flocks mid Sep to mid May. Southwards, numbers decrease sharply, but flocks of 500 recorded Zaria and 100+ at Kainji. Formerly sparse south of the great rivers: Lagos uncommon, max. 5; Onitsha and Ilorin; small flock at IITA Ibadan, Oct (A.M.N). Birds ringed in Nigeria (over 600) have been recovered in Finland, Sardinia and Russia (6). A bird ringed Finland recovered in northern Nigeria.

Gallinagininae

220. LYMNOCRYPTES MINIMUS   PM
(I.269)   Jack Snipe

Uncommon Palaearctic migrant to marshes, Nov-Mar. Mostly in north, Sokoto to Lake Chad, south to Ilorin; also at Lagos in drainage ditches, Jan-Feb (Gee & Heigham 1977) and Ife, "regular dry season" (R.F.). Unrecorded in southeast. Frequent winter visitor to Kano area with over 30 ringed there (Sharland 1980).

221. GALLINAGO GALLINAGO   PM
(I.266)   Common Snipe

Not uncommon Palaearctic migrant (*G. g. gallinago*) throughout to marshes and drying lake edges, late Aug to early Apr, and isolated records for all other months except Jul. Usually singly or in small parties (max. 16 in Ibadan rice fields). Numbers increase in northern wetlands, Mar-Apr, during northward spring passage. A bird ringed Kano was recovered in Russia.

222. GALLINAGO MEDIA   PM
(I.267)   Great Snipe

Locally common Palaearctic migrant to marshland, mainly north of the great rivers but also at several coastal localities from Lagos to Calabar. Most numerous on autumn passage, late Aug to Oct, when formerly large "bags" obtained, notably at Zaria and Jos. Less numerous through winter, increases in Apr. Reported as rare in the Hadejia Wetlands, 1989-1991 (M.D.). A bird ringed in Russia was recovered at Zaria.

Tringinae

223. LIMOSA LIMOSA   PM
(I.289)   Black-tailed Godwit

Common Palaearctic migrant (*L. l. limosa*) to wetlands of the north from Sokoto to Lake Chad, mainly Oct-Mar, a few remaining all year at Lake Chad and elsewhere. Flocks of 50-100 frequent, max. 1000 "over flooded firikis" in Chad basin (P.W.). Wintering population of up to 5000 recorded in Hadejia wetlands, 1989-1991 (M.D.). Also a few records from valleys of the great rivers and in addition mainly singletons on coastal mud flats at Bonny (P.A.S.) and Lagos (J.B.H.).

224. LIMOSA LAPPONICA   PM
(I.290)   Bar-tailed Godwit

Uncommon and irregular Palaearctic migrant (*L. l. lapponica*) mainly to coastal mudflats, late Aug to Feb. Usually in small parties, but flock of 100 in Niger Delta, 9 Oct 1963 (P.A.S.). Only 2 (undated) inland records: between Lau and Numan (Benue River) and at Ringim (R.E.S.).

225. NUMENIUS PHAEOPUS   PM
(I.204)   Whimbrel

Common Palaearctic migrant (*N. p. phaeopus*) to coastal lagoons and creeks with large winter flocks, e.g. of up to 1000 at Lagos. Flocks of 60+ remain all year. Rare inland records only of single birds: Malamfatori, Aug-Sep (A.J.H.); Kano, undated (R.E.S.); Ife, 17 Dec 1970 (R.F.). 2 recoveries of birds ringed in England (Gee & Heigham 1977).

226. NUMENIUS ARQUATA   PM
(I.291)   Eurasian Curlew

Uncommon Palaearctic migrant, probably mainly *N. a. arquata* though *N. a. orientalis* has been collected Kalkala (Bannerman 1951), Opobo (Serle 1957) and

Bida (Bates 1930). Usually singly in coastal mud flats and creeks, exceptionally 50 at Bonny, 1 Sep 1963 (Smith 1966). Coastal records Badagri to Bonny; also scattered records inland throughout, and in all months.

227. TRINGA ERYTHROPUS   PM

(I.286)   Spotted Redshank

Not uncommon Palaearctic migrant throughout, mainly to wetlands of the north and coastal muddy shores, all months except Jun, mostly Sep-Apr; usually singly or small parties – max. 30, Lagos (D.I.M.W.). At Sokoto "much commoner than Redshank" and 5 on 1 Jul in breeding plumage (Mundy & Cook 1972-73). A flock of 220 at Dumbari, 18 Feb 1987 (Ash 1990). Common in the Hadejia wetlands, 1989-1991, with flocks of up to 1500 (M.D.).

228. TRINGA TOTANUS   PM

(I.285)   Common Redshank

Uncommon Palaearctic migrant (*T. t. totanus*) throughout the country, mid Oct to mid Apr, but in some localities more common and recorded all months. Winters mainly on coastal muddy shore; elsewhere, especially across the north, chiefly on passage Oct and Mar-Apr. Lagos area, overall Jul-Mar, mainly Aug-Sep, max. 18 on two days (Alexander-Marrack *et al.* 1985). Bird ringed in U.K. recovered in southern Nigeria.

229. TRINGA STAGNATILIS   PM

(I.287)   Marsh Sandpiper

Not uncommon Palaearctic migrant to muddy shores, river banks and wetlands throughout, Sep-Apr, but Jun and Jul are only months without records. Mostly singly or small parties, especially inland. Flocks of up to 30 in Niger Delta (P.A.S.) and 10+ inland at Sokoto (Mundy & Cook 1972-73), Lake Chad, (A.J.H.) and Chad basin boreholes (P.H.).

230. TRINGA NEBULARIA   PM

(I.288)   Common Greenshank

Common Palaearctic migrant throughout in wetlands of all types, mainly mid Oct to early May, a few remaining all year. Usually singly or in small parties though, exceptionally, a flock of 30 Sokoto, 1 Jul (Mundy & Cook 1972-73). One recovery in southern Nigeria of bird ringed in Netherlands.

231. TRINGA FLAVIPES   V

(Not in MP&G)   Lesser Yellowlegs

North American vagrant. D.I.M.W. claims 4 sightings, possibly of same individual, Lagos 15/16 Feb 1969, 10 Mar 1969, 18 Mar 1969 and one in same area Nov 1970.

232. TRINGA OCHROPUS PM
(I.282)   Green Sandpiper

Not uncommon Palaearctic migrant throughout, chiefly along wooded streams, mainly mid Sep to early May, but recorded all months. Usually solitary, but 4 together Logomani (F.C.S.) is exceptional.

233. TRINGA GLAREOLA PM
(I.283)   Wood Sandpiper

Common Palaearctic migrant throughout in wetlands and muddy shores of lakes and reservoirs, less common on tidal shores, mainly mid Oct to early Apr, occasionally as early as mid Jul. A few may remain all year at Lake Chad and elsewhere in north. Mid-season flocks up to 50 frequent. A bird ringed Kano recovered in the Crimea; one from Sweden recovered Kano (R.E.S.).

234. XENUS CINEREUS VPM
(I.280)   Terek Sandpiper

Rare Palaearctic migrant, at the western extremity of its wintering range. In autumn only at 2 localities: collected by P.I.R. Maclaren at Lagos, 7 Oct 1947, and another sighted in following Oct (Bannerman 1951); "at least 4 different birds 21 Aug – 2 Sep with one staying until 19 Sep" 1968 at Malamfatori (Dowsett 1969). Regular but rare in Chad, Aug-Sep, (Newby 1979) and Abidjan, Ivory Coast, Dec (Thiollay 1985).

235. ACTITIS HYPOLEUCOS PM
(I.281)   Common Sandpiper

Common Palaearctic migrant, mainly mid Sep to Apr; but recorded all months though only in small numbers May-Jul. Mainly seen on northward and southward passage north of the great rivers but southwards and on coast throughout the year. Found on all types of shore but favours stonework of dam and harbour walls. A bird ringed in Germany recovered at Ondo (R.E.S.).

Arenariinae

236. ARENARIA INTERPRES PM
(I.279)   Ruddy Turnstone, Turnstone

Uncommon Palaearctic migrant (*A. i. interpres*), possibly increasing, recorded late Aug to Feb. Only on coastal mud flats, Lagos to Niger Delta, singly or small parties – max. 15 at Bonny (Smith 1966) – except one, 1 Jun 1965, Lake Chad shore at Malamfatori (A.J.H.), and another at Kuzu Daguana, 9 Jan 1987 (Ash 1990). Extra-limital records indicate most arrive via the coast with large numbers in Senegal; small numbers in Mali, Niger, Chad and even Zaïre.

Phalaropodinae

237. PHALAROPUS LOBATUS   VPM

(Not in MP&G)   Red-necked Phalarope

New species for Nigeria. One observed by Wandert Bentham at an oasis at Tulotulowa (13°21′N, 10°59′E), 29 Sep 1988 (M.D.).

238. PHALAROPUS FULICARIUS   VPM

(I.293)   Grey Phalarope

Vagrant. One record: 12 birds close to the West Mole of Lagos Harbour entry, 30 Mar 1973 (Brown 1974) and, presumably the same group, still there next day (J.B.H.). No new records from Nigeria but elsewhere in West Africa most sporadic encounters have been coastal but also well inland in Mali (Bie & Morgan 1989).

STERCORARIIDAE

239. STERCORARIUS POMARINUS   PM

(I.303)   Pomarine Skua

Rare Palaearctic migrant, regular on the West African coast to W. Nigeria. At least 7 records from Lagos, Aug-Mar (Gee & Heigham 1977), and a surprising inland sighting from Lake Kainji: "a dark phase Pomarine Skua ... seen at Shagunu ... 28th May 1966" (Wells 1966). Several sightings from seismic ship in Gulf of Guinea, Jun/Jul 1992, including group of 3; one adult with prolonged tail-feathers, 10 Jul 1992 (Capt.F.S.).

240. STERCORARIUS PARASITICUS   V

(I.302)   Arctic Skua

Vagrant from Holarctic. Serle (1957) thought one from Calabar (Bannerman 1931) was not collected so far east. A number of sightings since, at Lagos, Aug-Mar, including an "injured adult (dark phase) 26th Feb to 2nd Mar" in 1968 (Wallace 1969).

241. STERCORARIUS LONGICAUDUS   V

(Not in MP&G)   Long-tailed Skua

Vagrant. An immature at Lagos, 2 Jul 1967 (Pettitt 1968), accepted as "undoubtedly this species" by Wallace (1973), who claimed sight of 2 "harrying *Sterna fuscata*" at sea due south of Lagos near the Equator.

242. CATHARACTA SKUA   V

(Not in MP&G)   Great Skua

Vagrant. Previously only a single sighting at Lagos, 10 Jan 1971, "during an influx of Palaearctic terns; the bird was clearly nominate *skua* from appearance, and thus its most southeasterly occurrence" (Wallace 1973). Recently one (racially undetermined) heading south, sighted from seismic ship in Gulf of Guinea, 25 Jul 1992 (Capt.F.S.). One recovery in Ivory Coast of bird ringed in Scotland (Thiollay 1985). In the 1981 Checklist this bird was un-numbered but in view of the recent sighting full status is now justified.

LARIDAE

243. LARUS MINUTUS   V

(Not in MP&G)   Little Gull

Vagrant (Wallace 1973): Lagos "up to three at any one time (five individuals), from 19 January to 16 February 1969, and 15 December to 18 January 1970. All birds were sub-adult". Previously recorded in West Africa from Sierra Leone (Field & Owen 1969) and subsequently recorded Mauritania (Gee 1984) and Senegal (Dupuy 1984).

244. LARUS SABINI   V

(I.309)   Sabine's Gull

Vagrant. Known only from the Lagos area: first recorded 25 Nov 1967 (Pettitt 1967); subsequently singletons 11 Jan 1970, 27 Feb, 28 Mar and perhaps a single individual 12-25 Apr, all 1971 (Wallace 1973).

245. LARUS CIRROCEPHALUS   ?RB

(I.307)   Grey-headed Gull

This species was inadvertently omitted from the 1st edition; it is regular and not uncommon at Lake Chad and other lakes and pools in the Chad basin, e.g. up to 20 at Lake Alo near Maiduguri (P.H.). Several records for Kainji, with a max. of 15 birds over the spillway, Apr (Geerling and Afolayan 1974). A temporary pool at Kazaure had several, max. 15, throughout Dec 1977 (R.E.S.). Max. 50 birds at Dagona Waterfowl Sanctuary, 14 Jan 1987 (P.H.), but recorded as uncommon in the Hadejia Wetlands, 1989-1991 (M.D.). There are no breeding records.

246. LARUS RIDIBUNDUS   PM

(I.308)   Black-headed Gull

Palaearctic migrant, frequent visitor to Zaria in the dry season. First noted Malamfatori, 22 Mar 1963 (J.H.E. and others), and subsequently often at Lake Chad, sometimes reaching "several dozen birds all in winter plumage" (S.Pedler); also at several dams and pools southwards to Kainji, notably during Dec 1977 at Kazaure where up to 45 occurred with *L. cirrocephalus* (R.E.S.) and to Yankari, Dec 1990 (I.D.). Regular in the Hadejia Wetlands, 1989-1991, but uncommon; one flock of 140+ (M.D.).

247. LARUS GENEI   V

(I.306)   Slender-billed Gull

Vagrant. One record only: "a sub-adult, probably first winter" Lagos, 18 Jan 1970 (Wallace 1973). The only other record south of Senegal is from the Ivory Coast in 1990 (Demey & Fishpool 1991).

248. LARUS FUSCUS   PM

(I.305)   Lesser Black-backed Gull

Locally common Palaearctic migrant all months, especially at Lagos, along coast from Badagri to Calabar, and many inland localities, mainly along the great rivers (several Kainji – Wells & Walsh 1969) at Lake Chad and one at Nguru, Jan 1992 (S.R.). Described as "uncommon, regular" in Hadejia Wetlands, 1989-1991 (M.D.). Usually in small parties, but 200+ regular at Lagos Nov-Apr (400 in Dec – Wallace 1973), and on passage "peaking at 45 per day on 16 August" at Malamfatori (R.J.D.). Numbers have increased dramatically at Lagos since Sander (1956) found it "scarce". Both nominate *fuscus* and *graelsii* have been secured; their proportions vary seasonally at Lagos (Wallace 1973). 3 birds ringed in Denmark (*L. f. fuscus*) recovered in Nigeria.

249. LARUS ARGENTATUS   V

(I.304)   Herring Gull

Vagrant. 2 adults at Lighthouse Beach, Lagos, 2 Feb 1969, and again 9 Feb 1969, with one remaining till 16 Feb 1969 (Wallace 1973). Single sub-adult Lagos, 12 Jan 1978 (D.I.M.W.).

STERNIDAE

250. GELOCHELIDON NILOTICA   PM

(I.311)   Gull-billed Tern

Uncommon Palaearctic migrant (*G. n. nilotica*), mainly Sep-Apr, to lakes and reservoirs in northernmost areas from Kano to Lake Chad, where most numerous (up to 100) Oct and Mar, coinciding with peaks of trans-Saharan passage. Not uncommon (max. 20 together) at Kainji dam, but only occasional records elsewhere, e.g. Sokoto, Lagos, Falgore and recently (1992) between Kano and Lake Chad (S.R.).

251. STERNA CASPIA   PM, ?AfM/NB

(I.312)   Caspian Tern

Uncommon, probably mainly migrant from the Palaearctic, to estuaries and inland lakes and large rivers, mostly Aug-May. Provenance uncertain, but birds recovered in Northern Nigeria have been ringed in Finland (6) and Sweden (2).

Breeding. No records, but breeds on islands off Senegal and Guinea-Bissau so may reach Nigeria from there.

252. STERNA MAXIMA ?

(I.317) Royal Tern

Status uncertain. Not uncommon (*S. m. albidorsalis*) along the entire coast from Badagri to Calabar. Parties up to 20 in all months at Lagos (Gee & Heigham 1977), elsewhere mostly Apr-Nov. No inland records.

Breeding. Not recorded in Nigeria but could occur; breeds notably Apr-Jul in Mauritania and Senegambia, when species seems prominent in Nigeria.

[STERNA BERGII V

(Not in MP&G) Swift Tern

A single sight record at Lighthouse Beach, Lagos, 27 Feb 1969 (Wallace 1973).]

253. STERNA SANDVICENSIS PM

(I.316) Sandwich Tern

Common Palaearctic migrant (*S. s. sandvicencis*) only at Lagos (on beaches and harbour buoys), though recorded along coast from Badagri to Burutu. No inland records. Present Lagos all months, 50+ Nov-Mar. "Adults outnumbered immatures from September to January, and their subsequent spring passage to the west is marked in March and May" (Wallace 1973). Birds ringed in U.K. (25), France (1), Germany (4) Denmark (1) and Netherlands (2) have been recovered in the Lagos area.

254. STERNA DOUGALLII PM

(I.315) Roseate Tern

Palaearctic migrant (*S. d. dougallii*) at Lagos, unrecorded elsewhere in Nigeria. Previous records sparse, but Wallace (1973) found it present "in every month but regular only in winter, with total population reaching three figures in January" There have been recoveries in the Lagos area of birds ringed in S.W.Ireland (3) and U.K. (4) (R.E.S.). Population decline reported in 1985 "may be part of an overall decline in the Western Palaearctic population" (Alexander-Marrack *et al.* 1985).

255. STERNA HIRUNDO PM, RB

(I.313) Common Tern

Not uncommon Palaearctic migrant (*S. h. hirundo*) along the entire coastline, and regularly found in small numbers (max.10) at Lighthouse Beach, Lagos (Alexander-Marrack *et al.* 1985). Present all months without significant seasonal pattern of numbers or proportion of immatures, and possibly including breeding birds in rains; "a quite exceptional count of 440 birds on 2 December 1967" (Wallace 1973). No inland records except two ringing recoveries at Aba and near Zaria. Mainly Palaearctic origin, viz: recoveries of birds ringed in U.K.(7), Sweden (2), Finland (3), Germany (6), and Holland (2).

Breeding. Breeds annually in Jul at mouth of River Dodo, Nigeria (BoA).

256. STERNA PARADISAEA   PM

(I.314)   Arctic Tern

A Holarctic migrant only recently shown to be present regularly at Lagos (Wallace 1973), on beaches and in the harbour, 25+ Jan and Feb, 10+ on passage May and Oct/Nov, but a few present in all months. Former West African records are sparse but include birds captured inland at a crater lake in Cameroon close to the Nigerian border. Birds ringed in U.K.(12), Denmark (3), Finland (3), Norway (1) and Germany (1) have been recovered along the coast, and U.S.A.(1) recovered at Ikibiri, the only inland recovery in Nigeria.

257. STERNA ANAETHETUS   V

(I.321)   Bridled Tern

Probably vagrant. Though Bannerman (1951) called it "a regular and numerous visitor to the beach and harbour at Lagos", he later (1953) said its status was doubtful and Wallace (1973) had "no certain record" in 4 years and doubted the earlier records. There is a sight record of a party of 6 at Burutu, 3 May 1953 (R.E.S.).

Breeding. No records. Known to breed in Pagalu (Annobon) and increasingly elsewhere in Gulf of Guinea, but it is certainly not "regular and numerous" in Nigeria.

258. STERNA FUSCATA   V

(I.320)   Sooty Tern

Vagrant (said to be *S. f. fuscata*); about 10 records. Apart from Lagos (6 records) the others have been exhausted birds at inland localities. 6 birds ringed in U.S.A. recovered in the mid-west and eastern Nigeria.

Breeding. No records, but breeds on Ascension and Principé, and Senegal in 1980 (Dupuy 1984).

259. STERNA BALAENARUM   AfM/NB

(I.319)   Damara Tern

Trans-equatorial migrant to the Nigerian coast from breeding areas in the south. Numbers noted only at Lagos; also recorded Burutu (R.E.S.). Wallace (1973) at Lagos noted small numbers Apr-Jun, rising to over 100 Jul-Oct, fewer again Nov-Jan, none Feb-Mar.

Breeding. "Breeding season Nov-Jan SW coast Africa" (BoA).

260. STERNA ALBIFRONS   RB

(I.318)   Little Tern

Not uncommon resident (*S. a. guineae*) along the great rivers and regularly seen, seasonally, south to the coast from Badagri to the Niger Delta. The few northern localities include Sokoto – "probably resident" (Mundy & Cook 1971-73) – and Lake Chad, where it breeds (R.J.D.). Subject to local movement due to river water level changes. Uncommon, Lighthouse Beach, Lagos, max. 2 in breeding plumage, Jun 1979 (Alexander-Marrack *et al.* 1985).

Breeding. Mainly on sand banks of great rivers, Apr-Jun, but later at Lake Chad, young being fed until Sep (R.J.D.).

261. CHLIDONIAS HYBRIDUS   PM
(I.324)   Whiskered Tern

Locally not uncommon Palaearctic migrant (*C. h. hybridus*) on inland waters, mostly Lake Chad and environs, with up to 15 in a day and 6 together (R.J.D.) from mid Jul to Apr. Recorded as "common winter resident and on passage" in Hadejia Wetlands, 1989-91 (M.D.). Up to 40 together Kainji (F.W.). Noted Lagos, Nov, Jan, Feb and Aug (D.I.M.W.). In full breeding plumage, Jul and Aug.
Breeding. No records, but could possibly occur in the Chad area (R.J.D.).

262. CHLIDONIAS NIGER   PM
(I.322)   Black Tern

Previously abundant Palaearctic migrant (*C. n. niger*) present all year at Lagos both on beaches and over lagoons, mainly immatures. The few inland records are during migration, mainly Sep and Apr, usually in breeding plumage and in company of *C. leucopterus*. Marked decline noted by Wallace in 1978; lack of records noted in all months Sep-Mar in Lagos area and elsewhere in 1985 and 1987 (Ash 1990), but present in numbers up to 200 in Jul and Aug each year 1988-1992 (P.H.).

263. CHLIDONIAS LEUCOPTERUS   PM
(I.323)   White-winged Black Tern

Locally common Palaearctic migrant to lakes and wetlands north of the great rivers; max. flocks in Sep, up to 1000 at Kazaure (R.E.S.), 600 at Lake Chad (R.J.D.) and 500 at Kainji (F.W.). Recorded as "common winter resident and on passage" in Hadejia Wetlands, 1989-1991 (M.D.). In the south occurs at Lagos, in small numbers in most months and 2 immature birds over lake at IITA, 6 Aug 1988 and 15 Sep 1989 (P.H.). Northern records are for all months. Breeding plumage is acquired during Apr, when numbers diminish till Sep.

264. ANOUS MINUTUS   V
(I.326)   Black Noddy

Vagrant (*A. m. atlanticus*), only 2 records: one collected by Jardine (1846) at mouth of the Bonny River (Serle 1957); a sighting by J. F. Brown, Lagos, 16 Jun 1974 (Gee & Heigham 1977).
Breeding. No records. Breeds on Pagalu, so the paucity of Nigerian records is surprising.

265. ANOUS STOLIDUS   ?
(I.325)   Brown Noddy

Status obscure. Few records (*A. s. stolidus*), collected only at Lagos (Bannerman

1951), and several sightings there without any seasonal pattern, as well as in the Niger Delta (Dodo River and Forcados), never more than 2 together. One came "on board" seismic ship in Gulf of Guinea, 23 Jul 1992 (Capt.F.S.).

Breeding. No records. Breeds on islands in the Gulf of Guinea; absence from Nigeria probably due to lack of rocky coastline.

RYNCHOPIDAE

266. RYNCHOPS FLAVIROSTRIS   RB

(I.327)   Skimmer

Formerly a local resident along the great rivers and major tributaries, at least seasonally when water levels were favourable, and single regular sightings were reported in coastal lagoons and large estuaries, Lagos to Calabar. Although reported from other West African countries, no records in recent years for Nigeria until Sep 1989, single bird at IITA, Ibadan (J.B.).

Breeding. Eggs, usually C/3, Apr-May, on sandbanks of the Niger, Benue and lower Kaduna, but no recent records.

PTEROCLIDAE

267. PTEROCLES EXUSTUS   AfM/B

(I.332)   Chestnut-bellied Sandgrouse

Seasonally not uncommon intra-African migrant (*P. e. exustus*) in sandy arid scrub of the Sudan and Sahel savannas, mainly north of 13°N, from Sokoto to Lake Chad, in flocks of up to 40, Oct-Apr. Most move north into Niger during the rains.

Breeding. Nest C/3, near Bulatura oases, Mar 1991 (P.H.).

268. PTEROCLES QUADRICINCTUS   Afm/B

(I.335)* Four-banded Sandgrouse

Seasonally common breeding intra-African migrant on open plains and thorn scrub, especially on ironstone soil, through most areas north of the great rivers. Several records further south at Ilorin and Kainji Lake Nat. Park. Moves north in the rains mainly to the Sudan zone, more sparsely to the Sahel and into Niger. No locality known to have species present in all months.

Breeding. Oct-May in Guinea Savanna: C/2 Zaria, Nov; B/3 Bauchi, Dec (Bannerman 1951); chick with adult Potiskum, Mar (P.B.); breeding Yankari, Oct, Nov and Jan (Crick and Marshall 1981).

*Named *Eremialector quadricinctus* by MP&G.

COLUMBIDAE

Treroninae

269. TRERON CALVA   RB

(I.362)   African Green Pigeon

Common resident in mangroves, high forest, secondary forest and gallery forest north to the great rivers; also in relict forest on the southern slopes of the Jos Plateau and montane forest at the Obudu and Mambilla Plateaux. West of the lower Niger and on the Jos Plateau escarpment it is *T. c. sharpei*; east of the lower Niger *T. c. calva*.

Breeding. Protracted, Jan-Aug, but mostly Jan-Apr. Nest building in Oban Hills, Oct 1987 (Ash 1990).

270. TRERON WAALIA RB

(I.360) Bruce's Green Pigeon

Common resident in well-wooded northern savannas where it replaces the more southerly *T. calva*, its most southerly localities being Ilorin, Gboko and Gashaka-Gumti Nat. Park. Its considerable dependence on figs makes it less common northwards and subject to local movements for food.

Breeding. Bauchi, Mar (Bannerman 1951); Kaduna, Apr (M.S.); "building in riparian woods," Kainji Lake Nat. Park, Aug (Wells & Walsh 1969).

Columbinae

271. TURTUR BREHMERI RB

(I.358) Blue-headed Wood Dove

Uncommon resident (*T. b. infelix*) in mature lowland forest from Lagos to Calabar north to Gambari, Ife and Ikom, but mostly from Edo (Bendel) State, where more high forest persists than elsewhere.

Breeding. "N.W. Benin Province", Dec (Mason 1940); "breeding condition" Lagos, Jan (Sander 1956).

272. TURTUR TYMPANISTRIA RB

(I.354) Tambourine Dove

Common resident in mangroves, secondary forest and high forest edges throughout the forest zone and northward in gallery forest to southern slopes of the Jos Plateau. Noted also in montane forest at Obudu Plateau. [The record from Luma Island, Lake Chad (Bannerman 1931) is suspect.]

Breeding. 2 adults with young squab Ibadan, 25 Feb 1964 (J.H.E.); juv. Sapele, 8 Jun 1975 (J.B.H.), and Nindam, Oct 1980 (Dyer *et al.* 1986).

273. TURTUR AFER RB

(I.355) Blue-spotted Wood Dove

Common resident in forest clearings, gallery forest and dense savanna woodland from the coast north to the great rivers, occurring north to near Kaduna, to well wooded areas of the Jos Plateau and its southern escarpment, and east to Serti where it overlaps with *T. abyssinicus*, which progressively replaces it northwards.

Breeding. Through the dry season, Oct-Mar.

274. TURTUR ABYSSINICUS   RB

(I.356)   Black-billed Wood-Dove

Common resident in wooded savannas north of the great rivers, abundant Falgore (Wilkinson & Beecroft 1985). Occurs southward, overlapping with *T. afer*, to Igbetti and Kishi in the west and Nsukka and Enugu (S.G.C.) in the east, and noted Lagos 1970 (D.I.M.W.).
Breeding. Through the dry season, Oct-Mar.

275. OENA CAPENSIS   Afm/B

(I.353)   Namaqua Dove

A common clearly defined "northern concertina" intra-African breeding migrant (Elgood *et al.* 1973). Present all year in the Sahel, migrates south to the great rivers, to breed Sep-Apr, sometimes as far south as Ilorin and Gboko. Found in all types of savanna, including farmland.
Breeding. From Sokoto south to Ilorin, Oct-Apr.

276. COLUMBA IRIDITORQUES   R(B)

(I.342)   Western Bronze-naped Pigeon

Not uncommon resident in high forest of southwest from Benin to Lagos. Easily overlooked unless voice is known, may well occur right across the country.
Breeding. No records. Nest found in Cameroon. Liberia, laying Mar and breeding indicated Apr, Jul and Sep (BoA).

277. COLUMBA LARVATA   R(B)

(I.359)   Lemon Dove

New species for Nigeria. Not listed as endemic in Nigeria in BoA but this montane species considered likely to occur there (Elgood 1976). A single specimen netted in the montane secondary woodland at Obudu Cattle Ranch, 17 Nov 1985 (Ash & Sharland 1986). Widespread on Mt. Gangirwal "1950-2200 m, near streams, some in song. Also singing Ngel Nyaki c. 1600 m." (Ash *et al.* 1989).
Breeding. No records. Cameroon, Jan, Aug, Oct (BoA).

278. COLUMBA SJOSTEDTI   R(B)

(I.338)   Cameroon Olive Pigeon

Not uncommon montane resident of the Obudu Plateau in flocks of up to 10 (M.D.); occurs in gallery mist forest of the Gashaka-Gumti Nat. Park up to 2500 m., where it is abundant in Mar (Ash *et al.* 1989).
Breeding. No records. Breeds Cameroon, May (BoA).

279. COLUMBA UNICINCTA   R(B)

(I.341)   Afep Pigeon

New species for Nigeria. Large numbers of pale grey pigeons, which must have been *C. unicincta* as they were definitely not the similar large sized *C. sjöstedti*, were seen on several occasions by Ash in the Oban area. 100+ in a loose flock at Neghi, 26 Sep, and several sightings of small groups in early Oct (Ash 1990). Although Ash regards this as unconfirmed since no specimen or photograph is available, the probability that these were *C. unicincta* seems high.

Breeding. No records. Breeds Gabon in dry season, Jun-Sep (BoA).

280. COLUMBA GUINEA   RB
(I.337)   Speckled Pigeon

Abundant (*C. g. guinea*) in urban areas and farmed land throughout the Guinea and Sudan savannas, less numerous in the Sahel. Strictly stationary, but is extending its range southward; first recorded Ibadan late 60's (J.M.) where it is now common at IITA, and not uncommon Lagos (P.H.). No records yet in southeast.

Breeding. Probably all months, mostly in dry season, Sep-Apr.

281. STREPTOPELIA SEMITORQUATA   RB
(I.347)   Red-eyed Dove

Abundant resident in mangroves, at forest edges and clearings and in gallery forest of the Southern Guinea zone, and at Lagos (D.I.M.W.). Progressively less common northward, but still not uncommon at Zaria and Yankari and formerly noted in wooded moist areas as far north as Hadejia but not recorded 1989-1991 (M.D.).

Breeding. From the coast north to Zaria and Vom, eggs reported in almost all months; no peak breeding month.

282. STREPTOPELIA DECIPIENS   RB
(I.349)   African Mourning Dove

Common resident (*S. d. shelleyi*), typically in gallery woodland from the great rivers north to the northern border wherever wooded streams occur. Although reported since 1969 in at least 3 areas of Lagos in almost all months (Gee and Heigham 1977), no records Lagos 1987-1993 in spite of being well known (P.H.).

Breeding. From Kainji Lake Nat. Park north to Sokoto and Kano, in almost all months.

283. STREPTOPELIA VINACEA   RB
(I.350)   Vinaceous Dove

Abundant resident in wooded areas of Guinea Savanna, less common in Sudan and Sahel zones. Progressively less common southwards until virtually absent in the south of the derived savanna and the forest zone; reappears in coastal savanna from Badagri to Lagos, where it is uncommon.

Breeding. In most months from Badagri north to Zaria and Vom.

284. STREPTOPELIA ROSEOGRISEA   AfM/?NB

(I.351) African Collared Dove

Essentially a sub-Saharan species (*S. r. roseogrisea*) that migrates south into northernmost areas of thorn-scrub savanna from Sokoto to Lake Chad in the dry season, mid Oct to May. In the rains it moves to north of Nigeria. Probably resident in most northern areas of Kano State, occurs at Gaya, Kirikasama and Kazaure (Sharland & Wilkinson 1981), and recorded as a common resident in Hadejia Wetlands, 1989-1991 (M.D.).
   Breeding. No records. Mali every month; Chad Sep-Oct (BoA).

285. STREPTOPELIA TURTUR   PM

(I.344) European Turtle Dove

A locally common Palaearctic migrant (*S. t. turtur*, though North African *S. t. arenicola* could occur) to northernmost areas from Sokoto to Lake Chad, usually in woodlands near water, mid Sep to early Apr. Often large flocks, max. 1000+ at Kazaure, Jan (R.E.S.); smaller flocks south to Zaria; individuals, with other doves, straggle south to Kainji (Wells & Walsh 1969), Pandam (C.S.) and Yankari (C.G.).

286. STREPTOPELIA HYPOPYRRHA   RB

(I.345) Adamawa Turtle Dove

Resident dove of the Jos/Bauchi Plateau, although less common than *S. senegalensis* and *Columba guinea* at Bukuru (M.Ho.). A few found southwest to near Kaduna (C.H.F.) and northeast to Kari and Potiskum (P.B.). Rare in the Nindam F.R. (Dyer *et al.* 1986) but frequent at Falgore (Wilkinson & Beecroft 1985). Though reported at Maiduguri in the rains (P.H.) and on the Mambilla Plateau in the dry season (D.P.E.), movements are probably only local.
   Breeding. Season probably extended; eggs Mar-Nov in the Jos area. "Dec; but probably Aug-Mar" (BoA).

287. STREPTOPELIA SENEGALENSIS   RB

(I.352) Laughing Dove

Abundant resident (*S. s. senegalensis*) in towns, villages, farms and cultivated areas throughout, but not in small clearings in the forest zone and uncommon in areas of natural vegetation. Probably sedentary, though numbers fluctuate seasonally in some areas.
   Breeding. Throughout, in all months, peaking in dry season, Oct- Mar; C/2 Ijebu-Ode, Jan and Apr 1991 (Sodeinde 1993).

PSITTACIDAE

Psittacinae

288. PSITTACUS ERITHACUS   RB

(I.400) Grey Parrot

Locally not uncommon resident (*P. e. erithacus*) where large enough areas of mature high forest remain, and in mature mangroves, only from Lagos to Calabar north to Ife and Ogoja. Becoming less numerous through human persecution and forest destruction.

Breeding. Jan, Mar. C/3 Yenagoa, 7 Jan 1955 (Serle 1957). Widespread offer of fledglings for sale from Feb.

289. POICEPHALUS ROBUSTUS   V

(I.401)   Brown-necked Parrot

Rare (*P. r. fuscicollis*) and local in savanna woodlands, probably no more than a casual visitor. Bannerman (1953) states it is "a visitor to the Plateau Province in April and May" Records are: between Kano and Zaria, Sep 1969; Damaturu, Dec 1970 (D.I.M.W.); 4 birds Jos, 16 Mar 1964 (M.H.); 2 birds Jos, August 1990 (M.Ho.); 6 sightings at Aliya, Nov-Dec (K.&Co.). The extended date range suggests a casual visitor rather than an African migrant.

Breeding. No records. Breeds Gambia, Feb, Apr.

290. POICEPHALUS SENEGALUS   Afm/B

(I.404)   Senegal Parrot

Widespread and common resident in the Guinea savannas of southwest and north and widespread in Gashaka-Gumti Nat. Park. Up to 8 birds, which were perhaps feral, Ikoyi Park and Tarkwa from 1980 (Alexander-Marrack *et al.* 1985), and small parties not uncommon now Ikoyi (A.M.N.). A partial migrant: southerly records to Oyo and Ibadan are in dry season, Sudan zone records mainly in the rains. White recognises 2 races; nominate *senegalus* in northern areas and *versteri* in the south, due to a southward cline of increasing underpart redness.

Breeding. Young leaving nest Jos, 10 Oct (J.R.L). "Begins Nigeria (Bauchi) Oct . . . also nestlings N. Nigeria Oct, Nov" (BoA).

Loriinae

291. AGAPORNIS PULLARIA   RB

(I.407)   Red-headed Lovebird

Uncommon resident (*A. p. pullaria*), mainly gregarious in riparian habitats with fruiting grasses or fig trees in wooded savanna. Caged birds are for sale surprisingly in most main towns, yet field records are not numerous and flocks of over 10 seldom met. Mostly found in coastal southwest, Badagri to Lagos, north to Zaria and the Jos Plateau, in southeast at Enugu, Onitsha floodplain and Owerri, and flock of 40 Gashaka-Gumti Nat. Park in 1988 (Green 1990).

Breeding. B/4 Enugu, 5 Oct 1954 (Serle 1957); 2 adults feeding 3 juvs. Lagos, Oct (J.B.H.).

292. PSITTACULA KRAMERI   RB

(I.406)   Rose-ringed Parrakeet

Uncommon but widespread resident (*P. k. krameri*) in savanna woodland, from the great rivers north to Sokoto and Lake Chad, south of the middle Niger to

Ilorin and south of the Benue to Gboko. Numerous Lagos records probably refer to a resident population almost certainly established from escapes, but a coastal savanna population could be one extending east from the Dahomey Gap.

Breeding. Two fledglings Gboko, Feb (H.H.G.). Nigeria, Feb, May (BoA).

MUSOPHAGIDAE

Corythaeolinae

293. CORYTHAEOLA CRISTATA   RB

(I.395)   Great Blue Turaco

Locally not uncommon resident where good-sized areas of forest remain (e.g. Okomu F.R. in Edo State), mainly from Ipake to Calabar, although the population is greatly depleted by forest felling. Outlying populations in gallery forest near Makurdi (H.H.G.), inselberg pediment forest near Abuja (D.C.H.) and relict forest on southern escarpment of the Jos Plateau. "Common resident Nindam" (Dyer *et al.* 1986).

Breeding. Probably irregular: juv. "head and neck still covered with down" Mamu Forest, 15 Nov; female with oviducal egg Mamu Forest, 30 May (Serle 1957).

Tauracinae

294. TAURACO PERSA   R(B)

(I.385)   Green Turaco

Not uncommon resident (*T. p. persa*), widespread in the forest zone in the canopies of high forest and secondary growth; also in montane gallery forest at the Obudu Plateau, with relict populations in the forested areas of southern slopes of the Jos Plateau west to near Kaduna (Anara F. R.) and frequent Gashaka-Gumti Nat. Park (Green 1990).

Breeding. No records, but is strictly stationary. Breeds Cameroon, May-Jun, Aug (BoA).

295. TAURACO MACRORHYNCHUS   R(B)

(I.388)   Yellow-billed Turaco

Uncommon resident (*T. m. verreauxii*) in lowland mature forest, from Sapele ("not uncommon" – J.B.H.) and Benin eastward to Oban, the montane forest at the Obudu Plateau (Serle 1957), and the gallery forest at 1500 m. Gashaka-Gumti Nat. Park (Green 1990). A sight record from Ibadan, 23 Mar 1974 (T.R-S.) emphasises its similarity to *T. persa*, which may mean it has been overlooked in the past. The most common Turaco along the Lekki Peninsula (P.H.).

Breeding. No records. Breeds Cameroon Jan, Jun-Aug (BoA).

296. TAURACO LEUCOLOPHUS   RB

(I.390)   White-crested Turaco

Locally not uncommon resident in "wet Guinea Savanna and gallery forest near streams" (H.H.G.). Only occurs from Ibi on the Benue south to Takum and Lissam eastward to Gashaka-Gumti Nat. Park and the Mambilla Plateau, its main range being east of Nigeria.

Breeding. C/2 Lissam, Aug (Serle 1939).

297. MUSOPHAGA VIOLACEA   RB

(I.393)   Violet Turaco

Locally not uncommon resident in gallery forest throughout the Guinea zone, south to Ibadan (A.P.) in west; across the north in the Sudan zone along well wooded streams from Sokoto to Potiskum; in the east south to Makurdi and Gashaka-Gumti Nat. Park (Green 1990) but absent from the southeast savanna woodlands.

Breeding. B/2 Serakin Pawa, 19 Apr 1938 (Serle *in* Bannerman 1955); Kabba, Aug (Brown 1948); juvs. Kainji Lake Nat. Park, Nov (Wells & Walsh 1969); Jun (BoA).

Criniferinae

298. CRINIFER PISCATOR   RB

(I.396)   Western Grey Plantain-eater

Common and widespread resident in wooded areas of the Guinea Savannas to Mambilla Plateau in the east, and derived savanna of the southwest, reaching to the coast at Lagos, but sparse in the southeast. Much less common in the Sudan zone and rare in the Sahel, probably due to paucity of suitable large trees.

Breeding. Extended or variable; recorded most months, peaking Apr-May. Building Ibadan, 29 Oct 1987 (Ash 1990).

CUCULIDAE

Cuculinae

299. OXYLOPHUS JACOBINUS   Afm/B

(I.373)   Jacobin Cuckoo

Not uncommon intra-African breeding migrant in savanna woodland north of the great rivers, Apr-Oct. Generally considered to be *O. j. picta* in West Africa, but there is a skin in the University of Michigan Museum of Zoology of *O. j. serratus* collected 31 Aug 1968, 8 km northwest of Zaria (R.B. Payne). Southerly records, all dry season, are sparse: female with "much subcutaneous fat" Enugu, 6 Dec 1954 (Serle 1957); Gambari, 19 Jan 1961 (J.H.E.); Lagos, Mar and Dec (Gee & Heigham 1977); Iwo, 3 Dec 1961 (J.H.E.). Their scarcity suggests movement, presumably to further southeast.

Breeding. Females in breeding condition Gadau, May (Bannerman 1951), Zaria, May (C.H.F.): juvs. fed by *Turdoides plebejus* Zaria, Jul (C.H.F.); fed by *Pycnonotus barbatus*, Jun and Jul (A.P.), and fledgling Nov (BoA).

300. OXYLOPHUS LEVAILLANTII   Afm/B

(I.372)   African Striped Cuckoo,

Seasonally common intra-African migrant in wooded savanna throughout most of the country, including suburban gardens of large towns; but uncommon in forest zone and in extreme north. Recorded mainly in coastal savanna north to the great rivers in the dry season, Oct-Mar; moves north of the great rivers in the rains, but the migratory pattern is still obscured by many "out of season" occurrences (Elgood et al. 1973).

Breeding. Female "with large yolking eggs" Enugu, 23 Apr (Serle 1957); female "with hypertrophied oviduct" Kainji, 4 Sep (Wells & Walsh 1969); numerous associations of juvs with *T. plebejus*, which is main (possibly only) host, Ilorin to Kano, Mar-Sep. Apr-Sep, probably to Oct-Nov (BoA).

301. CLAMATOR GLANDARIUS   Afm/B, ?PM

(I.371)   Great Spotted Cuckoo

Not uncommon in wooded savanna north of the forest zone and less so in coastal savanna at Lagos. Whether some are Palaearctic migrants is unproven. Almost every local observer has regarded it as migratory with slow northward passage Feb-Jun, but no clear pattern has emerged (Elgood et al. 1973).

Breeding. From Ibadan north to Sokoto, Apr-Jul. The only known host is *Corvus albus*.

302. PACHYCOCCYX AUDEBERTI   ?RB

(I.370)   Thick-billed Cuckoo

Records from both forest in south and gallery forest in savanna. First recorded Gambari, a pair 13 Oct 1963 (J.H.E.); also Pandam Wildlife Park, Nov (R.E.S) and "a few birds displaying" Jan and Apr (C.S.); Zaria, Nov (M.H.). Seen regularly at Nindam and present all months except Feb, Mar, Jul and Aug (Dyer et al. 1986). Recent sighting Lekki Peninsula, 1 May 1991 (P.H.).

Breeding. Young at Kagoro, rains 1979 (M.D.). Breeds Cameroon, Mar (Bannerman 1953). Hosts thought to be *Prionops caniceps*.

303. CUCULUS SOLITARIUS   Afm/(B)

(I.365)   Red-chested Cuckoo

Not uncommon intra-African migrant (*C. s. solitarius*) in high forest throughout the year. A clear "southern concertina" migrant (Elgood et al. 1973), it moves north during the rains, mainly Apr-Sep, to northern limits of the Guinea Savanna and even to Sokoto (Mundy & Cook 1972-73) and near Potiskum (P.B.).

Breeding. Nigeria, Aug (BoA). Said to parasitise a range of small passerines.

304. CUCULUS CLAMOSUS   R(B), Afm

(I.366)   Black Cuckoo

Not uncommon, probably the non-migratory *C. c. gabonensis*, in high forest and secondary growth throughout the year, though numbers diminish Oct-Feb. North of the derived savanna there are records May-Oct (Zaria), Feb, Apr-Jul and Nov (Nindam). Even further north it is thought to be mostly the nominate *clamosus*, a wet season visitor from southern Africa.

Breeding. No records in Nigeria, but is known to parasitise a number of passerines found in Nigeria and to be present all year. Breeds Cameroon, Sep (BoA).

305. CUCULUS CANORUS   PM

    (I.363)   European Cuckoo

Rare Palaearctic migrant (possibly overlooked) that could occur anywhere within the country. Collected at Owerri by Marchant (1953) and at Enugu by Serle (1957). A single sighting Falgore, Mar (Wilkinson & Beecroft 1985), another Okomu F.R., 23 Oct 1987 (Ash 1990). Sightings from Sokoto to Lake Chad suggest it may enter Nigeria at any point.

306. CUCULUS GULARIS   Afm/B

    (I.363)   African Cuckoo

Not uncommon breeding intra-African migrant in wooded savanna, seasonal movements not yet fully elucidated. Dry season records from as far south as Burutu (R.E.S.) and Lagos (Gee & Heigham 1977), and rainy season records as far north as Sokoto (Mundy & Cook 1972-73) and Potiskum (P.B.). From no locality are there records all year, e.g. recorded Kainji Lake Nat. Park, 17 Jan-22 Jun (Wells & Walsh 1969), Falgore, Jun and Sep, (Wilkinson & Beecroft 1985) and frequent Gashaka-Gumti Nat. Park, Nov-Apr (Green 1990).

Breeding. Female collected Enugu, 16 Feb 1954, had "greatly enlarged ovary" with "two recently erupted follicles" (Serle 1957); fledgling fed by pair of *Corvinella corvina* on several days Kishi, late Apr to early May (A.P.).

307. CERCOCOCCYX MECHOWI   R(B)

    (I.367)   Dusky Long-tailed Cuckoo

Uncommon resident in high forest; mostly collected specimens from the least disturbed central forest areas, from Benin to Umuagwu. Heard at Kagoro (R.E.S.) and recorded Nindam F.R., Apr-Dec (Dyer *et al.* 1986). Sightings in 1987 extended eastwards to Okwango F.R. and Oban Hills F.R. (Ash 1990).
Breeding. No records. Breeds Cameroon, Dec-Feb (BoA).

308. CERCOCOCCYX OLIVINUS   R(B)

    (I.368)   Olive Long-tailed Cuckoo

Uncommon resident in high forest from Ipake (J.A.B.) to Owerri (Bannerman 1951).

Breeding. The record of a juv. being fed by *Ploceus cucullatus* in a Lagos garden (Forrester 1971) is uncertain because of unlikely habitat. In nearby relict forest at Ishieri a bird imitated the call of *Neocossyphus finschii*, 26 Feb 1972, which could well be the host (Gee & Heigham 1977). Cameroon, young in post-juvenal moult, Feb (BoA).

309. CHRYSOCOCCYX CUPREUS   Afm/B

(I.374) African Emerald Cuckoo

Common (*C. c. cupreus*) in forest, including secondary growth, throughout the year. Common at Falgore and Nindam and elsewhere north of the forest zone, where it is a rains migrant, regularly reaching Zaria and occasionally, presumably in wetter years, even Kano and Kari. Whether it breeds outside the areas of continuous occurrence is unknown.

Breeding. Female with oviducal egg Ibadan, 13 May 1961 (F.C.S.). Breeds Liberia, Aug-Sep, Cameroon, Jan, Mar, Nov (BoA).

310. CHRYSOCOCCYX FLAVIGULARIS   ? R(B)

(I.377) Yellow-throated Cuckoo

Noted at Kagoro on 11 Nov 1979 and 26 Nov 1979 (C.H.F., R.E.S., M.D. and M.G.) and probably resident Nindam (Dyer *et al.* 1986). One seen feeding on a swarm of black caterpillars in umbrella trees at Okomu F.R., 26 Nov 1985 (Ash 1990).

Breeding. No records from anywhere in the species' range in West Africa.

311. CHRYSOCOCCYX KLAAS   Afm/B

(I.376) Klaas' Cuckoo

Not uncommon seasonally throughout, except the Sahel zone. Present all year in southern areas, north to the Jos Plateau's southern escarpment, migrating north in the rains-Sokoto, May-Oct (Mundy & Cook 1972-73), Maiduguri, Jul-Sep (P.H.). Noted Obudu Plateau Aug, (M.D.) and Falgore Apr-Aug (Wilkinson & Beecroft 1985).

Breeding. Female in breeding condition Aba, 9 Jul 1954 (Serle 1957); juv. fed by *Sylvietta virens* Calabar, 14 Oct 1977 (P.M.). Nigeria, Mar-Sep (BoA).

312. CHRYSOCOCCYX CAPRIUS   Afm/B

(I.375) Didric Cuckoo

Common seasonally in forest clearings and wooded savanna throughout the country. Present throughout the year south of the great rivers, some moving into the north, May-Oct, where its abundance depends on the local rainfall of the year; a "southern concertina" migrant (Elgood *et al.* 1973).

Breeding. From coastal areas north to Sokoto, mostly Apr-Sep, but overall Jan-Oct. Main hosts *Ploceus cucullatus* and *P. nigricollis*.

Phaenicophaeinae

313. CEUTHMOCHARES AEREUS   RB

(I.384) Yellow-bill

Common resident in forest and thick secondary growth throughout the forest zone and northward in gallery forest to Kainji (Wells & Walsh 1969), noted at Gadau, Jul (P.B.), and during the rains in Anara F.R. and Old Birnin Gwari (Gartshore 1982). East of the lower Niger nominate *aereus* occurs, to the west *C. a. flavirostris*; but no northern birds have been collected for racial determination. Possibly moves northwards in the rains.

Breeding. Female collected Mamu Forest, 21 Aug "had just finished laying a complete clutch of three eggs" (Serle 1957); C/2 Ilaro, 10 Jun 1963 (J.A.B.). Cameroon, Nov (BoA).

Centropodinae

314. CENTROPUS LEUCOGASTER   RB

(I.379)   Black-throated (or Great) Coucal

Common resident (*C. l. leucogaster*) in undergrowth of secondary forest right across the country, north to Ibadan, Ife and Enugu in relict forest patches. Strictly stationary.

Breeding. "Southern Nigeria, June and August" (MP&G), but source not identified. Cameroon, Jun, Aug-Nov (BoA).

315. CENTROPUS GRILLII   Afm/B

(I.378)   Black Coucal

Uncommon seasonal breeding migrant, typically in wide grassy river valleys in savanna. Some southerly sightings are suspect through confusion with melanic *C. s. senegalensis* (q.v.) – (Elgood 1955, 1973). Bates (1930) collected a juv. at Lagos, where it has been seen Jan, Apr-Jun and Sep, suggesting present all year. Northerly records, e.g. Zaria, Apr-Oct (C.H.F.), are during the rains, probably a "southern concertina" migrant (Elgood *et al.* 1973).

Breeding. Female with enlarged ovary (15 mm ovum) Ilorin, 13 Jun 1960 (F.C.S.); 3 juvs. Jos area, Sep (V.S.); "strong presumptive evidence" of breeding near Sokoto, Sep (Bannerman 1951).

316. CENTROPUS SENEGALENSIS   RB

(I.382)   Senegal Coucal

Common resident (*C. s. senegalensis*) in savanna thickets and scrub and in forest clearings, covering most of the country. Strictly stationary. The melanic (rufous) form (*epomidis*) comprises 40% of all birds at Lagos, the proportion diminishing northward to disappear about 200 km from the coast (Elgood 1973).

Breeding. Throughout, mainly Mar-Aug, i.e. in the rains when grass is lush enough to provide building material and cover.

317. CENTROPUS MONACHUS   RB

(I.381)   Blue-headed Coucal

Probably not uncommon resident throughout (*C. m. fischeri*) in marshes and lush grass near water, from Lagos to Lake Chad. Resemblance to *C. senegalensis* has obscured status and distribution, though in some places easily separable ecologically and found to be common; e.g. at Malamfatori *monachus* is found in wet grassland near the lake margin, *senegalensis* in drier scrub away from the lake.

Breeding. "Nest building 28 March", Ife (R.F.). Nigeria, Mar, Jun; Cameroon, Jan, Apr-Sep (BoA).

TYTONIDAE

318. TYTO ALBA   RB

(I.473)   Barn Owl

Not uncommon resident (*T. a. affinis*) in southwest and north, much less numerous in southeast, avoiding forest but found in wooded savannas and often in suburban situations. Strictly stationary.

Breeding. Sapele to Maiduguri, Nov-Jan.

STRIGIDAE

319. OTUS SCOPS   RB, PM

(I.479)   Common Scops Owl

Resident (*O. s. senegalensis*) and not uncommon in wooded savanna and suburban situations north of the great rivers throughout, south to Abeokuta and Ife, but unrecorded in southeast. The Palaearctic migrant *O. s. scops* has been netted and collected often enough Nov-Mar to suggest it is not uncommon in savanna woodland and suburban gardens as far south as Ibadan (J.H.E.) and Enugu (Serle 1957).

Breeding. C/3 near Kano, 20 Apr 1922; "young birds, 17 May", Dan Kaba (Bannerman 1933); young in same tree hole Ife, Feb 1973 and Feb 1976 (R.F.).

320. OTUS LEUCOTIS   RB

(I.482)   White-faced Scops Owl

Not uncommon resident (*O. l. leucotis*) throughout the entire country in forest clearings and all types of savanna with some good-sized trees, including suburban areas. Strictly stationary.

Breeding. Jan-Mar in all areas; also Oct (BoA).

321. BUBO AFRICANUS   RB

(I.492)   Spotted Eagle-Owl

Not uncommon resident (*B. a. cinerascens*) in savanna woodland throughout the area north of the great rivers, less common southward but recorded at Ibadan, Enugu, Abakaliki, Obudu Plateau and Gashaka-Gumti Nat. Park (Green 1990).

Breeding. Most records Kainji Lake Nat. Park, Zaria, the Jos Plateau and Yankari Nat. Park, Dec-May; young fledged Zaria, 8 Jun (C.H.F.), although BoA gives laying dates Aug, Dec-Apr.

322. BUBO POENSIS   RB

(I.496)   Fraser's Eagle-Owl

Few records, from Bonny to Ibadan, but probably an uncommon, not rare, resident (*B. p. poensis*) in lowland forest and difficult to locate. One heard in Oban West, 14 Apr (F.D-L. & R.D.). Juvs were not infrequently offered to Ibadan Zoo, so probably less rare than the paucity of localities suggests.

Breeding. Captive bird laid an egg Ibadan Zoo, 11 Oct (R.H.P.). Breeds Ghana, Nov; Cameroon, Jul, Sep, Dec (BoA).

323. BUBO LACTEUS   RB

(I.493)   Verreaux's Eagle-Owl

Uncommon resident in wooded savanna mainly north of the great rivers, mostly in the northeast, Potiskum to Lake Chad, one recorded at an oasis north of the wetlands, Jul 1990 (M.D.). South of the great rivers one near Kabba (Brown 1948), and the Obudu Plateau (Ash & Sharland 1986), although this distribution is not included in the map for this species in BoA Vol.3.

Breeding. C/1 Minna, 7 Jan 1936 (Bannerman 1951); Lake Alo, near Maiduguri, Feb/Mar (P.H.). A pair of newly fledged juvs. Obudu Plateau, 2-3 Apr (Ash *et al.* 1989).

324. BUBO LEUCOSTICTUS   R(B)

(I.495)   Akun Eagle-Owl

Rare resident in lowland forest. Only 3 records: Lagos, undated (Bates 1930) and Iju, near Lagos, undated (Bannerman 1933) – both collected; sighted 5 Sep 1965 "asleep in mid-morning on an exposed horizontal branch about 20 feet up" Gambari (Bass 1967).

Breeding. No records. Breeds Sierra Leone, Nov-Dec; Liberia, Apr, Sep, Dec; Gabon, Nov, Jan (BoA).

325. SCOTOPELIA PELI   RB

(I.497)   Pel's Fishing-Owl

Uncommon resident in gallery forest along rivers in the Guinea savannas.

Breeding. "A few pairs nesting" Pandam Wildlife Park, Aug and Oct (C.S.); nest with single pullus Pandam, Feb (M.G.).

326. SCOTOPELIA BOUVIERI   R(B)

(I.499)   Vermiculated Fishing-Owl

Rare resident along rivers of the forest zone, although not listed as endemic resident in Nigeria in BoA Vol 3. Only 4 records: collected Okitipupa, 30 Aug 1939 (Bannerman 1951); a young bird kept in captivity at Ogun River, near Lagos, till adult plumage developed (Sander 1957); sighting Lagos, 27 Mar 1969 (D.I.M.W.); probable sighting Ishieri, Lagos, undated (J.P.G.).

Breeding. The only records are from Gabon (May-Oct) and Zaïre, probably Nov-Dec (BoA).

144 Strigidae

327. GLAUCIDIUM PERLATUM RB

(I.486) Pearl-spotted Owlet

Not uncommon resident (*G. p. perlatum*) in wooded savannas throughout the area north of the great rivers and south to the coast at Lagos and in some suburban areas. Unrecorded in southeast and eastern half of the southwest. Photograph showing ear-tufts taken by R.Farmer at Tarkwa Bay in 1989.
Breeding. Oviducal egg Kano area, Apr (Bannerman 1933).

328. GLAUCIDIUM SJÖSTEDTI ?

(I.490) Chestnut-backed Owlet

New species for Nigeria. A forest owl not previously known further west than Cameroon Mountain (Louette 1981) and Korup Nat. Park (Agland 1985) adjoining border with Nigeria. Heard 9 Apr 1988 in primary forest in the Ikpan Block, and "prolonged and close views" of 2 in the Oban West forest, 15 Apr (Ash *et al.* 1989).
Breeding. No records. Breeds Cameroon, Feb, May, Aug, Nov and Dec (BoA).

329. STRIX WOODFORDII RB

(I.478) African Wood Owl

Probably not uncommon resident (*S. w. nuchalis*) in forest right across the country. Recorded Pandam Wildlife Park, Obudu Cattle Ranch, Boshi-Okwango F.R. (Cross River Nat. Park), Okomu and Nindam, where calls indicate presence all year (Dyer *et al.* 1986), Gashaka-Gumti Nat. Park (Green 1990) and Lekki Conservation Centre 13 Jul 93 (P.H.). Young are not infrequently offered for sale.
Breeding. Female with yolking eggs collected Nkpologu, 8 Dec 1953 (Serle 1957); half-grown juv. handled Lagos, Feb (J.H.E.); juv. just able to fly netted Ife, Dec (R.F.).

[ASIO FLAMMEUS VPM

(I.476) Short-eared Owl

Palaearctic migrant (*A. f. flammeus*), twice collected at "Lake Chad", probably just extra-limital in both cases. Sight records from the Jos Plateau, where *A. capensis* is not uncommon, so that confusion is possible (Ebbutt *et al.* 1964).]

330. ASIO CAPENSIS RB

(I.477) Marsh Owl

Locally not uncommon resident (*A. c. tingitanus*) in grassy valleys and swamps north of the great rivers, especially on the Jos and Mambilla Plateaux. The only southern records are sightings at Lagos, 18 May 1969 and 11 Jun 1970 (Gee & Heigham 1977).
Breeding. "Nests containing eggs have been seen between 1st October and

12th January" on Jos Plateau (V.S.); Vom, Oct (R.M.Gambles). Newly fledged young with adults at Rayfield (near Jos), 28 Jan 1992 (J.B.).

CAPRIMULGIDAE

Caprimulginae

331. CAPRIMULGUS NATALENSIS   RB

(I.506)   Swamp Nightjar

Probably locally a not uncommon resident in grassland, at only a few scattered localities. In eastern areas *C. n. natelensis* has been collected at Okigwi (Marchant 1953) and around Lake Chad. Recorded near Mambilla Plateau at c. 1500 m "at least ten (mostly singing males)", Mar (Ash *et al.* 1989). In central areas, sightings only and these may intergrade with *C. n. accrae*. This race is "restricted to two small areas (at Lagos) . . . in open grassland, but nowhere numerous" (Sander 1957).
   Breeding. Eggs Lagos (*accrae*), Apr and May (Sander 1957).

332. CAPRIMULGUS CLIMACURUS   Afm/B

(I.515)   Long-tailed Nightjar

Common and widespread resident in all types of savanna throughout. *C. c. sclateri* is present all months in coastal savanna at Lagos with an extensive breeding period, Jan-Oct. Elsewhere in south, as at Ibadan, it is present as a non-breeding migrant from the north, Nov-Feb. In far north is a resident population, *C. c. climacurus*. Movement and racial pattern obscure in intermediate areas.
   Breeding. Lagos, Jan-Oct with peak in May; Kainji Lake Nat. Park and north of the great rivers (*sclateri* and nominate *climacurus* not differentiated), May-Aug.

333. CAPRIMULGUS NIGRISCAPULARIS   R(B)

(I.501)   Black-shouldered Nightjar

Not uncommon resident in secondary growth in the forest zone right across the country; also at southern edge of the Jos Plateau and (not certainly) at Yankari Nat. Park. The persistent characteristic call indicates continuous presence, though silent during part of the rains in most areas.
   Breeding. Sings southern Nigeria, Jul-Mar. Breeds Zaïre, Jan, Feb, Apr-Aug, Dec (BoA).

334. CAPRIMULGUS INORNATUS   Afm/B

(I.505)   Plain Nightjar

Not uncommon seasonally in open savanna throughout. At Lagos, probably in south generally, present all months; elsewhere definitely seasonal, with migration northward in rains (Elgood *et al.* 1973).
   Breeding. Male in breeding condition Sokoto, Apr (Bannerman 1951); fledgling Enugu, Apr (Serle 1957).

335. CAPRIMULGUS TRISTIGMA RB

(I.504)   Freckled Nightjar

Locally not uncommon resident (*C. t. sharpei*) on inselbergs of the Southern Guinea zone north to Kari (P.B.) and the Jos Plateau, strongly stenotopic at bare rock surfaces. All West African birds placed in *C. t. sharpei* by White, but Parker & Benson (1971) have created the race *pallidirostris* for birds from the Jos Plateau.

Breeding. C/2 Upper Ogun Estate, 31 Jan 1965 (J.H.E.); Gugurugi and Ossara, both May (Brown 1948).

336. CAPRIMULGUS AEGYPTIUS AfM/NB

(I.509)   Egyptian Nightjar

Probably locally not uncommon on open sandy ground. The only specimen (*C. a. saharae*) "was obtained near the mouth of the Yo river", 24 Feb 1905 (Bannerman 1933); at nearby Malamfatori, frequent Aug-Oct, once 6 together (A.J.H.). White mentions Lake Chad as an area visited in off-season by both nominate *aegyptius* and *saharae*, so both races could occur on Nigerian shores of the Lake.

337. CAPRIMULGUS EUROPAEUS PM

(I.500)   European Nightjar

Probably uncommon Palaearctic migrant. Almost all records from the east and only *C. e. europaeus* recorded. Birds identified in the hand Ibadan, 11 Dec 1944 (H.F.M.); near Abuja, 24 Oct 1958 (M.H.); near Vom, 20 Apr 1967 – one collected from 100 nightjars noted, others of which could have been *europaeus* (J.R.Lang); Gombe, undated (R.H.P.); Kano, 2 netted during Oct 1976 (R.E.S.).

338. CAPRIMULGUS RUFIGENA AfM/NB

(I.502)   Rufous-cheeked Nightjar

Rare non-breeding trans-equatorial migrant from southern Africa recorded during the rains from only 4 localities: Yola, collected by Bates, 17 Aug 1925 (Bannerman 1933); Jos Plateau, "occasional" (E.H.S.& S); Kano (R.E.S.); one Falgore, May (Wilkinson & Beecroft 1985).

339. MACRODIPTERYX LONGIPENNIS Afm/B

(I.513)   Standard-winged Nightjar

Intra-African migrant, common seasonally in open savanna throughout, but its migrations, in relation to breeding, are complex and not fully understood (Elgood *et al.* 1973). Broadly, present only in the dry season south of the great rivers and in the rains to the north in Niger, but both movement and breeding seem influenced by the rain pattern of individual years. Passage migration noted Yankari Nat. Park mid Oct (Green 1989).

Breeding. In south, Benin and Sapele, Feb and Mar; central areas, Ilorin, Wamba and Yankari, Mar and Apr; in north, Zaria C/2, 24 May (C.H.F.),

Gadau, Jun (Bannerman 1951). Although a northward progression of breeding time seems fairly clear, a few records fail to fit the pattern.

340. MACRODIPTERYX VEXILLARIA AfM/NB
(I.514) Pennant-winged Nightjar

Uncommon non-breeding trans-equatorial migrant in the rains. Earliest Enugu, 5 Apr 1954 (Serle 1957); latest, male in breeding plumage Sapele, 10 Aug 1975 (J.B.H.), Sankwala, 7 Aug 1993 (M.K.), Lagos "late August" (Sander 1957) and Pandam Jul 1992 (J.B.). Most northerly record is near Potiskum, May (P.B.).

APODIDAE

Apodinae

341. RHAPHIDURA SABINI R(B)
(I.607) Sabine's Spinetail

Uncommon resident, locally not uncommon above forests, sight records only. A singleton Yankari, Nov (C.G.). Up to 10, sometimes in association with *Neafrapus cassini*, in the Oban Hills and Okwango Sectors of Cross River Nat. Park and Okomu F.R., Sep-Jan (Ash 1990).
Breeding. No records. Breeds SW Cameroon, Mar (Serle 1981).

342. TELACANTHURA MELANOPYGIA V
(I.604) Black Spinetail

Rare vagrant, first sighted Nigeria in 1975, a westward extension from Cameroon, but now also reported from Ghana. Max. 6 birds sighted daily in lowland forest clearings at Nikrowa, near Benin, 29 Mar-1 Apr 1975 (J.B.H. & C.S.P.), 2 over Okomu F.R., 26 Oct 1985 (Ash 1990); small numbers often present in flocks of *Neafrapus cassini* in Okomu F.R. (P.H.).
Breeding. No records anywhere in West Africa.

343. TELACANTHURA USSHERI RB
(I.603) Mottled Spinetail

Uncommon, perhaps locally not uncommon, resident (*T. u. ussheri*), easily overlooked through general similarity to abundant *Apus affinis*. Widespread from Lagos – 14 sightings Mar-Jun (J.H.E.) – Ikom, 16 Apr 1954 and Calabar (see below), in the south, north to Yankari Nat. Park, Zaria and Kano.
Breeding. Nesting on buildings in Calabar, 6 Apr 1988 (Ash et al. 1989).

344. NEAFRAPUS CASSINI R(B)
(I.605) Cassin's Spinetail

Not uncommon resident in lowland forest. Max. 30 at Calabar, 19 Sep 1976 (P.M.). In the southeast up to 20 frequently seen together at Ekang and in the

Okwango, Oban Hills and Boshi Sectors of Cross River Nat. Park, Sep-Jan (Ash 1990). Also recorded from Niger Delta and 4 forest reserves of southwest Nigeria (Elgood 1977).

Breeding. No records anywhere in West Africa.

345. CYPSIURUS PARVUS RB

(I.602)   African Palm Swift

Common resident throughout wherever various species of palms occur. In south the darker race *C. p. brachypterus* associates with Cocoanut (*Cocos*) and Oil-Palm (*Elaeis*); through the Guinea zone birds that are probably racially intermediate associate with Borassus palm; in the Sudan zone nominate *parvus* is found at Dum Palms (*Hyphaene*).

Breeding. Mar-Aug in south; mainly Jun-Aug in north.

346. APUS BARBATUS ?

(I.592)   African Black Swift

Only one record (*A. b. sladeniae*), over montane grassland: one collected 19 Mar 1961 at Obudu Plateau by F.C.Sibley was labelled *A. apus* until re-identified 10 years later by Parker (1971). May easily be overlooked since its range includes adjacent southwest Cameroon.

347. APUS PALLIDUS ?PM

(I.590)   Pallid Swift

Locally not uncommon Palaearctic migrant; sight records only. Thought to be *A. p. brehmorum*, which breeds in the Palaearctic, but could be nominate *pallidus* which breeds in northernmost Sahara. Recorded from Lagos (D.I.M.W.) to Malamfatori (R.J.D.), mid Sep to May (a few in Jun). Regular spring passage Zaria, Apr-May (A.P.), up to 150 there (C.H.F.).

[APUS UNICOLOR ?

(I.591)   Plain Swift

Not included in the First edition, the only record was of a single sighting Lagos, 1 Dec 1970 (D.I.M.W.). Previously considered an accidental on mainland Africa – Morocco – further sightings Morocco and recently Mauritania, 25 Apr 1988 (Meininger *et al.* 1990), make its occurrence on the West African coast less problematical.]

348. APUS APUS PM

(I.589)   European Swift

Palaearctic migrant (*A. apus*), abundant on spring passage Apr, less numerous in autumn and local during 'winter', seldom remaining long in any area, mid Aug to early May, earliest 9 at Kainji, 3 Aug (F.W.), latest 29 May in same area. Flocks of 200+ are frequent, especially after early rain. On a 100 km journey (Oyo-Ilorin), 19 Mar 1956, a few to many seen continuously (J.H.E.). Recorded feeding in flight over all habitats including high forest.

349. APUS BATESI ?

(I.595) Bates's Swift

Sightings from Kagoro on southern escarpment of Jos Plateau, "probable" sighting, 29 Sep 1979, and "certain" sighting with 2 other observers, 17 Feb 1980 (M.D.); Obudu Plateau, seen with 2 swallow species, 7 Aug 1980 (M.D.); recent records from the southeast of parties up to 10 and also sightings over forest Okomu F.R. (Ash 1990) suggest it may have been overlooked previously.
Breeding. No records. Breeds Cameroon, May-Jun (BoA).

350. APUS CAFFER RB

(I.600) White-rumped Swift

Not uncommon but local resident near streams in savanna. Mostly in the west, from coastal savanna at Badagri north to Zaria and Kano; in the east only at Calabar, Mambilla Plateau and Malamfatori along the border. Also locally frequent on the Jos Plateau.
Breeding. B/2 Abeokuta, Apr; C/2, Jun (Serle 1950); Vom area, Apr (V.S.); Zaria, Jul (A.P.).

351. APUS HORUS ?

(I.601) Horus Swift

Treated as unsubstantiated in the first edition as it is difficult to distinguish from *A. caffer* and *A. affinis*. Sight records must be treated with caution, but possibly overlooked in the past. Dobbs (1959) accepted records by Macgregor at Sokoto and gave status as "Rare, on Passage" However, recent sightings of c. 30 between Mambilla and Serti (elevation 1250 m), 12 Nov 1985, others at 4 nearby sites and c. 20 below Obudu Cattle Ranch (elevation 1400 m), 14-18 Nov 1985 (Ash 1990), confirm its occurrence in Nigeria.
Breeding. Thought to breed in Chad, Nov-Feb (BoA). Birds near Obudu, Nov 1985, were seen to enter holes and one was excavating or clearing out hole (Ash 1990).

352. APUS AFFINIS RB, PM

(I.599) Little Swift

Abundant resident (*A. a. aerobates*) around towns and large villages throughout, but apart from reservoirs infrequent in rural areas. The Palaearctic race (*A. a. galilejensis*), collected near Kano (Bannerman 1933) may well prove not uncommon in the north, where few birds have been handled.
Breeding. All the year and in all areas, but peak seasons vary locally and annually.

353. TACHYMARPTIS AEQUATORIALIS ?

(I.598) Mottled Swift

Status obscure, but probably very local and irregular. The only known specimens are 4 collected at Wase Rock (M.Horwood), 12-14 Apr 1964, from a flock of 1000 max. present Nov-Jun, which proved to be *T. a. lowei*. Sight records from central areas and Mambilla Plateau include flock of 200+ Apr-May 1988, at the western end of the Jos Plateau near Kurra (J.B.). Flocks of 500+ at Yankari Nat. Park, Feb (A.P.), and c.30 at Mada River Bridge, 23 Jul 93 (M.Ho.). Large flocks present over Kamale Pinnacle, Mandara Mts. (on Nigerian/Cameroon border), 4 Dec 1982 (P.H.). Whether all birds are *lowei* or include some *T. a. bamendae* is unknown.

Breeding. May breed Wase Rock, Nov-Jun; probably breeds Ghana, Jun and Oct (BoA).

354. TACHYMARPTIS MELBA ?PM

(I.597) Alpine Swift

Probably an irregular Palaearctic migrant (*T. m. melba*), though *T. m. tuneti* and other races which breed in eastern Africa cannot be ruled out. Mostly in upland areas or around inselbergs, associating with other swifts. Extreme dates: c. 40 at Numan, 7 Nov 1958 (R.E.S.); single bird at Zaria inselberg, 21 May 1963 (C.H.F.). Largest flock 200 at Mambilla Plateau, Feb (D.P.E.).

COLIIDAE

355. UROCOLIUS MACROURUS RB

(I.518) Blue-naped Mousebird

Now uncommon resident (*U. m. macrourus*) in thorn scrub and *Salvadora* of the Sudan and Sahel savannas from Sokoto to Lake Chad. An unrepeated sighting Zaria, Jan 1973 (J.H.E.) was probably due to a long sequence of exceptionally dry years. Decrease in population in Kano State noted over last 20 years (R.E.S. 1981), although reported as "locally common in orchards and acacia woodland" around Nguru, 1989-1991 (M.D.), and flocks of 6-8 birds around Maiduguri (P.H.).

Breeding. "Around Lake Chad", May-Jun (Bannerman 1933); female in breeding condition Yo, May (BMNH).

356. COLIUS STRIATUS RB

(I.516) Speckled Mousebird

Not uncommon resident locally (*C. s. nigricollis*), restricted to the eastern savanna woodlands, not yet found west of the Lower Niger nor west of the Jos Plateau. Occurs on the Obudu and Mambilla Plateaux, but most commonly on the Jos Plateau and in savanna between Enugu and Afikpo.

Breeding. Eggs Jos area, Apr-May and Aug; in breeding condition Enugu, Aug-Sep (Serle 1957).

TROGONIDAE

357. APALODERMA VITTATUM   R(B)

(I.522)   Bar-tailed Trogon

Not uncommon resident regularly seen in montane forest at Obudu Plateau; small numbers in montane forests (1500-2050 m) Mambilla Plateau, Mar (Ash *et al.* 1989). Collected by Serle (1957) and F.C.Sibley.
Breeding. No records. Breeds Cameroon, Oct (BoA).

358. APALODERMA NARINA   R(B)

(I.520)   Narina's Trogon

Uncommon resident in forest, but recorded from Ilaro to Calabar, including a "much mutilated 'spirit specimen' " regarded as *A. n. constantia* from Calabar (Bannerman 1933). Also more widely but thinly spread records from gallery forest, as far north as the relict forest of the Jos Plateau southern escarpment, near Potiskum (P.B.) and at Yankari and Gashaka-Gumti Nat. Parks, Feb and Mar (Green 1990). A specimen from between Jos and Bauchi identified by BMNH as *A. n. brachyurum* (R.E.S.).
Breeding. No records anywhere in West Africa.

359. APALODERMA AEQUATORIALE   ?

(I.521)   Bare-cheeked Trogon

New species for Nigeria. Male heard in Ikpan Block on 10 Apr 1988 in primary forest, and attracted by a tape (Chappuis 1981) from Gabon, to give clear sight record. Female also thought to be present. The same, or a second pair, found 1 km distant, 12 Apr 1988 (Ash *et al.* 1989).
Breeding. No records. Gabon, Jan-Feb; Zaïre (Ituri), nestling Aug (BoA).

ALCEDINIDAE

Daceloninae

360. HALCYON BADIA   RB

(I.429)   Chocolate-backed Kingfisher

Uncommon resident in high forest, near streams and in swamp forest, from Lagos to Calabar north to Olokemeji and Benin.
Breeding. At Isheri, a relict forest near Lagos, male collected by J.P.Gee, 12 Feb 1972, was in breeding condition.

361. HALCYON LEUCOCEPHALA   Afm/B

(I.428)   Grey-headed Kingfisher

Common (*H. l. leucocephala*) seasonally throughout, but subject to a remarkable migration/breeding cycle (Skinner 1968 and see Elgood *et al.* 1973). Present in the forest zone, Nov-Feb, then moves north into Guinea savanna to breed, Mar-

May, to move again northward to the extreme north and into Niger, Jun-Sep, returning south in Oct. (This pattern is not strictly followed by all birds, nor in all years, e.g. present along Lekki Peninsula throughout year (P.H.)).

Breeding. Mar-May or early Jun, but Bannerman (1933) reported 9 nests Ilorin, Jan. Breeding Rayfield (Jos), Apr-May (J.B.).

362. HALCYON MALIMBICA RB

(I.426) Blue-breasted Kingfisher

Common resident (*H. m. forbesi*) in mangroves, forest clearings and gallery forest north to the limits of the derived savanna. Much less common further north, but occurs in mature gallery forest at Zaria and Yankari Nat. Park. No clear evidence of migration, though most northerly records are during the rains.

Breeding. From the coast north to Lokoja, Jan-Jun; juvs. Jul-Aug.

363. HALCYON SENEGALENSIS Afm/B

(I.425) Woodland Kingfisher

Abundant resident (*H. s. fuscopilea*) all months in mangroves, forest clearings, edges and outliers of the forest zone and in derived savanna intergrading with *H. s. senegalensis* at the forest/savanna interface (BoA). Less common in savanna woodlands north to the great rivers. A "southern concertina" migrant (Elgood *et al.* 1973). Moving into all northern areas Sokoto to Lake Chad, May-Oct, with fewest in extreme north.

Breeding. From coast north to Vom and Kari, Apr-Aug.

364. HALCYON CHELICUTI RB

(I.430) Striped Kingfisher

Not uncommon resident (*H. c. chelicuti*) in savanna woodlands of the Guinea zone, south to Ibadan and Abeokuta in west and Enugu in east. Birds from the Sahel and around Lake Chad belong to *H. c. eremogiton*; Bannerman (1933) considered birds from Kano and Sokoto would belong to this race but this still needs confirmation. Possibly only migratory to some northern localities, e.g. "partial rains migrant", Maiduguri (P.H.); present Potiskum area, Nov-Apr (P.B.).

Breeding. Co-operative. C/3 Bassa, 16 Apr 1938 (Bannerman 1951); feeding young in nest Ibadan, Apr (J.H.E.).

Alcedininae

365. CEYX LECONTEI R(B)

(I.424) African Dwarf Kingfisher

Rare or very local resident. A pair netted Ogba, near Benin City, 28 Apr 1975, again 4 Jul 1975 (D.N. Johnson); photographed at Sapele, Jun (C.S.P.); sighted Ife University Campus, undated (R.F.). Recent records are: single birds at Oban, 30 Sep 1987 and Ibadan, 30 Oct 1987, where sighted at 3 localities (Ash 1990); several netted Okomu F.R. (P.H.).

Breeding. No records. Breeds Cameroon Feb (BoA).

366. CEYX PICTA   RB

(I.423) African Pygmy Kingfisher

Common resident (*C. p. picta*), widespread throughout but rather more numerous in the south, in mangroves, forest edges and clearings, wooded savanna and suburban gardens. Seasonal movements in some areas of extreme north: present Malamfatori Jul to mid Sep (R.J.D.); Maiduguri, "pronounced rains migrant" (P.H.); Potiskum area, "commonest at start and end of dry season" (P.B.).

Breeding. Mostly in south, through rainy months, Mar-Oct; few records for north, all May (at start of rains).

367. CORYTHORNIS LEUCOGASTER   R(B)

(I.422) White-bellied Kingfisher

Uncommon resident, perhaps locally not uncommon, along forest streams mainly in the forest zone but also in relict forest at Pandam Wildlife Park (C.S.). Often taken in mist nets, (Kagoro 10-15, M.D.), but few have been identified racially. Specimens at Sapele (Bannerman 1933) and Mberubu (Serle 1957) were "*C. l. batesi*"; at Zaria, 1 May 1967, surprisingly "nearer *bowdleri*" (C.H.F.). As White has merged *batesi* in nominate *leucogaster* and says it intergrades with *bowdleri* in southwest Nigeria it seems that a cline exists.

Breeding. No records. Breeds Cameroon, Jul and Oct (BoA).

368. CORYTHORNIS CRISTATA   RB

(I.421) Malachite Kingfisher

Common resident (*C. c. galerita*) throughout wherever there are coastal brackish mangrove creeks, inland lakes, rivers and open pools in marshes. Local movements in north when favoured pools dry out.

Breeding. From the coast at Badagri north to Zaria, Apr-Oct, later in the north than the south (BoA).

369. ALCEDO QUADRIBRACHYS   RB

(I.420) Shining-blue Kingfisher

Uncommon but widespread resident now seldom recorded north of the great rivers (apart from streams running from the Jos Plateau to the Benue). A specimen from Ikom was *A. q. guentheri* and so probably are all birds of the mangrove creeks from Badagri to Calabar. Bannerman (1933) assigns a specimen from just north of the Niger to *A. q. quadribrachys*, which he says is "widely though sparingly distributed in Northern Provinces" as far north as Sokoto.

Breeding. Entering nest hole Ughelli, 5 Nov (H.F.M.); young juv. Shaffini Swamp Forest (Kainji), 28 Oct 1969 (F.W.).

Cerylinae

370. MEGACERYLE MAXIMA   R(B)

(I.418) African Giant Kingfisher

Not uncommon resident along wooded rivers and wooded lakesides throughout.

Subject to local movement in some areas. Uncommon in coastal mangrove creeks and absent from the Sahel and, apparently, from Lake Chad shores although recorded Komadugu-Yobe River near Geidam, Dec 1973 (P.H).
Breeding. No records. Breeds Liberia, Dec-Jan; Cameroon Dec (BoA).

371. CERYLE RUDIS   RB

(I.417)   Pied Kingfisher

Common, even locally abundant, resident (*C. r. rudis*) throughout at all types of waterside with trees or artificial perches including mangrove creeks. Numbers fluctuate seasonally in many areas, probably associated with seasonal movements of fish.
Breeding. Co-operative. Many records Nov-Mar, previously only from valleys of great rivers and northward, but in late 1980s and early 1990s nesting colony on Lekki Peninsula in banks of a stream and nearby man-made fish ponds (A.M.N.).

MEROPIDAE

372. MEROPS BREWERI   RB

(I.447)   Black-headed Bee-eater

Rare or very local resident, only 3 records: male collected Mamu Forest, 25 May 1953 (Serle 1957); collected just west of the Lower Niger near Idah, undated (H.Volsoe); 3 adults at nest between Idah and Lokoja (at 7°30′N, 6°50′E) – see below.
Breeding. Co-operative. 3 adults feeding young in nest between Idah and Lokoja, 23 Mar 1980 (M.D. – the first record for Africa). Breeds Zaïre, Mar, nestlings Mar-Apr (BoA).

373. MEROPS MUELLERI   RB

(I.444)   Blue-headed Bee-eater

Rare resident (*M. m. mentalis*). Previous records are: male Umuagwu, 6 Nov 1949 (Marchant 1953); Osomba, undated (H.Volsoe); Owena, 25 Dec 1952 (J.H.E.); feeding young Calabar, 24 Apr 1977 (P.M.). Recent records from 4 localities within Okwango F.R. and Oban Hills "indicate that this species is more widespread and commoner than previously believed" (Ash 1990).
Breeding. Only the Calabar record (above) of feeding young; Cameroon, Jan (BoA).

374. MEROPS GULARIS   RB

(I.445)   Black Bee-eater

Locally not uncommon resident (*M. g. gularis*) at forest edges and clearings from Okitipupa and Owena to the Niger Delta, uncommon west to Lagos and east to Calabar. This present pattern probably reflects the intensity of deforestation in different areas. Subject to local movements, birds appearing and disappearing irregularly.

Breeding. Benin-Ifon Rd, May (Bannerman 1951); Okitipupa, Mar (H.F.M.); Sapele, Apr and May (Serle 1958).

375. MEROPS PUSILLUS RB

(I.439)   Little Bee-eater

Not uncommon resident (*M. p. pusillus*) locally throughout, particularly at grassy river and reservoir banks, in marshy savanna and, less often, farmlands. Usually singly, in pairs or very lax groups. May be a partial migrant but probably movements are only local.

Breeding. All areas, Feb-Jul.

376. MEROPS VARIEGATUS RB

(I.441)   Blue-breasted Bee-eater

Very local resident (presumably *M. v. loringi*) mainly in open montane grassland. Regular on the Obudu and Mambilla Plateaux, with several netted (race not determined) at the latter (H.B. and P.H.); also sight record of 3 from lowland forest at Sapele, 10 Jun 1976 (C.S.P.).

Breeding. Breeds Cameroon, Feb-Mar (BoA).

377. MEROPS HIRUNDINEUS RB

(I.446)   Swallow-tailed Bee-eater

Uncommon resident (*M. h. chrysolaimus*), but well distributed in savanna woodlands of the Guinea zone. Usually several together, but not in flocks. Local movements noted but with no clear migratory pattern (Elgood *et al.* 1973).

Breeding. Co-operative (Fry 1984). Juv. collected Kishi, 27 Jun 1961 (F.C. Sibley); juvs. in Kainji Lake Nat. Park, May-Sep (Wells & Walsh 1969). Breeds Gambia, May-Jul immediately before the rains (Gore 1981).

378. MEROPS BULLOCKI RB

(I.442)   Red-throated Bee-eater

Common resident locally (*M. b. bullocki*) in erosion gullies and along high-banked streams in Northern Guinea Savanna, less common in Southern Guinea Savanna south to Ilorin and Enugu and reported in coastal savanna at Lagos (D.I.M.W.); also northward into the Sudan zone from Sokoto to Maiduguri but not into the Sahel.

Breeding. Co-operative. Ilorin to Gorgoram and Hadejia, Dec-Mar, but most colonies peak in Feb (Fry 1966).

379. MEROPS ALBICOLLIS Afm/B

(I.437)   White-throated Bee-eater

Abundant seasonally throughout, but a clearly defined migrant with well separated breeding and off-season areas. Present in the forest zone and just north of it in derived savanna, Oct to early May. Breeds in the Sahel, mainly just north of Nigeria, Jun and Jul. In intermediate areas mainly in large flocks, on unhurried passage, especially southward, Sep-Oct; but in well wooded areas, e.g. southern escarpment of the Jos Plateau, flocks may remain through the off-season.

Breeding. Mainly just north of Nigeria, but small colonies between Yo and Malamfatori, Jun (P.W.) and Jul (Fry 1966).

380. MEROPS ORIENTALIS   RB

(I.433)   Little Green Bee-eater

Common resident (*M. o. viridissimus*) in light woodland of the Sudan and Sahel zones from Sokoto to Lake Chad. Seldom met further south, records only from Yankari Nat. Park.

Breeding. Kano and Potiskum, Apr (C.H.F.); breeds Nguru (M.D.).

381. MEROPS PERSICUS   Afm/B

(I.432)   Blue-cheeked Bee-eater

Locally not uncommon migrant around both Lake Chad and Kainji Dam, with isolated scattered sightings across the north. Handled birds have all been *M. p. chrysocercus*, but *M. p. persicus* possibly occurring cannot be ruled out. Occurs Lake Chad, Oct-Mar, and at Kainji "extreme dates 1 Apr-29 Jul" (Wells & Walsh 1969), which suggests the birds could migrate between the two areas.

Breeding. Eggs Kainji, (c. 20 pairs), May (F.W.); nests with young Lake Chad, Jun/Jul 1980 (M.D.).

382. MEROPS APIASTER   PM

(I.431)   European Bee-eater

Uncommon Palaearctic migrant seen mainly on passage mid Sep to Oct and Mar-Apr, but some overwinter. Noted in all areas from the coast north to Sokoto and Lake Chad. Usually in flocks of less than 20 but "perhaps a hundred", Karu (Bannerman 1933).

383. MEROPS MALIMBICUS   Afm/B

(I.434)   Rosy Bee-eater

Common seasonal migrant, breeding on sandbanks along the great rivers Apr-Jun, dispersing to coastal and forest zones rest of year, flocks of 10-50. In some years may not uncommonly arrive early or depart late from off-season areas, and at Kwale (on the Lower Niger) may remain all year and possibly breed.

Breeding. All known colonies are relatively central, from Eggan (middle Niger) to Ibi (Benue), Onitsha (Lower Niger) and Kaduna River below Bida (A.M.N.). Largest colony reported is 37,000 birds at Eggan, May (Brown 1948). Overall dates, Mar-Jun.

384. MEROPS NUBICUS   Afm/B

(I.435)   Carmine Bee-eater

Common breeding migrant (*M. n. nubicus*) throughout open savannas, strongly attracted to bush fires. In dry season, mainly Dec-Feb (the time of bush fires), flocks of 1000 may be encountered away from the breeding areas, e.g. Moshi River, Dec (J.H.E.); infrequently met as far south as Ibadan and Owerri. In the rains, mainly Jul-Sep after breeding before moving south, not uncommon as far north as Sokoto and Lake Chad.

Breeding. Mainly middle Niger and Benue river banks, Apr-Jun; Gadau, Jul (P.B.). Largest colony, 12,000 nests Eggan, May (Bannerman 1951).

CORACIIDAE

385. CORACIAS NAEVIA   Afm/B

(I.413) Rufous-crowned Roller

Not uncommon seasonal breeding migrant (*C. n. naevia*), from the great rivers north to Sokoto and Potiskum, unrecorded in extreme north. Data conforms with "hump-back bridge" pattern of movement (Elgood *et al.* 1973). All records south of the great rivers to Ilorin, Ife and Serti are Sep-Mar (with one from Lagos, 4 Oct 1970 – D.I.M.W.), while most northernmost records are May-Aug.

Breeding. Virtually nothing recorded: Yankari, Jun (Dyer & Gartshore 1974). Senegambia Aug-Sep; Ghana "rolling" display Mar and Sep; laying, Mar (BoA).

386. CORACIAS CYANOGASTER   R(B)

(I.414) Blue-bellied Roller

Locally not uncommon resident in little disturbed savanna woodland, mainly of the Guinea zone, south to Owo and north to Kari; occurs on the Jos Plateau, and mainly in the west. A record east of the Niger between Idah and Lokoja, 3 Oct 1990 (P.H.). Appears to leave some areas seasonally, but no real evidence for migration.

Breeding. No records. Breeds Ivory Coast, Feb-Sep; Togo, May (BoA).

387. CORACIAS ABYSSINICA   Afm/B

(I.410) Abyssinian Roller

Common and widespread, seasonally, throughout savannas with trees or artificial perches. Dry season records as far south as Ife (Feb), Lokoja (Jan) and Ogoja (Mar); present all year in north at Sokoto, Kano and Malamfatori and wet season record in the south, Lanlate, May (P.H.). Marked seasonal increases and decreases in intervening area – a "northern concertina" migrant (Elgood *et al.* 1973).

Breeding. Mostly Zaria, also from Kuta north to Kari, Mar-Jun, a very narrow belt, but probably breeds further north and south.

388. CORACIAS GARRULUS   PM

(I.409) European Roller

Uncommon Palaearctic migrant (*C. g. garrulus*) mainly to forest edge habitat, Sep-Apr. Usually singles, an occasional pair, from Lagos to Calabar in forest zone, north to derived savanna at Ibadan, Ife and Enugu. Also autumn passage Malamfatori area ("20+ flying singly southward over Acacia belt", P.W.) and at Kano. No spring passage recorded.

389. EURYSTOMUS GULARIS   RB

(I.416) Blue-throated Roller

Common resident (*E. g. gularis/neglectus*) in high forest and relict forest patches from Lagos to Calabar north to Ibadan and Enugu; also in forest on southern slopes of Jos Plateau at Kagoro. Few specimens have been racially determined: Ibadan (west) "nearer *neglectus*" (F.C.Sibley); Ubiaja (central) *neglectus* (Bannerman 1933); Oban (east) intermediate (Bannerman 1933).

Breeding. Data scanty, all refer to feeding young at nest holes: Ilaro, Feb (J.A.B.); Ibadan, Apr (J.H.E.); Calabar, Sep (P.M.), inferring a protracted season.

390. EURYSTOMUS GLAUCURUS   Afm/B

(I.415) Broad-billed Roller

Seasonally common (*E. g. afer*) from the coast north to Sokoto and Maiduguri, but not found in extreme north and Sahel. Intra-African migrant, with clear "hump-back bridge" pattern of movement (Elgood *et al.* 1973): present in coastal and southern forest areas, Oct to early May; in Northern Guinea and Sudan zones, May to early Oct; in intervening area (Ibadan, Enugu and well wooded areas of southern escarpment of Jos Plateau) present all year.

Breeding. After the northward shift, May-Jul, from Ilaro and Ibadan north to Kano.

PHOENICULIDAE

391. PHOENICULUS CASTANEICEPS   R(B)

(I.471) Forest Wood-Hoopoe

Uncommon resident (*P. c. castaneiceps*) in high forest only in the southwest, from Lagos to Warri and Sapele; unrecorded from east of the Lower Niger.

Breeding. No records anywhere in West Africa. Ovary slightly enlarged Zaïre, Nov (BoA).

392. PHOENICULUS BOLLEI   RB

(I.469) White-headed Wood-Hoopoe

Uncommon resident (*P. b. bollei*) in high forest from Lagos to Benin north to relict patches at Ibadan – overall "dispersed, frequent" in southwest forests (Elgood 1977), but only once recorded at the Lekki Conservation Centre in the 1990s. Only one sight record outside this area: Obudu Plateau, Mar, quite probably *P. b. okuensis* (F.C.Sibley).

Breeding. Pair feeding young at nest Ondo, 22 Jan 1961 (F.C.S.); copulation Ife, 3 Oct 1976 (R.F.); female "ovary with 1 large yolked egg" Ilaro, 24 Sep 1943 (Serle 1950).

393. **PHOENICULUS PURPUREUS** RB, ?Afm/B

(I.468) Green Wood-Hoopoe

Locally common resident (*P. p. guineensis*), widespread through wooded savannas of southwest and north but surprisingly absent from southeast, Serti being the only locality south of the Benue. Uncommon in coastal savanna at Lagos. Little evidence to support Bannerman's (1951) suggestion that it is a dry season migrant to the coast as it is recorded at Ikoyi, Lagos, all year (P.H.).

Breeding. Co-operative (Grimes 1975, Ligon 1978). C/3 and C/4 Abeokuta, Feb (Serle 1950); feeding fledgling Ibadan, Feb, also copulation there Apr (J.H.E.) and fledglings Sep (A.P.); fledgling Maiduguri, Jan (C.H.F.). Breeding is probably protracted.

394. **PHOENICULUS ATERRIMUS** Afm/B

(I.470) Black Wood-Hoopoe

Uncommon, perhaps locally not uncommon, resident (*P. a. aterrimus*), in savanna woodlands north of the great rivers. Not uncommon at Molai and Sambisa, Borno State (P.H.). More southerly records to Ibadan, Ishan and Enugu are Oct to mid Apr, suggesting dry season southward migration, but one exception, Ibadan, 28 Jun 1952 (H.F.M.).

Breeding. Young being fed at nest Kari, Apr (P.B.); "Lake Chad area, probably May and June" (MP&G).

UPUPIDAE

395. **UPUPA EPOPS** RB, PM

(I.466) Hoopoe

Not uncommon throughout northern areas south to Kaduna and the Jos Plateau, less numerous southwards to Ado-Awale and Enugu and once Lagos, 30 Oct 1973 (J.B.H.). Mostly racially undetermined sightings but both *U. e. epops* and *U. e. senegalensis* collected at Enugu by Serle (1957). Many more sightings Oct-Mar suggest immigration of *U. e. epops* from the Palaearctic, but *U. e. senegalensis* may be more conspicuous as it breeds then and may well have moved southward to do so.

Breeding. C/1 Nkpopgu, 8 Feb 1955 (Serle 1957); nest under observation Jos Plateau, mid Jan to end Feb and feeding 2 juvs. till 3 Apr (Smith 1966); Sokoto, Mar (Mundy & Cook 1972-73); juvs. Kishi, Apr (A.P.).

BUCEROTIDAE

396. **BUCORVUS ABYSSINICUS** RB

(I.465) Abyssinian Ground Hornbill

Uncommon resident in savannas, especially with rocky outcrops, throughout the area north of the great rivers. Recorded at Serti (P.H.) and Mambilla (Green 1990). Recorded several times south of the Middle Niger, notably Kainji Lake Nat. Park.

Breeding. C/2 near Kaduna, 21 Mar 1937 and 9 Apr 1938; C/2 near Zaria, Apr (Bannerman 1951).

160   Bucerotidae

397. TOCKUS ALBOCRISTATUS   R(B)
(I.453) White-crested Hornbill

Not uncommon resident (*T. a. cassini*) in high and secondary forest right across the country, ranging north in relict forest patches in the west to Ilorin and Kabba; recently recorded from gallery forest 50 km south of Akwanga (P.H.).
Breeding. No records. Breeds Ghana, Jan; Liberia Nov (BoA).

398. TOCKUS HARTLAUBI   RB
(I.462) Black Dwarf Hornbill

Uncommon resident (*T. h. hartlaubi*) in high forest, extending across the country. A silent species, probably overlooked.
Breeding. Adults feeding juvs. Ife, Dec (R.F.); young juv. thought to be just from nest Calabar, Aug (P.M.), and "Nigeria, Oct" (BoA).

399. TOCKUS CAMURUS   RB
(I.463) Red-billed Dwarf Hornbill

Not uncommon resident in the forest zone right across the country wherever sizeable areas of high or secondary forest remain; heard more often than seen.
Breeding. No records. Male in breeding condition Owerri, 26 Sep 1948 (Marchant 1953); females in breeding condition Ghana, Feb (BoA).

400. TOCKUS ERYTHRORHYNCHUS   RB
(I.457) Red-billed Hornbill

Common resident (*T. e. erythrorhynchus*) in wooded areas of the Sudan and Sahel Savannas, locally not uncommon in more arid areas of the Northern Guinea zone south to Kainji, Yankari Nat. Park, Wase G.R.; present, all seasons, in high rainfall habitat on the Jos Plateau (M.Ho.).
Breeding. From Kano to Potiskum, Sep-Nov. Nigeria, Apr-Jun (BoA).

401. TOCKUS FASCIATUS   RB
(I.460) African Pied Hornbill

Abundant resident (*T. f. semifasciatus*) in the forest zone from western border to Owerri, where forms intermediate with *T. f. fasciatus* occur (Marchant 1953); while further east at Calabar birds are close to *T. f. fasciatus* (R.E.S.). Ranges northward, becoming less numerous, in gallery forest to Ilorin and Enugu with records from Kainji, Bida, Agenebode (P.H.) and several forest patches on the southern escarpment of the Jos Plateau.
Breeding. Visiting nest holes, Jan-May.

402. TOCKUS NASUTUS   Afm/B
(I.456) African Grey Hornbill

Seasonally common (*T. n. nasutus*), even abundant in some areas, throughout

Sudan and Guinea zones. Mainly resident in Sudan zone, where numbers increase during the rains by immigration from the Guinea zone, from which it is mainly absent late May to early Oct. Migration visible, especially southwards in Oct, parties 50+. The population in southwest coastal and derived savanna appears sedentary.

Breeding. From Lagos north to Katsina, Feb-Jul overall, later in north than south.

403. CERATOGYMNA FISTULATOR   RB

(I.449) Piping Hornbill

Not uncommon resident in both the forest zone, mainly edges and clearings, and in gallery forest north to Kainji, Abuja and Keffi, and in the forested areas of southern escarpment of the Jos Plateau. East of the Niger is *C. f. sharpii*, and west is *fistulator*. Serle (1957) found intermediates at several south-eastern areas, but most records are sightings racially undetermined.

Breeding. "Nigeria (active nest July)" (BoA).

404. CERATOGYMNA SUBCYLINDRICUS   R(B)

(I.452) Black-and-white-casqued Hornbill

Uncommon resident, (*C. s. subcylindricus*) west of the Niger and *subquadratus* to the east. Occurs southwest from near Ibadan to Benin, and only once recorded east of the Niger, a male at Elele, 15 May 1953 (Serle 1957). Sightings in gallery forest north to between Kabba and Abuja including "up to 30 in one day", 12 Dec 1963 (M.H.), and recorded all months Nindam (Dyer *et al.*1986).

Breeding. No records. Breeds Zaïre, Jan-Mar (BoA).

405. CERATOGYMNA CYLINDRICUS   RB

(I.450) Brown-cheeked Hornbill

Not uncommon resident (*C. c. albotibialis*) in the larger remnants of high forest; numbers are diminishing through forest erosion. Bannerman (1933) has records from gallery forest near Abuja and localities in "Niger Province" Recently reported Pandam Wildlife Park, Sep 1991 (P.H.).

Breeding. Co-operative. "Nigeria (birds in breeding condition July)" (BoA).

406. CERATOGYMNA ATRATA   R(B)

(I.455) Black-casqued Wattled Hornbill

Rare resident in high forest from Benin east to Calabar, but not uncommon in Okomu F.R. (P.H.). No recent records from further southwest, though Bannerman (1933) had records from Meko near the western border and, surprisingly, from Ilorin Province north of the forest zone. "Common and noisy" above forest in Korup Nat. Park (Thomas 1991) in southwest Cameroon, adjacent to the Nigerian border.

Breeding. No records. Breeds Gabon, Nov-Dec (BoA).

407. CERATOGYMNA ELATA   R(B)

(I.454)   Yellow-casqued Wattled Hornbill

Now mainly a rare resident of the high forest zone, particularly from Benin eastward; as numbers greatly reduced through forest destruction. In 1992 considered an "uncommon resident in Okomu F.R. with very few records over the last 5 years" (P.H.). "Common and noisy above the forest and along rivers" in Korup Nat. Park (Thomas 1991) in southwest Cameroon, adjacent to Nigerian border. Collar & Stuart (1985) consider it a threatened species.

Breeding. No records. Breeds Cameroon; suggested laying Jan-Feb, emergence Feb-May, nest-hole sealed by male in Jul; Liberia, fledglings Aug, (BoA).

CAPITONIDAE

408. GYMNOBUCCO PELI   RB

(I.536)   Bristle-nosed Barbet

Probably not uncommon resident (*G. p. peli*) in forest right across the country, but resemblance to *G. calvus* may have caused it to be overlooked. Certainly much less common than *G. calvus* (Elgood 1977). Not recently reported Lagos area (Alexander-Marrack *et al.* 1985).

Breeding. Nesting in same tree with *G. calvus* near Lagos, Jun (J.P.G.), and breeding reported Okomu F.R., 23 May 1993 (P.H.).

409. GYMNOBUCCO CALVUS   RB

(I.535)   Naked-faced Barbet

Common resident (*G. c. calvus*), locally abundant, in forest, including relict patches, right across the country.

Breeding. Colonial, up to 250 pairs occupying holes in a single tree. Protracted, activity at colonies throughout the year (but not necessarily breeding all months). Feeding young at nesthole Lekki Peninsula, 27 Feb 1990 (A.M.N.).

410. POGONIULUS SCOLOPACEUS   RB

(I.547)   Speckled Tinkerbird

Common resident (*P. s. scolopaceus*) in forest and secondary growth right across the country from the coast, north to Ibadan, Ife and Enugu. Birds from extreme southeast may be intermediate between *P. s. scolopaceus* and *flavisquamatus* (Serle 1957).

Breeding. Records only of feeding young, both at nest and free flying, in most months, Feb-Nov. Laying probably Jan, Feb-Nov (BoA).

411. POGONIULUS CORYPHAEUS   R(B)

(I.541)   Western Green Tinkerbird

Not uncommon resident (*P. c. coryphaeus*) in montane forest at Obudu Plateau and highlands of the Mambilla Plateau, particularly at 1900-2300 m (Ash *et al.* 1989).

Breeding. No records. Breeds Banso in Cameroon, Oct (Serle 1950).

412. POGONIULUS ATROFLAVUS   RB

(I.543)   Red-rumped Tinkerbird

Uncommon resident in lowland forest, though probably overlooked; known localities such as Ibadan and Calabar suggest it extends right across the country.

Breeding. Female collected Imesi-Ile, 19 Mar 1963 had enlarged ovary (T.Ludlow). Gonadal data Nigeria, Feb-May; Cameroon, juvs. Apr-May, subadults Aug-Nov, reported breeding Mar (BoA).

413. POGONIULUS SUBSULPHUREUS   RB

(I.546)   Yellow-throated Tinkerbird

Not uncommon resident (*P. s. flavimentum*) in high forest and old secondary growth right across the country, unrecorded north of the forest zone and much less numerous east of the Niger.

Breeding. Nigeria, records all year (BoA).

414. POGONIULUS BILINEATUS   RB

(I.544)   Yellow-rumped Tinkerbird

Common resident (*P. b. leucolaima*) at forest edges and clearings and in gallery and relict forest in derived savanna right across the country. Gallery forest records extend north to Kainji and southern escarpment of the Jos Plateau and eastwards to the Obudu Plateau (P.H.).

Breeding. B/2 just hatched Abeokuta, 27 Mar (Serle 1950); Nigeria, reported Mar-Apr (BoA).

415. POGONIULUS CHRYSOCONUS   RB

(I.542)   Yellow-fronted Tinkerbird

Common, even locally abundant, resident (*P. c. chrysoconus*) in wooded savanna north of the great rivers and less commonly south to Ilorin, Kabba and Serti. Occasional records even further south in the west to Meko and Ibadan, but only to Serti south of the Benue.

Breeding. C/2 Lokoja, 26 Aug 1932; "fresh holes seen" Vom, Feb-Apr (V.S.); nestlings Zaria, Nov (A.P.); feeding young in nest Bukuru, 6 Oct 1992 (M.Ho.).

416. BUCCANODON DUCHAILLUI   RB

(I.540)   Yellow-spotted Barbet

Locally common resident (*B. d. duchaillui*) in swamp forest from Lagos east to Owerri and Calabar (Mackenzie 1979) in the southeast, but also at Ayangba, Mar 1981 (M.D.), and common in the Oban Hills and Mambilla reaching 2050 m on Gangirwal (Ash *et al.* 1989). Easily overlooked unless the voice is known.

Breeding. B/4 Yenagoa, Jan (Serle 1957). Jun, Dec-Jan, also moult Mar (BoA).

417. TRICHOLAEMA HIRSUTA   RB

(I.532)   Hairy-breasted Barbet

Not uncommon resident (*T. h. hirsuta*) in forest, including relict patches, of south-west Nigeria. Rather less common east of the Niger where it is said to hybridise with *T. h. flavipunctata* (White 1965).

Breeding. Ibadan, Jan-Feb (J.H.E.); immature at Ife, Oct and female at nest, Dec-Jan (R.F.). Excavating hole in dead tree Lekki Peninsula, 16 Oct 1988 (A.M.N.).

418. LYBIUS VIEILLOTI   RB

(I.529)   Vieillot's Barbet

Common resident (*L. v. rubescens*) in savanna throughout the country, more local and less common in derived savanna and coastal savanna.

Breeding. Mainly Apr-Jul, Ibadan to Sokoto, east to Vom; also at Ibadan, Nov-Dec (H.F.M.).

419. LYBIUS LEUCOCEPHALUS   RB

(I.528)   White-headed Barbet

Uncommon resident (*L. l. adamauae*) in wooded savanna of the Northern Guinea and Sudan zones. Extends west to Zaria and Funtua, the westernmost end of its range.

Breeding. Possible pre-breeding display Taboru, 28 Mar 1992 (J.B.). Breeding indications Nigeria, Feb (BoA).

420. LYBIUS BIDENTATUS   RB

(I.525)   Double-toothed Barbet

Uncommon and local resident (*L. b. bidentatus*) at forest edges and in gallery forest, mostly in southwest. Not recorded in southeast by Serle (1957), but a pair at Obudu Plateau, 8 Aug 1980 (M.D.); Serti (P.H.) and Danko F.R. (Ash 1990) are the only localities south of the Benue. Few records north of the great rivers, mainly from the forested slopes of the southern edge of the Jos Plateau.

Breeding. Ibadan, Sep (J.H.E.) and "reported Sep, Dec-Mar" (BoA).

421. LYBIUS DUBIUS   RB

(I.523)   Bearded Barbet

Common resident in wooded savanna (and gardens) throughout the area north of the great rivers; also south of the rivers to Ilorin, Igbetti, Sankwala (M.K.) and Gashaka-Gumti Nat. Park (Green 1990).

Breeding. Zaria to Jos Plateau and south to Kainji, Mar-Jul. Juvs. Jun, reported Sep, moult Apr-Aug (BoA).

422. TRACHYPHONUS PURPURATUS　　　　　　　　　　　　　　　　　RB

　　(I.550)　Yellow-billed Barbet

Common resident (*T. p. togoensis*) in forest, including old secondary growth and relict patches, west of the Niger, becoming less common eastward. *T. p. purpuratus* has been found generally uncommon east of the Niger, though in the Owerri area it proved "quite common" (Marchant 1953); occurs also in montane forest at Obudu Plateau (P.M.).

　　Breeding. Protracted – hole inspection, feeding young in nest, etc., Jan-Jul and Oct.

423. TRACHYPHONUS MARGARITATUS　　　　　　　　　　　　　　　RB

　　(I.549)　Yellow-breasted Barbet

Not uncommon resident (*T. m. margaritatus*) in the Sahel of the extreme northeast. Described as "not uncommon" in the thorn scrub of the Hadejia wetlands, 1989-91 (M.D.), which may be its western and southern limits.

　　Breeding. "Bates found it breeding near Lake Chad in May and June" (Bannerman 1933) – possibly extra-limital.

INDICATORIDAE

424. PRODOTISCUS INSIGNIS　　　　　　　　　　　　　　　　　　　RB

　　(I.562)　Cassin's Honeybird

Uncommon resident in lowland forest, right across the country, nominate *insignis* east of the Niger and *P. i. flavodorsalis* in southwest, though one specimen from Benin (Bannerman 1951) is nominate race. A small tree-top species, it may be overlooked.

　　Breeding. Moulting adults Nigeria, Apr. Breeds Ghana, Dec and Cameroon, Oct-Dec (BoA).

425. PRODOTISCUS REGULUS　　　　　　　　　　　　　　　　　　　RB

　　(I.561)　Wahlberg's Honeybird

Rare resident (possibly overlooked), recorded only at Enugu (Serle 1957) in savanna. Serle states "single birds observed on four occasions at Enugu in the trees in savanna country and farmland"

　　Breeding. Single female collected with oviducal eggs, 27 Sep 1954 (Serle).

426. MELICHNEUTES ROBUSTUS　　　　　　　　　　　　　　　　　R(B)

　　(I.559)　Lyre-tailed Honeyguide

Rare resident in a few lowland forest localities east of the Niger. Seen or heard at Port Harcourt, Owerri (Bannerman 1951), Umuagwu (Marchant 1953) and Calabar (Serle 1957).

　　Breeding. No records. Indicated Zaïre, Apr, Aug; reported breeding Mar-Sep (BoA).

166   Indicatoridae

427. INDICATOR MACULATUS   R(B)

(I.553)   Spotted Honeyguide

Rare resident (*I. m. maculatus*) in lowland forest including gallery forest. Only 5 records: Ondo, 1 Aug 1937, collected, skin in BMNH (Ffoulkes-Roberts); Badagri, 13 Jan 1965, netted in dense bush (not forest) (Button 1965); Gashaka (near Serti) "netted in riverine bush", Dec (Hall 1977); sighted Kagoro in relict forest on southern escarpment of the Jos Plateau, 11 Nov 1979 (C.H.F.,R.E.S., M.D.& M.G.); netted Kagoro 19 Apr 1987 (P.H.).

Breeding. No records. Ivory Coast, Jun. Cameroon, juvs. Jun, Aug reported Nov, moult Sep (BoA).

428. INDICATOR INDICATOR   RB

(I.551)   Greater Honeyguide

Not uncommon resident in savanna north of the great rivers. Regular south of the middle Niger from Borgu to Ilorin, occasionally south to Ibadan and the coast at Lagos; south of the Benue formerly common at Enugu (Serle 1957) and recorded at Serti (P.H.). Nearly all southerly records are for the dry season, but Elgood *et al.* (1973) did not regard it as migratory.

Breeding. Numerous records Jan-Jul with hosts *Merops bullocki, M. pusillus, M. persicus, Halcyon leucocephala* and *Hirundo semirufa*.

429. INDICATOR MINOR   R(B)

(I.554)   Lesser Honeyguide

Now separated from *I. conirostris* (*q.v.*) with which it is considered to form a superspecies. Not uncommon and widespread resident (*I. m. senegalensis*) in woodlands north of the forest zone, but reaching cleared forest in the south.

Breeding. No records. Cameroon, "moult May" (BoA).

430. INDICATOR CONIROSTRIS   RB

(I.554)   Thick-billed Honeyguide

Forms a superspecies with *I. minor*. Uncommon resident (*I. c. conirostris*) in woodlands south of the great rivers. Previously records from this area were thought to be probably all *I. m. conirostris*, which is now considered a distinct species from *I. minor* (*q.v.*), although the two species "probably interbreed in S-central Nigeria" (BoA).

Breeding. Thought to parasitise *Gymnobucco calvus* and probably other *Gymnobucco* species. Breeds Cameroon, Oct, Feb (BoA).

431. INDICATOR EXILIS   RB

(I.555)   Least Honeyguide

Uncommon resident (*I. e. exilis*) in lowland forest right across the country, though the separation of *I. willcocksi* has obscured the issue, since many earlier workers assigned specimens to "*I. e. hutsoni*", now named *I. willcocksi hutsoni*. (The view is taken here that *exilis* is a forest species; *willcocksi* occurs in rather more northerly gallery forest and savanna woodlands.)

Breeding. Female netted Ilaro, 20 Nov 1962 – "while in captivity overnight the bird dropped a pink soft shelled egg" (Button 1967).

432. INDICATOR WILLCOCKSI   RB

(I.556) Willcocks's Honeyguide

Rare resident *I. w. willcocksi* in savanna woodlands and gallery forest, intergrading in north with *I. w. hutsoni*. Differentiated by Alexander in 1901, but not recognised by Bannerman, who quotes (1933) the type specimen *I. willcocksi hutsoni* (from Tatara in the former Benue Province) as *I. exilis hutsoni*. (See *Indicator exilis*). Netted at Kagoro, Jun 1977, on the southern escarpment of the Jos Plateau, but released without being sub-specifically identified. Also netted Kagoro on 19 Apr 1987 (P.H.). Recently 2 sighted Taboru feeding at tree hole in company with 2 *I. indicator*, 9 Nov 1991 (M.Ho.& J.B.) and 3 Kwakwi, 9 Oct 1993 (M.Ho).

Breeding. Probably nest parasitic. Nigeria, "gonadal data Jan, May, reported Feb" (BoA).

PICIDAE

Jynginae

433. JYNX TORQUILLA   PM

(I.587) Eurasian Wryneck

Now considered to form a superspecies with *J. ruficollis* (*q.v.*). Uncommon but regular Palaearctic migrant (*J. t. torquilla*) to wooded savanna throughout the area north of the great rivers, late Aug to mid Apr. Several observers in north report southward passage there in autumn, but there are many "mid-winter" records. However, the few southerly records, Ife twice Dec and Mar (R.F.), Enugu, Jan (Serle 1957) and Serti, Nov-Dec (P.H.), suggest overwintering there. Perhaps some pass through Nigeria southeastward.

434. JYNX RUFICOLLIS   R(B)

(I.588) Rufous-breasted Wryneck

Now considered to form a superspecies with *J. torquilla* (*q.v.*). Possibly not uncommon (*J. r. pulchricollis*, which includes *thorbeki*) along the Cameroon border in savanna woodland. First records: specimen netted Mambilla Plateau, no date (P.Ward); Abong, no date (P.H.); "in very open savanna" Serti, 16/17 Dec 1974 (P.H.).

Breeding. No records anywhere in West Africa.

Picumninae

[SASIA AFRICANA   Rejected

(I.586) African Piculet

Bannerman (1933) mentions a nest at Lokoja, 6 Oct 1931 (see Jourdain & Shuel

(1935) for details). Chapin (1939) and subsequently Bannerman (1951) doubted its authenticity, but it is noteworthy that Shuel had the birds in view for some days before taking an egg. Serle (1950b) collected the species at Kumba and other places in Cameroon, so that the Lokoja record would represent a westward range extension of 400 km.]

Picinae

435. CAMPETHERA PUNCTULIGERA   RB

(I.572)   Fine-spotted Woodpecker

Common and widespread resident (*C. p. punctuligera*) in woodlands of the Guinea Savanna, less common northward, but recorded from Kano to Lake Chad. South of the middle Niger noted sporadically south to Ibadan and Abeokuta; and south of the Benue to Enugu and Serti. No seasonal movements.

Breeding. From Abeokuta to Potiskum, Mar-Apr. Senegambia to Nigeria generally May-Aug, Nigeria also Feb (BoA).

436. CAMPETHERA CAILLIAUTII   R(B)

(I.565)   Green-backed Woodpecker

Uncommon resident (*C. c. permista*) at forest edges and relict forest patches from Lagos east to Owerri, with a single example collected in gallery forest near Jebba (F.C.Sibley); but locally not uncommon, being met regularly (and netted) on Lagos University Campus (J.H.E.). Relict forest at Kagoro on southern escarpment of the Jos Plateau is the most northerly record.

Breeding. No records. Juvs. and gonads enlarged central Zaïre, Mar-May and Sep (BoA).

437. CAMPETHERA TULLBERGI   R(B)

(I.569)   Tullberg's Woodpecker

Not uncommon resident (*C. t. tullbergi*) in montane forest at the Obudu Plateau, unrecorded elsewhere in Nigeria.

Breeding. No records. Post breeding moult Cameroon, Apr (BoA).

438. CAMPETHERA NIVOSA   RB

(I.567)   Buff-spotted Woodpecker

Not uncommon resident (*C. n. nivosa*) in the lower strata of lowland forest right across the country from Lagos to Calabar, from the coast north to Mekko, Ibadan, Ife, Enugu and Serti and netted in relict forest at Kagoro, 16 Sep 1979 (M.D.).

Breeding. C/1 Mekko, 17 Apr 1942 (Serle 1950).

439. CAMPETHERA CAROLI   R(B)

(I.566)   Brown-eared Woodpecker

Rare in forest (*C. c. caroli*). Unrecorded until 2 sightings by D.N.Johnson in high forest near Benin, Apr and Jun 1975 (Heigham 1976); recently one Okomu F.R., 26 Nov 1985 (Ash 1990).

Breeding. No records. Young in nests with unhatched egg (probably infertile) Cameroon, Jan-Feb (BoA).

440. DENDROPICOS ELACHUS R(B)
(I.575)   Little Grey Woodpecker

Uncommon resident in *Acacia* woodland of the Sahel, almost entirely in extreme northeast between Lake Chad and Maiduguri, with a single record from Aliya.
Breeding. No records. Nesting reported Niger, Mar-May (BoA).

441. DENDROPICOS POECILOLAEMUS R(B)
(I.576)   Speckle-breasted Woodpecker

Only one known record, a specimen netted "on the edge of cultivation" at Serti, 11 Oct 1974 (Hall 1977c).
Breeding. No records. Juvs. and gonads enlarged Zaïre, May-Sep (BoA).

442. DENDROPICOS GABONENSIS RB
(I.577)   Gabon Woodpecker

Uncommon resident (presumably *D. g. reichenowi*), usually in secondary forest undergrowth right across the country from Lagos to Calabar. A Lagos specimen was intermediate between *reichenowi* and *lugubris* of Ghana (Gee & Heigham 1977).
Breeding. 2 collected at Umuagwu in Oct had slightly enlarged gonads (Marchant 1953). Male drilling nesthole Lekki Peninsula, 15/16 Oct 1988 (photographed by I.G.N.).

443. DENDROPICOS FUSCESCENS RB
(I.574)   Cardinal Woodpecker

Uncommon resident (*D. f. lafresnayi*), widespread in woodlands of the Guinea Savanna, south into derived savanna to Ibadan, Enugu and Serti and north into the Sudan zone at Potiskum. Also recorded in forest clearing near Benin.
Breeding. Young in nest Kainji Lake Nat. Park (Wells & Walsh 1969); "drilling nesthole near Potiskum, 29 Oct to 5 Nov" (P.B.); hole excavation Benin, Mar (J.B.H.); juvs. at Enugu, 9 Feb and 31 Mar (Serle 1957).

444. DENDROPICOS PYRRHOGASTER RB
(I.582)   Fire-bellied Woodpecker

Common resident in the forest zone right across the country, mostly in high forest or mature secondary growth, but also in relict patches north to Ibadan and to Akure in the southwest; not reported north of the forest in the southeast.
Breeding. "Young peering from hole" Ilaro, 8 Sep (J.A.B.); hole excavation Ibadan, Nov (J.H.E.); pair feeding young Ife, Jan-Feb (R.F.); male drumming Lekki Peninsula, 16 Oct 1988 (A.M.N).

445. DENDROPICOS XANTHOLOPHUS   R(B)

(I.584)   Yellow-crested Woodpecker

Rare resident in high forest. Undated sight records of a "pair seen very clearly" in forest near Sapele on 2 occasions. "The yellow on the crown stood out very clearly against the median black" (in the male) and "left me in no doubt of the identity" - C.S.Porteous. Also sighted at Oban Hills, 1 Aug 1980 (D&G).

Breeding. No records. Juvs. and adults in breeding condition Cameroon, Oct-Mar (BoA).

446. DENDROPICOS ELLIOTII   RB

(I.585)   Elliot's Woodpecker

Not uncommon resident (*M. e. johnstoni*) in montane forest at the Obudu Plateau and Mambilla Plateau (Ash *et al.* 1989).

Breeding. No records, but a female collected at Obudu, 17 Mar 1961, had a 3 mm ovary (F.C.Sibley), while birds collected in Cameroon, Oct-Nov, were in breeding condition (MP&G).

447. DENDROPICOS GOERTAE   RB

(I.581)   Grey Woodpecker

Common and widespread resident (*M. g. goertae*) in all types of savanna from coast at Warri and at Lagos (in mature mangroves) to Sokoto and Lake Chad.

Breeding. In many areas, Jan-Mar.

448. PICOIDES OBSOLETUS   RB

(I.579)   Brown-backed Woodpecker

Not uncommon resident (*P. o. obsoletus*) in undisturbed woodlands of the Guinea Savanna south to Old Oyo Nat. Park and Enugu, and single records as far south as Ibadan and the Lekki Conservation Centre 31 Oct 92 (P.H.), with Potiskum the most northerly locality.

Breeding. Widespread records Dec-Mar, with hole excavation as early as Oct. Laying dates Feb-Mar (BoA).

PASSERINES

EURYLAIMIDAE

449. SMITHORNIS RUFOLATERALIS   R(B)
(I.610)   Red-sided Broadbill

Uncommon resident (*S. r. rufolateralis*) in high forest right across the country from Ilaro to Calabar.
Breeding. No records. Breeds Cameroon, Dec and Jan (MP&G).

450. SMITHORNIS CAPENSIS   R(B)
(I.609)   African Broadbill

New species for Nigeria. Uncommon resident, only recorded in 2 montane forest areas on the Mambilla Plateau, but occurs both east and west of Nigeria. Identified from voice sonagrams by F.D-L. and R.J.D.
Breeding. No records for West Africa.

PITTIDAE

451. PITTA ANGOLENSIS   R(B)
(I.613)   African Pitta

Rare resident (*P. a. pulih*) in 2 lowland forest areas: near Benin (Bannerman 1936) and relict forest near Ibadan from which at least 3 birds have been brought to different ornithologists. Recently recorded from Mbe Mts. in north of Cross River State (P.J.). The East African race *longipennis* tends to be migratory.
Breeding. No records. Breeds Sep and Oct in Cameroon (BoA).

ALAUDIDAE

452. MIRAFRA CANTILLANS   AfM/?NB
(I.615)   Singing Bush-Lark

Not uncommon intra-African migrant (*M. c. chadensis*) along the western shores of Lake Chad, mainly in dry season, Sep-Apr (A.J.H.); also there Jun (P.W.). Elsewhere, recorded in Hadejia wetlands area (M.D.), Katsina (I.D.) and, perhaps due to Sahel drought of the early 1970s, also noted Zaria, Jan 1975 (C.H.F.) and Nov-Dec 1975 (M.D.).
Breeding. Probably moves north into the sub-desert in the rains to breed extralimitally, but MP&G state it breeds in Nigeria, Jun-Aug, and BoA gives laying date Aug.

453. MIRAFRA AFRICANA   R(B)
(I.618)   Rufous-naped Lark

Uncommon and very local resident (*M. a. batesi*) on dry grassy uplands of the Jos to Bauchi area (where Bates collected the original specimens). Locally common on Mambilla Plateau grassland (race not determined but possibly *bamendae*) (Ash *et al.* 1989). One has also been collected from Lake Chad area, racially undetermined, probably *kurrae* from Darfur or *stresemanni* from northern Cameroon, though it is possible *batesi* ranges east to Lake Chad.

Breeding. Not recorded north of the equator, though there is no evidence for migratory movements.

454. MIRAFRA RUFOCINNAMOMEA RB

(I.619) Flappet Lark

Not uncommon resident locally (*M. r. buckleyi*) in open savannas of the southwest and north; intergrades in the Benue valley with *M. r. serlei*, the race found in the southeast to Enugu and Okigwi. No records for extreme north except one rains record, Maiduguri (P.H.), though supposedly not migratory. Not uncommon in southwest coastal savanna from Lagos to Badagri but does not reappear northward until near Ilorin.

Breeding. B/1,C/2,C/2 Zaria, Jun-Jul (Bannerman 1936) and also Dec-Feb (C.H.F.).

[MIRAFRA RUFA ?

(I.621) Rusty Bush-Lark

A single sighting, east mole of Lagos Harbour, 12 Jun 1948. "Close observation led to a detailed description best fitted by this species. Definitely not *rufocinnamomea*. As a sub-Saharan species the record is regarded as dubious" (Sir Hugo Marshall).]

455. PINAROCORYS ERYTHROPYGIA Afm/B

(I.624) Rufous-rumped Lark

Locally not uncommon resident mainly in Northern Guinea savanna but reaching as far south as Mekko in the west and Enugu in the east through the dry season. Seems to overfly the Sudan zone to pass the rains in the Sahel, mainly north of Nigeria.

Breeding. Young birds taken at Ibi, Apr (Bannerman 1936); nest with "one small blind chick and one addled egg" Enugu, 22 Jan (Serle 1957).

[AMMOMANES DESERTI Rejected

(I.627) Desert Lark

Mentioned because White (1961) gives the range of *A. d. geyri* as "Southern edge of the Sahara from Tillia to Damergou and Kano in northern Nigeria" The Kano record has not been confirmed. Hall and Moreau (1970) have no location south of 15°N in western Africa.]

456. CALANDRELLA BRACHYDACTYLA PM
(I.634)   Greater Short-toed Lark

Locally common Palaearctic migrant (*C. b. brachydactyla*) in open savanna of the extreme northeast from Lake Chad to Maiduguri, Nov to mid Mar, with flocks up to 400 (D.A.Holmes); also between Gashua and Geidam (D.I.M.W.). All specimens have been nominate race but *longipennis* from S.W.Asia probably occurs too.

457. CALANDRELLA CINEREA RB
(I.635)   Red-capped Lark

Uncommon and very local resident (*C. c. saturatior*), apparently occurring only on upland grasslands in a small area of the Jos plateau, near Jos (Sharland 1959). Although thought to migrate in other parts of Africa (Moreau 1966), the Jos birds seem stationary, but they may be dry season breeding migrants.
   Breeding. Two pairs "showing imminent signs of breeding; one pair seen carrying grass", Bokkos (southern edge of Jos Plateau) (Smith 1965).

458. CALANDRELLA RUFESCENS PM
(Not numbered by MP&G)   Lesser Short-toed Lark

Rare Palaearctic migrant known only from grasslands of the Jos Plateau, where one was ringed (without racial determination) and others seen (R.E.S.). MP&G cause confusion in stating a "single bird was ringed at Calabar" giving a *Nigerian Field* (July 1960) reference; the latter gives no locality but shows it in a Table as ringed in Northern Nigeria (i.e. Jos) and not Eastern Nigeria (i.e. Calabar).

459. GALERIDA MODESTA Afm/B
(I.630)   Sun Lark

Locally not uncommon resident (*G. m. modesta* – formerly *G. m. giffardi*) in open savanna, especially farmland, in the Northern Guinea and Sudan zones, but subject to some migration. Southern limits in the dry season are Igbetti, Ilorin to Wukari, but only recorded at Malamfatori Jun-Sep (A.J.H.).
   Breeding. Zaria, Mar (Bannerman 1951); nests Ririwai, Oct-Nov, and fledglings, Dec (P.B.).

460. GALERIDA CRISTATA RB, Afm
(I.629)   Crested Lark

Common and widespread resident (*G. c. alexanderi*) in open savanna and farmland of the northern Guinea, Sudan and Sahel zones, from Zaria and the Jos Plateau north to the northern border; numbers reduced in Zaria in wet weason, probably by northerly migration into Niger (Fry 1965, Newby *et al.* 1987).
   Breeding. Mostly Nov-Mar, once in May.

461. EREMOPTERIX LEUCOTIS   Afm/B

(I.631) Chestnut-backed Sparrow-Lark

Not uncommon resident seasonally (*E. l. melanocephala*), widespread from the great rivers and Kainji Lake Nat. Park to the northern border; common locally in open grassland on stony soils. A "northern concertina" migrant (Elgood *et al.* 1973): southerly records (e.g. Kainji) are dry season Nov to late Mar, in the northern breeding season, though as yet not proven to breed in the south.

Breeding. Zaria and Jos Plateau north to Sokoto and Kari, mainly Jan but overall Oct-Mar.

462. EREMOPTERIX NIGRICEPS   ?

(I.632) Black-crowned Sparrow-Lark

New species for Nigeria. Formerly this species was not uncommon in Niger 160 km north of the Nigerian border (R.E.Sharland pers.comm). Progressive southward march of the sub-Sahara – 'the Sahel drought' – in recent years has brought the species into Nigeria where it is now not uncommon alongside *E.leucotis* notably in the wetland round Nguru. Not unlikely to be discovered much further west and east of this area, since both species range from upper Senegal to the Nile valley with *nigriceps* north of the range of *leucotis*.

HIRUNDINIDAE

463. PSALIDOPROCNE NITENS   R(B)

(II.1027) Square-tailed Saw-wing

Uncommon resident (*P. n. nitens*) in lowland forest, but being difficult to distinguish from immature *P. obscura* may have been overlooked. Collected only at Oban (Bannerman 1939), sightings are also mostly from the southeast triangle between Calabar, the Mambilla Plateau and Owerri. There are 7 sightings from Lagos (D.I.M.W.).

Breeding. Not reported, but occurs Jan-Jul in Cameroon (MP&G).

464. PSALIDOPROCNE OBSCURA   Afm/B

(II.1026) Fanti Saw-wing

Not uncommon locally, often near water, with flocks of up to 50 recorded, from the coast at Lagos and Warri, where it is resident, north to Enugu. Not found north of c. 11°N, and at Zaria is a clear rains migrant present mid Apr to mid Oct. In other intermediate areas under continuous observation (e.g. Ibadan and Ife) is sporadic, but may be classed as a "southern concertina" migrant (Elgood *et al.* 1973).

Breeding. In the rains May-Oct, when population is extended, from near the coast at Sapele to northern limit of range at Kari.

465. PSALIDOPROCNE PRISTOPTERA   R(B)

(II.1025) Black Saw-wing

Not uncommon resident (*P. p. petiti*) over montane grassland at both Obudu and Mambilla Plateaux; also at Serti below and adjacent to Mambilla, but only in the rains (P.H., Green 1990).
Breeding. Not reported, but Apr-Jun and Nov in Cameroon (Serle 1950). (See *P.fuliginosa*).

466. PSALIDOPROCNE FULIGINOSA   R(B)
    (II.1028)   Mountain Saw-wing

Sight records claimed independently by J.H.E., T.R-S. and P.M., all in montane forest on the Obudu Plateau have been supported by more recent sightings in the same place by M.G. (also mist-netted), and by Ash *et al.* (1989). Confusion with *P. p. petiti* cannot be ruled out, but the species is known from Mount Cameroon and Bioko (Fernando Po), so occurrence at Obudu is not unlikely.
Breeding. In "Fernando Po, dates unspecified" (MP&G) where it "has become almost a House Swallow"; breeds west Cameroon, Oct-Mar (Serle 1981); Mt. Cameroon, Oct, Dec-Mar, one clutch recorded each month (BoA).

467. RIPARIA PALUDICOLA   RB
    (II.1017)   African Sand-Martin

Locally not uncommon resident (*R. p. minor*) over or near water from the valleys of the great rivers north to Sokoto and Lake Chad in almost all months. Sight records for the Mambilla Plateau have not been racially determined, but could be *R. p. newtoni*, the race at Bamenda and elsewhere in the Cameroon Highlands. The only record from the southwest is unconfirmed – 3 with other hirundines Ibadan, Jan (Ashford 1968). No clear evidence of migration but subject to some local dispersal, only a dry season visitor to Kano State (Sharland & Wilkinson 1981).
Breeding. At several localities between Zaria and Lokoja, Oct-Feb.

468. RIPARIA RIPARIA   PM
    (II.1015)   Sand Martin

Locally abundant Palaearctic migrant (*R. r. riparia*) usually near or over water, early Sep to late Apr, right across the north with northward passage at Lake Chad formerly estimated at 100,000 a day during Mar (A.J.H.) and autumn passage only slightly less spectacular, but a large decrease in numbers by the early 1990s (P.H.). Midwinter flocks of 2000 at Nguru (R.E.S.). Most birds must overfly the south as there are few southern records (Lagos and Ibadan) and none in southeast. Main wintering area unknown. Birds ringed in Nigeria have been recovered in Czechoslovakia, Germany, Cyprus, Malta and Tunisia; one ringed Denmark recovered Malamfatori.

469. RIPARIA CINCTA   AfM/?NB
    (II.1018)   Banded Martin

Uncommon non-breeding intra-African migrant (*R. c. cincta*) to open grasslands with standing water, almost exclusively early May to mid Nov north of the great rivers, mostly on the Jos Plateau area. Southern records come from Oyo and

Enugu; also Lagos where Feb and Mar (D.I.M.W.) records do not conform with the rains migrant pattern.

Breeding. No records for West Africa, but a pair at Shendam were carrying grass and thought to be building (R.S.McClelland) and c.20 were seen at holes on a river bank at Kaduna but thought merely to be roosting (M.S.). Probably breeds south of the equator.

470. **PSEUDHIRUNDO GRISEOPYGA** Afm/B

(II.1009) Grey-rumped Swallow

Has been confused with *H. spilodera*, making some records of both species suspect. Local resident (*P. g. griseopyga*), mostly from the Niger valley, Kainji to Onitsha, north to Kano and Lake Chad, and on the Mambilla Plateau, in grassy or wooded savanna usually near water. Elgood *et al.* (1973) said "a scarce and/or highly local swallow which is prone to make brief and sporadic appearances, so that its migratory status is difficult to assess" Present status unchanged.

Breeding. Most records from the Niger valley, Nov-May. Nest building Falgore, late Nov (Wilkinson & Beecroft 1985).

471. **HIRUNDO SEMIRUFA** Afm/B

(II.1006) Red-breasted Swallow

Seasonally not uncommon (*H. s. gordoni*) throughout, but essentially in towns, not often met in open country. A "southern concertina" migrant (Elgood *et al.* 1973) present all year in south, moving north to Kano and Maiduguri only in the rains; Kari is the most northerly breeding locality.

Breeding. Well documented. One of the few species known to be double brooded, nests Apr-Sep, from the coast at Lagos north to Kari.

472. **HIRUNDO SENEGALENSIS** Afm/B

(II.1005) Mosque Swallow

Uncommon and very local, mostly near towns, villages or inselbergs, at only a few localities, none in the southeast. All specimens have been from the north and have been *H. s. senegalensis*, but most in the south are probably *H. s. saturatior*. Moreau (1966) considered it migratory north of the equator but it is certainly present all year at some central Nigerian localities.

Breeding. Only nest building data: Gadau, May (Bannerman 1939); Ibadan, May (H.F.M.); Zonkwa, Jul (P.B.); Yankari Nat. Park, Jun-Aug (Green 1989).

473. **HIRUNDO ABYSSINICA** Afm/B

(II.1008) Lesser Striped Swallow

Locally common (*H. a. puella*) at least seasonally, along rocky streams and near towns and villages in the west from Abeokuta and Ondo north to Sokoto and Maiduguri. A few records from the southeast (none collected), but some could be (*H. a. maxima*) at the southwestern edge of their range (BoA). Migratory pattern not clear, but movement occurs in central areas around Kafanchan (Serle 1940) and the range expands northward in the rains while breeding.

Breeding. Well documented, many localities, Abeokuta north to Gadau, east to Jos Plateau and Maiduguri. Nests from Mar, but mainly May-Jul. Probably double brooded.

474. HIRUNDO DAURICA   Afm/B

(II.1004)   Red-rumped Swallow

Common and widespread (*H. d. domicella*) particularly along eroded river valleys in Northern Guinea and Sudan zones. Moreau (1966) regarded it as migratory in the northern tropics; Bannerman (1939) thought it non- migratory in West Africa; in Nigeria numbers change seasonally at Zaria (C.H.F.) and it is mainly a dry season visitor to Yankari (Green 1989). Southern records also suggest migration (Serle 1950). No evidence for an influx of *H. d. rufula* from the Palaearctic. Rock-perching birds with more rufous underparts seen at Taboru (Jos Plateau) may be *kumboensis* (M.Ho.,J.B.).
Breeding, Kainji north to Kano, Nov-Feb. Pair at nest Obudu Plateau, Nov (Ash 1990). [A record from Muregi, May (Bannerman 1939) is doubtful as it refers to "saucer-shaped nests", whereas this species builds a retort-shaped nest.]

475. HIRUNDO FULIGINOSA   R(B)

(II.1013)*   Dusky Cliff Swallow

Not uncommon in lowland forest in adjacent Cameroon but until recently no unequivocal record for Nigeria though admitted by Parker (1969). Sightings Oban and 25km south of Obudu town (M.G. with R.E.S.), and Oban Hills F.R., Sep (Ash 1990).
Breeding. Cameroon: Apr-Jun, (young Nov, Jan) (BoA).
*Named *Petrochelidon fuliginosa* by MP&G.

476. HIRUNDO PREUSSI   RB, ?Afm

(II.1012)   Preuss's Cliff Swallow

Sporadically locally abundant resident with flocks up to 1000 not infrequent, usually near rivers and inselbergs north of Abeokuta in the west, and Port Harcourt (D.I.M.W.), the Obudu Plateau (M.G.) and Serti (Ash *et al.* 1989) in the east. Whether migratory or subject to post-breeding dispersal is not clear, though northernmost records are for the rains; birds appear and disappear irregularly and are known not to breed in same area in consecutive years.
Breeding. Colonies of up to 400 pairs often under bridges from Abeokuta, Dec, and Oyo north to the Jos Plateau, Mar-Jul; nest-building Kazaure, Feb and May (Sharland and Wilkinson 1981), and colony of c. 100 pairs there at least until 'summer' 1991 (I.D.).

477. HIRUNDO FULIGULA   RB

(II.1021)   Rock Martin

Not uncommon resident (*H. f. bansoensis*) around inselbergs in southwest and north, in the Ogoja/Obudu area in southeast and in Gashaka-Gumti Nat. Park on the Cameroon border (Green 1990). Stenotopic and non-migratory.

178   Hirundinidae

Breeding. Both May-Jun and Oct-Dec. Normally at cliffs, but B/4 on artifical "cliffs" of Ife University buildings, Oct and again in same nest, May (R.F.). Bannerman (1953) says it prefers native houses to rock faces.

478. HIRUNDO SMITHII   RB

(II.1002)   Wire-tailed Swallow

Not uncommon resident (*H. s. smithii*) along savanna streams (attracted to culverts) especially in the Guinea zone, also south to Ibadan and Abeokuta in southwest, Ogoja and Serti in southeast and northward to Kano and Kari. Although said to be probably migrant north of the equator (Moreau 1966), is probably sedentary in Nigeria.

Breeding. Nests, usually under culverts, found over wide area, Oct-May.

479. HIRUNDO NIGRITA   RB

(II.1001)   White-throated Blue Swallow

Not uncommon resident along rivers in the forest zone from Lagos to Calabar. Some records for tidal waters but none for wooded streams in savanna north of the forest, the most northern localities being Olokemeji, Anambara Creek and Itu.

Breeding. Mostly Jan and Feb, but C/2 Sapele, Aug (Serle 1958) suggests season may be extensive.

480. HIRUNDO LEUCOSOMA   RB

(II.999)   Pied-winged Swallow

Uncommon resident in grassy savanna, farmland and near small towns from the coast at Badagri north to about 11°N. Most northerly records are for the rains, so may prove to be partial migrant.

Breeding. Pair feeding young Nsukka, 26 Jun (Serle 1957); chicks Ibadan, 4 May (H.F.M.): nesting Falgore Game Reserve, Jun (R.E.S.).

481. HIRUNDO AETHIOPICA   RB

(II.998)   Ethiopian Swallow

Common, even locally abundant resident (*H. a. aethiopica*) particularly in urban and suburban areas throughout the north and southwest; in the southeast recorded only in the Benue valley and Ogoja area where it is present Feb-Oct (Heaton and Heaton 1980), and on the Mambilla Plateau in Nov (Ash and Sharland 1987). Possibly overlooked.

Breeding. Well documented, mainly May-Jul, but overall Mar-Aug throughout.

482. HIRUNDO LUCIDA   ?RB

(II.994)   Red-chested Swallow

Status difficult to determine due to confusion with *H. rustica* of which it was formerly considered a sub-species. Collected at Jebba (Bannerman 1939). Reported rainy season sightings of *H. rustica* probably refer to this species.

Breeding. No records yet but Apr-Jul in Togo (Cheke 1982) and nest with young Niamey (Niger), early Oct (Paludan, 1936, vide Giraudoux *et al.* 1988).

483. HIRUNDO RUSTICA   PM

(II.993)   Barn Swallow

Common Palaearctic migrant (*H. r. rustica*) to wide variety of habitats, especially open areas and water, Sep-Apr, but in all areas most numerous on spring and autumn passage. Appears in south with other hirundines after the first rain. Large numbers winter in forest areas around Mbe Mountains, northern Cross River State. Birds ringed Nigeria recovered France, Germany and Spain; birds ringed Britain, France, Germany, Belgium, Denmark, Switzerland and Morocco recovered Nigeria.

484. DELICHON URBICA   PM

(II.1022)   House Martin

Uncommon Palaearctic migrant (*D. u. urbica*) to open areas near towns or water, all months except Jul, but mostly on autumn passage Sep-Oct or spring passage Mar-Apr. May overwinter on the Obudu Plateau but in view of the species abundance in the Palaearctic it is strangely sparse in Nigeria. Widely scattered records, but in southwest only at Ibadan and Ife. Bird ringed Britain recovered eastern Nigeria, late Feb.

MOTACILLIDAE

485. MOTACILLA FLAVA   PM

(II.642, 645, 646)   Yellow Wagtails

Common Palaearctic migrant to mown grass, cattle grazed areas, muddy shores of rivers, lakes and reservoirs. *M. f. flava* is widespread and predominant, *thunbergi, iberiae, cinereocapilla, feldegg* and *superciliaris*, more local and less numerous (Sharland and Wilkinson 1981). Claims for other races, notably *flavissima*, are not substantiated. The racial distribution pattern is complex (see Wood 1975). About 40,000 have been ringed in Nigeria and recoveries are numerous in North Africa from Morocco to Libya and in Europe from France to Turkey north to Finland and Russia. Birds ringed in Bulgaria, Denmark, Finland, Poland, Italy, Sweden and Russia have been recovered in Nigeria.

486. MOTACILLA CLARA   R(B)

(II.638)   Mountain Wagtail

Not uncommon resident (*M. c. chapini*) at the Obudu Plateau (independent sightings by at least 4 observers – F.C.S., J.H.E., T.R-S. & M.Ho.), and on the Mambilla Plateau (Ash 1990). Possibly an altitudinal migrant, e.g. sighted at Calabar at almost sea level (R.E.S.), in the Oban Hills at c.300 m, Aug 1980 (M.D.), at the Kwa Falls, Dec 1989 (A.M.N.) and in the Okwango F.R., Feb

(Ash 1990). Collected (just extralimital) by Preuss at Victoria (Cameroon) also at sea level. (Not regarded as montane in Sierra Leone – G.D. Field).
Breeding. No records from West Africa.

487. MOTACILLA ALBA   PM
(II.636)   White Wagtail

Not uncommon Palaearctic migrant (*M. a. alba*) to lake and river edges across the north from Sokoto to Lake Chad south to Zaria and the Jos Plateau, early Nov to late Mar. Southernmost locality is Kainji where it meets *M. aguimp*; but this is the only area of overlap and it is possible that juv. *aguimp* (with grey backs) have been mistaken there for *alba*.

488. MOTACILLA AGUIMP   RB
(II.637)   African Pied Wagtail

Common resident (*M. a. vidua*) at watersides, along roads and in suburban situations from the coast to the southern edge of the Guinea zone (to 10°N in the west), numbers diminishing northwards, but with several localities along the middle Niger. Less common in southeast where, apart from Serti (P.H.), it does not extend into the true savanna.
Breeding. Through the dry season, Oct-Apr, from the coast north to Nasarawa (Serle 1950).

489. ANTHUS NOVAESEELANDIAE   AfM/(B), ?VPM
(II.653)   Richard's Pipit

Uncommon, mainly in high grasslands, but easily overlooked by confusion with other pipits. Up to 15 sightings per day at Obudu Plateau, Aug 1980 (M.D.). Probably 3 separate populations are involved: (i) *A. n. richardi*, vagrant Palaearctic migrant in small numbers, Oct-Apr, around Lake Chad, although it is not yet established that Palaearctic birds cross the Sahara (BoA consider that the Lake Chad birds are smaller than *richardi* and may represent an undescribed local population); (ii) *A. r. lynesi*, probably an intra-African migrant from Cameroon, 2 collected, Obudu Plateau (Serle 1957), one at Mambilla Plateau (Ebbutt 1965); (iii) *A. r. cameroonensis*, also from Cameroon and which MP&G record on the Obudu Plateau: in BoA *cameroonensis* is restricted to Mt. Cameroon and Mt. Manenguba in Cameroon, but may well occur in other montane regions close to the Cameroon-Nigeria border. Main localities are the high plateaux (Mambilla and Obudu), between Maiduguri and Lake Chad, and has also been netted at Kano (*lynesi*). Apart from the specimens of *lynesi*, no others have been racially determined, so that a confusing situation remains.
Breeding. No records, but Feb-Apr in Cameroon Highlands (BoA).

490. ANTHUS CAMPESTRIS   PM
(II.647)   Tawny Pipit

Uncommon Palaearctic migrant to the north from Sokoto to Lake Chad, mid Oct to Apr, usually in dry open savanna or farmland, as far south as Yola and on Jos Plateau, where 20 seen in Feb (R.E.S.).

491. ANTHUS SIMILIS R(B)

(II.649) Long-billed Pipit

Uncommon resident on open upland grasslands. 2 separate populations may be involved: *A. s. josensis*, first collected Sep 1957 on the Jos Plateau by R.E.S. and only rarely sighted since; *A. s. bannermani*, female collected 15 Mar 1961 at Obudu Plateau by F.C.S. and, presumably the same race, quite common Gotel Mts. (Ash *et al.* 1989). (BoA lumps *josensis* in with *bannermani*).

Breeding. No records, but Feb-Apr in Cameroon Highlands; eggs in ovaries Niger Republic, Jun (BoA).

492. ANTHUS LEUCOPHYRS RB, ?Afm

(II.650) Plain-backed Pipit

Common and widespread resident in all months (*A. l. zenkeri*) in all types of open savanna and farmland from coastal savanna north to 11°N, Zaria and Jos Plateau. Nigerian data give little support to Moreau's (1966) statement that it moves north after breeding in the northern tropics, though occurrence near Lake Chad is for the rains and numbers change seasonally in some areas.

Breeding. Throughout the year in south, e.g. Ilaro in Jan, May, Sep and Dec (J.A.B.), but seems limited Mar-May at Zaria (C.H.F.).

493. ANTHUS TRIVIALIS PM

(II.654) Tree Pipit

Not uncommon Palaearctic migrant (*A. t. trivialis*) to wooded savanna and forest clearings, late Sep to early May, mainly on passage Sep-Oct and Mar in north, but small numbers over-winter in the south, on the Obudu Plateau and in Gashaka-Gumti Nat. Park (Green 1990). At Vom, where a few over-winter, 50 have been netted on autumn passage and 37 in spring (V.W.S.).

494. ANTHUS CERVINUS PM

(II.656) Red-throated Pipit

Common Palaearctic migrant to muddy shores in the north from Sokoto to Lake Chad south to Zaria and the Jos Plateau. Also common on montane grassland, Gangirwal (Gotel Mts.), Mar (Ash *et al.* 1989). Small numbers occur south to the coast in the west at Lagos but none further south than Onitsha in southeast. Mostly Jan to early May (Lake Chad, Oct), suggesting slow southward movement as wetlands to the north in Niger dry out.

495. MACRONYX CROCEUS RB

(II.658) Yellow-throated Longclaw

Common and widespread resident in open grass savanna and farmland from the coast to the southern edge of the Sudan zone, occasionally seen between Maiduguri and Lake Chad.

Breeding. Many records Lagos north to the Jos Plateau, all in the rainy season, Apr-Oct.

CAMPEPHAGIDAE

496. CAMPEPHAGA PHOENICEA Afm/B
(II.1032) Red-shouldered Cuckoo-Shrike

Uncommon resident (*C. p. phoenicea*) in well-wooded areas, perhaps seasonally not uncommon in some localities; gives a clear "hump-back bridge" pattern of migration (Elgood *et al.* 1973). Present all months in most of Southern Guinea zone and Enugu; moves south to the coast in west, Nov-Apr, to Calabar in east, Feb; moves north to Zaria, where present early May to early Nov (C.H.F.), Jos Plateau Mar-Aug (J.B.), Potiskum and Bornu.
Breeding. From Kainji Lake Nat. Park and Mbaakon and after northward migration, north to Zaria and Bornu, May-Sep.

497. CAMPEPHAGA PETITI R(B)
(II.1033) Petit's Cuckoo-Shrike

New species for Nigeria. Probably not uncommon in montane forest on Obudu Plateau (pair sighted by F.D-L.); and Gotel Mts. (3 sightings, Ash *et al.* 1989).
Breeding. No records for West Africa.

498. CAMPEPHAGA QUISCALINA R(B)
(II.1034) Purple-throated Cuckoo-Shrike

Sightings only in tree canopies in Nindam F.R., near Kagoro, an area on southern escarpment of Jos Plateau that has produced several forest rarities though well away from the forest zone (Dyer *et al.* 1986). Hall & Moreau (1970) show localities both east and west of Nigeria.
Breeding. No records but "about to breed" Feb, Ghana (BoA).

499. LOBOTOS LOBATUS ?
(II.1039) Western Wattled Cuckoo-Shrike

New species for Nigeria. One brief sighting and call heard in Ikpan primary forest by R.J.D., 11 Apr 1988 (Ash *et al.* 1989). Requires confirmation. Forms a superspecies with Eastern Wattled Cuckoo-Shrike *L. oriolinus* and we have followed BoA in placing the boundary between the two forms southeast of Nigeria. However, Dowsett (1993a) attributes his Nigerian record to *L. oriolinus*.

500. CORACINA CAESIA R(B)
(II.1037) Grey Cuckoo-Shrike

Not uncommon resident (*C. c. pura*) in montane forest at the Obudu Plateau; a record near Abeokuta, 4 Sep 1969 (D.I.M.W.), needs confirmation.
Breeding. No records, but breeds west Cameroon, Nov and Dec (Serle 1981); adult feeding juv. Cameroon, Mar (Tye 1992).

501. CORACINA PECTORALIS R(B)

(II.1035) White-breasted Cuckoo-Shrike

Not uncommon resident in mature savanna woodland of the Guinea zones, but seldom in degraded areas. Extends southward into Derived Savanna at Meko, Ibadan and Enugu; northward to Zaria and Kari. Strictly non-migratory.

Breeding. No records, but C/2 The Gambia, Jun (*vide* Gore 1990) and Ghana, Jan (Grimes 1987).

502. CORACINA AZUREA R(B)

(II.1038) Blue Cuckoo-Shrike

Not uncommon resident in the canopy of relatively undisturbed lowland forest west of the lower Niger, at Calabar to the east and just across the border at Korup in southwest Cameroon (Thomas 1991). Easily overlooked unless the voice is known and may prove not uncommon in high forest right across the country.

Breeding. No records, but "showed signs of breeding" near Benin, Feb (Mason 1940).

PYCNONOTIDAE

503. ANDROPADUS MONTANUS R(B)

(II.713) Cameroon Montane Greenbul

Uncommon resident (*A. m. montanus*) in montane forest at the Obudu Plateau, and in the Gotel Mts (Ash *et al.* 1989). A specimen collected 18 Dec 1962 by P. Ward at Obudu extended range west from Cameroon into Nigeria; 3 birds netted there Nov (Ash 1990).

Breeding. No records but in breeding condition Cameroon, Jan-Mar and Nov; bird with brood patch, Mar; juvs. Mar-Apr (BoA).

504. ANDROPADUS TEPHROLAEMUS R(B)

(II.711) Mountain Greenbul

Common resident (*A. t. bamendae*) in montane forest at the Obudu and Mambilla Plateaux and in the Gotel Mts. Serle (1957) collected the first series at Obudu and it has been collected, netted and sighted there often since, in all seasons. Ash *et al.* (1989) found it locally very common on Mambilla Plateau and adjoining Gotel Mts.

Breeding. No records, but laying dates in Cameroon mainly dry season, possibly all year (Serle 1981).

505. ANDROPADUS VIRENS RB

(II.722)* Little Greenbul

Abundant resident (*A. v. erythropterus = grisescens*) in secondary forest, near streams and swamps, right across the country north to Ibadan, Ife and Enugu; in gallery forest at the Upper Ogun Estate, near Akure and near Kainji and in relict forest at southern escarpment of the Jos Plateau at Kagoro and Shendam. Widespread in Gashaka-Gumti Nat. Park (Green 1990). Specimens at Owerri were regarded (Marchant 1953) "intermediate between *grisescens* and the nominate race", the latter occurring from Cameroon eastward.

Breeding. Breeding condition near Lagos, Sep (J.P.G.), 2 juvs. with gapes, Dec (D.I.M.W.); breeding condition eastern Nigeria, May-Jun and Sep (BoA).
*Named *Eurillas virens* by MP&G.

506. ANDROPADUS GRACILIS RB

(II.718) Little Grey Greenbul

Not uncommon resident at forest edges, especially old secondary growth, *A. g. gracilis* east of the Lower Niger, *A. g. extremus* to the west. Recorded north of the true forest belt to Ibadan, Ife and Enugu, in montane forest at the Obudu Plateau (P.M.) and also at Nindam F.R. (Dyer *et al.* 1986).

Breeding. Females with large yolking eggs at Mamu, 21 Mar and Enugu, 5 Jul (Serle 1957).

507. ANDROPADUS ANSORGEI RB

(II.719) Ansorge's Greenbul

Probably not uncommon resident (*A. a. ansorgei*) in high forest and lush secondary growth of the southeast. The voice will probably prove to be distinctive, but scarcely distinguishable from *A. gracilis*. Only collected east of the lower Niger (several localities – Marchant 1953, Serle 1957) and just west of it at Sapoba (F.C.Sibley). Probably also occurs in forest zone of southwest.

Breeding. Nest and eggs undescribed. Specimens in breeding condition collected May and Dec (Marchant 1953).

508. ANDROPADUS CURVIROSTRIS R(B)

(II.720) Cameroon Sombre Greenbul

Not uncommon resident (*A. c. curvirostris*) in the lower strata of lowland forest west of the Lower Niger. Few records to the east, none east of Owerri.

Breeding. Nest and eggs undescribed. Owerri male had slightly enlarged testes, 1 Aug 1949 (Marchant 1953). Said to breed Aug-Dec, west Cameroon (Serle 1981).

509. ANDROPADUS GRACILIROSTRIS RB

(II.717)* Slender-billed Greenbul

Locally common resident (*A. g. gracilirostris*) high up in old secondary growth rather than high forest, from Ilaro to Owerri, north to Ibadan, Ife and near Nsukka. Also recorded north of the great rivers at Nindam F.R. (Kagoro) by Dyer *et al.* (1986).

Breeding. Male in breeding condition Lagos area, Jun and juvs. in Jul (G&H); breeds Sierra Leone, Sep-Jan (Field 1993).
*Named *Stelgidillas gracilirostris* by MP&G.

510. ANDROPADUS LATIROSTRIS   RB

(II.723)*   Yellow-whiskered Greenbul

Common resident at forest edges and lush secondary growth right across the country. Specimens from east of the Lower Niger north to near Onitsha are *A. l. latirostris*; from southwest north to Ibadan and Ife are *A. l. congener*; from the Benin forests (Edo State) are racially undetermined but probably *congener*.

Breeding. "... a female that had just laid a complete clutch of two eggs" Mamu, 30 May (Serle 1957); "specimens taken in May were in breeding condition" near Lagos (G&H).

*Named *Stelgidocichla latirostris* by MP&G.

511. CALYPTOCICHLA SERINA   RB

(II.721)   Golden Greenbul

Rare resident in forest, including secondary growth and relict patches, across the whole forest zone. Although one of the few readily distinguishable bulbuls, noted only at 4 localities. First collected at Umuagwu, 1 Aug 1949 (Marchant 1953)); sighted at Gambari (J.H.E., F.C.S.), near Akure (F.C.S.) and 4 at Calabar (P.M.).

Breeding. Marchant's specimen (Aug) was a male with somewhat enlarged testes. West Cameroon, Mar and Aug (Serle 1981).

512. BAEOPOGON INDICATOR   RB

(II.695)   Honeyguide Greenbul

Not uncommon resident (*B. i. indicator*) at forest edges and in secondary growth right across the country, more common locally in the west, north to Ibadan, Ife and Enugu; also at Kagoro and Tayu on southern slopes of the Jos Plateau. A specimen from Lagos (Sander 1957) was "indistinguishable" from *B. i. leucurus*, which White (1962) and BoA place from Togo west to Sierra Leone.

Breeding. No nests reported, but specimens in breeding condition have been collected through dry season, Sep (Marchant 1953) to Mar (MP&G).

513. BAEOPOGON CLAMANS   R(B)

(II.696)   Sjöstedt's Honeyguide Greenbul

A sighting in the Oban Hills lowland forest, 2 Aug 1980 (G&D), has been confirmed by Ash *et al.* (1989) who found it fairly common in the Ikpan Block and Oban West in Apr. Brought into view by playback of call.

Breeding. Unrecorded in West Africa.

514. IXONOTUS GUTTATUS   RB

(II.697)   Spotted Greenbul

Very local resident (*I. g. guttatus*), not uncommon in patches of lowland forest, usually near water, right across the country but not far north from the coast.

Breeding. Not positively reported, but "Southern Nigeria, Jun-Sep (building)" (MP&G). Breeds, west Cameroon Mar-May and Aug (Serle 1981).

515. CHLOROCICHLA SIMPLEX   RB

(II.694)   Simple Greenbul

Common resident in secondary growth, gardens and abandoned farms in the Forest and Derived Savanna zones from the coast north to Ilorin, Enugu and the Serti area, most numerous in the south.

Breeding. From the coast north to Ibadan, mostly Jun-Aug but 2 Jan records and bird on nest photographed Okomu Forest, 3 Feb 1991 (I.G.N.).

516. CHLOROCICHLA FLAVICOLLIS   RB

(II.692)   Yellow-throated Leaf-love

Locally common resident (*C. f. flavicollis*) in gallery forest and well-wooded suburban gardens of the Derived Savanna and Guinea zones from Abeokuta, Ibadan, Enugu and the Mambilla Plateau north to Zaria, the Jos Plateau, Yankari and Kari. Isolated records Lagos (D.I.M.W.), Birnin Kudu (R.E.S). Non-migratory.

Breeding. Probably co-operative, reported from Ilorin north to Zaria, May-Aug.

517. THESCELOCICHLA LEUCOPLEURA   R(B)

(II.691)   White-tailed Greenbul

Locally common resident in swamp forest and along forest streams with *Raphia* palms, right across the country. A few gallery forest records (also with *Raphia*), at Kabba (Mrs Dudley), Ogoja (Serle 1957) and Kagoro on southern escarpment of the Jos Plateau (M.D.).

Breeding. No records, probably co-operative; BoA gives "Cameroon, Feb, May, Jul, (breeding condition Oct), in rainy season".

518. PYRRHURUS SCANDENS   RB

(II.693)   Leaf-love

Uncommon and local resident (*P. s. scandens*) in gallery forest, sometimes at forest edges, especially in southeast, from near coast at Lekki peninsula (P.H.) and Sapele north to Kainji, Zaria and Kagoro; also at the Obudu Plateau and in the Gashaka-Gumti Nat. Park (Green 1990).

Breeding. No records, but females collected in breeding condition, 13 Oct and 26 Nov (Serle 1957); nest building Togo, Mar (Walsh 1990).

519. PHYLLASTREPHUS BAUMANNI   RB

(II.706)   Baumann's Greenbul

Not uncommon resident (*P. b. baumanni*) at forest edges and in secondary growth right across the country, possibly less numerous in southeast, north to Ibadan, Ife and Enugu. Also netted at Pandam (C.S.) in gallery forest at southern edge of the Jos Plateau, but no other Guinea zone records.

Breeding. No records, but female breeding condition Awgu, Dec (Marchant 1953).

520. PHYLLASTREPHUS POENSIS RB

(II.702)   Cameroon Olive Greenbul

Common resident in montane forest at the Obudu and Mambilla Plateaux and in the Gotel Mts (Ash et al. 1989).
Breeding. A captured bird was said to have been taken while incubating on 20 Dec 1962 (J.H.E.); in Cameroon, Nov-Apr, mainly Nov-Jan in dry season (BoA).

521. PHYLLASTREPHUS ICTERINUS RB

(II.710)   Icterine Greenbul

Not uncommon resident (*P. i. icterinus*) in the lower strata of high forest right across the country, though surprisingly not yet near Lagos. Not found north of the true forest zone.
Breeding. Nest building Owerri, Jan; birds in full breeding condition, Nov and Jan (Marchant 1953).

522. PHYLLASTREPHUS ALBIGULARIS RB

(II.707)   White-throated Greenbul

Not uncommon resident (*P. a. albigularis*) at forest edges and clearings and in secondary growth right across the country, extending north of the forest zone to Ede, Ife and Enugu. Several netted at Kagoro in relict forest on southern escarpment of the Jos Plateau; collected nearby at Kagum.
Breeding. No nests, but specimens with somewhat enlarged gonads, Aug-Nov (Marchant 1953).

523. PHYLLASTREPHUS POLIOCEPHALUS R(B)

(II.708)   Grey-headed Greenbul

Not uncommon resident in montane forest at the Obudu Plateau; unrecorded anywhere else. Formerly regarded as race of *P. flavostriatus* but now given full specific status following BoA.
Breeding. No records, but west Cameroon, Feb (Serle 1981).

524. BLEDA SYNDACTYLA R(B)

(II.688)   Red-tailed Bristlebill

Uncommon, presumed resident, in high forest from west (Ilaro) to east (Calabar) and north to Ibadan. West of the Lower Niger is nominate *syndactyla*, to the east is *B.s.multicolor = ogowensis*.
Breeding. No records, but in Cameroon, Oct-Dec (BoA).

525. BLEDA EXIMIA R(B)

(II.689)   Green-tailed Bristlebill

Common (*B. e. notata*) in lower storey of lowland primary forest in the extreme southeast, probably the species western limit. Collected by Talbot in 1909 (Serle 1957) near Oban, more recently netted in the same area, Jul 1980 (D&G), and recorded in the Ikpan block (Ash *et al.* 1989) and in Okwango Forest Reserve (Ash 1990).

Breeding. No records for Nigeria but Cameroon, egg-laying May, Jul-Aug, probably all year (BoA).

526. BLEDA CANICAPILLA RB
(II.690) Grey-headed Bristlebill

Common resident in lowland forest, close to the ground, right across the country and in relict forest patches north to Ibadan, Ife and Enugu. Also frequently netted in lowest forest stratum at Kagoro (Dyer *et al.* 1986) and there is a single record (Koeman *et al.* 1978) from gallery forest at Aliya (11°N) which needs substantiation.

Breeding. C/2 Mamu, 16 Jun 1953 (Serle 1957).

527. CRINIGER BARBATUS RB
(II.685) Western Bearded Greenbul

Not uncommon resident (*C. b. ansorgeanus*) in the lower strata of high forest right across the country but most numerous east of the Lower Niger and in the main forest zone; Bannerman (1936, 1951) has localities also as far north as Ibadan and Ilesha.

Breeding. Female Yenagoa, 6 Jan, "had just laid one egg and was soon to lay a second" (Serle 1957).

528. CRINIGER CHLORONOTUS R(B)
(II.685) Eastern Bearded Greenbul

New species for Nigeria. Known only from two specimens collected in Oban forest, 18 Jul 1981 (M.D.). Also occurs just over the border at Korup, Cameroon (Thomas 1991). Sometimes treated as a race of *C. barbatus* but separated in BoA on the basis of its white throat and vocal differences.

Breeding. No records for Nigeria but Cameroon, breeding condition Mar (BoA).

529. CRINIGER CALURUS R(B)
(II.686) Red-tailed Greenbul

Common resident mainly in the lower strata of high forest of the true forest zone right across the country, but also north to Ibadan and Ife (*?verreauxi*) in southwest. Around Benin eastward it is nominate *calurus*, and in southwest (Lagos) is *C. c. verreauxi*; but the line of intergradation has not been determined.

Breeding. Surprisingly, for such a common species, there are no breeding records. However, breeds Bioko, Feb-Mar and Nov, and Cameroon, Feb, Apr-Aug and Dec (BoA).

530. CRINIGER NDUSSUMENSIS R(B)
(II.687)   White-bearded Greenbul

Possibly not uncommon resident in lowland forest east of the lower Niger (see Serle (1957) below). Now distinguished from *C. olivaceus* and given full specific status following Hall and Moreau (1970) and BoA. Mainly distinguished from *C. calurus* by thinner bill but Serle (1957) failed to find this distinction in a series of 34 male and 22 female specimens. However, the call may be distinctive (Chappuis 1975, BoA).
Breeding. No records for West Africa.

531. PYCNONOTUS BARBATUS RB
(II.684)   Common Bulbul

Common, locally abundant, resident in man-made habitats throughout, but also enters old secondary forest. White (1962) attributes birds from southern areas to *P. b. gabonensis* (=*nigeriae*), those from the north to *inornatus*, but a cline almost certainly exists. Strictly non-migratory, but appears in new man-made areas, e.g. cattle ranch and hotel at Obudu Plateau, first noted late 1961.
Breeding. All months throughout, peaking in rains, Apr-Jul.

TURDIDAE

532. STIPHRORNIS ERYTHROTHORAX RB
(II.842)   Forest Robin

Not uncommon resident (*S. e. erythrothorax*) in lowland forest from Lagos to Owerri, in gallery forest in the Niger/Benue valleys and in relict forest on southern slopes of the Jos Plateau at Kagoro, where it was the most commonly netted bird (Dyer *et al.* 1986), and Pandam.
Breeding. Female taken at nest Mamu Forest, 3 Apr 1953 (Serle 1957).

533. SHEPPARDIA BOCAGEI R(B)
(II.833)   Bocage's Akalat

The collection of a specimen (*S. b. granti*) in montane forest at Obudu Plateau, 19 Mar 1961 (F.C.Sibley), extended the range of this species west into Nigeria.
Breeding. Not recorded, though Sibley's specimen was a female with a 5mm ovary. West Cameroon, Jan (Serle 1981) and Cameroon, Dec-Mar (BoA).

534. SHEPPARDIA CYORNITHOPSIS R(B)
(II.841)   Lowland Akalat

New species for Nigeria. The only record is one netted in secondary lowland rain forest at Okomu F.R., 25 Jul 1988 (P.H.). Requires substantiation but occurs both west (Liberia) and east (Cameroon) of Nigeria.
Breeding. No records, but Liberia males in breeding condition Jun-Sep, recently fledged juv., Oct (BoA).

535. LUSCINIA LUSCINIA VPM

(II.860) Sprosser, Thrush Nightingale

Vagrant Palaearctic migrant to savanna undergrowth. Only 2 records, both mist-netted at Kano; the first by J.R. Best, Sep 1975, the second by R.E. Sharland, Oct 1976.

536. LUSCINIA MEGARHYNCHOS PM

(II.859) Nightingale

Common Palaearctic migrant (*L. m. megarhynchos*) in savanna scrub, gardens and forest clearings, in all areas except coastal, other than Badagri to Lagos. Arrives in north early Sep, moving slowly south to reach Ibadan and Lagos early Nov. Few remain to winter in north. Northward passage is more rapid, late Mar to early Apr, and some in May. A bird ringed Tunisia recovered at Akure (R.E.S.).

537. LUSCINIA SVECICA PM

(II.858) Bluethroat

Uncommon Palaearctic migrant (mainly *L. s. svecica*) early Dec to Mar. First record Sokoto, 27 Dec 1953 (Dobbs 1959), more than 20 records since mainly in northernmost areas, Sokoto, Kano, Hadejia Wetlands area (M.D.) and Potiskum, but one from Ibadan (Ashford 1969). C.H. Fry found it common in Jan 1967 at Gwadabawa (north of Sokoto).

538. COSSYPHICULA ROBERTI R(B)

(II.840) White-bellied Robin-Chat

Uncommon resident (*C. r. roberti*) in montane forest at the Obudu Plateau. A specimen (male with very small testes) obtained at Obudu by F.C. Sibley, 20 Mar 1961, extended the range west into Nigeria. Three pairs were sighted at 1300 m on the SW escarpment at Obudu, 4 Apr 1988, (Ash *et al.* 1989).

Breeding. Nest and eggs unknown. Breeding condition Cameroon, Mar (BoA) and west Cameroon, Nov (Serle 1981).

539. COSSYPHA ISABELLAE RB

(II.831) Mountain Robin-Chat

Not uncommon resident (*C. i. batesi*) in montane forest at Obudu Plateau, Gotel Mts. and Chappal Hendu (Ash *et al.* 1989).

Breeding. N/2 Chappal Hendu, Mar (Ash *et al.* 1989). Cameroon "many family parties of spotted young" Mar and Jun, and C/2 perhaps out of season, 8 Sep 1948 (Bannerman 1951).

540. COSSYPHA POLIOPTERA R(B)

(II.832) Grey-winged Robin-Chat

Rare resident (*C. p. nigriceps*) in savanna woodland and dense gallery forest in

only a few localities in a central part of the Guinea savanna, mostly south of the Jos Plateau but with Birnin Gwari the most north and west locality (C.H.F.), to Loko on the Benue in the south (Bannerman 1936), Pandam in the east (M.G.), and 2 (one heard only) at Assop, 27 Aug 1993 (M.Ho.). Recently, 8 noted at Leinde Fadali, (Mambilla Plateau) on the Cameroon border (Ash *et al.* 1989).
   Breeding. No records. Breeding condition Liberia, Jan (BoA).

541. COSSYPHA CYANOCAMPTER   R(B)
   (II.834)   Blue-shouldered Robin-Chat

Uncommon and very local resident (*C. c. cyanocampter*) in dense secondary growth at forest edges, only in southwest, from Ilaro to Ibadan and Oshogbo, except one record in east at Umuagwu (Marchant 1953). (That it is "regular" at Sokoto (Dobbs 1959) is highly improbable). Easily overlooked unless the voice is known, it may prove to occur right across the forest zone.
   Breeding. Breeding condition, May (BoA) and in Cameroon, Mar, Jul and Oct (BoA).

   [COSSYPHA HEUGLINI   ?
   (II.830)   White-browed Robin-Chat

A probable pair sighted in an orange grove at Wulgo, 13 Mar 1961, where they remained in view some time, to reappear in same place later (J.H.E.). This would represent a northwestward extension of known range of less than 200 km.
   Breeding. No records, the nearest being "Gabon (breeding condition) April" (MP&G).]

542. COSSYPHA NATALENSIS   RB
   (II.835)   Red-capped Robin-Chat

Locally not uncommon resident, but known only from relict forest at Kagoro on southern escarpment of the Jos Plateau, where 24 were netted and released (Dyer *et al.* 1986), and from Chappal Waddi (Gotel Mts.) above 1400 m (Ash *et al.* 1989). Race unknown but White (1962) and BoA give *C. n. larischi* as extending west to Cameroon whereas MP&G attribute Cameroon birds to *C. n. intensa*, a race also recognised by White and BoA.
   Breeding. C/3 Nindam Forest Reserve, 15 Jun 1980 (Dyer *et al.* 1986).

543. COSSYPHA NIVEICAPILLA   RB, Afm/B
   (II.837)   Snowy-crowned Robin-Chat

Locally common resident (*C. n. niveicapilla*) all year in suburban gardens of the forest zone and in gallery woodland from coast north to the great rivers; from there north to Sokoto, Kano, Potiskum and Maiduguri it is a rains migrant, May-Oct, with a marked influx at Zaria in late Apr (C.H.F.).
   Breeding. From the coast at Lagos north to Kaduna and the Jos Plateau (probably at the extreme north of its range), May-Aug.

544. COSSYPHA ALBICAPILLA   RB

(II.836)   White-crowned Robin-Chat

Uncommon resident (*C. a. giffardi*) in thick scrub along small rivers from c. 20 localities mostly in a central belt of the Guinea zone, but ranging right across the country from Kishi to Serti, from along the middle Niger and Benue valleys north to Kaduna and Aliya.

Breeding. C/2 Afue hills (near the Benue), 7 Jul 1938 (Serle 1940).

545. ALETHE DIADEMATA   R(B)

(II.843)   Fire-crested Alethe

Probably not uncommon resident (*A. d. castanea*) near ground level in mature lowland forest, across the country from Lagos to Calabar and Oban Hills, north to Ife in the west and Okwango Forest Reserve (Ash 1990) in the east. At Calabar 6 seen together at an ant trail (P.M.). Although furtive, can be mist-netted, with consequent revision of known range and frequency.

Breeding. No records. Cameroon, May, Aug, Oct (juvs. Nov) (BoA).

546. ALETHE POLIOCEPHALA   RB

(II.845)   Brown-chested Alethe

Probably not uncommon resident, from Lagos to the Obudu Plateau and the Serti area. Serle (1957) identified a specimen from Mamu Forest as *A. p. poliocephala*. Mason (1940) found it "fairly common" (race uncertain) in the forest near Benin. The single specimen from Lagos was also not identified racially. However BoA class all Nigerian birds as *A. p. compsonota* and restrict *A. p. poliocephala* to Sierra Leone to Ghana.

Breeding. Male Lagos, collected 6 Jun 1971, was in breeding condition (Gee & Heigham 1977).

547. NEOCOSSYPHUS POENSIS   RB

(II.807)   White-tailed Ant-Thrush

Not uncommon and local resident (*N. p. poensis*), usually near ground in lowland forest, right across the forest zone from Lagos to Calabar. Mostly collected or mist-netted, indicating its elusive habits.

Breeding. 2 fledglings netted Ilaro, 14 Jul (J.A.B.).

548. NEOCOSSYPHUS FRASERI   R(B)

(II.757)   Rufous Flycatcher-Thrush

Only recorded from the Oban Hills (M.D.), where 2 birds have been netted (Ash and Sharland 1987). In BoA it is given separate specific status from *N. finschi* and is at the extreme northwest of its range (*N. fraseri rubicunda*).

Breeding. No records. Cameroon Aug, Oct and Dec (BoA).

Plate 1. Great White Pelicans in the Hadejia Wetlands near Gorgoram with domestic cattle and Acacia forest in the background. (A. P. Leventis)

Plate 2. Cattle Egrets in full breeding plumage. (M. E. Gartshore)

Plate 3. Hadada on the floodplain of the Gaji River, Yankari National Park. (A. P. Leventis)

Plate 4. White-faced Whistling-Duck and Garganey, IITA. (I. G. Nason)

Plate 5. Male Pygmy Goose on the lake at IITA. (I. G. Nason)

Plate 6. White-backed Vulture above its nest in a *Borassus* palm at Yankari National Park. (I. G. Nason)

Plate 7. Bateleurs at Yankari National Park, showing both light and dark colour phases. (I. G. Nason)

Plate 8. Grasshopper Buzzard taking flight, Gorgoram, northeast Nigeria. (A. P. Leventis)

Plate 9. Fox Kestrel near Wase Rock, central Nigeria. (I. G. Nason)

Plate 10. Clapperton's Francolin, Sambisa G.R. (A. P. Leventis)

Plate 11. African Crake, Agenebode. (A. P. Leventis)

Plate 12. Allen's Gallinule, IITA, Ibadan. (A. P. Leventis)

Plate 13. Arabian Bustard near Bama. (A. P. Leventis)

Plates 14 & 15. Spotted Thick-knee in Acacia Forest, Sahel-savanna zone, near Maiduguri (A. P. Leventis) and chicks near Zaria. (M. E. Gartshore)

Plate 16. Greater Painted-Snipe in rice paddies, IITA. (I. G. Nason)

Plate 17. White-crowned Plover, IITA, Ibadan. (I. G. Nason)

Plates 18 & 19. Egyptian Plover (left) and Grey Pratincole at IITA, Ibadan, where they appear as 'occasionals' when the Great Rivers are in flood. (I. G. Nason)

Plate 20. Rock Pratincoles on the Osse River, Ifon Forest Reserve. (A. P. Leventis)

Plate 21. Forbes' Plover in a fallow rice paddy at IITA, Ibadan. (I. G. Nason)

Plate 22. Cream-coloured Courser between Yusufari and the Bulatura oases. (A. P. Leventis)

Plates 23 & 24. Four-banded Sandgrouse, male (right) and female at Kainji Lake National Park. (I. G. Nason)

Plate 25. Female Namaqua Dove near Kano. (I. G. Nason)

Plate 26. Spotted Eagle Owl, the dark-eyed race *B. a. cinerascens*, near the Hadejia Wetlands Project Headquarters at Nguru. (I. G. Nason)

Plate 27. Standard-winged Nightjar on a laterite road near Idah, central Nigeria. (A. P. Leventis)

Plate 28. Grey-headed Kingfisher near Agenebode. (A. P. Leventis)

Plates 29 & 30. Adult Malachite Kingfisher (left) in the Hadejia Wetlands, and a black-billed juvenile on the Lekki Peninsula. (I. G. Nason)

Plate 31. Rosy Bee-eaters near nesting grounds, Kaduna River. (I. G. Nason)

Plate 32. Carmine Bee-eaters near Zaria. (M. Dyer)

Plate 33. Abyssinian Roller, Hadejia Wetlands. (I. G. Nason)

Plate 34. Vieillot's Barbet, Nguru, northern Nigeria. (I. G. Nason)

Plate 35. White-crested Hornbill in degraded forest, Lekki Peninsula. (A. P. Leventis)

Plate 36. Gabon Woodpecker excavating nesthole, Lekki Peninsula, near Lagos. (I. G. Nason)

Plate 37. Plain-backed Pipit, Lekki Peninsula. (I. G. Nason)

Plate 38. Yellow-throated Longclaw, IITA, Ibadan. (I. G. Nason)

Plate 39. Northern Ant-eater Chat near Dagona. (I. G. Nason)

Plate 40. Rufous Scrub-Robin at its nest. (M. E. Gartshore)

Plate 41. Rufous-crowned Eremomela in forest canopy, Okomu F.R. (A. P. Leventis)

Plate 42. Brown-throated Wattle-eye in a Lagos garden. (A. P. Leventis)

Plate 43. Red-headed Rockfowl on the nest in high forest near Bashu village, Kanyang/Sonkwala Mountains, S. E. Nigeria. (A. P. Leventis)

Plate 44. Beautiful Sunbird in a Kano garden. (A. P. Leventis)

Plate 45. Blue-eared Glossy Starling, Nguru. (I. G. Nason)

Plate 46. Yellow-billed Shrike in farmland, IITA, Ibadan. (I. G. Nason)

Plate 47. Red Bishop on farmland at Agenebode, south-central Nigeria. (A. P. Leventis)

Plate 48. Red-billed Fire-finch on the Jos Plateau. (A. P. Leventis)

549. NEOCOSSYPHUS FINSCHI RB

(II.757)   Finsch's Flycatcher-Thrush

Not uncommon resident in lower storey trees of lowland forest from Lagos to Owerri. Not recorded north of Ibadan, Ife and Mamu Forest near the edge of the forest zone.
Breeding. "Noted building in February" (Marchant 1953).

550. CERCOTRICHAS GALACTOTES RB,AfM/B,PM

(II.854)   Rufous Scrub-Robin

Locally common resident (*C. g. minor*) in degraded savanna and farmland in northernmost areas from Sokoto to Lake Chad, south to Zaria. Sharland and Wilkinson (1981) suggest that *minor* may be migratory in the Kano/Zaria area moving north in the wet season. There is a single record of the Palaearctic race *C. g. galactotes*, netted at Kano, 2 Nov 1978 (Wilkinson 1979).
Breeding. C/3 Sokoto, 17 Apr (Bannerman 1951); C/2 Bagauda, 7 Apr (Sharland and Wilkinson 1981).

551. CERCOTRICHAS PODOBE RB

(II.856)   Black Scrub-Robin

Not uncommon resident (*C. p. podobe*) in arid savanna with *Hyphaene* palms and thorn scrub of the northernmost areas, from Sokoto to Lake Chad.
Breeding. "Lake Chad region", Apr-Jun (Bannerman 1936); building Maiduguri, Mar (J.H.E.).

552. PHOENICURUS PHOENICURUS PM

(II.857)   Common Redstart

Common Palaearctic migrant (*P. p. phoenicurus*) in shrubby savanna north of the great rivers, mainly late Sep to mid Apr. Rarely noted in south: Ibadan twice, netted 12 Jan 1966 (R.W.A.) and present 4 weeks continuously in a garden, Jan 1956 (J.H.E.); Burutu, Dec 1952 (R.E.S.). Of 10 birds ringed at Kano 2 were retrapped following year (R.E.S.). One bird ringed in Kano trapped in Algeria.

553. SAXICOLA TORQUATA RB

(II.828)   Common Stonechat

Common resident (*S. t. salax = adamauae*) of montane grassland and montane forest edge on both Obudu and Mambilla plateaux and could occur in other highland areas of the Nigeria/Cameroon border. No evidence of immigration from the Palaearctic.
Breeding. Fledgling with both parents Obudu plateau, 4 Mar 1960 (J.H.E.).

554. SAXICOLA RUBETRA PM

(II.829)   Whinchat

Common to locally abundant Palaearctic migrant, late Sep to early May, throughout the main savannas, preferring degraded savanna and farmland; less common in coastal savanna of southwest and in southeast noted only at Calabar, and the Obudu and Mambilla plateaux (Ash and Sharland 1987). Passage is conspicuous spring and autumn in some areas, especially in the north, where few overwinter. Birds ringed Nigeria recovered at Tripoli and in Poland.

555. OENANTHE LEUCOPYGA ?V

(II.816)   White-crowned Black Wheatear

Only 2 sightings: Malamfatori, 30 Aug 1963 (A.J.H.) and near Maiduguri, undated (J.A.B.).

556. OENANTHE OENANTHE PM

(II.811)   Northern Wheatear

Common Palaearctic migrant (*O. o. oenanthe*), late Sep to mid Mar, on bare ground of farmland and degraded savanna throughout the area north of the great rivers; a few straggle south of the Middle Niger to Ibadan (J.H.E.) and the coast at Lagos (J.B.H.), but south of the Benue only reported at Calabar (R.E.S.) and on the Mambilla Plateau (P.H.). Near Lake Chad passage is earlier in autumn and later in spring than elsewhere.

557. OENANTHE HISPANICA PM

(II.814)   Black-eared (Spanish) Wheatear

Uncommon but regular Palaearctic migrant (*O. h. hispanica*) to arid savanna across the north from Sokoto to Lake Chad. Both white- and black-throated phases occur. At Kano a bird stayed in one place, Jan-Mar 1964, to reappear (?same bird) in Nov, was ringed 11 Dec 1964 and remained till mid Feb; it returned to same site autumn 1965, staying till late Feb 1966 (R.E.S.). The only positive record of *O. h. melanoleuca* is from the Jos Plateau, the most southerly record for the species (MP&G), where the nominate race has also been sighted. This requires substantiation since BoA gives the winter range of *melanoleuca* as "Sahel west to Mali . . ."

558. OENANTHE DESERTI ?V

(II.813)   Desert Wheatear

Only a few records, racial determination and provenance unknown but likely to be *O. d. homochroa* (BoA). Sightings at Malamfatori, 15 Feb 1965 (A.J.H.), male Sokoto, Jan (Mundy & Cook 1972-3), 2-3 sightings in Hadejia wetlands area (M.D.) and Bama ridge (south of Maiduguri), Feb (P.H.).

559. OENANTHE BOTTAE Afm/B

(II.817)   Red-breasted Wheatear

Seasonally not uncommon (*O. b. heuglini*) in degraded savanna, markedly on recently burnt ground, throughout the area north of the great rivers. A single

Nov record from Obudu town (Heaton & Heaton 1980) requires substantiation. Almost all data fit the pattern of a "hump-back bridge" migrant (Elgood *et al.* 1973) – present in northern Guinea Savanna Oct-Mar (when it breeds), moving north in rains to Sudan and Sahel zones. Local movements to recently burnt areas obscure the broad migration picture.

Breeding. From Zaria and various localities on the Jos Plateau to Kari, Jan-Apr; double brooding in the same nest (D.E.McGregor).

560. OENANTHE ISABELLINA   PM

(II.812)   Isabelline Wheatear

New species for Nigeria. Uncommon but regular Palaearctic migrant to the dry area north of the Hadejia Wetlands in recent years (M.D.), perhaps as a consequence of the southerly spread of the Sahel drought zone. Recently, single Katsina, 7 Feb 1994 (I.D.).

561. CERCOMELA FAMILIARIS   RB

(II.820)   Red-tailed Chat

Locally common resident (*C. f. falkensteini*) on bare rocky ground and along erosion gullies in the Guinea Savanna, notably over much of the Jos Plateau. Extends north in the Sudan zone to Sokoto, Katsina and Gwoza in the Mandara Mts. and southward to Igbetti just south of the Middle Niger and to Ogoja and the approaches to the Obudu Plateau south of the Benue.

Breeding. Zaria to Kari and the Jos Plateau, south to the Benue, Mar-May.

562. MYRMECOCICHLA AETHIOPS   RB

(II.826)   Northern Ant-eater Chat

Common resident (*M. a. aethiops*) in open savanna and farmland of the Sudan and Sahel zones and in parts of the Jos Plateau as far south as Kurra (M.Ho).

Breeding. 7 nests with eggs Sokoto, Jun-Jul (M&C); feeding young Jos area, May (V.S.).

563. MYRMECOCICHLA NIGRA   R(B)

(II.825)   Sooty Chat

Uncommon and very local resident in grassy savanna. Sightings only from Sokoto to Zaria in west, Yankari Nat. Park (Green 1989), the Gashaka-Gumti Nat. Park (Green 1990), and the Mambilla plateau, where it is "widespread and frequent" (P.H.). Usually reported singly, but "2 pairs Katabu 22 Apr 1967 and several along Potiskum-Maiduguri road 22 Dec 1960" (M.S.).

Breeding. No records anywhere in West Africa.

564. MYRMECOCICHLA ALBIFRONS   RB

(II.821)   White-fronted Black Chat

Not uncommon resident (*M. a. frontalis*) locally in savanna woodland, especially along erosion gullies throughout the Guinea zone. Sparse in southwest, recently recorded Lekki Peninsula near Lagos (Ash and Sharland 1987), and Okomu oil-palm plantation (P.H.), but common in southeast at Enugu, Owerri and Serti; several times observed around Calabar and in the central south around Warri and Sapele. An isolated (unconfirmed) sighting at Malamfatori is the only northerly record.

Breeding. Mostly from Zaria and the Jos Plateau, Dec-Apr, but adults feeding fledglings (twice) at Sapele in Mar (J.B.H.) shows it also breeds in the south of its range.

565. MYRMECOCICHLA CINNAMOMEIVENTRIS   RB

(II.823) Mocking Cliff-Chat

Not uncommon resident (*M. c. coronata*) around inselbergs, mainly in the Guinea savannas, less common north to Sokoto, Katsina, Kano, and to south of the middle Niger to Igbetti and Eruwa; south of the Benue only on the Obudu Plateau.

Breeding. Dec-May (BoA); Jos Plateau, mainly Mar-May.(V.S.).The merging of *M. coronata* in *M. cinnamomeiventris* (White 1962 and BoA), regarded by Bannerman and MP&G as separate species, is still open to debate. Gray (1968) noted both at Obudu, with *cinnamomeiventris* "at 3000 ft on rocks along the approach road" while *coronata* "occurs at a higher altitude (4200 ft) in the same area" They may simply be colour morphs however.

566. MONTICOLA SAXATILIS   PM

(II.808) Mountain Rock Thrush

Uncommon but widespread and regular Palaearctic migrant, late Oct to early Apr, in open savanna (not necessarily rocky) throughout the area north of the great rivers and also Igbetti in south (F.C.S.).

567. MONTICOLA SOLITARIUS   VPM

(II.809) Blue Rock Thrush

Rare, perhaps vagrant, Palaearctic migrant (*M. s. solitarius*) to inselbergs, rocky places and perhaps quarries. Only 4 localities, all westerly: Igbetti, collected 3 Dec 1960 (F.C.S.); sightings Sokoto (Dobbs 1959) and once 2 together there (Mundy & Cook 1972-73); Zaria, 24-29 Mar 1966 (C.H.F.) and 29 Oct 1967 (N.J.S.); and Shasha (in forest zone) (S.G.C.). All records late Oct to late Mar.

568. ZOOTHERA CROSSLEYI   RB

(II.801) Crossley's Ground-Thrush

Uncommon resident (*Z. c. crossleyi*) in montane forest in the southeast. A male was collected at the Obudu Plateau (Serle 1957) and there have been several sightings there since (P.M. & M.D.); 2 birds trapped there, Nov 1985 (Ash and Sharland 1987). Recorded in the Gotel Mts and on the Mambilla Plateau by Ash et al. (1989).

Breeding. Not reported, but "Kupe (Cameroon) and Obudu (breeding condition), April to June" (MP&G).

[ZOOTHERA PRINCEI   RB

(II.804)   Grey Ground-Thrush

A single sighting: "Umuagwu, on 3 August 1953, in primary forest a thrush was seen momentarily but clearly as it returned to its nest.... It was not *Z. cameronensis* Sharpe: it was almost certainly *Z. princei*" (Serle 1957). Hall & Moreau (1970) have a map locality for *cameronensis* at this point which is likely to be an error. No other records, nor for *cameronensis*, but *princei* was netted once at Korup, just over the Cameroon border (Thomas 1991).

Breeding. The nest mentioned above had C/3 but "Two days later ... appeared deserted" and the bird was therefore not met again.]

569. TURDUS PELIOS*   RB, Afm/B

(II.796)   African Thrush*

Locally common resident (*T. p. saturatus*), often suburban, from the coast north to the limits of the Guinea zone; less common north to Kano and Nguru where a singing male present Jul 1990 (M.D.). Also a partial migrant, numbers increase in wet season at Zaria (C.H.F.) and Kano (R.E.S.) and similarly increase to form flocks at Ibadan in the dry season (J.H.E.).

Breeding. Lagos to Kano, Apr-Sep.

*The species is called *T. libonyanus* (Kurrichane Thrush) by Bannerman, *T. olivaceus* (Olive Thrush) by MP&G, while White includes it in *T. pelios*, to which MP&G give the name African Thrush. The English name African Thrush is preferred since the other two English names are used commonly for different thrush species in other parts of the continent.

SYLVIIDAE

[CETTIA CETTI   Rejected

(II.873)   Cetti's Warbler

The Kano record of 2 birds mist-netted, Apr 1964 (R.E.Sharland), reported in Elgood (1981) has since been withdrawn by the observer on the grounds of possible misidentification.]

570. BRADYPTERUS BABOECALA   RB

(II.884)   African Bush-Warbler

Rare and very local resident, but probably overlooked since it skulks in swamps and reed beds. Known from the following localities: Onitsha, where Serle (1957) collected 3 specimens of *B. b. centralis*; Kazaure and Kano where R.E.S. reports it "resident locally in reed beds", racially undetermined; and Obubra where Serle heard it singing. White (1960) recognises *B. b. chadensis* from "Lake Chad" but there is no positive record within Nigeria.

Breeding. One of the Onitsha birds was a juv. male, taken 24 May. Breeds west Cameroon, Jun and Aug (Serle 1981).

571. BRADYPTERUS LOPEZI* R(B)

(II.891)   Cameroon Scrub-Warbler

Perhaps not uncommon resident (*B. l. bangwaensis*) in bracken and brambles at the Obudu Plateau, where it was collected by Serle (1957) and has been sighted by others since (P.M., M.D. and Ash *et al.* 1989). Also common in the ground stratum of montane forest and adjacent rank growth in the Gotel Mts. and Leinde Fadali (Mambilla Plateau), where further specimens were collected (Ash *et al.* 1989).

Breeding. No records, but "Cameroun (breeding condition), July and August" (MP&G).

* Dowsett-Lemaire and Dowsett (1989), on the basis of morphology and voice, consider *bangwaensis* is more closely allied to *B. lopezi* than to *B. cinnamomeus*, and may even warrant full specific status.

572. MELOCICHLA MENTALIS RB

(II.989)   Moustached Grass-Warbler

Not uncommon resident (*M. m. mentalis*) in rank grass with bushes, usually near water, in the Guinea Savanna and the Derived Savanna. Southward, a very few records to the coast at Badagri and Bonny, northwards to c.11°N at Zaria and Aliya.

Breeding. From Ibadan north to Zaria and the Jos Plateau, Apr- Jul.

573. SCHOENICOLA BREVIROSTRIS R(B)

(II.904)   Fan-tailed Grassbird

Probably locally not uncommon resident (*S. b. alexinae*) in coarse grass hollows along mountain streams. Collected or mist-netted on "steep slopes of Mt. Kolukoshon at about 4500 feet" (Serle 1957), at Obudu Plateau (F.C.Sibley) and on the Mambilla Plateau (P.H.).

Breeding. No records but "Sierra Leone (breeding condition), July" (MP&G).

[LOCUSTELLA NAEVIA ?VPM

(II.875)   Grasshopper Warbler

A single sight record: in marsh grass at Ilorin Reservoir, 2 Jan 1975 (H.E.Axell). Possible confusion with a *Cisticola* sp means record needs substantiation. However, 5 netted Ghana, 1985, 1987 (Hedenstrom *et al.* 1990).]

574. LOCUSTELLA LUSCINIOIDES PM

(II.876)   Savi's Warbler

Uncommon Palaearctic migrant (*L. l. luscinioides*) to swampy places in the northernmost areas. Birds have been mist-netted as follows: 3 at Malamfatori; 3 at Kano (2 in reed beds, 1 in suburban garden) (R.E.S.); 6 at Jekara between Nov 1981 and Feb 1982 (Wilkinson and Aidley 1983). One of the Jekara birds was in advanced state of primary moult (22 Nov) suggesting at least temporary residence.

575. ACROCEPHALUS SCHOENOBAENUS   PM
(II.882)   Sedge Warbler

Locally abundant Palaearctic migrant, mostly Oct-Apr, overall Sep-May, to reed-beds and wetland grasses throughout the area north of the great rivers. An increase in numbers at Kano in Mar-Apr may represent birds on passage (Sharland and Wilkinson 1981). In southwest several have been netted at Ibadan (J.A.Br), one near Abeokuta (J.A.B.), once sighted Lagos (D.I.M.W.) and Lekki peninsula 4 Jan 1991 (A.M.N.); only records in southeast, Onitsha (Serle 1957) and Serti (P.H.). A bird ringed Malamfatori was recovered in Russia. At Kano several birds have been retrapped in subsequent years.

576. ACROCEPHALUS SCIRPACEUS   PM
(II.878)   Eurasian Reed Warbler

Common Palaearctic migrant (*A. s. scirpaceus*) in reed-beds and marshes, but also in dry bush areas, chiefly on spring passage in the northernmost areas from Sokoto to Lake Chad. Most do not stay, as few are met further south, though recorded to the coast at Lagos and Calabar and "mid-winter" occurrences at Ibadan and Enugu are regular. A bird ringed in Austria was retrapped near Maiduguri and another ringed in Belgium was recovered in south-eastern Nigeria (Dowsett *et al.* 1988).

577. ACROCEPHALUS BAETICATUS   R(B),?Afm/B
(II.881)   African Reed Warbler

Status unclear through close similarity to *A. scirpaceus* (Dowsett-Lemaire and Dowsett 1987). Has been mist-netted at 4 localities since first recorded "Lake Chad" (Bates 1930): Malamfatori, Mar 1963 (J.H.E.) and Mar-Apr 1967 and 1968 (Lake Chad Expedition); Ibadan, 14 Mar 1969 (J.H.E. with R.W.A.); Serti "netted occasionally through Oct and Nov in a small marshy area" (P.H.); Jekara Dam, netted every month from Oct 1981 to Jun 1982, and again in Oct 1982 (Wilkinson and Aidley 1983). The Jekara records suggest that it may be a local migrant (as it is elsewhere in Africa).

Breeding. No records for anywhere in West Africa, but Fry *et al.* (1974) state "were ready to breed from April onward" at Malamfatori and at Jekara "2 heavy birds caught on 6 April and 3 May may have been females about to lay eggs" (Aidley & Wilkinson 1987b).

[ACROCEPHALUS DUMETORUM   Rejected
(II.880)   Blyth's Reed Warbler

Birds collected at Malamfatori, Mar 1963 (J.H.E., P.W. and A.J.H.) and Mar-Apr 1967 and 1968 (Lake Chad Expeditions) formerly believed to be *A. dumetorum* (vide Elgood 1982) are now considered to represent a population of *A. baeticatus* (Fry *et al.* 1974).]

578. ACROCEPHALUS PALUSTRIS   PM
(II.879)   Marsh Warbler

Probably rare Palaearctic passage migrant. MP&G state "This Warbler can hardly be distinguished from the Reed Warbler", and "No definite records [in West Africa], but almost certainly occurs" if only on passage to southern Africa. One bird netted at Malamfatori, 7 Sep 1965 (R.J.D.) was identified as *palustris*, and at Pandam Wildlife Park they were said to be "fairly common around Lake, Sep-Oct" (C.Smeenk). N.B. the Kano record given in Elgood (1981) was later withdrawn (Sharland and Wilkinson 1981) since there was insufficient evidence to separate it from Eurasian Reed Warbler.

579. ACROCEPHALUS ARUNDINACEUS   PM
(II.877)   Great Reed Warbler

Regular and common Palaearctic migrant (*A. a. arundinaceus*) in reed-beds and grassy wetlands, mainly to southern areas, Oct-Mar, but also met in central and northern areas. Persistent song makes it more conspicuous than its congeners. A bird ringed in Austria was recovered in southeast Nigeria (Dowsett *et al.* 1988), and there has also been a recovery of a bird ringed in Germany.

580. ACROCEPHALUS RUFESCENS   RB
(II.892)   Greater Swamp Warbler

Common resident *A. r. rufescens* in reed-beds, papyrus and grassy wetlands throughout the country. Birds from Malamfatori and Nigerian shores of Lake Chad are possibly *A. r. chadensis*, though this has not been proven.

Breeding. Numerous records, all south of the great rivers; 8 nests Sapele, Apr-Oct (Serle 1958), perhaps double-brooded.

581. ACROCEPHALUS GRACILIROSTRIS   RB
(Not in MP&G)   Lesser Swamp Warbler

A new species for Nigeria. First "netted in *Typha* reed beds at Jekara in May 1981 (D.J.A.) and repeatedly from November 1981 until August 1982" (Wilkinson & Aidley 1982). No other records from Nigeria but Hall and Moreau (1970) show a locality on the northern shore of Lake Chad. Probably overlooked elsewhere in similar habitat.

Breeding. Nestling Jekara, 21 Apr 1983; female Jekara, laid egg whilst confined in bird bag, 23 Apr 1983 (R.E.S.); juvs. netted Jekara, May-Jun (Aidley & Wilkinson 1987b).

582. HIPPOLAIS PALLIDA   PM, RB
(II.872)   Olivaceous Warbler

Two distinct populations: (i) *H. p. laeneni* (formerly called Pallid Tree Warbler *H. p. pallida*), a not uncommon breeding resident in acacia woodland across the north from Sokoto to Lake Chad south to Zaria and the Jos Plateau; (ii) *H. p. opaca* (formerly called Opaque Tree Warbler), a not uncommon Palaearctic migrant throughout, south to Lagos and Sapele, in a wide range of open habitats. Netted Kano, Jan, Mar, May, Jun (Sharland & Wilkinson 1981). At Malamfatori, of 26 ringed on autumn passage, 24 were definitely *H. p. opaca*, 2 could have been another Palaearctic migrant *H. p. elaeica* (Dowsett 1969).

Breeding. Only noted near Malamfatori (*H. p. laeneni*), Mar-Jun (R.J.D., C.H.F., J.H.E.).

583. HIPPOLAIS OLIVETORUM   VPM

(Not in MP&G)   Olive-tree Warbler

Vagrant Palaearctic migrant. A single record: netted Kano, 22 Oct 1971 (R.E.S.).

584. HIPPOLAIS POLYGLOTTA   PM

(II.870)   Melodious Warbler

Not uncommon Palaearctic migrant in wooded savanna, forest clearings and suburban gardens south of the great rivers, Nov-Apr. In the north at Kano "common on autumn passage but rarely seen in spring" (Sharland & Wilkinson 1981), and "Most of the captures ... were between mid-September and late October, with occasional birds in November and from January to March" (Aidley & Wilkinson 1987a).

585. HIPPOLAIS ICTERINA   PM

(II.871)   Icterine Warbler

Not uncommon Palaearctic migrant, mainly on spring passage, Feb-May, throughout from Kano and Lake Chad south to the coast at Lagos and Calabar. On autumn passage, 3 Sep-19 Oct, at Malamfatori (R.J.D.) and netted Yankari, Dec (M&G). In the south, mostly in wooded savanna, or savanna-like forest enclaves.

586. CHLOROPETA NATALENSIS   R(B)

(II.753)   Yellow Flycatcher-Warbler*

Probably not uncommon resident (*C. n. batesi*) at the Obudu and Mambilla Plateaux; collected at Obudu (Serle 1957) and by F.C. Sibley and netted at Mambilla by P.Hall. Nigeria's eastern highlands lie at the extreme western edge of the known range, but there is a probable sighting at Mbaakon (H.H.G.) and a more dubious one of a pair at Zaria (J.H.E.).

Breeding. No records but Cameroon, Sep-Feb (MP&G).

* Placed by MP&G in *Muscicapidae* (*sensu strictu* = *Muscicapinae*) hence the inappropriate English name.

587. CISTICOLA ERYTHROPS   RB

(II.969)   Red-faced Cisticola

Locally common resident (*C. e. erythrops*) in rank grass of forest clearings, farms and suburban gardens from Calabar to Lagos, becoming more sparse northward to Kainji, Nsukka and Serti. Records north of the great rivers at Zaria (C.H.F.), Kaduna, Kafanchan, Jos Plateau (M.Ho.) and Falgore Game Reserve (Wilkinson and Beecroft 1985) in tall grass near rivers with forested banks.

Breeding. MP&G quote Apr-Oct, but adults seen with young juvs. Sapele, Jan (J.B.H.); C/3 Abeokuta, 26 Jun (Serle 1950).

588. CISTICOLA CANTANS RB

(II.968) Singing Cisticola

Common resident in rank grass usually near streams throughout the Guinea Savanna zone, south to Ibadan and near Lagos (Tarkwa) and to Enugu where Serle (1957) found it "extremely common", collecting a long series, clearly showing *C. c. swanzii* extends across most of Nigeria. In northeast between Maiduguri and Lake Chad *C. c. concolor* occurs, but demarcation line between races is unknown though in west, Zaria (11°N) and centrally, Kano (12°N) are most northerly localities of *concolor*.

Breeding. At north of known range (Kaduna, Zaria and Kano), Jun-Aug. Serle's Enugu series included specimens in breeding condition, one as late as Oct. No other southerly records.

589. CISTICOLA LATERALIS RB

(II.961) Whistling Cisticola

Locally not uncommon resident (*C. l. lateralis*) in wooded savanna bordering forest patches or near streams, from the coast at Lagos and Sapele north to Ibadan, Agenebode and Enugu with a few more northerly records to Kishi. Also found at Kagoro on southern slopes of Jos Plateau (Dyer *et al.* 1986) and at 1500 m on Chappal Waddi (Green 1990).

Breeding. No nests, but immatures with adults Sapele, May and Aug (J.B.H.); male in breeding condition Lagos, Jun (Sander 1957) and males with enlarged gonads Abeokuta, Oct and Nov (Serle 1950).

590. CISTICOLA ANONYMUS R(B)

(II.963) Chattering Cisticola

Common resident locally in reed beds and grasses flanking rivers in the forest zone right across the country from Lagos to Calabar, mainly in the sub-coastal area, but also north to Ife (R.F.).

Breeding. Male with enlarged testes Calabar, 24 Dec 1948 (Marchant 1953); west Cameroon, all months (Serle 1981).

591. CISTICOLA CHUBBI RB

(II.966) Chubb's Cisticola

Common resident in montane grassland with bracken, and forest edge at the Obudu and Mambilla Plateaux, the Gotel Mts. and Chappal Hendu. Earlier sightings at Obudu (J.H.E., T.R-S. and P.M.) substantiated by netting, Jul 1980 (M.D.). Recorded Chappal Hendu (Green 1990), Gotel Mts. and Leinde Fadali

(Ash *et al.* 1989). No specimens collected; race may be *discolor*, which occurs Mt. Cameroon (Eyckerman and Cuvelier 1982), or more probably *adametzi*.

Breeding. Feeding 2 fledglings Obudu, 17 Nov 1985 (Ash 1990); breeds west Cameroon, Nov, Dec, Mar and Apr, (Serle 1981).

592. CISTICOLA ABERRANS   RB

(II.964)   Rock-loving Cisticola

Locally not uncommon resident (*C. a. petrophila*) on inselbergs throughout the Guinea Savanna, especially on the Jos Plateau; also north to Rano (Beecroft and Wilkinson 1983) and Mubi (J.A.B.) and in southwest as far south as Idanre, but no records from southeast.

Breeding. C/3 Jos, 30 May 1964 (M.H.); C/2 Vom, 17 Jul (V.S.); feeding young Ririwai, Jun (P.B.)

593. CISTICOLA RUFICEPS   RB

(II.979)   Red-pate Cisticola

Locally not uncommon resident (*C. r. guinea*) in grassy thorn scrub across the north from Sokoto to Maiduguri and south to Zaria, where C.H.F. found it common, Kafanchan and the Jos Plateau.

Breeding. C/4 Kafanchan, 26 Aug (Bannerman 1951); fledgling Zaria, 1 Oct (C.H.F.).

594. CISTICOLA DORSTI   ?R(B)

(Not in MP&G)   Dorst's Cisticola

New species for Nigeria. Recently separated from *C. ruficeps* by bioacoustic analysis (Chappuis and Erard 1991), but found on collection to have morphometric difference chiefly in the greater length of the tail feathers. Range in Nigeria not yet clear but certainly from Gusau to Maiduguri.

Breeding. No data. Presumed to be resident breeding species like *C. ruficeps*.

595. CISTICOLA GALACTOTES   RB

(II.970)   Winding Cisticola

Common resident in swamps and reed-beds throughout from the coast to Sokoto and Lake Chad. There are positive records of *C. g. zalingei* in northeast and Zaria, and of *C. g. amphilecta* from the valleys of the great rivers south to the coast at Lagos and to Onitsha; probably the 2 races have this north and south distribution.

Breeding. From Sokoto to the coast, probably very protracted, Mar- Dec.

596. CISTICOLA ROBUSTUS   R(B)

(II.973)   Stout Cisticola

New species for Nigeria. Only recorded at Gangirwal and Chappal Waddi (Gotel Mts.) where common in rank growth above 1900 m (Ash *et al.* 1989).

Breeding. No records.

597. CISTICOLA NATALENSIS RB

(II.974) Croaking Cisticola

Common resident (*C. n. strangei*) in moist grassy areas and degraded farmland savanna of the Guinea zone, only sparse southwards to Abeokuta (Serle 1950), Lagos (Sander 1957), Okigwi (Serle 1957) and the Obudu Plateau. Northern limit is c.11°N at Zaria, Falgore and Zonkwa.
Breeding. Zaria south to Owerri, May-Oct; southerly records tend to be earlier.

598. CISTICOLA BRACHYPTERUS RB

(II.975) Siffling Cisticola

Locally common resident (*C. b. brachypterus*) in grassland with small trees (for song perches) from coastal savanna at Lagos north to Zaria, the Jos and Obudu Plateaux.
Breeding. Lagos, Abeokuta and Enugu north to Zaria and Ririwai, May-Sep.

599. CISTICOLA RUFUS R(B)

(II.977) Rufous Cisticola

Uncommon resident, perhaps overlooked, in grassy savanna with some trees (for song perches). Mostly in valleys of the great rivers, but also south to Eke (Serle 1957) and north to Maiduguri (Bannerman 1939) and Kirikasama, where collected (Sharland & Wilkinson 1981).
Breeding. No records. Ghana: adult carrying food, Jul; feeding fledglings, Nov (see Grimes 1987).

[CISTICOLA TROGLODYTES Rejected

(II.978) Foxy Cisticola

Not substantiated as a Nigerian species. Bannerman (1939,1953) in discussing range states "and Nigeria" without quoting any locality. There is no BMNH skin and Hall & Moreau (1970) have no Nigerian locality. The nearest reported record is a bird collected at 15°30'N, 3°18'E in Mali, Aug (Lamarche 1981). Though included in the Provisional Checklist (Elgood 1964) it should now be rejected.]

600. CISTICOLA JUNCIDIS RB

(II.953) Zitting Cisticola

Uncommon resident (*C. j. uropygialis*), usually in wet grassland, from Lagos to Sokoto and Malamfatori on Lake Chad, but only the Serti area south of the Benue (P.H. and Green 1990). May be overlooked despite conspicuous courtship flight as this occurs in the rains, when its habitat is difficult to approach.
Breeding. Reported only in north from Zaria, Kano and the Jos Plateau, Jun-Oct.

601. CISTICOLA ARIDULUS R(B)

(II.954) Desert Cisticola

Uncommon resident (*C. a. aridulus*) in dry short grass country right across the extreme north from Sokoto, Katsina and Kano to Lake Chad, south to Potiskum. May be overlooked since conspicuous only when breeding in the rains, when its habitat is difficult to approach.
Breeding. No records, but must breed at the peak of the rains, probably Jul-Sep. Nesting Niger Republic, Jun-Jul (Bates 1933).

602. CISTICOLA EXIMIUS RB

(II.958) Black-necked Cisticola

Not uncommon resident (*C. e. occidens*) in grassy valleys (fadamas) mainly in the Guinea savanna from Borgu south of the middle Niger to much of southeast (Enugu, Nsukka, Okigwi), north to Zaria, the Jos Plateau and Potiskum.
Breeding. Female with 3 "large yolking eggs in the ovary" Enugu, 9 Jul (Serle 1957); Zaria, C/4, 15 Nov and "pulli', 15 Sep (C.H.F.).

603. PRINIA SUBFLAVA RB

(II.982) Tawny-flanked Prinia

Common resident in grassy forest clearings and savanna grassy swamps through most areas of the entire country, *P. s. melanorhyncha* in south, *P. s. subflava* in north, but a cline probably obscures their racial boundary.
Breeding. Lagos north to Kano, Jun-Nov.

604. PRINIA LEUCOPOGON R(B)

(II.983) White-chinned Prinia

Probably uncommon resident (*P. l. leucopogon*) whose westward range limit just enters Nigeria. First recorded at forest edges at Calabar (netted, R.E.S., subsequently seen P.M.). At Mambilla Plateau "common at edges of *Eucalyptus* plantations" (P.H.).
Breeding. No records but "Cameroun, practically throughout the year" (MP&G).

605. PRINIA BAIRDII R(B)

(II.986) Banded Prinia

Probably uncommon resident (*P. b. bairdii*) but only recorded at montane forest edge at the Obudu Plateau, 3 together on each of 2 days, 16-17 Apr 1977 (P.Mackenzie); at least 4 pairs in similar locality, 4 Apr 1988 (F.D-L., R.J.D.).
Breeding. No records but "Cameroun at least from April to September" (MP&G).

606. PRINIA ERYTHROPTERA RB

(II.988) Red-winged Prinia

Locally common resident (*P. e. erythroptera*) in savanna woodlands of the

Guinea zone south to Ibadan and the Afikpo plains, north to Zaria and the Jos Plateau. One rains record near Kano, but no other evidence for a northward rains movement.
Breeding. Enugu north to Vom, Mar-Oct.

607. DRYMOCICHLA INCANA   R(B)

(II.923)   Red-winged Grey Warbler

New species for Nigeria. The only record is of "flocks .... feeding in *Brachystegia eurycoma* trees along the Yim river near Gumti village in February 1988" (Green 1990). This represents a small westerly range extension of a population in Cameroon.
Breeding. No records.

608. UROLAIS EPICHLORA   RB

(II.987)   Green Longtail

Common resident (*U. e. epichlora*) at the edge of montane forest at the Obudu Plateau, and also noted (by voice) at Chappal Wadi by F.D-L. (Ash *et al.* 1989).
Breeding. Adults feeding fledgling, Obudu, Apr (P.M.); breeds Dec, Mar, west Cameroon (Serle 1981).

609. SPILOPTILA CLAMANS   R(B)

(II.990)   Cricket-Longtail

Locally not uncommon resident in thorn-scrub savanna mostly in the Sahel and adjacent Sudan zone of extreme northeast between Nguru and Lake Chad, but "frequent in an *Acacia nilotica* plantation at Achilafia" (Sharland & Wilkinson 1981).
Breeding. No records but "Southern Sahara, November, also June and July" (MP&G); wet season breeder mainly, Chad (Newby 1980). Laying dates: Mauritania, Jun-Aug; Senegal, Jan-Nov (to be published in BoA).

610. APALIS PULCHRA   R(B)

(II.909)   Black-collared Apalis

Noted in Postscript of First Edition. First netted at the Mambilla Plateau by M.D. in early 1981 and subsequently found to be very common in the lower strata of montane forest on the Gotel Mts. and Mambilla Plateau (Ash *et al.* 1989).
Breeding. No records.

611. APALIS NIGRICEPS   R(B)

(II.914)   Black-capped Apalis

Rare resident (*A. n. nigriceps*) in lowland forest canopy. Only confirmed localities are pair at Sapoba, 28 Dec 1960 (seen independently by J.H.E. and F.C.S.) and one at Okomu F.R., 4 Dec 1988 (P.H.). Doubt is cast by Ash *et al.* (1989) on a

record from the Mambilla Plateau, sighted by P.W. (reported by P.H.), on the grounds that it was more probably *A. jacksoni*.
Breeding. No records, but west Cameroon, Oct (Serle 1981).

612. APALIS JACKSONI R(B)

(II.913) Black-throated Apalis

New species for Nigeria. Rare and local resident of montane forest. The only locality is Ngel Nyaki forest (Mambilla Plateau) where at least 6 duetting pairs were called into view by F.D-L. and R.J.D. by tape playback of their call (Ash *et al.* 1989).
Breeding. No records.

613. APALIS FLAVIDA RB

(II.911) Yellow-breasted Apalis

Uncommon resident (*A. f. caniceps*) in coastal mangroves from Lagos to Port Harcourt and in gallery forest north to Zaria and Yankari.
Breeding. B/2 Lagos, Aug (Bannerman 1951), 1 immature Lagos, early Oct (Alexander-Marrack *et al.* 1985).

614. APALIS RUFOGULARIS RB

(II.905) Buff-throated Apalis

Not uncommon resident in lianas of lowland forest, Lagos to Calabar, north to Ife, *A. r. rufogularis* in southeast, *A. r. sanderi* in southwest, but whether or not separated by the Lower Niger is not known. Netted and photographed Kagoro on southern slopes of the Jos Plateau, possibly a third race, but none collected (Dyer *et al.* 1986).
Breeding. Bird at a nest (later abandoned without laying) Abak, 10 Jun (H.H.G.), but Irwin (1987) disputes the identification of this nest as not the typical enclosed structure of *Apalis* spp. Breeds west Cameroon, Feb and Dec (Serle 1981).

615. APALIS CINEREA R(B)

(II.907) Grey Apalis

Common resident (*A. c. cinerea*) in montane forest (mainly upper strata) at the Obudu and Mambilla Plateaux and in the Gotel Mts. down to about 1300 m (Ash *et al.* 1989).
Breeding. No records. Breeds Fernando Po (Bioko), Nov (MP&G), and west Cameroon, Feb-Mar (Serle 1981).

616. PHYLLOLAIS PULCHELLA R(B)

(II.924) Buff-bellied Warbler

Uncommon resident in *Acacia* woodland, mostly in extreme northeast between Maiduguri and Lake Chad, but also west to Kano and south to Potiskum.
Breeding. No records anywhere in West Africa.

Sylviidae

617. CAMAROPTERA BREVICAUDATA   RB

(II.945)   Grey-backed Camaroptera

Abundant resident throughout outside high forest; may well be Nigeria's most numerous bird. *C. b. tincta* in south, perhaps confined to clearings of the forest zone, *C. b. brevicaudata* in north, but a cline certainly exists: Serle (1957) collected 14 at Enugu, half nearest to *tincta*, half nearest to *brevicaudata*.

Breeding. In all vegetation belts except Sahel, Apr-Sep and Nov-Jan; perhaps double-brooded.

618. CAMAROPTERA SUPERCILIARIS   R(B)

(II.946)   Yellow-browed Camaroptera

Uncommon resident in thick secondary growth close to high forest, well distributed in southwest from the coast north to Ibadan and Ife; in southeast, Calabar (P.M.), Umuagwu (Marchant 1953), Ikpan Block, Oban Hills and Forest, Boshi-Okwango Forest (Ash *et al.* 1989).

Breeding. No records. Breeds west Cameroon, Jan (Serle 1981).

619. CAMAROPTERA CHLORONATA   RB

(II.944)   Olive Green Camaroptera

Probably locally not uncommon resident (*C. c. chloronata*) in dense undergrowth of secondary forest occurring in the following localities: the southwest (where 9 netted in short period at Ilaro – J.A.B.); Kagoro on southern slopes of the Jos Plateau (Dyer *et al.* 1986); Enugu and Mamu Forest (Serle 1957); Ngel Nyaki and Leinde Fadali (Mambilla Plateau) (Ash *et al.* 1989); Oban Hills and Boshi-Okwango Forest Reserves (Ash and Sharland 1986).

Breeding. Lagos, "males in breeding condition netted Jan-Oct!" (G&H); 2 juvs., 7 Sep 1969 (D.I.M.W.).

620. POLIOLAIS LOPEZI   R(B)

(II.941)   White-tailed Warbler

Not uncommon resident in montane forest at the Obudu Plateau, unrecorded elsewhere. First sighted 10 Jun 1953 by Serle (1957) who said "The race is likely to be *manengubae*"; several subsequent sightings and once collected (but race not determined), 18 Mar 1961 (F.C.Sibley).

Breeding. No records. Breeds Fernando Po (Bioko), Nov; enlarged gonads west Cameroon, Nov, Jan, Feb (Serle 1981); nest with eggs Mt. Cameroon, 16 Jan 1984 (Tye 1992).

621. EREMOMELA ICTEROPYGIALIS   RB

(II.933)   Yellow-bellied Eremomela

Not uncommon resident (*E. i. alexanderi*) in large trees in arid savanna of the Sudan zone and probably also the Sahel, from Sokoto to Lake Chad.

Breeding. C/2 Achilafia, 2 Feb 1980 (Sharland & Wilkinson 1981).

622. EREMOMELA PUSILLA   RB

(II.935)   Senegal Eremomela

Common resident (*E. p. pusilla*) locally in savanna woodlands of the Guinea zone, south to Ibadan and Abeokuta in southwest, Okigwi, Ofikpo and Obudu (town) in southeast and northward to meet *E. icteropygialis*, with which it can be con- fused in the field, from Sokoto to Kano.

Breeding. C/2 Kafanchan, 22 Feb and 22 May (Bannerman 1951); fledglings netted Kano, 22 Oct (Sharland & Wilkinson 1981).

623. EREMOMELA BADICEPS   RB

(II.938)   Rufous-crowned Eremomela

Probably not uncommon resident (*E. b. badiceps*) in the high canopy of lowland forest, but sparse records only from Ilaro to Owerri. Also in secondary growth north of the main forest to Ife and near Ado-Ekiti.

Breeding. Nest with young high in forest canopy Okomu F.R., 1 Oct 1989, photographed by A.P.L. (P.H.).

624. SYLVIETTA VIRENS   RB

(II.928)   Green Crombec

Common resident at forest edges and clearings and in gardens with good cover, right across the country from the coast north to Ibadan, Akure and Enugu. Also recorded on Chappal Waddi at 1400 m (Green 1990). *S. v. flaviventris* occurs west of the Lower Niger, *S. v. virens* in southeast.

Breeding. Incubating Ibadan, 12 May 1973 (T.R-S); feeding young Calabar, Oct (P.M.).

625. SYLVIETTA DENTI   R(B)

(II.929)   Lemon-bellied Crombec

Perhaps an overlooked resident in dense forest undergrowth, being indistinguishable in the field from *S. virens* (especially *S. v. flaviventris*). Only 3 records: pair collected Sapoba, 28 Dec 1960, one collected Odo-Akure, 12 Jun 1961 (both F.C.Sibley); one heard and seen Ikpan Block by F.D-L., 10 Apr 1988 (Ash *et al.* 1989). The Sapoba bird was said (BMNH) to be nearer to *S. d. hardyi*, which White (1962) states is "known from Sierra Leone and Ghana" than to nominate *denti*, which ranges east from southern Cameroon.

Breeding. No records, but "Cameroun (breeding condition), March and April" (MP&G).

626. SYLVIETTA BRACHYURA   RB

(II.925)   Northern Crombec

Common and widespread resident (*S. b. brachyura*) in savanna woodlands north of the great rivers and in the Borgu area; occasional in southwest as far south as Ibadan and Mekko, and south of the Benue to Enugu, Obudu (town) and Serti.

Breeding. C/2 Argungu, 10 Jun (Bannerman 1951); B/2 Vom, 26 Mar (V.S.); C/2 Jos, 15 Apr (M.H.).

Sylviidae

627. MACROSPHENUS KEMPI — R(B)

(II.949)   Kemp's Longbill

The distinctive voice shows it to be a not uncommon resident locally in the forest of southwest from Lagos to Ife (and probably east to the Lower Niger). Regarded as a race of *M. flavicans* in Elgood (1981) but given full specific status in MP&G and BoA, and this is supported by bioacoustic evidence (Demey & Fishpool 1991).

Breeding. No records.

628. MACROSPHENUS FLAVICANS — RB

(II.947)   Yellow Longbill

Probably not uncommon resident (*M. f. flammeus*) locally in forest east of the Lower Niger.

Breeding. No records, but 2 males in breeding condition collected Owerri, Aug (Marchant 1953). Breeds west Cameroon, May (Serle 1981).

629. MACROSPHENUS CONCOLOR — RB

(II.948)   Grey Longbill

Not uncommon resident in lowland forest from Lagos to the Cameroon border. Surprisingly also in thick riverine forest near Kainji, but elsewhere only in the forest zone.

Breeding. No records. Birds in breeding condition, Nov-Jan (MP&G); west Cameroon, Mar (Serle 1981).

630. HYPERGERUS ATRICEPS — RB

(II.952)   Oriole Warbler (Moho)

Common resident in coastal mangroves of southwest, especially Lagos area. Unrecorded south of the Benue except for the Mambilla Plateau. Not uncommon in gallery forest and woods on inselberg bases from southwest coast north to Zaria and north of the Benue east to the Jos Plateau, Yankari and Aliya.

Breeding. C/2 Lagos, Oct (Sander 1957); 3 nests Vom, Jun-Oct (J.R.L.); breeding Yankari, Jul and Aug (Green 1989).

631. HYLIOTA FLAVIGASTER — RB

(II.760)   Yellow-bellied Hyliota

Locally not uncommon resident (*H. f. flavigaster*) in mature woodland of the Guinea savanna, but numbers seem to be decreasing with habitat erosion (e.g. Serle (1957) collected a long series at Enugu, but Cowper (1977) did not encounter it there). Absent north of the Guinea zone – Ilorin, Enugu and Serti indicate southward limits. More recent sightings: Falgore, 27 Sep 1980 (Sharland & Wilkinson 1981), Falgore uncommon May-Sep (Wilkinson & Beecroft 1985); Gashaka-Gumti Nat. Park, generally uncommon Sep-Apr but frequent Mar 1988 (Green 1990).

Breeding. No positive records, but Serle (1957) indicated a well-defined breeding season during the first half of the rains, evidenced by family parties, mainly Jul-Sep, and juvs. collected at that time.

632. HYLIOTA VIOLACEA   R(B)
(II.762)   Violet-backed Hyliota

MP&G map *H. violacea* across southern Nigeria but Hall and Moreau suggest a break in the range may occur since *nehrkorni* occurs in Ghana and nominate *violacea* from southeast Cameroun to Zaire. Greig-Smith (1977) mentions this species occurring once in "mixed feeding flocks" at Erin-Ijesha in high forest, but was not prepared to claim a "first for Nigeria" since the single sighting was not confirmable. Now Ash claims a sighting "in treetops of degraded forest" at Bashu Okpambe, 4 Feb 1986.

Morony *et al.* place the genus *Hyliota* in the Sylviinae, Bannerman and MP&G in Muscicapidae (i.e. Muscicapinae) and White in Monarchinae.

633. HYLIA PRASINA   RB
(II.1198)*   Green Hylia

Common resident in the lower strata of lowland forest right across the country and in relict forest patches north of the main forest zone to Ibadan, Ife and Enugu – *H. p. prasina* east of the lower Niger but in southwest said to intergrade with *H. p. superciliaris* (White 1962).

Breeding. Owerri "nest building in Oct and Nov but the nests never occupied except for roosting" (Marchant 1953); feeding young Ife, Dec (R.F.).
*Placed by MP&G (and Bannerman) in *Nectariniidae*.

634. PHYLLOSCOPUS HERBERTI   RB
(II.903)   Black-capped Woodland Warbler

Probably not uncommon resident (*P. h. camerunensis*) in montane forest. Noted at the Obudu Plateau by several observers and in Ngel Nyaki forest and Gangirwal (Ash *et al.* 1989).

Breeding. Female Obudu, with soft-shelled egg in oviduct, 20 Dec 1962 (J.H.E.). Breeds west Cameroon, Jan (Serle 1981).

635. PHYLLOSCOPUS TROCHILUS   PM
(II.895)   Willow Warbler

Common Palaearctic migrant (*P. t. trochilus*) to wooded savanna, forest clearings and even mature forest, mid Sep to early Apr. Mostly on autumn and spring passage in north, notably near Lake Chad, but wintering in south, with song especially before departure. A Nigeria ringed bird recovered Belgium; birds ringed France, Spain and Sweden recovered Nigeria.

636. PHYLLOSCOPUS COLLYBITA   PM
(II.896)   Eurasian Chiffchaff

Uncommon, possibly overlooked Palaearctic migrant (*P. c. collybita*), mainly in wooded savanna, late Sep (calling) Malamfatori (R.J.D. and A.J.H.) to Feb ("full song") Kano (R.E.S.). Almost all in north, Lake Natu to Lake Chad south to Zaria, with a single sighting from the south at Lagos (D.I.M.W.). Mostly silent, so probably overlooked. Degree of southward movement thought to vary annually. Netted at Malamfatori and Kano.

637. PHYLLOSCOPUS SIBILATRIX — PM
(II.897)   Wood Warbler

Not uncommon Palaearctic migrant throughout to all habitats with good tree cover, mostly on passage late Aug to Oct and Mar-May, most winter records coming from the south: Lagos (G&H), Owerri (Marchant 1953), Ipake Forest Reserve (J.A.B.) and Ife (R.F.), but at least until mid Dec at Bukuru (M.Ho). A Nigeria ringed bird recovered Greece.

638. PHYLLOSCOPUS BONELLI — PM
(II.898)   Bonelli's Warbler

Not uncommon Palaearctic migrant (*P. b. bonelli*) early Oct-Mar, in acacia woodland and riverine thickets of the extreme north from Sokoto to Lake Chad, once as far south as Zaria (netted 8 Dec 1966, C.H.F.). Mainly silent so probably overlooked, particularly its penetration southward.

639. SYLVIA ATRICAPILLA — PM
(II.864)   Blackcap

Uncommon but regular Palaearctic migrant (*S. a. atricapilla*), generally in thickets, gardens and forest clearings, mainly on autumn and spring passage Nov and Mar-Apr. More often in south but netted at the Jos Plateau, Kano and Malamfatori; also Kainji and Mambilla Plateau. A bird ringed Belgium recovered southwest Nigeria (Dowsett *et al.* 1988).

640. SYLVIA BORIN — PM
(II.863)   Garden Warbler

Common Palaearctic migrant throughout, mainly on passage in the north, overwintering in south. Earliest arrival 23 Aug, Malamfatori (R.J.D.) and some May records, but mainly mid Sep to late Apr. Occupies any habitat offering good cover. Never conspicuous but netting has shown it common south to the coast, and on Obudu and Mambilla Plateaux. Birds ringed Nigeria recovered Finland, Germany, Italy and Zaïre; birds ringed Britain, Germany and Switzerland recovered Nigeria.

641. SYLVIA COMMUNIS — PM
(II.862)   Greater Whitethroat

Common Palaearctic migrant (*S. c. communis*) early Oct to mid Apr, with some earlier and later, to thorn scrub savanna of northernmost areas from Sokoto to

Lake Chad and not uncommon as far south as Zaria and the Jos Plateau; south of the great rivers only to the Kainji Lake Nat. Park (W&W), Ibadan (J.A.Br.) and Ife (R.F.). However, there has been a considerable reduction in numbers as a result of the Sahel drought. Birds ringed Nigeria recovered Libya and Egypt, none yet north of the Mediterranean.

642. SYLVIA CURRUCA   PM

(II.861)   Lesser Whitethroat

Uncommon Palaearctic migrant (*S. c. curruca*), Oct-Mar, in acacia woodland. Most numerous between Maiduguri and Lake Chad, and noted west to Kano and Sokoto and one record from Jos, Nov (D.I.M.W.).

643. SYLVIA NISORIA   VPM

(Not in MP&G)   Barred Warbler

A single record: netted and ringed Malamfatori, 17 Oct 1968 (Dowsett 1968).

644. SYLVIA HORTENSIS   PM

(II.865)   Orphean Warbler

Rare, probably vagrant (*S. h. hortensis*) in acacia woodland of extreme north. Migrant from the western Palaearctic to southern Sahara, very few reaching Nigeria. 3 records: collected at Yo (Bannerman 1939); ringed Malamfatori (P. Jones); sighted Sokoto, 29 Dec 1953 (R.E.S. with K.D.).

645. SYLVIA MYSTACEA   VPM

(Not in MP&G)   Menetries's Warbler

A single record, Gaya Forest Reserve near Kano "in an overgrown dry river-bed", netted, ringed and photographed, 17 Apr 1974 (Best 1975).

646. SYLVIA CANTILLANS   PM

(II.868)   Subalpine Warbler

Not uncommon Palaearctic migrant, Oct-Mar, mostly to acacia woodland or suburban gardens of northernmost areas from Sokoto to Lake Chad south to Zaria. The few collected and the many netted have not been determined racially and may be nominate *cantillans* or *S. c. albistriata* or *S. c. inornata*, all of which White (1960) states winter further east.

MUSCICAPIDAE

647. MELAENORNIS (EMPIDORNIS) PALLIDUS   RB

(II.739)   Pale Flycatcher

Common and widespread resident (*M. p. modestus*) in the savannas south of the great rivers and in northwest. More sparse in northeast, mostly in the Guinea savannas, especially areas degraded by farming. Also south to the coast at Lagos and north into the Sudan zone to Sokoto and Ririwai.

Breeding. Kishi north to Sokoto, mostly May-Jul, overall Feb-Sep.

648. MELAENORNIS EDOLIOIDES   RB

(II.741)   Northern Black Flycatcher

Common and widespread resident (*M. e. edolioides*) in all types of well wooded savanna throughout the Guinea Savanna zone. Less common further south in coastal savanna from Lagos to Badagri and in the Sudan zone northward to Sokoto and Kano.

Breeding. Recorded only in the Guinea zone north of the great rivers, May-Jun.

649. MELAENORNIS (FRASERIA) OCREATUS   RB

(II.745)   African Forest-Flycatcher

Not uncommon resident locally (*M. o. ocreatus*) at forest edges and clearings, from the coast at Lagos and Port Harcourt northward inland to Benin and Ikom.

Breeding. 2 adults feeding juvs. Erin-Ijesha, 4 Oct 1975; female with large ovary and which "almost certainly had a nest" Umuagwu, 31 Oct 1949 (Marchant 1953).

650. MELAENORNIS (FRASERIA) CINERASCENS   RB

(II.746)   White-browed Forest-Flycatcher

Not uncommon resident locally, along small rivers in the forest zone of southwest from Lagos to near Benin. In gallery forest ranges well north of the forest to Kainji, Pandam and Kagoro. The first record for southeast is from Mberubu, north of the forest zone (Marchant 1953); one netted in Nindam F.R., 17 Feb 1980 (Dyer *et al.* 1986).

Breeding. Male in breeding condition Mberubu, 23 Nov 1949. C/2 Lagos, 23 Apr 1971 (J.P.G.), and 23 Apr 1972 (J.H.E.). Female with oviducal egg Kagoro, 17 Feb 1980 (M.G.).

651. MUSCICAPA STRIATA   PM

(II.725)   Spotted Flycatcher

Common Palaearctic passage migrant (only *M. s. striata* identified but probably *M. s. balearica* occurs also) both Sep-Nov and Mar-May, throughout the country, in all types of vegetation except within high forest. Some winter locally in southwest; few records from southeast and only on passage. Birds ringed in Britain, Belgium, Germany and Switzerland recovered in Nigeria.

652. MUSCICAPA GAMBAGAE   R(B)

(II.725)   Gambaga Flycatcher

Rare (or overlooked) resident in shrubby savanna in only 3 areas of northeast:

"50 miles N.E. of Yola" (Bannerman 1936); the Jos Plateau – Kigom Hills (Woods 1967) and Vom (V.S.); near Potiskum (P.B.).
Breeding. Only record: a group including several juvs. near Girei c. 25 km northeast of Yola, 20 Jul 1991 (M.Ho.).

653. MUSCICAPA INFUSCATA   RB
(II.751)   Sooty Flycatcher

Uncommon resident, but locally not uncommon, in lowland mature forest from Gambari to Calabar, usually close to the coast.
Breeding. C/2 near Benin, 17 May 1938 (Bannerman 1951); building Oct and feeding young out of the nest, Owerri, Nov (Marchant 1953); pair with juv. at Bashu 11 Oct 1987, (Ash 1990).

654. MUSCICAPA USSHERI   RB
(II.752)   Ussher's Flycatcher

Hall and Moreau (1970) regarded this form as a superspecies and allopatric with *M. infuscata*, and both White and MP&G give the range as Ghana and Sierra Leone; nevertheless they overlap in Nigeria. Sightings claimed earlier 3-4, mouth of Benin River (P.A.S.) and near Obudu town (H.H.G.) – but doubted by Marchant (1966), were strongly supported with the netting of one (others sighted) at Serti, 23 Dec 1974 (Hall 1977). These localities include lowland and gallery forest. Probably rare but is easily confused with *M. infuscata* which is also uncommon and local in lowland forest.
Breeding. Pair feeding fledgling near Butatong, 19 Nov 1985 (Ash 1990).

655. MUSCICAPA AQUATICA   RB
(II.729)   Swamp Alseonax

Not uncommon resident (*M. a. aquatica*) along wooded rivers and streams of the savannas north of the great rivers to Lake Chad; also south of the Middle Niger to Old Oyo Nat. Park but not south of the Benue.
Breeding. Pair at inaccessible nest thought to contain young at Yo, 25 Mar 1963 (J.H.E.).

656. MUSCICAPA OLIVASCENS   RB
(II.730)   Olivaceous Alseonax

Rare resident in lowland forest, possibly overlooked. A record from Umuahia (W.A. Fairbairn in Bannerman 1936) was queried by Serle (1957) and a sighting from near Mambilla Plateau (P.W.) is also dubious. However, D.N. Johnson has had occasional records for all months near Benin (J.B.H.) and recently noted by J.S.A. in Oban Hills (see below).
Breeding. A pair feeding fledgling in dense forest at Oban Hills sector of Cross River Nat. Park, 1 Oct 1989 (Ash 1990).

657. MUSCICAPA ADUSTA   R(B)

(II.728)   Dusky Alseonax

New species for Nigeria. Common resident of woodland or forest edge in Cameroon mountain area and Fernando Po (Bioko) (MP&G); status in Nigeria probably the same. First Nigerian sighting (by R.E.S., M.D. and R.W.) at Obudu Plateau, Apr 1981, which extends westward the known range of *M. a. sjöstedti*. Further sightings in Gashaka-Gumti Nat. Park, Nov and Dec 1987, where rare, but frequent in Mar 1988 (Green 1990).

Breeding. Cameroon Mt., Mar; season probably prolonged (MP&G). No records in Nigeria.

658. MUSCICAPA EPULATA   R(B)

(II.733)   Little Grey Alseonax

No unequivocal records until 1986, perhaps overlooked in lowland forest, but ranges from Ghana to Zaïre. Bannerman (1936) states "It has not yet been recorded from Nigeria" Greig-Smith (1977) noted it in mixed species flocks in "forest near Erin-Ijesha (c. 07°36′N, 04°45′E)", 4 Oct 1975, but subsequently said (*in litt.*) identification was not sufficiently certain to warrant a "first" for Nigeria. Recently reported as resident but uncommon in Nindam F. R. (Dyer *et al.* 1986).

Breeding. No records, but "Cameroun, at least March to July" (MP&G).

659. MUSCICAPA SETHSMITHI   RB

(II.734)   Yellow-footed Alseonax

A single specimen, from montane forest (perhaps also occurs in lowland forest as elsewhere) – male collected Obudu Plateau, 19 Mar 1961 (F.C. Sibley); an extension of range west from Cameroon into Nigeria. Netted by R.E.S. on Obudu Plateau, Apr 1981, and subsequent records there (M.G. 1984, unpublished MS).

Breeding. Pair feeding a fledgling near Boshi F.R., 20 Nov 1985 (Ash 1990).

660. MUSCICAPA COMITATA   RB

(II.749)   Dusky-blue Flycatcher

Uncommon resident in lowland forest, usually along streams, from Abeokuta to Calabar, north to Ibadan and Imesi-Ile; sighted also at Pandam in relict forest on southern escarpment of the Jos Plateau.

Breeding. May be prolonged (MP&G). Young in nest (an abandoned nest probably of *Malimbus scutatus*) Ibadan, 6 May 1964 (J.H.E.).

661. MUSCICAPA TESSMANNI   R(B)

(II.750)   Tessmann's Flycatcher

Rare resident, possibly overlooked through similarity to *M. comitata* since "both species occur side by side and no difference in habits has been noted" (MP&G). Bates (1930) quotes "measurements of five birds from Gold Coast, Nigeria and

Cameroun" but gives no locality. Bannerman (1936) refers to a specimen from "Shonga on the Niger (Captain Ferryman)" No recent records.
Breeding. Resident breeder in Ivory Coast (Thiollay 1985).

662. MUSCICAPA CASSINI   RB

(II.735)   Cassin's Alseonax

Common resident along rivers and streams of the forest zone west of the Lower Niger, but uncommon generally in southeast. Most records near the coast, but also north of the high forest to Asejire on Ibadan-Ife road and Iwo (J.H.E.).
Breeding. C/2 Imo river (Owerri), 4 Apr (Bannerman 1951); feeding young in nest Araromi, 16 Jun 1960 (J.H.E.); feeding juvs. Sapele, 5 Jun (W.S.); nest with young Sapele, 19 Feb (J.B.H.).

663. MUSCICAPA CAERULESCENS   RB

(II.736)   Ashy Alseonax

Uncommon resident (*M. c. brevicauda*) in lowland forest east of the lower Niger and sighted also (? confused with *M. seth-smithi*) in montane forest on the Obudu Plateau (T.R-S.). Only one certain record from southwest – one collected at Gambari, 23 Apr 1961 (F.C.Sibley), but also sighted in mixed species flocks at Erin-Ijesha, 4 Oct 1975 (Greig-Smith 1977).
Breeding. "Southern Nigeria (building), December" (MP&G).

664. MYIOPARUS GRISEIGULARIS   R(B)

(II.737)   Grey-throated Tit-Flycatcher

Rare resident, only 2 early records, both in lowland forest: Umuagwu (near Owerri), 12 Jun 1949, "The first Nigerian record, representing a westward extension of range" Marchant 1953); Ahoada (still further west), 29 Jun 1952 (Serle 1957). Two seen at the edge of the Ebe River in Ikpan Block 10 Apr, 1988 (Ash et al. 1989).
Breeding. Marchant's Jun specimen was a male with enlarged testes. Recorded as resident breeder in Ivory Coast (Thiollay 1985).

665. MYIOPARUS PLUMBEUS   RB

(II.738)   Grey Tit-Flycatcher

Uncommon but widespread resident (*M. p. plumbeus*) in savanna woodland, but not uncommon locally in gallery forest, from Lagos to Kano but mostly more centrally from Lake Kainji to Yankari, Aliya and Potiskum.
Breeding. Female "two large yolking eggs" Nibbo (near Nsukka), 27 Dec 1954 (Serle 1957); near Kaduna, Mar (C.H.F.).

666. FICEDULA HYPOLEUCA   PM

(II.726)   European Pied Flycatcher

Common and widespread Palaearctic migrant (*F. h. hypoleuca*), in all habitats with trees, avoiding high forest, Oct-Apr. Occurs mainly on passage in autumn and spring north of the great rivers but remains through winter in south (Elgood *et al.* 1966). One ringed Malamfatori recovered Cyprus.

667. FICEDULA ALBICOLLIS   PM

   (II.727)   Collared Flycatcher

Uncommon Palaearctic migrant (*F. a. albicollis*), Sep-Mar. All certain (handled) records are from north (Kano, Jos Plateau to Lake Chad) where perhaps up to 10% of all *Ficedula* flycatchers are this species (Elgood *et al.* 1966). Only 2 southern records: netted at Ife, possibly *F. a. semitorquata* (R.Farmer) and possibly sighted at Lagos (D.I.M.W.). All birds racially determined have been *F. a. albicollis* but *F. a. semitorquata*, which is difficult to distinguish from *F. h. hypoleuca*, may also occur, perhaps only in the south.

PLATYSTEIRIDAE

668. BIAS FLAMMULATUS   RB

   (II.758)   African Shrike-Flycatcher

Uncommon resident (*B. f. flammulatus*), mainly in forest canopy, mostly west of the lower Niger, but also met north of the forest zone in a well- wooded garden at Ibadan (J.H.E.) and in relict forest at Kagoro on southern escarpment of the Jos Plateau (M.D.).
   Breeding. Breeding pair collected Enugu, 14 Apr 1954 (Serle 1957); pair with enlarged gonads collected Idoani, 23 Jun 1961.

669. BIAS MUSICUS   RB

   (II.759)   Black-and-white Shrike-Flycatcher

Locally not uncommon resident (*B. m. musicus*) in the forest zone, not within forest but in clearings, gardens and farms, from Badagri to Calabar north to Ibadan and the approaches to the Obudu Plateau at 650m (Serle 1957).
   Breeding. Not recorded, but an Ibadan female collected 16 Apr 1961 had greatly enlarged ovary (F.C.Sibley).

670. BATIS SENEGALENSIS   RB

   (II.770)   Senegal Batis

Common resident in all types of savanna, virtually everywhere other than in high forest, from the coast at Lagos and Bonny (an old record queried by Serle 1957) to Sokoto and Lake Chad, but most numerous in the Guinea Savanna.
   Breeding. Enugu to Zaria, Feb-Jun.

671. BATIS ORIENTALIS   R(B)

   (II.768)   Grey-headed Batis

Probably uncommon rather than rare resident (*B. o. chadensis*). Very few records,

and only from 2 areas, which are the westernmost edges of its range: just west of Lake Chad from Arege to Malamfatori – skin in BMNH (Boyd Alexander) and sightings (J.A.B.,J.H.& A.J.H.); Mambilla Plateau, netted 11 Sep 1974 (P.H.).
Breeding. No records but "Darfur, April and May" (MP&G).

672. BATIS POENSIS   RB

(II.764)   Fernando Po Batis

Mainland specimens now considered to be a sub-species of *B. poenis* Alexander (*Bull.B.O.Cl.* 112A:280). Probably uncommon in middle storey of lowland high forest rather than rare resident because small and shy and so closely similar to other flycatchers that it may have been overlooked. Almost all specimens collected are from southwest, from Lagos to near Akure and Gambari.
Breeding. Males collected Ondo, 21 Jan 1961, and near Akure, 12 Jun 1961, had enlarged testes (F.C.Sibley). Pair building nest in degraded forest at Bashu, 11 Oct 1987 (Ash 1990).

673. PLATYSTEIRA CYANEA   RB

(II.771)   Brown-throated Wattle-eye (Scarlet-spectacled Wattle-eye)

Abundant resident (*P. c. cyanea*) in mangroves from Badagri to Calabar, less so in forest clearings and gardens, then northward in gallery forest in diminishing numbers to average limit at 10°N, occasionally as far north as Kaduna and Aliya. Noted on the Obudu Plateau. There is no confirmation for Bannerman's view that this species "moves south when the rains are over" (Elgood *et al.*1973).
Breeding. Only south of the great rivers, Dec-Aug, possibly all year.

674. PLATYSTEIRA (DIAPHOROPHYIA) CASTANEA   RB

(II.775)   Chestnut Wattle-eye

Uncommon resident (*P. c. castanea*) in the lower strata of lowland forest right across the country, north to relict forest patches at Ibadan and Enugu and in montane forest at the Obudu Plateau.
Breeding. C/2 near Abak, 26 May 1972 (H.H.G.); courtship Lagos, 11 Mar 1972 (J.H.E.).

675. PLATYSTEIRA (DIAPHOROPHYIA) TONSA   RB

(II.776)   White-spotted Wattle-eye

Rare or very local resident in the underscrub of lowland forest of a very small area in the southeast. Bannerman (1951), quoting Marchant, said it was "probably not uncommon" at Owerri, but it has occurred at only 3 other localities: a male at Omanelu, 5 Aug 1953 (Serle 1957); Umuagwu (BMNH skin); a male in Oban Hills F.R. in company with *P. castanea*, 30 Jan 1987 (Ash 1990). Fairly common in Ikpan Block and a few noted in Oban West, Apr 1988.
Breeding. A pair feeding a juv. Ikpan, 10 Apr 1988 (Ash 1990).

676. PLATYSTEIRA (DIAPHOROPHYIA) BLISSETTI   RB

(II.777)   Red-cheeked Wattle-eye

Uncommon resident in dense secondary forest and relict forest patches of southwest from Lagos to Sapele, north to Ibadan and Ife, and heard regularly at Kagoro on southern escarpment of the Jos Plateau. First record for Nigeria was a pair taken at Enugu, 27 May 1954 (Serle 1957), still the only known locality east of the Lower Niger.

Breeding. Feeding young Lagos, Mar (Sander 1957); 2 adults with 2 juvs. Ilaro, Jan (J.A.B.).

677. PLATYSTEIRA CONCRETA   R(B)

(II.779)   Yellow-bellied Wattle-eye

Rare resident. The 2 earlier records of 16 Jan 1949, "the first Nigerian record" (Marchant 1953), and the female on Obudu Plateau, 15 Mar 1961 (F.C.Sibley), have been supplemented as follows: 2 sightings in the Calabar area in Aug and Nov 1978 (Mackenzie 1979); 2 in forest on the southwestern escarpment of the Obudu Plateau on 4 Apr 1988; at least 5 pairs in forest understory in Oban West, east of Owai, 15 Apr (Ash *et al.* 1989). The sub-species, formerly considered to be *P. c. graueri* = *harterti* requires confirmation.

Breeding. No records in Nigeria. Resident breeder in Ivory Coast (Thiollay 1985).

MONARCHIDAE

678. ERYTHROCERCUS MCCALLII   R(B)

(II.755)   Chestnut-capped Flycatcher

Not uncommon resident (*E. m. nigeriae*) in middle storey and lianas of lowland forest of southwest from Lagos to Sapele, north to Ibadan and Ife. Only one record (*E.m.mccallii*) from southeast: Umuagwu (Serle 1957).

Breeding. No records, but "Cameroun (breeding condition), May, June, September and December" (MP&G).

679. ELMINIA LONGICAUDA   RB

(II.780)   African Blue Flycatcher

Apparently 2 distinct resident populations (*E. l. longicauda*): locally common in mangroves from Lagos to Badagri; and not uncommon in woodlands and gallery forest throughout the Guinea zone from Ilorin and Serti north to Zaria and the Jos Plateau. Only isolated records outside these 2 areas, as at Ofemiri and Obudu Plateau in southeast and Potiskum in northeast.

Breeding. Only reported definitely for the Guinea zone population, Jun-Aug; also building at Gboko, 16 Mar (H.H.G.); mangrove population, display (Lagos), 29 Feb 1972 (J.H.E.).

680. TROCHOCERCUS (ELMINIA) NIGROMITRATUS   RB
   (II.786)   Dusky Crested Flycatcher

Uncommon resident in lowland forest, from near Lagos to Oban (M.G.), also north to Gambari and Benin, but probably occurs wherever mature forest remains.
   Breeding. Pair feeding a fledgling in Okwango F.R., 11 Feb 1987 (Ash 1990).

681. TROCHOCERCUS (ELMINIA) ALBIVENTRIS   RB
   (II.785)   White-bellied Crested Flycatcher

Not uncommon resident (*T. a. albiventris*) in montane forest on the Obudu Plateau; recorded elsewhere only in Gashaka-Gumti Nat. Park in Mar, 1988 (Green 1990).
   Breeding. Female with enlarged ovary, 14 Mar 1961 (F.C.Sibley); male with enlarged testes, 19 Dec 1962 (J.H.E.).

682. TERPSIPHONE (TROCHOCERCUS) NITENS   R(B)
   (II.784)   Blue-headed Crested Flycatcher

Not uncommon resident (*T. n. nitens*) in thick secondary forest of southwest from Lagos to Sapoba, Ibadan and Ife. Only one record in southeast at Umuagwu (Serle 1957) and one in north at Yankari "in dense swamp" (C.G.).
   Breeding. Resident breeder in Ivory Coast (Thiollay 1985).

683. TERPSIPHONE RUFIVENTER   RB
   (II.791)   Black-headed Paradise-Flycatcher

Common resident at forest edges and clearings and in secondary growth right across the country, with rufous-backed *T. r. fagani* (= *T. smithii fagani*) west of the Lower Niger, and grey-backed *T.r.tricolor* in southeast, while those from Bendel State may be intermediate. Found north of the forest zone to Oshogbo (*fagani*), Enugu and the Obudu Plateau (*tricolor*).
   Breeding. Surprisingly little known: 3 females with enlarged ovaries Ilaro, Sep; female with oviducal egg Ede, 27 Sep 1943 (Serle 1950); building Calabar, 2 Apr (P.M.).

684. TERPSIPHONE VIRIDIS   Afm/B, RB
   (II.787)   African Paradise-Flycatcher

Seasonally not uncommon resident (*T. v. ferreti*) in most areas, although its migrations are unclear. In the dry season some move south into the forest zone in southwest to Ibadan, Ilaro and even Lagos; no similar movement reported in southeast. In the rains some move north to Sokoto and Lake Chad. The central savannas have birds present all year. Polymorphic: white-tailed birds conspicuous in forest patches of southwest. The former sub-species *T. v. rufocinerea*, now accorded full specific status, which was earlier reported common near Calabar, has not been recorded since 1979, but in view of these past records *T. v. rufocinerea* is likely to be found in the southeast.
   Breeding. Ilorin north to Maiduguri in the rains, May-Aug.

TIMALIIDAE

Timaliinae

685. ILLADOPSIS CLEAVERI RB

(II.679) Blackcap Illadopsis

Uncommon resident, found close to the ground in forest. Records mostly in southeast (Omanelu, Owerri, Calabar), where the race is *marchanti*. This has also been collected at Ipake F.R. (C.H.F.) in extreme west, suggesting it ranges right across the country. *I. c. batesi* was collected (Serle 1957) in montane forest at the Obudu Plateau, 2 adults with 2 juvs., 11 Jun 1953; the only record.

Breeding. Juvs. Obudu, Jun (above), juv. Omanelu, 5 Aug 1953 (Serle 1957).

686. ILLADOPSIS PUVELI R(B)

(II.677) Puvel's Illadopsis

Uncommon resident (*I. p. strenuipes*) in undergrowth of lowland forest across the forest zone from Lagos to Mamu, north to Ibadan and Ife in the west. Also 2 mist-netted at Kagoro on southern escarpment of the Jos Plateau, 24 Apr 1977 (J.H.E., R.E.S., M.D., M.G.).

Breeding. No records anywhere in Africa.

687. ILLADOPSIS RUFIPENNIS RB

(II.674) Pale-breasted Illadopsis

Not uncommon resident (*I. r. rufipennis*) in lower strata of lowland forest, right across the country from Lagos to Calabar, but not north of the forest zone proper.

Breeding. Not reported, but birds collected in breeding condition Owerri, Jun and Nov (Marchant 1953), and Lagos, (Gee & Heigham 1977). Breeds west Cameroon, Mar, Jul, Aug and Nov (Serle 1981).

688. ILLADOPSIS FULVESCENS RB

(II.678)* Moloney's Illadopsis

Not uncommon resident (*I. f. iboensis*) in thick undergrowth in high forest right across the country, north to Ibadan and Enugu. One mist-netted at Kagoro in relict forest on southern escarpment of the Jos Plateau was retrapped 39 months later in the same area (Dyer *et al.* 1986).

Breeding. Enugu, "two adults and two juveniles just fledged", 9 Aug (Serle 1957).

*White has merged this form in *I. fulvescens*, to which MP&G give the name Brown Illadopsis (II.673), while placing *iboensis* in *I. moloneyanum* (II.678-Moloney's Illadopsis).

689. ILLADOPSIS ABYSSINICA RB

(II.682) Abyssinian Hill-Babbler

New species for Nigeria. Resident, "Very common in understorey and mid-level

tangles of montane forest on Gangirwal and fairly common on Chappal Waddi, 1800-2300 m" (Ash *et al.* 1989). Absent from nearby lower altitude forest and not yet recorded elsewhere, but occurs just across the border in Cameroon (Louette 1981).
Breeding. C/2, 20 Mar 1988 (Ash *et al.* 1989).

690. KAKAMEGA POLIOTHORAX   R(B)

   (II.681)   Grey-chested Illadopsis

Common resident in ground stratum of montane forest at the Obudu Plateau and in the Gotel Mts. (Ash *et al.* 1989).
   Breeding. No records, but in breeding condition in Cameroon, Apr-May, and Nov, Apr in west Cameroon (Serle 1981).

691. TURDOIDES REINWARDTII   RB

   (II.655)   Black-cap Babbler

Locally common resident (*T. r. stictilaema*) in gallery forest in the Guinea savanna zones, extending south to Abeokuta and to coastal savanna near Lagos (Gee & Heigham) in southwest and to Enugu, Obudu (town) and Serti in southeast. Bannerman's (1936) record at Kano seems out of normal range, but also recorded as far north as Zaria and Falgore G.R.
   Breeding. Probably co-operative and protracted: Jagindi, Dec (Bannerman 1936); C/2 Abeokuta, 26 Jun 1942 (Serle 1950).

692. TURDOIDES PLEBEJUS   RB

   (II.661)   Brown Babbler

Common resident in all types of savanna from the great rivers northward and not uncommon in southern savannas, including the coastal strip at Badagri. Too few specimens to clarify distribution of races, but broadly north of the great rivers it is nominate *plebejus*, in southwest *T. p. platycircus* and in the southeast (Enugu) *T. p. cinereus*.
   Breeding. Co-operative; records mostly from the north, with nesting in almost all months.

693. KUPEORNIS GILBERTI   RB

   (II.671)   White-throated Mountain-Babbler

Common resident in montane forest on the Obudu Plateau where it was first discovered as a new species by Serle (1957). Met regularly since, flocks up to 10.
   Breeding. "On 10 June at Obudu, young were being fed by their parents" (Serle 1957); breeds west Cameroon, Oct and Nov (Serle 1981).

694. PHYLLANTHUS ATRIPENNIS   R(B)

   (II.668)   Capuchin Babbler

Not uncommon resident (*P. a. haynesi*), very locally in a small area of southwest encompassed by Lagos, Badagri, Abeokuta and Ibadan; surprisingly not elsewhere in the forest zone. Prefers forest edges and has been seen in gardens at Ibadan (J.H.E.). 4 netted in relict forest at Kagoro on southern escarpment of Jos Plateau, 16 Sep 1979 (M.D.), and sighted there 20 Apr 1987 (P.H.).

Breeding. No records. In Mali local hunters said it nests all year (Lamarche 1981), but this needs substantiation.

Picathartinae

695. PICATHARTES OREAS   RB

   (II.1140)   Red-headed Rockfowl

Undoubtedly the most exciting Nigerian ornithological "find" of the 1980's. First reported within Nigeria by Hall (1981). Subsequently shown by Ash (1987, 1990) to be locally common in undisturbed areas of southeast Nigeria bordering Cameroon – an area hitherto virtually unexplored ornithologically; requires forest habitat with overhanging bare rock faces.

Breeding. Ash (1990) speaks of "94 breeding sites, involving an estimated 500-1000 birds" which were located on two visits in Feb 1987 and Sep-Oct 1987. Breeding season at least Aug-Nov, Ash (1991).

PARIDAE

696. PARUS LEUCOMELAS   RB

   (II.1094)   Black Tit

Common resident (*P. l. guineensis*) in mature woodland of the Guinea and Sudan savannas south to Ilorin and Enugu, but shuns areas degraded by farming. Frequent near Obudu town (Heaton & Heaton 1980).

Breeding. Nest with young birds Kari, 24 Feb (P.B.).

697. PARUS ALBIVENTRIS   R(B)

   (II.1095)   White-breasted Tit

Sighted by P. Mackenzie first in forest near the foot of Obudu Plateau, 16 Apr 1977, and seen again by him on Obudu Plateau in Apr 1981. This species is sufficiently distinctive for this second sighting to confirm the westward extension of range from the Cameroon where it has been reported in several localities.

Breeding. No records anywhere in West Africa.

REMIZIDAE

698. ANTHOSCOPUS PUNCTIFRONS   R(B)

   (II.1099)   Sennar Penduline Tit

Uncommon resident in thorn scrub of the Sahel zone in extreme northeast, mostly close to Lake Chad. Pair collected Logomani, 10 Jul 1960 (F.C.Sibley).

Breeding. Sibley's pair were at a nest.

699. ANTHOSCOPUS PARVULUS   RB
    (II.1100)   Yellow Penduline Tit

Uncommon resident locally in savannas with large trees, mainly in the Sudan zone from Sokoto to Potiskum and Lake Chad but also south to Zaria and Kainji Lake Nat. Park.
Breeding. Argungu, Jun (Serle 1943).

700. ANTHOSCOPUS FLAVIFRONS   R(B)
    (II.1101)   Yellow-fronted Penduline Tit

Probably uncommon rather than rare resident (*A. f. flavifrons*) at forest edges and clearings "but most easily overlooked owing to small size" (Marchant 1953). Only 2 positive localities: 2 males Umuagwu, 17 Oct 1948 and 6 Nov 1949 (Marchant); female Itu, 12 Aug 1954 (Serle 1957). Also an unconfirmed record from near Lagos (J.P.G.), suggesting the range is across the whole forest zone.
Breeding. No records locatable, though MP&G state "Nigeria (breeding condition), November"

SALPORNITHIDAE

701. SALPORNIS SPILONOTUS   R(B)
    (II.1200)   Spotted Creeper

Uncommon resident (*S. s. emini*) in mature savanna woodland of the Guinea zone from Shaki, Enugu and Serti north to Zaria and Kari. Frequent in mixed flocks near Obudu town (Heaton & Heaton 1980).
Breeding. No records but "pairing behaviour (chasing, singing, soliciting) noted in Borgu Game Reserve" (now Kainji Lake Nat. Park), May (Wells & Walsh 1969).

ZOSTEROPIDAE

702. ZOSTEROPS SENEGALENSIS   RB
    (II.1141)   Yellow White-eye

Common resident (*Z. s. senegalensis*) in savanna woodlands, farmlands and gardens from the coast north to the Sudan zone, not recorded in the Sahel of extreme northeast. Found also in forest clearings, but avoids high and secondary forest. *Z.s.stenocricota* is not uncommon at the edge of montane forest at the Obudu Plateau (and possibly the Mambilla Plateau).
Breeding. From Lagos to Argungu, Nov-Jul.

NECTARINIIDAE

703. ANTHREPTES FRASERI   RB
    (II.1194)   Fraser's Scarlet-tufted Sunbird

Common resident (*A. f. cameroonensis*) in lowland forest of southeast (where Serle (1957) collected a long series), much less common in southwest though noted from Lagos north to Gambari (J.H.E.), and netted regularly at Benin (D.N.J.).

Breeding. No nests found, but females in breeding condition Apr and Nov, and juvs. "with unossified skulls" Jan, Apr, Jun, Jul, Aug and Oct (Serle 1957).

704. ANTHREPTES GABONICUS   RB

(II.1197) Brown Sunbird

Common resident in mangroves from Badagri to Port Harcourt (and probably Calabar). Uncommon inland, but noted in gallery forest near Iseyin (J.H.E.), near Kainji (Wells & Walsh 1969) and at Pandam Wildlife Park (C.S.).

Breeding. Niger Delta "many nests were seen", Jan (Serle 1957); Sapele area "nests in dry season" (J.B.H.).

705. ANTHREPTES LONGUEMAREI   RB

(II.1191) Violet-backed Sunbird

Uncommon resident (*A. l. longuemarei*) in savanna woodland of the Guinea zone north of the great rivers to Zaria and Kari, and south only of the Benue to Enugu, where Serle (1957) found it locally common, though not seen there recently (Cowper 1977), suggesting numbers have diminished, perhaps everywhere.

Breeding. Male "with greatly enlarged testes" Kafanchan area, Nov (Bannerman 1948); nest building Kainji area, Feb (F.W.) and B/2 there, 26 Feb 1966 (Wells 1966a).

706. ANTHREPTES RECTIROSTRIS   RB

(II.1189) Green Sunbird

Uncommon resident (*A. r. tephrolaema*) in lowland forest and secondary growth, from Ipake to Owerri north from the coast to Akure and Ife.

Breeding. Nest Umuagwu, 19 Jun 1949 (Marchant 1953); juvs. Sapele area, 6 Jul 1975 (J.B.H.).

707. ANTHREPTES COLLARIS   RB

(II.1188) Collared Sunbird

Common resident at forest edges and clearings right across the country, *A. c. subcollaris* west of the Lower Niger, *A. c. somereni* in southeast. Remains common north of the forest belt to Ibadan and Nsukka, becoming more sparse northward in gallery forest to Kainji, Kafanchan and Pandam Wildlife Park, but none racially determined.

Breeding. From the coast north to Kafanchan, recorded Jan, Apr, Jul, Sep, Oct and Dec.

708. ANTHREPTES PLATURUS   Afm/B

(II.1156) Pygmy Sunbird

Seasonally common resident (*A. p. platura*) in wooded savanna throughout the area north of the great rivers and south to Igbetti, Enugu and Serti in the dry season. Although clearly an intra-African migrant (Elgood *et al.* 1973), extending its range southward to breed in the dry season, its northward limits and movements are unclear, since it appears seasonally in some localities and is present all year in others.

Breeding. Kaduna and Kafanchan north to Malamfatori, mostly Dec-Feb, but as late as Apr.

[ANTHREPTES AURANTIUM   Rejected

(II.1192)   Violet-tailed Sunbird

Nigeria ("Ondo Province") is mentioned by Bannerman (1953), "Southern Nigeria" by MP&G (1973) and "South Nigeria" by White (1963), but these statements rest on the earlier misidentification of a BMNH specimen now rectified as *A. longuemarei*. I am indebted to Sir Hugo Marshall, who collected this specimen, for drawing my attention to the error.]

709. NECTARINIA SEIMUNDI   R(B)

(II.1196)   Little Green Sunbird

Probably uncommon rather than rare resident (*N. s. minor*) in lowland forest including secondary growth. Few records but extending from Ipake (J.A.B.) and Lagos (Maclaren 1943), to Umuagwu (Marchant 1953) and Oban (Bannerman 1948, Ash 1990). Said to be "very retiring and easily overlooked" (MP&G).

Breeding. No records, but "Coastal Cameroun, July and November (breeding condition)" (MP&G).

710. NECTARINIA BATESI   RB

(II.1183)   Bates' Sunbird

Uncommon resident in lowland forest, right across the country from Lagos (J.P.G.) to Umuagwu (Serle 1957), but difficult to differentiate in the field and may be overlooked.

Breeding. Breeding pair collected Umuagwu, no date, (Serle 1957) and "Eastern Nigeria (breeding condition), November, February, March" (MP&G).

711. NECTARINIA OLIVACEA   RB

(II.1182)   Olive Sunbird

Common to locally abundant resident (*N. o. cephaelis* = *ragazzii*) in lowland forest, secondary growth, relict patches and dense gallery forest. Most numerous in forest zone right across the country, also north to Kainji (F.W.) and Kagoro on southern slopes of the Jos Plateau (M.G.).

Breeding. Surprisingly little data: birds with enlarged gonads collected in many months from the coast north to Ibadan, e.g. female with oviducal egg Mamu Forest, 3 Apr (Serle 1957). A nest with two eggs in Oban Hills F.R., 30 Jan 1987 (Ash 1990). In West Africa as a whole, breeding season probably prolonged.

712. NECTARINIA REICHENBACHII R(B)

(II.1185) Reichenbach's Sunbird

Very locally not uncommon resident, mostly near rivers and lagoons, sometimes gardens, almost all records from the narrow swamp forest zone between mangroves and lowland forest in southwest, from Lagos to Burutu. The commonest sunbird along the Jamieson River at Sapoba and along tributaries of Ossa River at Okomu (P.H.).

Breeding. No records, but "Cameroun, June, October and other months, season irregular" (MP&G).

713. NECTARINIA ORITIS RB

(II.1180) Cameroon Blue-headed Sunbird

Not uncommon resident (*N. o. bansoensis*) in montane forest at the Obudu Plateau; seen Gashaka-Gumti Nat. Park, Mar, Nov and Dec (Green 1990).
Breeding. Adults feeding juv., Apr (P.M.).

714. NECTARINIA VERTICALIS RB

(II.1178) Green-headed Sunbird

Common resident (*N. v. verticalis*) in mangroves, forest edges and clearings and gardens from the coast north to Ibadan and Enugu, extending, but progessively less common, into gallery forest throughout the Guinea Savanna to Zaria and Yankari.

Breeding. Building Owerri, 3 Mar (Bannerman 1948); adult carrying food Barakin Ladi (Jos Plateau), 1 Aug (V.S.).

715. NECTARINIA CYANOLAEMA RB

(II.1181) Blue-throated Sunbird

Not uncommon resident (*N. c. octaviae*) in lowland forest, including edges, clearings and secondary growth right across the country, north to Ibadan, Ife and Mamu Forest.

Breeding. Mamu Forest, 21 Aug 1954, "fledgling with a soft gape and unossified skull" (Serle 1957); female at nest Lagos, 15 Nov 1981 (Alexander-Marrack *et al.* 1985).

716. NECTARINIA FULIGINOSA RB

(II.1172) Carmelite Sunbird

Common resident (*N. f.aurea*) in mangroves and open coastal areas, including gardens, from Badagri to Opobo, not yet noted in extreme southeast, though it must occur there. A single inland record at Abeokuta (Bannerman 1948).

Breeding. Lagos: nest, 30 Nov (H.F.M.); copulation, Mar and juvs. with adult pairs, Oct, Nov, (J.B.H.); building nest, 28 Jan 1990 (A.M.N.). Nest with 1 young ready to fly, Lekki Conservation Centre, 1 Oct 1992 (P.H.).

717. NECTARINIA SENEGALENSIS RB, ?Afm/B
(II.1176)   Scarlet-chested Sunbird

Common resident (*N. s. senegalensis*) throughout the area, including urban areas, north of the great rivers and not uncommon south of the Middle Niger to Igbetti, Ilorin and Okene; also south to Ife and even Lagos (noted 5 times by D.I.M.W.), but south of the Benue, only to Serti (P.H.) and Enugu (S.G.C.). Some evidence of northward movement in the rains (Elgood *et al.* 1973).

Breeding. Ilorin north to Kano, Feb-Oct, with clear evidence of 2-3 broods raised in same nest, e.g. 3 broods Ilorin, Mar-Oct (Brown 1948); broods at 6 month intervals Jos (R.Kemp).

718. NECTARINIA ADELBERTI RB
(II.1175)   Buff-throated Sunbird

Not uncommon resident (*N. a. eboensis*) in secondary forest and gardens especially attracted to trees with ant nests, right across the country and north to Ibadan, Ife, Ankpa, Onitsha and Ogoja. Rare dry season visitor in Nindam F.R. (Dyer *et al.* 1986).

Breeding. Most records from near coast, Oct-Mar.

719. NECTARINIA VENUSTA Afm/B
(II.1164)   Variable Sunbird

Seasonally common resident (*N. v. venusta*) in savanna woodland throughout the country, partially migratory. Noted all year in coastal savanna and gardens at Lagos, but absent from much of the south Apr-Oct, at which season it is a rains visitor at Kano (R.E.S.) and Malamfatori (A.J.H.). At many localities no seasonality has been noted; possibly only some individuals move north after breeding.

Breeding. Lagos north to Kafanchan, Oct-Jan, yet juvs. at Lagos, May-Jul (J.B.H.). Evidence of two broods being raised in one nest, Ikoyi (A.M.N.).

720. NECTARINIA BOUVIERI R(B)
(II.1162)   Orange-tufted Sunbird

Common resident at the edge of montane forest at both the Obudu and Mambilla Plateaux, unreported elsewhere.

Breeding. Not reported, but "Cameroun (building nest), October" (MP&G).

721. NECTARINIA PREUSSI RB
(II.1167)   Preuss's Sunbird

Abundant resident (*N. p. preussi*) in montane shrubby grassland at both the Obudu and Mambilla Plateaux, unreported elsewhere.

Breeding. Female building nest Obudu, 19 Dec 1962 (J.H.E.). Pair feeding young at nest Obudu Cattle Ranch, 16 Nov 1985 (Ash 1990).

722. NECTARINIA CHLOROPYGIA RB

(II.1168)   Olive-bellied Sunbird

Common resident (*N. c. chloropygia* in southeast, *N. c. kempi* in southwest) from the coast north to the limits of the derived savanna at Ibadan and Enugu. Also in forest clearings and edges and gardens. A few racially undetermined sightings in gallery forest north to Ilorin (J.H.E.) and even Pandam Wildlife Park, north of the Benue (C.S.).

Breeding. From the coast north to Ibadan and Enugu, some activity in almost all months, mainly May-Oct.

723. NECTARINIA MINULLA R(B)

(II.1169)   Tiny Sunbird

Rare at forest edges and clearings. Has been collected at only 3 localities, but its resemblance in the field to common *N. chloropygia* makes its status difficult to define: Degema, "presumably from the Ansorge collection" (Serle 1957); Lagos (Oshodi) (P.Roche); male Badagri, 12 Jan 1961 (F.C.Sibley); also several probable sightings from the Lagos area (J.H.E., J.P.G.).

Breeding. No records, but Cameroon, Apr-Jun (MP&G).

724. NECTARINIA CUPREA Afm/B

(II59)   Copper Sunbird

Seasonally common resident (*N. c. cuprea*) in wooded savanna and gardens from the coast to northern limits of the Guinea Savanna. Remains all year in the south but is a rains breeding migrant in the area north of the great rivers – a "southern concertina" migrant (Elgood *et al.* 1973).

Breeding. Ibadan and Enugu north to Jos Plateau, Aug-Oct.

725. NECTARINIA COCCINIGASTER Afm/B

(II.1160)   Splendid Sunbird

Seasonally common resident in forest clearings, gardens, derived savanna and savanna woodland from the coast to the great rivers; also further north, e.g. Zonkwa, but only in the rains. Also reported from the Obudu and Mambilla Plateaux, at Nindam (Dyer *et al.* 1986) and at Kwal, 7 Nov 1992 (M.Ho).

Breeding. Activity noted most months, mostly Mar-Jun, but noted only from the coast north to Ubiaja and Enugu.

726. NECTARINIA JOHANNAE ?

(II.1158)   Johanna's Sunbird

Previously only a single unconfirmed sighting (15 Jul 1951) in forest clearing near Lagos (H.F. Marshall) – a female (presumably *N. j. fasciata*) observed at close quarters (the female of this species is more distinctive than the male). Record accepted by Sander (1957) and by MP&G ("Upper Guinea from Sierra Leone to Nigeria"). Although White (1963) says "no recent records from Nigeria", he gives

Abomey, Nigeria (Jardine & Fraser 1852) as type locality which must be an error for Abomey, Benin (Dahomey). Recent sighting at Sabon Gida, Akanwe Village, Gongola State: a male clearly seen, 18 Sep 1985 (Gray 1986).
Breeding. No records, but Jul in Ghana (MP&G).

727. NECTARINIA SUPERBA   RB

    (II.1157)   Superb Sunbird

Not uncommon resident (*N. s. nigeriae**) at lowland forest edges and clearings from Lagos to the Niger Delta, north to Ibadan and Ife, but only noted at Enugu (Serle 1957) and Umuagwu (Marchant 1953) in southeast.
    Breeding. Building Sapele, Jul; nestlings Benin, 11 Jul 1974, copulation 23 Aug 1974 (all J.B.H.).
*Birds from Nigeria were formerly attributed to *N. s. ashantiensis*, but White (1963) restricts this race to "from Sierra Leone to Ghana"

728. NECTARINIA PULCHELLA   Afm/B

    (II.1154)   Beautiful Sunbird

Seasonally common resident (*N. p. pulchella*) throughout the wooded savanna, thornscrub and gardens north of the great rivers, but only at Ilorin and Kainji Lake Nat. Park to the south. Migrates furthest south Sep-Mar and furthest north mainly Apr-Oct, a "hump-back bridge" type of movement (Elgood *et al.* 1973). Males in eclipse (Nov-Mar) are difficult to recognise and blur the migration picture.
    Breeding. Most records Zaria to Katsina, Jun-Aug, but 4 southerly nests at Lokoja, Feb-Oct (Bannerman 1948) are confusing.

LANIIDAE

729. LANIUS COLLURIO   PM

    (II.1058)   Red-backed Shrike

Uncommon Palaearctic migrant, sightings at 2 localities: on recently reclaimed land at Lagos, 9 Nov 1969, 23 Nov 1970 and collected (sub-adult) 26 Nov 1970 (Gee & Heigham 1977); and in Obudu (town), 13 Dec 1978 and 2 Apr 1979 (Heaton & Heaton 1980).

730. LANIUS ISABELLINUS   PM

    (II.1058)   Isabelline Shrike

Not uncommon Palaearctic migrant in scrubby savanna across the north from Sokoto to Lake Chad becoming uncommon south of Kainji and Onitsha. Now generally given separate specific status from *L. collurio*. One collected near Zaria, 23 Mar 1964, proved to be *L. i. speculigerus* (C.H.F.).

731. LANIUS GUBERNATOR RB

(II.1059) Emin's Shrike

Locally uncommon resident in Guinea savanna; may be overlooked through confusion with *L. collurio*. Recorded from the following localities: collected Gajibo (near Lake Chad) and near Benin (Bannerman 1939); sightings Kabba/Lokoja road (L.H.Brown); near Kainji "recorded regularly" over 3 years (Wells & Walsh 1969); Kainji Lake Nat. Park 1988 and 1989 (P.H.); Serti "1 seen regularly throughout November" (P.H.); Taboru, in gallery forest lining erosion gullies, 1992 (M.Ho., J.B.); Yankari (M.D.), and 14 Jun 1991 (A.M.N.).

Breeding. Kainji "pair with young bird barely out of nest 16 June 68" (Wells & Walsh 1969).

732. LANIUS MINOR VPM

(II.1052) Lesser Grey Shrike

Vagrant Palaearctic migrant. Only 2 records: first sighted (no date) Malamfatori (A.J.H.) and one at Lagos, 2 Nov 1969, which remained for some days until collected 14 Nov 1969 as first Nigerian specimen (Gee & Heigham 1977).

733. LANIUS EXCUBITOR RB

(II.1050) Great Grey Shrike

Not uncommon (*L. e. leucopygos* = *L. elegans leucopygos* in MP&G) in the Sahel just west of Lake Chad where Boyd Alexander collected several (Bannerman 1939), with many sightings in thorn scrub in recent years. Also 2 sightings east of Hadejia, one at Jekara (Sharland & Wilkinson 1981) and one at Katsina (I.D.). A sighting at Lagos, 28 Oct 1951, (H.F.M.), may be confusion with *L. minor* which has been collected there.

Breeding. B/3 in thorn scrub south of Lake Chad, 28 Feb (D.A.Holmes).

734. LANIUS EXCUBITORIUS R(B)

(II.1051) Grey-backed Fiscal Shrike

Rare local resident (*L. e. excubitorius* = *tchadensis*) in thorn scrub of the Sahel zone west of Lake Chad, in the same area as *L. excubitor*, with which it can be confused. Specimens are mentioned by Bannerman (1939), and one was collected at Logomani, Jul 1960 (F.C.S.). A pair seen at Malamfatori, 31 Jul 1965 (C.H.F.), and recorded from Chingurmi-Duguma in the Chad Basin Nat. Park (P.H.).

Breeding. Co-operative. No records. Breeding condition Cameroon, Apr (MP&G).

735. LANIUS MACKINNONI R(B)

(II.1056) Mackinnon's Shrike

Not uncommon resident at edges of montane forest at Obudu Plateau (J.H.E., H.H.G., T.R-S, P.M., M.Ho). 9 sightings in Apr, Jun, Nov and Dec, including one "on a pole by the hotel" (P.M.), and often recorded on the tennis court fence beside the hotel in recent years (P.H.).

Breeding. No records. In "Cameroun, December and March, also a nestling in September" (MP&G); west Cameroon, Nov-Mar (Serle 1981).

736. LANIUS COLLARIS RB
(II.1053) Fiscal Shrike

Not uncommon but locally resident (*L. c. smithii*), almost always in suburban areas. Formerly common around Lagos but no recent reports (P.H.) and almost entirely absent from any other town in southwest; common at most townships of southeast from Calabar and Port Harcourt north to Enugu and Obudu (town). Further north occurs in Guinea Savanna woodland at Kainji Lake Nat. Park (Wells & Walsh 1969), around Jos, and is not uncommon on the Mambilla Plateau. Recent sighting of 2 at Hadejia Wetlands, Aug 1990 (I.D.).
Breeding. Lagos and southeast towns, mostly Mar-May, also Jul and Nov-Dec. Probably double-brooded.

737. LANIUS SENATOR PM
(II.1060) Woodchat Shrike

Common Palaearctic migrant (both *L. s. senator* and *L. s. badius*) to a wide variety of habitats other than forest throughout, mid Sep to mid Apr in the north, a rather shorter period in the south. Both races have been taken in north and south but *senator* less often than *badius* in the south. Although the races are separable in the field few sightings have been discriminated. A bird ringed at Kano recovered in Italy.

738. LANIUS NUBICUS PM
(II.1055) Nubian Shrike, Masked Shrike

Uncommon Palaearctic migrant recorded only from Lake Chad south to Bama and west to Nguru, mostly in Sahel thorn scrub near streams, Oct-Apr.

739. CORVINELLA CORVINA RB
(II.1061) Yellow-billed Shrike

Locally common resident (*C. c. togoensis*) in savanna woodland throughout the area north of the great rivers east to Damataru and south of the Middle Niger to Ibadan and Abeokuta, very occasionally at Lagos. In southeast common in "Tivland", only one record Enugu (Serle 1957) and "abundant" Obudu (town), but nowhere else (Heaton & Heaton 1980).
Breeding. Co-operative and protracted: all months except Nov and Dec, Ibadan to Kano.

MALACONOTIDAE

740. NILAUS AFER RB, ?Afm/B
(II.1049) Northern Brubru

Not uncommon, probably resident, (*N. a. afer*) in wooded savanna mainly of the

Guinea zone. Though considered a migrant in the northern tropics by Moreau (1966), Elgood *et al.* (1973) found data merely suggested a tendency for Sudan and Sahel records to be for the rains and the most southern to be for the dry season, though it is resident at Enugu (Serle 1957).

Breeding. Only reported at Kainji, Jan-Feb (Wells & Walsh 1969).

741. DRYOSCOPUS GAMBENSIS   RB

(II.1073)   Puffback-Shrike

Common resident (*D. g. gambensis*) in wooded areas throughout, less numerous northward as tree cover diminishes; also in mangroves, forest clearings (avoiding closed forest) and all types of savanna including farm land with standing trees. Some evidence for local movements but no true migration.

Breeding. From Enugu and Ibadan north to Wamba, mainly Apr-Jun also Sep, Oct and Dec.

742. DRYOSCOPUS SENEGALENSIS   R(B)

(II.1072)   Red-eyed Puffback-Shrike

Rare resident, only 3 records: collected Oshogbo (in derived savanna of southwest), 24 May 1938 (Bannerman 1951); collected Obudu Plateau (from bird army in montane forest), 17 Mar 1961 (F.C.Sibley); netted Obudu Plateau, 9 Aug 1980 (D&G).

Breeding. No records. Nestling Cameroon, Aug (MP&G); breeds west Cameroon, Nov (Serle 1981).

743. DRYOSCOPUS ANGOLENSIS   R(B)

(II.1074)   Pink-footed Puffback-Shrike

New species for Nigeria. Rare resident, only 2 records: Obudu Plateau, Oct 1981 (M.D.); one netted Obudu Cattle Ranch, 15 Nov 1985 (Ash and Sharland 1987).

Breeding. No records. Breeds west Cameroon, Apr (Serle 1981).

744. DRYOSCOPUS SABINI   R(B)

(II.1075)   Sabine's Puffback-Shrike

Uncommon resident (*D. s. sabini*) in high forest from near Lagos north to Ibadan and Ife and east to Benin; also east of the Niger but only at Umuagwu (Marchant 1953, Serle 1957).

Breeding. No records. Elaborate courtship display seen at Gambari, Jun (J.H.E.). Male collected with somewhat enlarged gonads Umuagwu, 31 Oct 1948 (Marchant). "Cameroun (breeding condition) November and December" (MP&G).

745. TCHAGRA MINUTA   RB, ?Afm/B

(II.1078)*   Black-cap Bush-Shrike

Uncommon and very local resident (*T. m. minuta*) in tall grass along savanna streams in derived savanna, from Abeokuta and Ibadan in west, from Enugu and Obudu Plateau in east north to Zaria, Falgore G.R, Yankari and Aliya, but also in coastal savanna near Lagos. Northern records are mostly for the rains when breeding, so some migration is possible.

Breeding. C/3 Kafanchan, 23 Jul (Bannerman 1939); "newly flown" juv. Enugu, 3 Jul (Serle 1957); "fledgling chicks" Ibadan, 18 Jun (H.F.M.).

*Named *Bocagea minuta* by MP&G.

746. TCHAGRA SENEGALA   RB

(II.1076)   Black-headed Bush-Shrike

Common resident (*T. s. senegala* = *pallida*) in degraded savanna, especially farmland, throughout the true savannas; less common in coastal savanna at Lagos, in derived savanna at Abeokuta, Ibadan and around Owerri in southeast. *T. s. notha* occurs across the north from Sokoto to Lake Chad. Apparently strictly stationary.

Breeding. Well documented in most vegetation zones, Feb-Sep, mostly May-Aug.

747. TCHAGRA AUSTRALIS   R(B)

(II.1077)   Brown-headed Bush-Shrike

Uncommon resident in secondary bush, (*T. a. ussheri* in southwest, *T. a. emini* in southeast, perhaps separated by the Lower Niger) from the coast north to Ibadan, the Obudu Plateau (P.M.), and Gashaka-Gumti Nat. Park (Green 1990).

Breeding. MP&G state "Nigeria, February and June to September", but this possibly refers only to areas of Cameroon formerly within Nigeria.

748. LANIARIUS LUEHDERI   RB

(II.1070)   Luehder's Bush-Shrike

Perhaps not uncommon resident (*L. l. luehderi*) in secondary forest of a very small area near Calabar, at western edge of species range. First recorded breeding, Sep 1955 (Serle 1959); and more recently several sightings (P.M.).

Breeding. C/1, 18 Sep 1955, C/2, 4 Oct 1955 (Serle 1959); juv., 1 Apr 1977 (P.M.).

749. LANIARIUS FERRUGINEUS   RB

(II.1067)*   Tropical Boubou

Locally not uncommon resident (*L. f. major*) in wooded savanna mainly in south of the Southern Guinea zone; also rare in coastal suburban gardens (Lagos, Burutu, Calabar) and recorded north of the great rivers only in gallery forest near Kaduna, on and near the Jos Plateau and at Yankari Nat. Park. Also recorded from IITA and the Mambilla Plateau (P.H.).

Breeding. C/2 Kafanchan, 15 Jun (Bannerman 1939); "female sitting, between 10 Feb and 7 Mar 1965", "Tivland" (H.H.G.).

*Named *L. aethiopicus* by MP&G and by Hall and Moreau (1970).

Malaconotidae

750. LANIARIUS BARBARUS   RB

(II.1063)   Gonolek (or Barbary Shrike)

Common resident in scrub savanna and suburban gardens throughout the area north of the great rivers; unknown south of the Benue but common south of the Middle Niger south to Ilorin, then absent (apart from Abeokuta – Serle 1950) until common again in coastal savanna from Badagri to Lagos.

Breeding. From the coast at Lagos north to Sokoto and Kano, mostly Jun-Aug, but juvs. as late as Nov at Lagos (J.B.H.).

751. LANIARIUS ERYTHROGASTER   R(B)

(II.1062)   Black-headed (or Abyssinian) Gonolek

Common resident in papyrus and along grassy river banks in extreme northeast from shores of Lake Chad south to Logomani, replacing *L. barbarus* in this extreme northeast area.

Breeding. No records anywhere in West Africa.

752. LANIARIUS ATROFLAVUS   R(B)

(II.1064)   Yellow-breasted Boubou

Not uncommon resident in montane forest along streams of the Obudu Plateau and once only in similar habitat on the Mambilla Plateau (P.H.). Also "common" on Chappal Hendu in the Gashaka-Gumti Nat. Park (Green 1990).

Breeding. No records. Cameroon highlands, Dec-Feb (MP&G); west Cameroon Nov and Mar (Serle 1981).

753. LANIARIUS LEUCORHYNCHUS   R(B)

(II.1065)   Sooty Boubou

Few records: male collected Umuagwu, 4 Dec 1949 (Marchant 1953). "Only noted in very dense secondary growth regenerating on old farms at Umuagwu but probably more widespread. More secretive and difficult to see but makes its presence known by a great variety of startling calls" This suggests Marchant encountered more than the bird collected. More recently, "about 5 skulked in thick secondary growth at 150 m elevation" near Bashu, Feb (Ash 1990).

Breeding. No records. Liberia, Oct (MP&G).

754. LANIARIUS POENSIS   R(B)

(II.1066)   Mountain Sooty Boubou

Common resident in montane forest at Obudu and Mambilla Plateaux (Ash 1990). Also recorded Gotel Mts. (Green 1990).

Breeding. No records. Cameroon, (breeding condition), Apr, Oct and Dec (MP&G); west Cameroon, Nov-Dec (Serle 1981).

755. TELOPHORUS SULFUREOPECTUS   RB, Afm/B

(II.1081)   Sulphur-breasted Bush-Shrike

Not uncommon resident seasonally (*T. s. sulfureopectus*) in savanna woodlands, gallery forest and woods at inselberg bases throughout the true savannas, all the year at the south of its range, from Abeokuta, Ibadan and Enugu. Is a rains migrant in far north, e.g. Sokoto, Kano, Maiduguri; a southern "concertina" migrant (Elgood *et al.* 1973).

Breeding. Building south of Kano, May (Bannerman 1939); eggs Ibadan, 27 May (H.F.M.).

756. TELOPHORUS MULTICOLOR   R(B)

(II.1079)   Many-coloured Bush-Shrike

Uncommon resident (*T. m. multicolor*) in high forest from Ilaro to Ife and Ikom, but also sighted at Kagoro on southern escarpment of the Jos Plateau, and in the Gashaka-Gumti Nat. Park (Green 1990). At Ilaro, Button (1965) noted all 3 morphs: 5 red-breasted, 3 orange-breasted, 1 black-breasted. One at IITA, 16 Aug 1992 (P.H.).

Breeding. No records but Nigeria (breeding condition) Nov and Dec (MP&G).

757. TELOPHORUS CRUENTUS   R(B)

(II.1089)   Fiery-breasted Bush-Shrike

Not uncommon resident in secondary growth and well-wooded gardens in the forest zone, locally only at Lagos, Ilaro, Ibadan and Ife in southwest, and much more sparsely in southeast from Ahoada to near Ikom.

Breeding. No records. Breeds Cameroon, Aug (MP&G) and west Cameroon, Jun and Nov (Serle 1981).

758. TELOPHORUS GLADIATOR   R(B)

(II.1087)   Green-breasted Bush-Shrike

Uncommon resident in montane forest, range extending westward from Cameroon into Nigeria at Obudu Plateau: one collected 19 Mar 1961 (F.C. Sibley). Further sight records also from Obudu Plateau (J.H.E. and P.M.), but no other locality.

Breeding. No records anywhere in Africa.

759. TELOPHORUS BLANCHOTI   RB, ?Afm/B

(II.1086)*   Grey-headed Bush-Shrike

Locally not uncommon resident (*T. b. blanchoti*) in the Guinea savannas in woodland and suburban gardens south to Meko (and possibly Ibadan) in southwest, but only just south of the Benue in southeast. The most northerly records, from Sokoto to Potiskum, are for the rains and all data suggest the species may spread northward at that season.

Breeding. Ilorin north to Sokoto, mainly Jan-Apr; also Jun (Sokoto and Kano) and Sep (Kafanchan).
*Named *Malaconotus hypopyrrhus pallidirostris* in MP&G.

760. NICATOR CHLORIS   RB

(II.1090)   Nicator

Common resident (*N. c. chloris*) in lowland forest, including dense secondary growth, right across the country and north to Ibadan, Agenebode and Enugu; also in relict forest at Kagoro on southern escarpment of the Jos Plateau.
Breeding. 2 males with enlarged testes Owerri, 7 Mar 1947 (Marchant 1953); female with greatly enlarged ovary Enugu, 27 May; female with oviducal egg Enugu, 12 Jun (Serle 1957); adult feeding young Oban Hills, 10 Oct (Ash 1990).

PRIONOPIDAE

761. PRIONOPS PLUMATUS   RB

(II.1044)   Straight-crested Helmet-Shrike

Not uncommon and widespread resident (*P. p. plumatus*) in savanna woodlands throughout the Guinea zone, less common south to Ibadan and Abeokuta in southwest, to Enugu, Obudu and Serti in southeast, and northward to Sokoto and Kano.
Breeding. Protracted and co-operative, Mar-Jun and Oct-Nov, from Ilorin north to Kano.

762. PRIONOPS CANICEPS   RB

(II.1047)   Red-billed Shrike

Common resident (*P. c. harterti*) in high forest, sometimes at edges and in relict patches, and sometimes in secondary forest, from near Lagos, where numbers have declined (P.H.), east to the Cameroon border.
Breeding. Very few data: feeding young near Ibadan, Oct (J.H.E.); flocks with young juvs. Ife, Jan-Mar (R.F.).

DICRURIDAE

763. DICRURUS LUDWIGII   RB

(II.1043)   Square-tailed Drongo

Not uncommon resident (*D. l. sharpei*) in gallery forest and woods around inselberg bases in the Guinea zone, mainly south of the great rivers, north to Kaduna and Zaria, southward to the coast at Lagos where it is uncommon at forest edges. Strictly stationary.
Breeding. Adults with fully fledged juvs. near Kainji, 12 Apr (Wells & Walsh 1969) and near Kaduna, 30 May (D&G).

764. DICRURUS ATRIPENNIS   RB

(II.1042) Shining Drongo

Uncommon resident in little disturbed lowland forest from Lagos to Ikom, always within true forest. Easily confused with *D. adsimilis coracinus*, the forest race; and may be commoner than records suggest. Strictly non-migratory.

Breeding. Females in breeding condition Mamu, Oct and Umuagwu, Nov (Serle 1957); but also "2 attempts at breeding, nests made and brooded, presumably eggs" Ilaro, May (J.A.B.).

765. DICRURUS ADSIMILIS   RB

(II.1040 & 1041) Drongo & Velvet-mantled Drongo

Drongos, of one type or another, are common residents outside the forest proper throughout the area south of the great rivers, less common northward in the Northern Guinea and Sudan zones and apparently absent from the Sahel. White's (1962) lumping of *D. adsimilis* (MP&G, 1040) with *D. modestus* (MP&G, 1041) has obscured the fact that forest zone and savanna drongos in Nigeria seem distinct in appearance and voice. Essentially *D. a. divaricatus* (whitish primary linings) is found in savanna woodland and *D. a. coracinus* at southern forest edges and clearings, while the possibly hybrid *D. a. atactus* occurs in extreme southwest.

Breeding. Co-operative. Nov-Jun, mainly Feb-Apr, mostly south of the great rivers.

CORVIDAE

766. PTILOSTOMUS AFER   RB, ?Afm/B

(II.1112) Piapiac (Black Magpie)

Locally common resident, flocks can exceed 30, in degraded savanna with *Borassus* palms throughout the area north of the great rivers. In southeast, only recorded just south of the Benue and is absent from the former Eastern Region. In southwest, common south to Ilorin, then absent until not uncommon in coastal savanna between Badagri and Lagos where they are common in gardens with mature trees (A.M.N.) and near Sapele (J.B.H.). Previously thought to be a partial migrant but with no clear evidence.

Breeding. Co-operative. Lagos to Sokoto, Apr-Jun. Red-billed immatures seen in Falgore G.R., Jan, Mar, May, Jun and Oct (Wilkinson & Beecroft 1985).

767. CORVUS ALBUS   RB

(II.1109) Pied Crow

Locally common, even abundant, resident of farms and suburban areas throughout the savannas, flocks of 100+; more local around most, but not all, townships in the forest zone, e.g. Lagos, "infrequent sightings of 1-3 birds, especially after summer rainstorms" (Gee & Heigham 1977). Scant evidence for migration; in fact Lagos data point against a northward shift in the rains, which is the breeding season.

Breeding. Ibadan to Sokoto, Mar-Jul, starting less early in north.

768. CORVUS RUFICOLLIS   ?

(II.1108)   Raven* (Brown-necked Raven)

Uncommon (*C. r. ruficollis*), possibly only a casual non-breeding visitor to the extreme north (being essentially a sub-desert species), mostly in the Sahel just west of Lake Chad; also collected at Sokoto (Bannerman 1948). Near Lake Chad reported "common 20 miles into French Niger" at all times; present at Yo (just within Nigeria) in dry and wet seasons, excluding seasonal movement (P.W.). Several sightings round Bulatura Oases (P.H.).

Breeding. No records, but Dec-Mar in Sudan (MP&G).

*MP&G place this form as a race of *C. corax*.

ORIOLIDAE

769. ORIOLUS ORIOLUS   PM, ?V

(II.1102)   Golden Oriole

Palaearctic migrant (*O. o. oriolus*), uncommon to rare (possibly only vagrant) with no clear habitat preference, Sep-Mar, but 3 noted on passage at Maiduguri, Jun (P.H.). Distinction from *O. auratus* in the field is difficult enough to make all records, other than the few collected or netted specimens (both from north and south), open to some doubt. Sightings range from Sokoto (Mundy & Cook 1971-72) and Lake Chad (A.J.H.) to Lagos (Gee & Heigham 1977).

770. ORIOLUS AURATUS   Afm, B

(II.1103)   African Golden Oriole

Not uncommon resident (*O. a. auratus*) in savanna woodlands of the Guinea zone. Southern records from Ibadan to Serti are for the dry season, except a Lagos specimen in Sep; conversely, almost all Sudan zone records from Sokoto, Kano and Potiskum are for the height of the rains. This suggests a "hump-back bridge" pattern of migration (Elgood *et al*. 1973), but some birds remain in north till late Dec.

Breeding. Only north of the great rivers, mainly Mar-Apr.

771. ORIOLUS BRACHYRHYNCHUS   RB

(II.1105)   Western Black-headed Oriole

Not uncommon resident (*O. b. laetior*) in lowland forest east of the Lower Niger and extending to the Obudu Plateau; uncommon in southwest but widely recorded, perhaps as common around Benin as in southeast. One record from Lagos, 26 Mar 1978 (Alexander-Marrack *et al*. 1985). Compared with *O. nigripennis*, where the 2 occur together, is usually nearer the ground.

Breeding. A juv. Calabar, Mar, is the only record (P.M.).

772. ORIOLUS NIGRIPENNIS   RB

(II.1106)   Black-winged Oriole

Common resident in the canopy of lowland forest, including secondary growth, in

southwest; uncommon east of the Lower Niger though met at the Obudu Plateau, and uncommon in the forests near Benin.
Breeding. Nest building, incubating on nest and young juvs., all Mar-Jun, between Lagos and Ife.

STURNIDAE

Sturninae

773. POEOPTERA LUGUBRIS   RB

(II.1133)   Narrow-tailed Starling

Uncommon resident in lowland forest and at edges and clearings, when first recorded west of the Lower Niger, though its range extends east to Zaïre. Reported from Okwango and Oban in 1986 and 1988 (Ash *et. al* 1989).
Breeding. Nest near Ife, Jan (F.C.S.); group exploring nest holes near Lagos, Aug (Sander 1957).

774. ONYCHOGNATHUS WALLERI   R(B)

(II.1130)   Waller's Chestnut-wing Starling

Common resident (*O. w. preussi*) at the edges of montane forest, only on the Obudu Plateau, flocks up to 15 (M.D.).
Breeding. No records anywhere in West Africa.

775. ONYCHOGNATHUS MORIO   RB

(II.1131)   Red-wing Starling

Locally not uncommon resident. Strongly stenotopic to inselbergs and rocky outcroppings, is known mainly from relatively few localities north of the great rivers, absent in the sandy Chad Basin of northeast. Recorded south of Benue only in Gashaka-Gumti Nat. Park, where relatively common Nov-Mar (Green 1990), and recently observed at inselbergs as far north as Safana and Runka, 75 km south-southwest of Katsina (I.D.).
Breeding. Several records, all from Jos Plateau area, Apr-May.

776. ONYCHOGNATHUS FULGIDUS   RB

(II.1129)   Chestnut-wing Starling

Common and widespread resident (*O. f. hartlaubii*) in forest clearings and edges, and in wooded gardens, from the coast north to Ibadan, Oyo and Enugu. Recorded from Calabar area all months (Mackenzie 1979).
Breeding. Very little known. Ibadan, Feb (H.F.M.); feeding young in nesting hole Oyo, May (J.H.E.); feeding young Ife, Feb and "building" Mar (R.F.).

Sturnidae

777. LAMPROTORNIS PURPUREICEPS   R(B)

(II.1124)   Purple-headed Glossy Starling

Uncommon resident in lowland forest from Lagos to Calabar, but north only to Gambari, Benin and Umuagwu.
Breeding. No records anywhere in West Africa.

778. LAMPROTORNIS PURPUREUS   RB

(II.1120)   Purple Glossy Starling

Not uncommon resident (*L. p. purpureus*) in wooded savanna of the Guinea zone, becoming uncommon in southwest to Ibadan and the coast from Lagos to Badagri; in southeast only at Serti (H.H.G.). Also north into the Sudan zone at Sokoto and Kano, but there is no seasonal movement pattern to support migration.
   Breeding. Feeding young in nest-hole "Niger province", late Jun (Bannerman 1948); young at Kishi, Apr (A.P.).

779. LAMPROTORNIS CHALCURUS   RB

(II.1118)   Bronze-tailed Glossy Starling

Uncommon resident (*L. c. chalcurus*) in savanna woodlands, but difficult to separate in the field from *L. chloropterus*, so possibly more common than records suggest. Mostly recorded in west from the coast at Badagri (J.A.B.) to Sokoto. Noted Jos Plateau, Yankari Nat. Park and non-breeding flocks at Serti, Nov-Jan, in extreme east (P.H.).
   Breeding. C/4 Sokoto, 8 Jun 1939 (Bannerman 1948); pair entering nest hole near Kaduna, 20 Mar 1955 (J.H.E.); juvs. netted Vom, May (J.R.L.).

780. LAMPROTORNIS CHALYBAEUS   RB

(II.1117)   Blue-eared Glossy Starling

Locally common resident (*L. c. chalybaeus*) in woodlands (especially plantations of Neem *Azadirachta indica*) in extreme north. The commonest starling around Sokoto (flocks of 100 – Mundy & Cook 1972-73) and from Maiduguri to Lake Chad. Also collected on the Jos Plateau and sighted at Zaria and Yankari.
   Breeding. B/3 Sokoto, Aug (Mundy & Cook 1972-73).

781. LAMPROTORNIS CHLOROPTERUS   RB

(II.1119)   Lesser Blue-eared (Swainson's) Glossy Starling

Locally common to abundant resident (*L. c. chloropterus*) in savanna woodland over much of the area north of the great rivers, also south to the Old Oyo Nat. Park in southwest and to Enugu and Serti in southeast. Flocks up to 100 not uncommon in off season, e.g. Zaria, Jun-Dec (C.H.F.).
   Breeding. Probably co-operative. Breeding condition Enugu, Mar (Serle 1957); Kainji Lake Nat. Park, Feb-Mar (Wells & Walsh 1969); eggs at Kari, Mar-Apr (P.B.).

782. LAMPROTORNIS SPLENDIDUS　　　　　　　　　　　　　　RB

(II.1121)   Splendid Glossy Starling

Common or locally abundant resident (*L. s. splendidus*) at forest edges, clearings and relict patches across the whole forest zone north to Ibadan, Ife and Afikpo. Flocks of 100+ not uncommon in some localities. Isolated populations occur on wooded slopes and in gullies from southern edge of the Jos Plateau as far north as Jos township. Also noted in Gashaka-Gumti Nat. Park, Feb-Mar (Green 1990). Although flocks perform conspicuous daily movements to roost and feed there is no evidence of migration.

Breeding.   Only in forest zone, Dec-Mar.

783. LAMPROTORNIS CAUDATUS　　　　　　　　　　　　　　　RB

(II.1125)   Long-tailed Glossy Starling

Common resident (*L. c. caudatus*) in savanna woodland and wooded suburban areas in the Sudan and Northern Guinea zones, more local in the Sahel, but noted at Malamfatori and at Nguru (M.D.). South of the great rivers is "locally frequent all months" in Kainji Lake Nat. Park (Wells & Walsh 1969), noted around Okene and Kabba (Brown 1948) and sighted once near Lagos "? vagrant or escape" (Gee & Heigham 1977).

Breeding.   Surprisingly little recorded for such a numerous and conspicuous bird: all records are from Kano, Sep-Oct (Bannerman 1948), none recent.

784. LAMPROTORNIS PULCHER　　　　　　　　　　　　　　　　RB

(II.1136)   Chestnut-bellied Starling

Locally common resident in degraded savanna including farmland and gardens of the Sudan and Sahel zones across the north from Sokoto to Lake Chad. Also collected at Zaria (Walker 1965) and sighted at Yankari (M.D.) and Wase Rock (Dunger 1965).

Breeding.   Co-operative. Recorded mainly Sokoto and Kano, Mar-Oct.

785. CINNYRICINCLUS LEUCOGASTER　　　　　　　　　　　　Afm/B

(II.1114)   Violet-backed (Amethyst) Starling

Locally common seasonally (*C. l. leucogaster*) in savanna woodlands and forest clearings throughout, flocks of 100+; absent extreme northeast. A "hump-back bridge" pattern of migration (Elgood *et al.* 1973) moving north after breeding in the rains (Jun-Sep). Thus at Lagos "common but somewhat erratic visitor in large flocks" Nov-May (Gee & Heigham 1977), whereas northernmost records (Sokoto, Kano, Maiduguri) are Jul-Sep.

Breeding.   Co-operative. From the coast north to Zaria, Mar-Jun, the Jun record being coastal at Badagri (J.A.B.) and not conforming to the otherwise fairly clear pattern of migration.

Buphaginae

786. BUPHAGUS AFRICANUS RB

(II.1137)   Yellow-billed Oxpecker

Not uncommon resident (*B. a. africanus*), associating with cattle, donkeys and wild game in degraded savanna and wooded savanna throughout the area north of the great rivers, though numbers feeding with cattle have diminished dramatically recently through improved veterinary care (mainly dipping). A few southerly records "northern Oyo to Kabba" (Brown 1948) and the Obudu and Mambilla Plateaux, mainly in dry season when cattle herds have moved south.
   Breeding. From Jos Plateau north to Sokoto, Kano and Potiskum.

PASSERIDAE

787. PASSER GRISEUS RB

(II.1207)   Grey-headed Sparrow

Common or locally abundant resident (*P. g. griseus*) in urban, suburban and farmland areas of savannas throughout, including coastal savanna, and in forest zone township areas. Seldom far from cultivation and most numerous wherever there are horses. White (1963) states that the subdesert race *P. g. laeneni* occurs south "to northern border of Nigeria"
   Breeding. Throughout year (except May-Jun) and throughout the country.

788. PASSER LUTEUS AfM/NB

(II.1208)   Sudan Golden Sparrow

Seasonally abundant resident (*P. l. luteus*) in thorn scrub savanna near water in the Sahel zone south to Hadejia and Maiduguri (A.J.H.) and to Sambisa (P.H.); but mainly only present Oct-Jun, birds moving north out of Nigeria in the rains to breed. Dry season flocks of 2000+ not uncommon, often associating and roost- ing with *Q. quelea*.
   Breeding. Not recorded within Nigeria. May occur near Lake Chad, but breeding season in West Africa is Jun-Sep when probably all have moved into Niger.

789. PETRONIA DENTATA Afm/B

(II.1211)   Bush Petronia

An African migrant seasonally common in savanna woodland through much of the country south to Igbetti (27 Dec 1953 – H.F.M.) and Enugu (Nov-Feb – Serle 1957) and north to the great rivers, through most of the year, though many move north into Niger, Jul-Oct (Elgood *et al.* 1973).
   Breeding. Only noted north of the great rivers and in Kainji Lake Nat. Park, Nov-Mar.

790. SPOROPIPES FRONTALIS   RB

(II.1212)   Speckled-fronted Weaver

Common resident (*S. f. frontalis*) locally in thorn-scrub savanna from Yelwa and Zaria east to Bauchi and north to Sokoto and Lake Chad. In 1992 reported rather common on the Jos Plateau (M.Ho).
   Breeding. Scanty and confusing data: building Sokoto, Jul-Aug (Mundy & Cook 1972-73): Kano, Jul (R.E.S.); C/1 Zaria, 26 Feb, pulli, 1 Feb (C.H.F.); nest with two eggs at Bagauda, 4 Apr 1980 (Sharland & Wilkinson 1981). MP&G state "over most of its area October to February"

791. PLOCEPASSER SUPERCILIOSUS   RB

(II.1203)   Chestnut-crowned Sparrow-Weaver

Not uncommon resident, widespread in degraded savanna scrubland of the Guinea zone south of the Middle Niger to Kishi (J.H.E.) north to Sokoto, Kano and Maiduguri, but absent south of the Benue. Also "no specimens, but noted at Ibadan consorting with Village Weavers in November (L.H.Brown)" (Bannerman 1949).
   Breeding. Kainji north to Sokoto, Apr-Aug.

PLOCEIDAE

792. BUBALORNIS ALBIROSTRIS   RB

(II.1201)   Buffalo-Weaver

Common resident (*B. a. albirostris*) in cultivated areas of the Sudan zone from Sokoto to Lake Chad, in west, south to Yelwa and Agwarra (Wells & Walsh 1969). At Malamfatori numbers increased in the rains (A.J.H.), but no real evidence of migration.
   Breeding. Some activity most of the year; eggs, Jun onward perhaps till Dec.

793. PLOCEUS BANNERMANI   RB

(II.1236)   Bannerman's Weaver

Not uncommon resident at edge of montane forest of the Obudu Plateau, a slight westward range extension from nearby Cameroon Highlands. Not collected until Aug 1980 (M.D.), but first sighted Dec 1974 (T.Russell-Smith); sighted c. 10 times, Nov 1976 to Jun 1977 (P.M.), and "12 pairs seen, one collected", Aug 1980 (M.D). Recorded in Gashaka-Gumti Nat. Park, Nov and Dec 1987 and Mar 1988 (Green 1990).
   Breeding. Only record a pair in Danko F.R. with nest and 2 eggs, 11 Nov 1985 (Ash 1990).

794. PLOCEUS BAGLAFECHT   R(B)

(II.1233)   Baglafecht Weaver

Uncommon resident (*P. b. neumanni*), mainly at the edge of montane forest on the Mambilla Plateau: first record, a pair netted, Oct 1974 (P.H.), and 15

sightings since in that area and in Gashaka-Gumti Nat. Park (Ash 1990, Green 1990).
Breeding. No records, but may perhaps breed in any month (MP&G).

795. **PLOCEUS PELZELNI** RB

(II.1232)   *Slender-billed Weaver

Locally not uncommon resident (*P. p. monachus*) in mangroves and swamp forest of the coastal and sub-coastal belt, from Lagos to Calabar. Also "at Egga (?Eggan) on the Niger (Forbes)" (Bannerman 1949) – Egga cannot be located, but if Eggan is intended this record suggests the species is not confined to the sub-coastal belt.
Breeding. Noted only near Lagos, e.g. 20 nests in mangroves, 8 Jul 1956 (J.H.E.), overall May-Oct.
*Bannerman called this species Little Weaver, the name MP&G confusingly gave to *P. luteolus*.

796. **PLOCEUS LUTEOLUS** RB

(II.1230)   Little Weaver

Common resident (*P. l. luteolus*) in savanna woodlands, especially with *Acacia* trees, also gardens and farmland with large trees, in the Northern Guinea and Sudan zones, but only in Kainji Lake Nat. Park south of the great rivers.
Breeding. From Kainji north to Sokoto and Kano, Jun-Oct, also Maiduguri (P.H.).

797. **PLOCEUS OCULARIS** R(B)

(II.1224)   Spectacled Weaver

Probable first sighting, a pair at edge of montane forest on Obudu Plateau, March 1961 (F.C. Sibley). Further sightings at Oban Hills F.R.: a female on 30 Jan 1987 and a pair at same site 29 Sep 1987 (Ash 1990); netted in Gashaka-Gumti Nat. Park, Mar 1988 (Green 1990).
Breeding. Cameroon, Jan (MP&G).

798. **PLOCEUS NIGRICOLLIS** RB

(II.1223)   Black-necked Weaver* or (Swainson's) Spectacled Weaver

Common resident (*P. n. brachypterus*) in forest clearings, farms and wooded savanna from the coast north to the great rivers and not uncommon in gallery forest northward to Zaria, the Jos Plateau and Gadau.
Breeding. Nests usually solitary, breeding activity most months with a peak Jun-Sep, from the coast north to the Jos Plateau.
*The West African race *brachypterus* has no black on the "neck" or other upper parts, being instead bright olive-green. Black marks through the eyes make the name "Spectacled Weaver', by which it is most often at present known in West Africa, seem more suitable. See *P. ocularis*.

799. PLOCEUS MELANOGASTER RB
(II.1226) Black-billed Weaver

Not uncommon resident (*P. m. melanogaster*) near the ground within montane forest on the Obudu Plateau. Reported uncommon in Gashaka-Gumti Nat. Park, Mar 1988 (Green 1990).
Breeding. Nest Obudu Plateau, 11 Dec 1977 (P.M.).

800. PLOCEUS AURANTIUS RB
(II.1229) Orange Weaver

Locally not uncommon resident (*P. a. aurantius*) in swamps and along creeks in the coastal belt from Badagri to Bonny (and probably beyond), inland as far as Warri and Okitipupa; but since it occurs far from the coast in Zaïre it may do so in Nigeria.
Breeding. Recorded Feb, Jun, Sep, Nov and Dec, often in mixed colonies (with *P. cucullatus* and *P. nigerrimus*) in towns.

801. PLOCEUS HEUGLINI RB
(II.1216) Heuglin's Masked Weaver

Not uncommon resident in savanna woodlands and farms, often near villages throughout the area north of the great rivers, less numerous southward to the margin of the Guinea zone at Ilorin, Enugu and Serti. Hall & Moreau (1970) regard it as a superspecies with *P. velatus*, but the 2 overlap in the Sudan zone between Sokoto and Lake Chad.
Breeding. Only north of the great rivers, May-Oct, e.g. 45 nests Sokoto, 27 Jul to 5 Oct (Mundy & Cook 1972-73), i.e. in the same areas as *P. velatus*. Colonies usually derive protection from association with wasps, large birds, even Man (Elgood & Ward 1960, Grimes 1973).

802. PLOCEUS VELATUS RB
(II.1218) Vitelline Masked Weaver

Not uncommon resident (*P. v. vitellinus*) in thorn scrub savanna near swamps mainly of the Sudan zone, from Sokoto to Lake Chad and southward only in Kainji Lake Nat. Park. 7 records in the early 1990s from different parts of Jos Plateau (M.Ho)
Breeding. Throughout (including Kainji), Jun-Sep, e.g. 29 nests Sokoto, 5 Aug-25 Sep (Mundy & Cook 1972-73).

803. PLOCEUS CUCULLATUS RB
(II.1213) Village Weaver

Abundant resident (*P. c. cucullatus*) near towns and villages throughout, especially near standing water, including forest clearings, but avoiding closed forest.
Breeding. Colonial, often with other weavers, several hundred nests common. Some activity at nests almost all year in south, stimulated by any rain

shower; eggs mainly Jun-Aug; in area north of the great rivers rather later, with peak in Sep.

804. PLOCEUS NIGERRIMUS   RB
(II.1244)   Vieillot's Black Weaver

P. n. castaneofuscus is an abundant resident near villages and in swampy areas of southwest, from the coast north to Oyo and Akure and through most of the southeast from the Niger Delta to Calabar and north to Owerri. At Enugu, intermediates between *castaneofuscus* and nominate *nigerrimus* were collected by Serle (1957). *P. n. nigerrimus* is an uncommon and apparently very local resident in the southeast, its main range being east of Nigeria, Cameroon to Zaïre. Collected at Oban (Bannerman 1949) and Ikom (Serle 1957), sighted at the escarpment to the Mambilla Plateau (D.E., P.H.) and at Serti (P.H.) but reported fairly common in the southeast including Butatong, Oban Hills F.R., though uncommon Bashu and Okwango F.R. (Ash 1990).

Breeding. *P. n. castaneofuscus* like *P. cucullatus*, vigorous nest building occurs most of the year after rain, but eggs mainly May-Aug. Colonies of up to 300 pairs with *P. cucullatus* and sometimes *P. aurantius*. *P. n. nigerrimus* in a mixed colony with *P. cucullatus* near Mambilla Plateau, 24 Feb 1965 (D.Ebbutt). Large colonies, nest building Butatong, Nov 1985 and Sep 1987 (Ash 1990).

805. PLOCEUS MELANOCEPHALUS   RB
(II.1220)   Black-headed Weaver

Locally common resident (*P. m. capitalis*) on river banks with *Zizyphus* and *Mimosa* bushes, mostly along the Niger and Benue and their major tributaries, in many areas north of the great rivers from Sokoto to Lake Chad and south to Onitsha; old records are quoted by Serle (1957) for the Niger Delta. At Maiduguri (Hall 1977) "partially migratory, large numbers passing in July" but no other evidence of migration.

Breeding. Onitsha north to Sokoto and Kazaure, mainly Jul-Oct, but May at Onitsha (Serle 1957).

806. PLOCEUS TRICOLOR   RB
(II.1242)   Yellow-mantled Weaver

Not uncommon resident (*P. t. tricolor*) in lowland forest, forest edges, clearings and secondary growth of southwest from the coast north to Ibadan, Ife and Akure: less common in southeast, all the few localities being well to the east, including Calabar.

Breeding. Mainly Oct-Mar, but Ibadan, May (A.P.) and Lagos, Jun (H.F.M.). Colonies of 5-10 pairs.

807. PLOCEUS ALBINUCHA   R(B)
(II.1247)   White-naped Weaver

Uncommon resident (*P. a. holomelas*) in lowland forest from Ipake (J.A.B.) to Ikom (F.C.S.) and Owerri (Marchant 1953), inland as far as Gambari (J.H.E.) and Ikom. Not uncommon Okomu F.R. (P.H.).

Breeding. No records in Nigeria; resident breeder in Ivory Coast (Thiollay 1985).

808. PLOCEUS BICOLOR   R(B)
(II.1222)   Dark-backed Weaver

Not uncommon resident (*P. b. tephronotus*) at the edge of montane forest on the Obudu Plateau, not reported elsewhere.
Breeding. No records anywhere in West Africa.

[PLOCEUS PREUSSI   ?
(II.1240)   Golden-backed Weaver

A single very probable sighting of this distinctive species, in montane forest at Obudu Plateau, 21 Nov 1976 (P. Mackenzie). Ranges from Sierra Leone to Zaïre in lowland forest and so is likely to occur in Nigeria.]

809. PLOCEUS INSIGNIS   R(B)
(II.1239)   Brown-capped Weaver

Not uncommon resident in montane forest on the Obudu Plateau, also recorded in Gashaka-Gumti Nat. Park, Nov-Dec 1987 and Mar 1988 (Green 1990).
Breeding. No records, but "Cameroun, probably June to December" (MP&G) and building at Bambulue (Cameroon), Mar (J.H.E.).

810. PLOCEUS SUPERCILIOSUS   RB
(II.1237)   Compact Weaver

Not uncommon but local resident, subject to appearances and disappearances without seasonal pattern in many localities. Mostly in grasslands within the forest and derived savanna zones or in the valleys of the great rivers, but also Zaria (breeding) and Aliya.
Breeding. From the coast north to Zaria, Aug-Oct.

811. MALIMBUS RACHELIAE   RB
(II.1254)   Rachel's Malimbe

Resident in lowland forest of southeast, formerly only within 20 km of Calabar. Since 1987 reported frequent to common inside forest and at forest edge in Calabar and in the Oban Hills. Fairly common over a wide area of primary forest in the Ikpan block and Oban West (Cross River Nat. Park), 9-15 Apr 1988, with up to 10 birds seen in a day (Ash *et al.* 1989).
Breeding. Nests observed in Calabar area, Nov, Apr and Jun (Mackenzie 1979). Pair building Ikpan, 11 Apr 1988, and dependent juvs. being fed in Ikpan and Oban West, 12 and 15 Apr (Ash *et al.* 1989).

250   Ploceidae

812. MALIMBUS SCUTATUS   RB
(II.1253)   Red-vented Malimbe

Common resident (*M. s. scutopartitus*) of forest edges, clearings and secondary growth, especially those with *Eleais* and *Raphia* palms, right across the country from the coast, north to Ibadan, Ife, Ubiaja, near Nsukka and Enugu.
   Breeding. Some activity (mainly building) noted all months, mostly Sep-Feb.

813. MALIMBUS IBADANENSIS   RB
(II.1256)   Ibadan (Elgood's) Malimbe

Locally not uncommon resident mainly of forest edges and secondary growth – though first collected and described from an Ibadan garden (Elgood 1958) – in a small area of the southwest circumscribed by Ibadan, Ife, Iperu and Ilaro. Nigeria's only endemic species. Not sighted from 1980 until 2 Nov 1987 (Elgood 1988); latest record of pair building nest at Moniya, near Ibadan, 5 Mar 1988 (P.H.).
   Breeding. Nesting Ibadan, May, Jun and Oct (J.H.E.); eggs described Ilaro, Jul (J.A.Button) also Sep; building at Ife, Feb and Dec, juvs. early Nov, adults feeding young, May (R.F.).

814. MALIMBUS ERYTHROGASTER   RB
(II.1255)   Red-bellied Malimbe

Not uncommon resident in lowland forest canopy east of the Lower Niger from Degema to Calabar, mainly recorded by Marchant (1953) – "quite common in high bush . . . rarely coming low"
   Breeding. "2 pairs nesting with *M. rubricollis*" Umudin, Jul (Boulter 1965).

815. MALIMBUS NITENS   RB
(II.1250)   Blue-billed Weaver

Common resident in lowland forest and secondary growth subject to seasonal flooding, right across the country from the coast north to Ibadan, Ife and Enugu; also in gallery forest between Nasarawa and the Benue River (Serle 1940) – the only record north of the forest.
   Breeding. Over water, but not necessarily in wettest months. Overall Feb-Nov but mainly Apr-Jul.

816. MALIMBUS MALIMBICUS   RB
(II.1248)   Crested Malimbe

Not uncommon resident in lower strata of lowland forest (sometimes in secondary growth), right across the country from the coast north to Ibadan, Ife, Mamu Forest and Ikom. *M. m. nigrifrons* occurs west of the Lower Niger, *M. m. malimbicus* to the east, intergrading in southern Nigeria (White 1963); clinal intermediacy has been reported from Owerri (Marchant 1953).
   Breeding. Juv. netted Ilaro, 8 Feb 1964 (J.H.E.); building Ife, Feb (R.F.).

817. MALIMBUS RUBRICOLLIS RB
(II.1249) Red-headed Malimbe

Common resident of lowland forest edges and clearings, secondary growth and small forest outliers in farmland, right across the country from the coast north to Ibadan, Ife and Awgu. *M. r. nigeriae* occurs west of the Lower Niger, *M. r. rubricollis* to the east (White 1963), though Serle (1957) could not distinguish them – possibly Nigerian birds exhibit the middle range of a cline.

Breeding. Some activity most of year, mainly in drier months, Nov-Apr.

818. ANAPLECTES RUBRICEPS RB
(II.1259) Red-headed Anaplectes

Locally not uncommon resident (*A. r. leuconotus*) in "Doka" woodland of the Northern Guinea Savanna, from Kainji Lake Nat. Park and Zaria to Yankari, Kari and the Jos Plateau. A male seen near a nest in savanna woodland between Serti and Beli on 31 Mar 1988 (Ash *et al.* 1989). First record south of Benue in Nigeria.

Breeding. Nov-May, but building still in progress Zaria, 21 Jun 1960 (J.H.E.).

819. QUELEA ERYTHROPS RB
(II.1263) Red-headed Quelea

Locally common resident, mostly in moist grasslands south of the great rivers, also on coast at Lagos, Sapele, Warri and Calabar, and north of the great rivers at Zaria, the Jos Plateau and Pandam Wildlife Park. Subject to sporadic movements (rather than true migration) obscured by the fact that only the male nuptial plumage is distinctive in mixed flocks of small weavers. Flocks usually small, but once Sapele 500+, 28 Jun 1975 (J.B.H.).

Breeding. "Several hundred pairs" Abeokuta, Aug (Bannerman 1951); small colony Zaria, Jun (P.W.).

820. QUELEA QUELEA RB
(II.1262) Red-billed Quelea

Abundant (*Q. q. quelea*) in extreme northeast all year from Maiduguri to Lake Chad and south to Sambisa (P.H.), but no more than common across the Sudan Zone from Maiduguri west to Sokoto. Probably the world's most abundant species. Germination of food grains at the onset of rain leads to a "reverse" southward migration (Ward 1971), and birds may reach as far south as Zaria and the Benue River near the Cameroon border, Jun-Jul.

Breeding. Colonies of up to several million pairs in Chad basin, Aug-Nov, but peak Sep-Oct.

821. EUPLECTES AFER RB
(II.1270) Yellow-crowned Bishop

Common resident (*E. a. afer*) in grassy marshes, especially those bordering per-

manent rivers, throughout, but more frequent from the great rivers northward than towards the coast.
Breeding. From the coast at Lagos north to Kano, mostly Jul-Sep.

822. EUPLECTES HORDEACEUS   RB

(II.1266)   Black-winged Red Bishop

Common resident (*E. h. hordeaceus*) in tall grass and scrub near water throughout the Guinea Savanna, north to Kano (I.D.) and Aliya, less common progressively southward; no recent records for Ibadan or Lagos (old skins in BMNH and Liverpool Museum respectively) and absent south of Enugu and Serti in southeast.
Breeding. North of the great rivers and in Kainji Lake Nat. Park, Aug-Oct.

823. EUPLECTES ORIX   RB

(II.1265)   Red Bishop

Common to locally abundant resident (*E. o. franciscanus*), in rank grasses near water, from around Ilorin and Enugu, northward to Sokoto and Lake Chad, and previously further south to Ibadan and Abeokuta in southwest, Awgu and Afikpo in southeast, but very few recently, e.g. 4 at Lagos, 13-20 Oct 1973 (Gee & Heigham 1977).
Breeding. Only from the great rivers northward, Jul-Oct.

824. EUPLECTES CAPENSIS   R(B)

(II.1268)   Yellow (or Black-and-yellow) Bishop

Common resident (*E. c. phoenicomerus*) in montane grassland on the Obudu and Mambilla Plateaux, unrecorded elsewhere.
Breeding. No records, but males in full breeding plumage at Obudu, Nov (J.H.E.); "Cameroun, September to January" (MP&G).

825. EUPLECTES AXILLARIS   R(B)

(II.1271)   Fan-tailed Widow-bird

Uncommon, perhaps rare resident (*E. a. bocagei*), until recently known only from the Sahel just west of Lake Chad, but as only the male in nuptial plumage is distinctive (at a season when the rains make observation difficult), is possibly less rare than the few records suggest: 3 males collected Logomani, 7 Jul 1960 (F.C. Sibley); occasional in the rainy season, 4 seen together Malamfatori (A.J.H.). Uncommon in the Jeribowl floodplain, 10 km east of Maiduguri, during the rains (P.H.).
Breeding. One of Sibley's birds had slightly enlarged testis; "Cameroun, September and October" (MP&G).

826. EUPLECTES MACROURUS   RB

(II.1272)   Yellow-mantled Widow-bird

Common resident (*E. m. macrourus*) in wet grassy valleys of the Guinea Savanna, north to Zaria, Zonkwa, the Jos Plateau and Birnin Kudu and south to the coast from Calabar to Lagos. Possibly prone to some local movements when its habitat dries out, but these are obscured by some difficulty in distinguishing males in eclipse at that time.

Breeding. From the coast at Lagos north to the Jos Plateau, Jul-Oct.

827. EUPLECTES ARDENS   RB

(II.1275)   Red-collared Widow-bird

Locally not uncommon resident (*E. a. concolor*), confined to upland grassland of the Jos, Obudu (flocks up to 100, Aug – M.D.) and Mambilla Plateaux only. Not strictly montane and since only male in nuptial plumage is distinctive, could have been overlooked elsewhere.

Breeding. Copulation Obudu, Nov (J.H.E.); young just flying Jos, Oct (J.R.L.).

828. EUPLECTES HARTLAUBI   ?

(II.1274)   Marsh Whydah

New species for Nigeria. Although recorded in Cameroon by 1981, first recorded in Nigeria in 1988 at three localities on the Mambilla Plateau: one seen near Nwajai, 12 Mar 1988; 5 or 6 at Papa near Mayo Ndaga on 27 Mar; up to 20 seen daily near Yelwa, 28-30 Mar. All were in rank streamside vegetation in montane grassland at 1500-1600 m. (Ash *et al.* 1989). Status hard to define until further records become available.

Breeding. No record in Nigeria. Said to breed only in wet areas with a dense growth of fine wiry grass up to eighteen inches high. Recorded in southeastern Zaïre, Jan to Mar (MP&G).

829. ANOMALOSPIZA IMBERBIS   R(B)

(II.1306)   Parasitic Weaver

Uncommon and very local (possibly overlooked) resident in open grassy valleys, mostly from the Jos Plateau, from Jos and Vom to the River Gongola, and once a small flock at Zaria, 23 Jun 1966 (C.H.F.); most northerly record: a male netted Jekara Dam, 26 May 1982 (Wilkinson & Aidley 1982).

Breeding. No West African data but elsewhere known to parasitize warblers (*Prinia* and *Cisticola*) and other small passerines.

830. AMBLYOSPIZA ALBIFRONS   RB

(II.1260)   Grosbeak Weaver

Locally not uncommon resident in rank grass and reed beds near rivers in southwest from the coast north to Ibadan, Ife and Asaba, with one old record from Ilorin and one from Awgu in southeast (both Bannerman 1949). Probably most are *A. a. saturata* but some from extreme southwest (Lagos and Abeokuta) are *A. a. capitalba*; too few skins collected for clear racial distribution.

Breeding. Mostly Jun-Aug, but some as late as Oct.

ESTRILDIDAE

831. PARMOPTILA WOODHOUSEI   RB

(II.1282)   Flower-pecker Weaver-Finch

Rare resident (*P. w. woodhousei*), near ground in lowland forest, perhaps with preference for swamp forest. Small and shy, possibly overlooked; almost all records refer to collected specimens. Recorded only at 5 localities: near Cameroon border at Calabar (Bannerman 1949); Ikom (Serle 1957); Lagos, 11 Mar 1972 (J.P.Gee); one in rain forest at Bashu, 8 Oct 1987 (Ash 1990); one netted at Okomu F.R., 20 Nov 1988 (P.H.). Records suggest it occurs right across the forest belt.

Breeding. Gee's Lagos specimen was female in breeding condition; feeding young out of nest Calabar, May (P.M.).

832. NIGRITA FUSCONOTA   RB

(II.1287)   White-breasted Negro-Finch

Uncommon resident in little disturbed lowland forest, usually at canopy level, so may be overlooked, *N. f. uropygialis* west of the Lower Niger and *N. f. fusconota* to the east. In southwest extends from coast north to Ife and Akure, in southeast from Calabar to Umuahia and Umuagwu. Other records: 3 singles around Okwango F.R., 19-21 Nov 1985; 2 Oban Hills F.R., 1 Oct 1987; one at Bashu, 9 Oct 1987 (Ash 1990).

Breeding. Breeding condition Lagos, 4 Jan (Bannerman 1949); building Ife, 18 Apr 1972 (R.F.).

833. NIGRITA BICOLOR   RB

(II.1286)   Chestnut-breasted Negro-Finch

Not uncommon resident (*N. b. brunnescens*) in mangrove scrub and lowland forest including secondary growth, usually near ground level, right across the country from the coast north to Ibadan and Ife in southwest, but not north of Owerri in southeast, where it may be uncommon. Readily taken in mist nets.

Breeding. C/3 Ibadan, 8 May (H.F.M.); nest Sapele, 16 Mar 1975 (J.B.H.); building Lagos, Mar (B.N.F.).

834. NIGRITA LUTEIFRONS   R(B)

(II.1285)   Pale-fronted Negro-Finch

Uncommon resident (*N. l. luteifrons*) in lowland forest edges and clearings usually at a lower height than *N. canicapilla*, similarity to which may have caused *luteifrons* to be overlooked. Almost all records are from southwest, from Lagos to the Niger Delta, north to Ibadan and Ife. The only easterly records (Serle 1957) are "Ansorge's specimen from the Lower Niger" and one obtained at Okpo just north of the former Eastern Region.

Breeding. Not recorded, but "Fernando Po, October. Cameroun, June" (MP&G).

835. NIGRITA CANICAPILLA   RB
   (II.1284)   Grey-headed Negro-Finch

Common resident (*N. c. canicapilla*) of lowland forest canopy, secondary growth, edges, clearings and gardens right across the country from the coast north to Ibadan, Ife, Akure, Nsukka and Enugu. Also Oban Hills; one building, 1 Oct 1987 (Ash 1990).
Breeding. In almost all months, mostly in rainy season, Apr-Oct.

836. NESOCHARIS SHELLEYI   R(B)
   (II.1335)   Fernando Po Olive-back

Probably not uncommon (not known whether *N. s. shelleyi* or *N. s. bansoensis*) at the edge of montane forest at Obudu Plateau but unrecorded elsewhere. Records are: male (first sighting), 20 Dec 1962 (J.H.E.); sighting, Dec 1974 (T.R-S.); pair seen, 21 Nov 1976; pair netted, 26 Jun 1977 (P.M.); pair seen, 8 Aug 1980 (M.D.); one or 2 at 3 sites on Obudu Cattle Ranch, 15-18 Nov 1985 (Ash 1990); pair seen and photographed at 2 sites at Obudu Cattle Ranch, 24-26 Dec 1989 (I.G.N.). The netted pair were not racially determined.
Breeding. No records in West Africa.

837. NESOCHARIS CAPISTRATA   RB
   (II.1336)   Grey-headed Olive-back

Uncommon resident in grassy savanna with some bushes, usually near water, mostly within the Guinea zone, north of the great rivers from Kaduna, Jos Plateau and Yankari Nat. Park to Kari, south of the Middle Niger to Abeokuta, but the only record south of the Benue is one in thick woodland between Serti and Beli 30 Mar 1988 (Ash *et al.* 1989).
Breeding. Nest building (nest almost complete) Abeokuta, 3 Jul 1959 (J.H.E.); 2 nests being built Birnin Gwari, Jun (D&G).

838. PYTILIA PHOENICOPTERA   RB
   (II.1309)   Red-winged Pytilia

Not uncommon resident (*P. p. phoenicoptera*) in scrub and tall grass savanna of the Northern Guinea zone from Kainji Lake Nat. Park and north of the great rivers into the Sudan zone at Sokoto, Kano and Potiskum.
Breeding. C/4, 15 Nov 1937; C/4, 21 Dec 1937; B/2 and C/2, 1 Feb 1938, all Kafanchan (Bannerman 1949). C/2, 16 Dec and C/3, 22 Dec, Kari (P.B.); female with oviducal egg Kainji Lake Nat. Park, 8 Sep (Wells & Walsh 1969).

839. PYTILIA MELBA   RB
   (II.1312)   Melba Finch

Not uncommon resident (*P. m. citerior*) in grassy patches of thorn scrub usually near water in the Sudan and Sahel zones from Sokoto to Lake Chad.
Breeding. C/3 Kano, 31 Aug 1936, 1 Sep 1936 (Bannerman 1949); building Sokoto, Jul (Mundy & Cook 1972-73); C/3 Kano, 1 Mar 1979 (hatching 9 Mar) (Sharland & Wilkinson 1981).

840. PYTILIA HYPOGRAMMICA RB

(II.1310)   Yellow-winged Pytilia

Not uncommon resident in savanna woodland and former farmland of the Guinea zone south to Kishi, Enugu and Serti and north to Zaria.
   Breeding. C/3 Enugu, 18 Jan 1955, with details of identification (Serle 1957).

841. MANDINGOA NITIDULA RB

(II.1308)   Green-backed Twin-spot

Previously only a single old record (*M. n. schlegeli*): Ibadan, "a bird found dead" by Foulkes-Roberts (Bannerman 1949). Said to be "silent elusive little birds of dense thickets and secondary forest" (MP&G). Recently recorded in Oban Hills.
   Breeding. 2 juvs. netted and photographed at Oban Hills F.R., 30 Jan 1987 (Ash 1990).

842. CRYTPTOSPIZA REICHENOVII RB

(II.1298)   Red-faced Crimson-wing

Uncommon resident (*C. r. reichenovii*) at the edge of montane forest on the Obudu Plateau, unknown elsewhere. Male and female netted on successsive days, Dec 1962 (J.H.E.); several sightings there since (T.R-S. and P.M.).
   Breeding. The netted pair, taken in the same small area, had enlarged gonads, and were probably nesting.

843. PYRENESTES OSTRINUS RB

(II.1295-7)   Seed-cracker

Uncommon resident (*P. o. ostrinus*) at forest edges and in gallery forest from the coast to the great rivers and sparsely north to Kaduna and Pandam Wildlife Park.
   Breeding. Building (Warri, Calabar, Ibadan), Jul-Sep; adults feeding juvs. Sapele, Jan-Mar (J.B.H.).

844. SPERMOPHAGA HAEMATINA RB

(II.1291)   Blue-bill

Common resident near ground level in thick undergrowth of lowland forest, especially young secondary growth, *S. h. togoensis* west of the lower Niger, *S. h. pustulata* to the east. Mostly met from the forest zone at the coast, north to Ibadan, Ife and Enugu, but also in relict forest along southern escarpment of the Jos Plateau at Kagoro and Pandam Wildlife Park and perhaps also in dense gallery forest between these 2 main areas. Readily taken in mist nets.
   Breeding. C/3 Sapele, 2 Sep (Serle 1958); Ndian, Aug-Oct (Macdonald 1959).

845. CLYTOSPIZA MONTEIRI R(B)

(II.1288) Brown Twin-spot

Not uncommon resident in one small area close to the Cameroon border near 7°N in both montane and lowland grassy areas. First record, 3 netted Abong, 11 May 1974 (P.W.), extending known range west into Nigeria. Since found "quite common" at Serti and sighted on the nearby Mambilla Plateau (P.H.).
Breeding. No records for anywhere in West Africa, but Apr in Gabon (MP&G).

846. EUSCHISTOSPIZA DYBOWSKII RB

(II.1289) Dybowski's Dusky Twin-spot

Uncommon and very local resident in upland grassy savanna of only 3 areas: the Jos Plateau, where only old records until recent sighting Tayu, 18 Sep 1993 (M.Ho); between Serti and the Mambilla Plateau where it has been netted and found to be quite common (P.H.); one seen on slopes of Obudu Plateau at 1200 m, 4 Apr 1988 (Ash *et.al* 1989).
Breeding. A male seen beside riverine vegetation in Kagoro Hills on 4 Feb 1987 and a female and at least 2 juvs. in the same locality next day. An overnight fire destroyed this habitat and it was not until 17 Feb that this or a different family party was located again downstream of the original locality (Wilkinson *et al.* 1987). No records elsewhere in West Africa.

847. LAGONOSTICTA RUFOPICTA RB

(II.1317) Bar-breasted Fire-Finch

The common resident Fire-Finch (*L. r. rufopicta*) of the south and some well wooded central areas. Not uncommon in grassy forest clearings and open areas from the coast from Badagri to Calabar north to the great rivers, and beyond from Zaria to Yankari, where it is largely replaced by *L. senegala*.
Breeding. C/4 Epe, 15 Aug 1928 and nests Kafanchan, 19 Jul and 5 Oct (Bannerman 1949); C/6 Lagos, 16 Sep (H.F.M.); C/5 Ibadan, 16 May 1954 (J.H.E.).

848. LAGONOSTICTA SENEGALA RB

(II.1316) Red-billed Fire-Finch

Abundant resident (*L. s. senegala*) in open savanna, especially farmland and near villages throughout the area north of the great rivers, south of the Middle Niger to Ilorin and south of the Benue to Enugu and Serti, but never very numerous southward. An old record from Lagos could refer to an escape.
Breeding. Some activity most months, mainly May-Oct.

849. LAGONOSTICTA RARA RB

(II.1320) Black-bellied Fire-Finch

Locally not uncommon resident (*L. r. forbesi*) of grassy savanna farmland and the edge of gallery forest in the Guinea zone from Iseyin, Enugu and Serti north to Zaria and Kari.

Breeding. C/4 Kafanchan, 21 Jul 1937 (Bannerman 1949); female with 3 yolked eggs Enugu, 4 Oct 1954 (Serle 1957).

850. LAGONOSTICTA RUBRICATA   RB

(II.1313)   African Fire-Finch

Locally not uncommon resident (*L. r. polionota*) in thickets and dense grass, perhaps preferring upland areas, mostly in the Guinea zone southward to Idanre (an elevated area), Enugu and Serti, north to Ririwai and Aliya, with records from Jos and Obudu Plateaux.
Breeding. C/4 Kafanchan, 20 Aug 1937 (Bannerman 1949).

851. LAGONOSTICTA LARVATA   RB

(II.1319)   Black-faced Fire-Finch

Locally not uncommon resident (*E. l. togoensis*) in damp areas of savanna woodland such as *Raphia* thickets and along streams, mostly in the Northern Guinea Zone, but south to Kishi and Iseyin in southwest and Enugu and Serti in southeast. Also noted at Sokoto and Ririwai, but Zaria and 11°N are normal limit.
Breeding. C/4 Kafanchan, 9 Jul, C/3 Nasarawa, 12 Aug (Bannerman 1949).

852. URAEGINTHUS BENGALUS   RB

(II.1339)   Red-cheeked Cordon-bleu

Abundant resident (*E. b. bengalus*) in degraded savanna around farms and villages of the Northern Guinea and Sudan zones and in some localities in the Sahel to Lake Chad. Still common southward to the great rivers and Kainji Lake Nat. Park and regular in southwest to Igbetti and Ilorin, and once Ibadan (10 Dec 1967 – J.Mackenzie), though this last could have been an escape. South of the Benue noted at Gboko and Serti.
Breeding. Mostly Jul-Oct, overall Jun-Nov.

853. ESTRILDA CAERULESCENS   RB

(II.1322)   Red-tailed Lavender Waxbill

Locally not uncommon resident in dense scrub (especially wet areas with *Raphia* thickets) of Guinea and Sudan savannas, south of the Middle Niger from Kainji Lake Nat. Park to Kaiama, but not south of the Benue, and north to Kano and Maiduguri. Flocks 20+ not infrequent.
Breeding. Nest building Graya, near Kano, Oct 1979 (R.E.S.). Flock with juvs. being fed Zaria, 1 Dec (M.D.).

854. ESTRILDA POLIOPAREIA   RB

(II.1329)   Anambra Waxbill

Not uncommon resident in a very few localities from the Lower Niger to extreme southwest, in long grass on river or lagoon sand banks. "Discovered by Robin

Kemp at the Anambra Creek" (Bannerman 1949) and subsequently Serle (1957) collected a series at Onitsha (30 km southeast). Sighted at Badagri (C.H.F., J.A.B.) and Forcados area ("small parties, several times" - H.F.M.); 2 clearly identified at Asaba, opposite Onitsha, 24 Jan 1987 (Ash 1990).

Breeding. "A female collected (Onitsha) on 19 June had yolking eggs" (Serle 1957).

855. ESTRILDA MELPODA   RB

(II.1327)   Orange-cheeked Waxbill

Common to locally abundant resident (flocks 50+ frequent) from the coast north to the limits of the Northern Guinea zone, in rank grass near water in savanna and forest clearings. Also present near Lake Chad and on the Mambilla and Obudu Plateaux.

Breeding. From the coast north to Zaria and the Jos Plateau, Apr-Oct, peak in Jul.

856. ESTRILDA TROGLODYTES   RB

(II.1325)   Black-rumped Waxbill

Locally common resident (*E. t. troglodytes*) in dry grassy savanna and abandoned farmland from Kainji Lake Nat. Park and the great river valleys, north to the northern borders from Sokoto to Lake Chad. Flocks of 50+ frequent, sometimes, with other seed-eating species, in really large numbers, e.g. several hundreds at a threshing waste Pategi, 21 May 1960 (J.H.E.). Abundant in Sambisa in the dry season (P.H.).

Breeding. 3 nests Zaria, mid Jul to mid Aug; Kano undated (Bannerman 1949). Nest with seven eggs at Kano, Aug 1978, and fledglings netted there, Nov and Dec (Sharland & Wilkinson 1981).

857. ESTRILDA ASTRILD   R(B)

(II.1323)   Waxbill

Not uncommon resident (*E. a. occidentalis*) in grassland, but very local, apparently mainly in east and near border with Cameroon. Recently netted at Mambilla (H.B.,P.H.) and Obudu Plateaux (P.M.). Bannerman (1949) mentions "little flocks" at Jos as a "not very satisfactory record", but it has been sighted there since, and at Kaduna (J.R.L.); also Calabar (R.E.S.) and Potiskum (P.B.).

Breeding. No records, but "Cameroun, November" (MP&G).

858. ESTRILDA NONNULA   R(B)

(II.1333)   Black-crowned Waxbill

Locally abundant resident (flocks 60+) in montane grassland, usually near montane forest edge at Obudu and Mambilla Plateaux, unrecorded elsewhere. Bannerman (1950) assigned Cameroon highlands birds to *E. n. nonnula* and MP&G state this race occurs at Obudu Plateau; but White (1963) distinguished birds from "Fernando Po and southwest Cameroons" as *E. n. elizae*. Obudu and Mambilla birds need to be racially determined.

Breeding. No records, but "Cameroun, September to November" (MP&G).

859. AMANDAVA SUBFLAVA　　　　　　　　　　　　　　　　　　　RB

(II.1334)　Goldbreast

Locally common resident (*A. s. subflava*) in grasses, usually near water (including rice), over a wide area from Oyo and Iwo in southwest to Onitsha on the Lower Niger, north to Sokoto, Kano and Maiduguri. Common on Mambilla Plateau near Yelwa at 1600 m 28-30 Mar 1988 (Ash *et.al* 1989). Possibly a seasonal migrant in some areas but no clear evidence.

Breeding. C/5 Kafanchan, 18 Nov 1937 (Serle 1938); adults with 4 juvs. near Potiskum, 1 Jan (P.B.).

860. ORTYGOSPIZA ATRICOLLIS　　　　　　　　　　　　　　　　RB

(II.1303)　Quail-Finch

Common resident (*O. a. atricollis*) in short grass areas such as air-strips and farmland stubble, from the coast at Lagos north to Sokoto and Lake Chad but in southeast only known from Enugu and Okigwi. Flocks of 30+ frequent.

Breeding. From Lagos to Zaria and Kano mostly Sep-Dec, but noted as late as Feb.

861. LONCHURA MALABARICA　　　　　　　　　　　　　　　　　RB

(II.1281)　Silver-bill

Common resident (*L. m. cantans*) in dry sandy savanna, especially around villages, right across the north from Sokoto to Lake Chad and south to Kainji Lake Nat. Park, the Jos Plateau and Yankari. An isolated population in Lagos "residential suburbs may have originated from escapes but now seems well established" (Gee & Heigham 1977).

Breeding. Protracted and perhaps variable, Sep-May, not yet noted south of Zaria.

862. LONCHURA CUCULLATA　　　　　　　　　　　　　　　　　　RB

(II.1277)　Bronze Mannikin

Common to locally abundant resident (*L. c. cucullata*) in grassy areas from the coast north to Zaria and the Jos Plateau, much less common northward to Kano. Unlike *L. bicolor* is infrequent in grassy forest clearings.

Breeding. Prolonged, with 2 or 3 broods in same nest (J.R.L.) on Jos Plateau; from coast north to Zaria and Jos Plateau, overall Apr-Dec, mostly Jun-Sep.

863. LONCHURA BICOLOR　　　　　　　　　　　　　　　　　　　RB

(II.1278)　Black and White Mannikin

Common resident (*L. b. bicolor*) in grassy areas of forest clearings in southwest, rather less common in southeast; mainly from the coast to Ibadan, Ife and Akure in southwest but only on Obudu and Mambilla Plateaux at any distance from coast in southeast. Only 2 northern localities: Zungeru (Bannerman 1949) and the Jos Plateau (Ebbutt *et al.* 1965).

Breeding. Numerous records from the coast north to Ibadan, Mar-Sep.

864. LONCHURA FRINGILLOIDES   RB
    (II.1280)   Magpie Mannikin

Uncommon local resident, possibly overlooked through similarity to *L. cucullata* with which it associates. Noted in only 6 localities: 2 sighted Uyo (near Calabar), 11 Jul 1954 (Serle 1957); Epe, 10 Aug 1952 (H.F.M.); BMNH skin (collected R.G. Newell) from Panshanu, 26 Jul 1962; "2 pairs nest building" Shaffini Swamp Forest, Lake Kainji, 11 Feb (F.W.); "parties up to 20" several times at Serti, Sep-Jan (P.H.); small flock Tayu, 18 Sep 1993 (M.Ho.).
    Breeding. Lake Kainji (see above); building Serti, Nov.

865. AMADINA FASCIATA   Afm/B
    (II.1302)   Cut-throat

Locally common resident (*A. f. fasciata*) all year in thorn scrub of the Sudan zone from Sokoto to Maiduguri. More southerly records to Zaria and Kainji Lake Nat. Park are for dry season only, while numbers in Sahel (Malamfatori) increase in the rains, both indicating short range migration. Great increase in numbers at Zaria in recent years, thought to be consequence of the Sahel drought of the early seventies (C.H.F.).
    Breeding. Zaria, Jan (Stickley 1966).

866. PHOLIDORNIS RUSHIAE   RB
    (II.1199)*   Tiny Tit-Weaver

Locally not uncommon resident in the canopy of lowland forest (*P. r. rushiae*) from Lagos to Calabar, but sparsely recorded.
    Breeding. Adults feeding young, Ife Dec (R.F.).
*Placed in *Nectariniidae* by MP&G and in *Estrildinae* (*Ploceidae*) by Bannerman.

VIDUIDAE

Much work has been done since 1981 on the species now included in this family (Payne 1982, 1985 and 1993) and is still proceeding, especially in relation to the indigobirds, but finality in distinguishing all the species occurring in Nigeria has not yet been reached. In accordance with our stated aim of following the sequence and nomenclature followed by the authors of *Birds of Africa* we have included here only those species shown in the Preliminary Working List of Species to be included in Volume VII of *Birds of Africa* (in prep.) as adopted at an editorial meeting held in August, 1993, which gives no English names. The English names we show in this section are those used by R.B. Payne in his contribution on "Brood Parasitism in Nigerian Birds" (p. 53). In consequence of this, 3 species of indigobird viz. *Vidua larvaticola, V. nigeriae* and *V. camerunensis* which Payne includes as occurring or likely to occur in Nigeria are omitted. It is to be hoped that continuing fieldwork will enable these differences to be resolved in the near future.

867. VIDUA CHALYBEATA RB

(II.1340) Village Indigobird

Not uncommon resident (*V. c. neumanni*) in grassy savanna north of the great rivers and south of the Benue to Enugu and Serti. Less common in southwest but met all year at Lagos (Gee & Heigham 1977). Parasitises and mimics *Lagonosticta senegala*.

Breeding. Jul to Oct. Specific dates and locations not recorded but in view of its wide distribution in areas also occupied by *L. senegala* breeding clearly takes place in Nigeria (Payne 1968a, 1982 and 1985).

868. VIDUA RARICOLA RB

(Not in MP&G) Goldbreast Indigobird

Uncommon resident in grassy savanna. Specimens from Enugu, Kogum and Zaria. Parasitises and mimics *Amandava subflava*.

Breeding. Young at Zaria, Nov 1975 (M.G.). Other specific dates and locations not recorded but breeding likely as in previous species (Payne 1982 and 1985).

869. VIDUA FUNEREA R(B)

(II.1342) Variable Indigobird

Uncommon resident (race not defined) recorded Aug to Dec in savanna in Nindam F.R. (Dyer *et al.* 1986). *V. f. maryae* recorded only in the area of the Jos Plateau, though other subspecies known in Sierra Leone and Cameroon. Parasitises and mimics *Lagonosticta rubricata* whose distribution in Nigeria is more widespread, both north and south of the Jos Plateau. Payne accords the Nigerian bird specific status as *V. maryae*, Jos Plateau Indigobird.

Breeding. No precise records in Nigeria but birds in breeding plumage with enlarged testes on Jos Plateau in Aug. Breeding likely as in preceding species in view of records of mimicry of *L. rubricata* at Panshanu and Kagoro. Nests with young found in Sierra Leone, Nov (Payne 1982).

870. VIDUA WILSONI RB

(II.1342) Bar-breasted Firefinch Indigobird

Ranges in West Africa from Gambia to Cameroon. Resident but not common in Nigeria, recorded as far north as Falgore Game Reserve, Kano State (Wilkinson & Beecroft 1985), south to Enugu, west to Ibadan and Abeokuta and east to Yankari. Parasitises and mimics *Lagonosticta rufopicta*.

Breeding. As in other indigobird species the breeding season falls late in the rains. Birds at Zaria mated in Aug but no young out of the nest by early Sep (Payne 1982).

871. VIDUA MACROURA R(B)

(II.1344) Pin-tailed Whydah

Common resident in grassy savanna and grassy clearings within the forest zone including the Jos, Mambilla and Obudu Plateaux. No clear evidence of migration, though most northerly records are in the rainy season, e.g. Falgore G.R. (Wilkinson & Beecroft 1985), but elsewhere local appearances are sporadic. When not breeding, flocks of 100+ are common.

Breeding. No positive data other than breeding plumage and display, Apr-Oct. Elsewhere known to parasitise *Estrilda nonnula, E. astrild, E. troglodytes* and *E. melpoda* (Payne 1994).

872. VIDUA ORIENTALIS   R(B)

(II.1346)   Sahel Paradise Whydah

Common resident (*V. o. aucupum*) in savanna woodlands of northeast from Birnin Kudu to Lake Chad; not uncommon through rest of the area north of the great rivers and south to Kainji and Igbetti in the west and to Enugu and Serti in the east. Bannerman (1949) states that *aucupum* intergrades with nominate *orientalis* around Maiduguri; Serle (1957) collected 3 males at Enugu which he identified as *Steganura paradisea interjecta*, which White (1963) placed in *V.(=S.)orientalis*, locating it only from Cameroon eastward.

Breeding. No records, but males in breeding plumage in Kano State, Jun-Feb (Sharland & Wilkinson 1981). Serle (1987) stated there was strong presumptive evidence that an egg discovered in the nest of *Pytilia hypogrammica* on 18 Jan belonged to this parasitic weaver. Known to parasitise the nest and mimic the song of *P. melba* (Payne 1985).

873. VIDUA INTERJECTA   R(B)

(II.1346)   Exclamatory Paradise Whydah

Considered by Bannerman (1953) and Mackworth-Praed and Grant (1973) to be a subspecies of *V.(=Steganura) orientalis* but shown by Payne (1985) as a separate species, males with long tails being observed in Nigeria at Zaria and Yankari Nat. Park between Jul and Nov. Specimens taken at Enugu, Yola and Zaria.

Breeding. No records but probably breeds in rainy season like its congeners. Parasitises *Pytilia phoenicoptera* and probably also *P. hypogrammica*.

FRINGILLIDAE

874. SERINUS LEUCOPYGIUS   RB

(II.1355)   White-rumped Seed-eater

Locally common resident (*S. l. riggenbachi*) in open grassy savanna and farmland mainly of the Sudan zone to Maiduguri, Sambisa, Zaria, the Jos Plateau and Yankari. Lagos records are almost certainly of escapes.

Breeding. C/4, 25 Jul, C/3, 8 Aug, both Kano; C/4 Sokoto, 4 Aug (Bannerman 1948); Zaria, Dec (C.H.F.).

875. **SERINUS MOZAMBICUS** RB

   (II.1348) Yellow-fronted Canary

Locally common resident (*S. m. caniceps*) in open savannas and farmland north of the great rivers, south only to IITA Ibadan in the west, but to Enugu and Afikpo in southeast. Surprisingly absent (or very uncommon) in large tracts of suitable country; numbers may be diminishing through persecution, being a locally popular cage-bird. Southern records from Ife, Lagos and Warri ("local in gardens and thickets all year" - F.E. Warr) may refer to escapes.

   Breeding. North of the great rivers and in Kainji Lake Nat. Park, Apr-Dec.

876. **SERINUS GULARIS** RB

   (II.1353) Streaky-headed Seed-eater

Uncommon resident (*S. g. canicapilla*) in degraded farmland savanna of the Guinea zone, south to Enugu and north to Zaria. Serle (1957) collected a long series at Enugu, but it has not been found there recently (S.G.C.) and nowhere now can it be regarded as more than "locally frequent", e.g. in Kainji Lake Nat. Park (Wells & Walsh 1969). Occasional in Yankari Nat. Park (Green 1989); one Anara F.R., 1 Apr 1991 (M.D. & A.M.N.).

   Breeding. No records, but in breeding condition Loko, Jul (Bannerman 1948).

877. **SERINUS BURTONI** RB

   (II.1358) Thick-billed Seed-eater

Possibly uncommon rather than rare highland resident (*S. b. burtoni*). Sightings on Obudu Plateau: first record 22 Dec 1967 (Gray 1969); 19 Nov 1976 (P.M.); common Nov 1987 (Ash 1990) and in Gashaka-Gumti Nat. Park (Green 1990).

   Breeding. A pair nest-building Obudu Plateau, 17 Nov 1985; 2 adults feeding fledgling at same place, 9 Feb 1987 (Ash 1990).

878. **LINURGUS OLIVACEUS** R(B)

   (II.1361) Oriole-Finch

Not uncommon resident (*L. o. olivaceus*) at the edge of montane forest on the Obudu Plateau. Sighted on Mambilla Plateau (Stuart 1986, Ash 1990) and in Gashaka-Gumti Nat. Park (Green 1990).

   Breeding. No records, but "Cameroon Mt., November to January" (MP&G).

EMBERIZIDAE

879. **EMBERIZA HORTULANA** PM

   (II.1366) Ortolan

Uncommon Palaearctic migrant to open grassy areas with bare rock patches from around Zaria and the Jos Plateau only, Dec-Apr. Several have been netted and more sighted, but the small total suggests that northern Nigeria is south of the normal wintering range.

880. EMBERIZA TAHAPISI　　　　　　　　　　　　　　　　　　　　　　　　Afm/B

(II.1369)   Rock-Bunting

Common to locally abundant resident (*E. t. goslingi*) in open savanna with rock outcrops and erosion gullies throughout the area north of the great rivers, but with a "hump-back bridge" pattern of migration (Elgood *et al.* 1973). Recorded south of the great rivers in the dry season to Kabba, Enugu, Mambilla and Obudu Plateaux. It is a locally popular cage-bird, so coastal records from Lagos, Burutu and Port Harcourt may refer to escapes. In the Sudan and Sahel zones it is a rains migrant with strong passage noted at Malamfatori, Sep (R.J.D.).

Breeding. May be protracted, mostly Sep-Feb (29 nests Zaria, 24 Sep to 11 Dec-M.G.), but C/3 Kano, Jul (R.E.S.). All records north of great rivers.

881. EMBERIZA FLAVIVENTRIS　　　　　　　　　　　　　　　　　　　　　　　RB

(II.1364)   Golden-breasted Bunting

Not uncommon resident (*E. f. flavigaster*) in combretum scrub and open savanna of the Sudan zone from Sokoto to near Lake Chad, and south of 12°N only at Aliya.

Breeding. C/2, 2 nests near Sokoto, Jun (Bannerman 1948); juvs. Sokoto, Aug (Mundy & Cook 1972-73).

882. EMBERIZA AFFINIS　　　　　　　　　　　　　　　　　　　　　　　　R(B)

(II.1365)   Brown-rumped Bunting

Uncommon and local resident (*E. a. nigeriae*) in degraded and grassy savanna, mostly in the Sudan zone from Katsina to Maiduguri, south into the Northern Guinea zone to Yankari Nat. Park (Green 1989), Pandam Wildlife Park and Yola, and south of the great rivers only at Kainji Lake Nat. Park.

Breeding. No records anywhere in West Africa.

883. EMBERIZA CABANISI　　　　　　　　　　　　　　　　　　　　　　　　RB

(II.1363)   Cabanis' Bunting

Local resident (*E. c. cabanisi*) rather than uncommon, mainly in farmland and degraded savanna. Serle (1957) collected a long series at Enugu; common in Kainji Lake Nat. Park (Wells & Walsh 1969), uncommon both at Falgore G.R., Kano State (Wilkinson & Beecroft 1985) and in Gashaka-Gumti Nat. Park (Green 1990). Elsewhere irregular but widespread, mostly in the Guinea Savanna, but south to Ibadan and Port Harcourt.

Breeding. Building near Owerri, 28 Jul (Bannerman 1948); C/1 (?incomplete) Ririwai, 5 Sep (P.B.).

POSTSCRIPT

[ANAS PLATYRHYNCHOS – Mallard] (unnumbered, preceding No. 63)

Very recently a substantiated record, 1 adult male at Dagona Waterfowl Sanctuary, 12 Dec 1993 (I.D.).

APPENDIX 1

ANALYSIS OF AVIAN FAMILIES RECORDED IN NIGERIA

RB = Resident breeds   R(B) = Resident, breeding not proven
PM = Palaearctic Migrant   Afmig = All intra-African migrants whether breeding or not

	Genera	Spp	Aquatic	Marine	Forest	Savanna	Montane	RB	R(B)	PM	Afmig	Other
Non-Passerines												
Struthionidae	1	1				1		1				
Procellariidae	1	2		2								2
Hydrobatidae	2	2		2								2
Podicipedidae	2	2	2					1		1		
Sulidae	1	2		2								2
Phalacrocoracidae	1	2	2					2				
Anhingidae	1	1	1					1				
Pelecanidae	1	2	2					2				
Ardeidae	11	19	18			1		12	2	7	2	1
Scopidae	1	1	1					1				
Ciconiidae	5	8	8					2	1	2	3	
Threskiornithidae	4	6	6					3	1	2		
Phoenicopteridae	1	1	1								1	
Anatidae*	11	24	24					8	3	11		2
Accipitridae*	31	49	1		7	41		20	7	10	12	
Sagittaridae	1	1				1		1				
Falconidae	1	10				10		5		5		
Phasianidae	6	14			3	11		9	2	1	2	
Turnicidae	2	3				3		1			1	1
Rallidae	10	17	7		4	6		7		4	2	4
Gruidae	3	3				3		1		2		
Heliornithidae	1	1	1					1				
Otididae	3	6				6		2			3	1
Jacanidae	2	2	2					1	1			
Rostratulidae	1	1	1								1	
Haematopodidae	1	1		1						1		
Recurvirostridae	2	2	2							1	1	
Burhinidae*	1	4	1			3		2	1	1		
Glareolidae	3	8	5			3		5		2	1	
Charadriidae	3	19	17			2		7		8	4	
Scolopacidae	12	27	25	2						26		1
Stercorariidae	2	4		4						1		3
Laridae	1	7		7						2		5
Sternidae*	4	17	5	12				2		9	1	6
Rynchopidae	1	1	1					1				
Pteroclidae	1	2				2					2	
Columbidae	5	19			4	13	2	12	2	1	2	2
Psittacidae	4	5			1	5		3			1	1
Musophagidae	4	6			3	3		4	2			
Cuculidae	8	19			6	13		5	4	1	9	
Tytonidae	1	1				1		1				
Strigidae*	6	13	2		4	7		9	2	2		1
Caprimulgidae	2	10			1	9		2	1	1	6	
Apodidae*	6	15			4	9	2	4	2	3		6
Coliidae	1	2				2		2				
Trogonidae	1	3			2		1	2				1
Alcedinidae	6	12	3		4	5		7	3	2		
Meropidae	1	13			2	10	1	8		1	4	
Coraciidae	2	6			2	4		1	1	1	3	
Phoeniculidae	1	4			2	2		2	1		1	
Upupidae	1	1				1		1		1		
Bucerotidae	3	12			8	4		7	4		1	
Capitonidae	6	16			10	5	1	15	1			
Indicatoridae	3	9			5	4		7	2			
Picidae	4	16			5	9	2	8	7	1		

	Genera	Spp	HABITAT					STATUS				
			Aquatic	Marine	Forest	Savanna	Montane	RB	R(B)	PM	Afmig	Other
Passerines												
Eurylaimidae	1	2			1		1	2				
Pittidae	1	1			1			1				
Alaudidae*	6	13				13		3	1	2	4	3
Hirundinidae	5	22	5		2	13	2	8	4	3	7	
Motacillidae	3	11				9	2	3	2	5	1	
Campephagidae	3	7			3	2	2		5		1	1
Pycnonotidae	11	29			22	3	4	18	11			
Turdidae*	16	40			10	25	5	18	8	10	1	3
Sylviidae*	25	81	12		15	42	12	33	23	22		3
Muscicapidae	4	21	2		10	7	2	13	5	3		
Platysteiridae	3	10			7	3		8	2			
Monarchidae	4	7			4	2	1	4	2		1	
Timaliidae	6	11			6	2	3	8	3			
Paridae	1	2				1	1	1	1			
Remizidae	1	3			1	2		1	2			
Salpornithidae	1	1				1			1			
Zosteropidae	1	1				1		1				
Nectariniidae*	2	26			15	8	3	16	4		5	1
Laniidae	2	11				10	1	4	2	5		
Malaconotidae	6	21			5	12	4	10	11			
Prionopidae	1	2			1	1		2				
Dicruridae	1	3			1	2		3				
Corvidae	2	3				3		2				1
Oriolidae	1	4			2	2		2		1	1	
Sturnidae	5	14			4	9	1	11	2		1	
Passeridae	4	5				5		3			2	
Ploceidae*	8	39			13	18	8	30	8			1
Estrildidae	18	36			10	23	3	30	5		1	
Viduidae	1	7				7		3	4			
Fringillidae	2	5				3	2	4	1			
Emberizidae	1	5				5		2	1	1	1	

*Families which include species in square brackets

APPENDIX 2

PUBLISHED RECOVERIES OF BIRDS RINGED ELSEWHERE AND RECOVERED IN NIGERIA UP TO THE END OF 1993

SPECIES	RINGED	RECOVERED
Sula capensis	2 Rep. of S. Africa	East Nigeria
Nycticorax nycticorax	1 Hungary	North Nigeria
	1 France	North Nigeria
	1 Yugoslavia	North Nigeria
	1 Czechoslovakia	North Nigeria
Ardeola ralloides	3 Yugoslavia,	North Nigeria
	1 Bulgaria	North Nigeria
Egretta garzetta	3 USSR	1 North Nigeria
		2 South Nigeria
Ardea purpurea	1 USSR, 1 Germany	1 North, 1 South
Ardea cinerea	3 USSR, 1 Germany,	3 North, 2 South
	1 Hungary	
Ciconia ciconia	20 Spain, 8 France,	All North
	9 Germany, 1 Morocco,	
	1 Portugal, 1 Greece,	
	4 Tunisia, 2 Algeria,	
	1 Estonia	
Anas querquedula	1 Latvia, 1 USSR	North Nigeria
	1 India	
Pandion haliaetus	1 Germany, 12 Finland,	Scattered
	11 Sweden	
Pernis apivorus	1 Sweden, 1 Netherlands	South Nigeria
Milvus migrans	1 Switzerland, 1 Germany	South Nigeria
Circus pygargus	1 Sweden	Yola
Falco tinnunculus	1 France	6°48′N, 6°03′E
Charadrius dubius	1 Germany	Nguru
Calidris canutus	1 Sweden	5°48′N, 7°02′E
Calidris ferruginea	1 Austria	4°40′N, 7°10′E
Philomachus pugnax	1 Finland	12°53′N, 11°05′E
Gallinago media	1 USSR	Zaria
Numenius phaeopus	2 UK	6°27′N, 3°22′E
		4°44′N, 7°05′E
Tringa totanus	1 UK	7°53′N, 5°24′E
Tringa nebularia	1 Netherlands	4°18′N, 6°16′E
Tringa glareola	1 Sweden	Kano
Actitis hypoleucos	1 Germany	Ondo
Larus fuscus	3 Denmark	S Nigeria
Sterna caspia	6 Finland, 2 Sweden	All inland, Malamfatori to Kainji
Sterna sandvicensis	25 UK, 1 France	All coastal
	4 Germany, 1 Denmark,	
	2 Netherlands	
Sterna dougallii	4 UK, 3 Ireland	All coastal
Sterna hirundo	2 Sweden, 6 Germany,	All coastal except
	3 Finland, 7 UK,	one at
	2 Netherlands	11°51′N, 6°47′E
Sterna paradisaea	1 USA, 12 UK	All coastal
	3 Denmark, 3 Finland,	
	1 Norway, 1 Germany	
Sterna fuscata	6 USA	E Nigeria
Riparia riparia	1 Denmark	Malamfatori
Hirundo rustica	22 UK, 11 Germany,	All SE Nigeria except
	11 France, 6 Belgium	11°30′N, 13°42′E
		and 12°54′N, 10°30′E

Appendix 2   269

SPECIES	RINGED	RECOVERED
Delichon urbica	1 Channel Islands, 1 Denmark, 2 Switzerland, 1 Morocco 1 UK	Anambara
Motacilla flava	3 Sweden, 2 USSR, 7 Italy, 1 Bulgaria, 8 Finland, 2 Poland, 1 Denmark	4 S Nigeria, 11 Vom, 6 Ibadan, 2 Kano, 1 Malamfatori
Luscinia megarhynchos	1 Tunisia	Akure
Acrocephalus scirpaceus	1 Austria, 1 Belgium	Maiduguri and E Nigeria
Acrocephalus arundinaceus	1 Germany, 1 Austria	E Nigeria
Phylloscopus trochilus	2 France, 1 Spain, 1 Sweden	E Nigeria
Sylvia atricapilla	1 Belgium	6°30′N, 3°30′E
Sylvia borin	2 Germany, 1 Switzerland 1 UK	E Nigeria
Muscicapa striata	4 UK, 1 Switzerland, 1 Belgium, 1 Germany	E Nigeria

Footnote: Disparities may occur due to changes in international boundaries.

APPENDIX 3

RECOVERIES OF BIRDS RINGED IN NIGERIA AND RECOVERED ELSEWHERE UP TO END OF 1993

SPECIES	RINGED	RECOVERED
Anas querquedula	6 Kano/Kazaure	1 Greece, 1 Poland, 4 USSR
Charadrius hiaticula	1 Kano	Malta
Philomachus pugnax	3 Kano, 1 Nguru	1 Sardinia
	4 Malamfatori	1 Finland, 6 USSR
Gallinago gallinago	1 Kano	1 USSR
Tringa glareola	1 Kano	1 USSR
Riparia riparia	4 Malamfatori	Malta, Tunisia,
	1 Kano	Czechoslovakia, Cyprus, Germany
Hirundo rustica	7 Calabar	2 Spain, 2 France, 3 Germany
Motacilla flava	40 Kano, 51 Vom,	1 France, 36 Italy,
	7 Ibadan,	13 Malta, 5 Tunisia,
	2 Malamfatori	4 Algeria, 4 Poland, 1 Morocco, 7 USSR, 1 Turkey, 8 Greece, 1 Cameroon, 1 Roumania, 1 Yugoslavia, 2 Austria, 4 Libya, 1 Estonia, 1 Latvia, 9 Finland
Phoenicurus phoenicurus	Kano	Algeria
Saxicola rubetra	2 Vom	1 Libya, 1 Poland
Acrocephalus schoenobaenus	Malamfatori	USSR
Phylloscopus trochilus	Kano	Belgium
Phylloscopus sibilatrix	Malamfatori	Greece
Sylvia borin	2 Kano, 2 Jos	Italy, Finland, Zaïre, Germany
Sylvia communis	Malamfatori	1 Egypt, 2 Libya
Ficedula hypoleuca	Malamfatori	Cyprus
Lanius senator	Kano	Italy

Footnote: Disparities may occur due to changes in international boundaries.

APPENDIX 4

PALAEARCTIC MIGRANTS RINGED IN NIGERIA (SHARLAND 1983)

Non-Passerines

*Ixobrychus minutus	7	
Ardeola ralloides	5	
Ciconia ciconia	3	
Anas crecca	8	
A.acuta	7	
A.querquedula	158	(6)
A.clypeata	4	
Circus macrourus	1	
Coturnix coturnix	1	
Himantopus himantopus	19	
Charadrius dubius	56	
C.hiaticula	26	
C.alexandrinus	1	
Calidris alba	1	
C.minuta	372	
C.temminckii	14	
C.ferruginea	17	
Philomachus pugnax	622	(8)
Lymnocryptes minimus	31	
Gallinago gallinago	78	(1)
G.media	1	
Limosa limosa	4	
Tringa erythropus	13	
T.totanus	2	
T.stagnatilis	18	
T.nebularia	10	
T.ochropus	34	
T.glareola	572	(1)
Xenus cinereus	1	
Actitis hypoleucos	193	
Sterna hirundo	1	
Chlidonias leucopterus	1	
Streptopelia turtur	1	
*Clamator glandarius	4	
*Otus scops	13	
Caprimulgus europaeus	2	
*Upupa epops	20	
Jynx torquilla	88	

Passerines

Calandrella rufescens	1	
Riparia riparia	1539	(5)
Hirundo rustica	1468	(8)
Delichon urbica	2	
Motacilla flava	38329	(100)
M.alba	36	
Anthus campestris	3	
A.trivialis	134	
A.cervinus	134	
Luscinia luscinia	1	
L.megarhynchos	512	
L.svecica	6	
*Cercotrichas galactotes	1	
Phoenicurus phoenicurus	346	(1)
Saxicola rubetra	504	(2)
Oenanthe oenanthe	35	
O.hispanica	1	

Appendix 4

Monticola saxatilis	8	
M.solitarius	1	
Locustella luscinioides	12	
Acrocephalus schoenobaenus	2448	(1)
A.scirpaceus	619	
A.arundinaceus	152	
Hippolais pallida	225	
H.olivetorum	1	
H.polyglotta	158	
H.icterina	203	
Phylloscopus trochilus	1009	(1)
P.collybita	6	
P.sibilatrix	188	(1)
P.bonelli	27	
Sylvia atricapilla	24	
S.borin	2443	(4)
S.communis	3152	(3)
S.curruca	191	
S.hortensis	1	
S.mystacea	1	
S.cantillans	251	
Muscicapa striata	284	
Ficedula hypoleuca	270	(1)
F.albicollis	23	
Lanius collurio	6	
L.senator	49	(1)
Oriolus oriolus	4	
Emberiza hortulana	6	

Totals ringed = 57223
Total extra-limital recoveries (in brackets) = 144

* Species with African breeding populations as well as Palaearctic breeding populations. Probably the majority of these birds were 'local'.

APPENDIX 5

NEW SCIENTIFIC NAMES USED IN THE SECOND EDITION AND THE CORRESPONDING NAMES USED IN THE FIRST EDITION

New No.	Scientific name in new edition	Old No.	Scientific name in First edition
3	Puffinus griseus	3	Procellaria grisea
6	Tachybaptus ruficollis	2	Podiceps ruficollis
8	Sula capensis	7	Sula bassana capensis
12	Anhinga melanogaster	11	Anhinga rufa
19	Gorsachius leuconotus	16	Nycticorax leuconotus
23	Bubulcus ibis	22	Ardeola ibis
26	Egretta gularis	29	Egretta garzetta gularis
35	Mycteria ibis	33	Ibis ibis
49	Phoeniconaias minor	46	Phoenicopterus minor
69	Marmaronetta angustirostris	55	Anas anguirostris (error)
78	Chelictinia riocourii	111	Elanus riocourii
83	Necrosyrtes monachus	74	Neophron monachus
84	Gyps africanus	72	Gyps bengalensis
87	Aegypius occipitalis	76	Trigonoceps occipitalis
94	Polyboroides typus	85	Polyboroides radiatus
98	Micronisus gabar	93	Melierax gabar
100	Accipiter tachiro	92	Accipiter toussenelii
118	Spizaetus africanus	103	Hieraaetus africanus
133	Guttera pucherani	137	Guttera edouardi
159	Aenigmatolimnas marginalis	153	Porzana marginalis
160	Amaurornis flavirostris	150	Limnocorax flavirostra
172	Ardeotis arabs	165	Otis arabs
220	Limnocryptes minimus	218	Gallinago minima
234	Xenus cinereus	212	Tringa terek
242	Catharacta skua	—	[Stercorarius skua]
250	Gelochelidon nilotica	248	Sterna nilotica
251	Sterna caspia	251	Sterna tschegrava
261	Chlidonias hybridus	244	Sterna hybrida
262	Chlidonias niger	247	Sterna nigra
263	Chlidonias leucopterus	245	Sterna leucoptera
264	Anous minutus	237	Anous tenuirostris
269	Treron calva	266	Treron australis
276	Columba iriditorques	257	Columba malherbii
278	Columba sjöstedti	255	Columba arquatrix
286	Streptopelia hypopyrrha	260	Streptopelia lugens
299	Oxylophus jacobinus	290	Clamator jacobinus
300	Oxylophus levaillantii	291	Clamator levaillantii
306	Cuculus gularis	293	Cuculus canorus gularis
315	Centropus grillii	301	Centropus toulou
329	Strix woodfordii	307	Ciccaba woodfordii
333	Caprimulgus nigriscapularis	319	Caprimulgus pectoralis
341	Rhaphidura sabini	326	Chaetura sabini
342	Telacanthura melanopygia	325	Chaetura melanopygia
343	Telacanthura ussheri	327	Chaetura ussheri
344	Neafrapus cassini	324	Chaetura cassini
353	Tachymarptis aequatorialis	328	Apus aequatorialis
354	Tachymarptis melba	334	Apus melba
355	Urocolius macrourus	337	Colius macrourus
367	Corythornis leucogaster	344	Alcedo leucogaster
368	Corythornis cristata	343	Alcedo cristata
370	Megaceryle maxima	341	Ceryle maxima
372	Merops breweri	353	Bombylonax breweri
381	Merops persicus	364	Merops superciliosus
397	Tockus albocristatus	388	Tropicranus albocristatus
403	Ceratogymna fistulator	379	Bycanistes fistulator

Appendix 5

404	Ceratogymna subcylindricus	380	Bycanistes subcylindricus
405	Ceratogymna cylindricus	378	Bycanistes cylindricus
417	Tricholaema hirsuta	394	Lybius hirsutus
—	[Sasia africana]	—	[Verreauxia africana]
444	Dendropicos pyrrhogaster	427	Mesopicos pyrrhogaster
445	Dendropicos xantholophus	428	Mesopicos xantholophus
446	Dendropicos elliotii	425	Mesopicos elliotii
447	Dendropicos goertae	426	Mesopicos goertae
448	Picoides obsoletus	423	Dendropicos obsoletus
452	Mirafra cantillans	438	Mirafra javanica
455	Pinarocorys erythropygia	439	Mirafra nigricans
476	Hirundo preussi	453	Hirundo spilodera
488	Motacilla aguimp	468	Motacilla alba vidua
530	Criniger ndussumensis	492	Criniger olivaceus ndussumensis
533	Sheppardia bocagei	540	Cossypha bocagei
538	Cossyphicula roberti	546	Cossypha roberti
549	Neocossyphus finschii	566	Stizorhina fraseri finschii
568	Zoothera crossleyi	567	Turdus gurneyi crossleyi
—	[Zoothera princei]	—	[Turdus princei]
571	Bradypterus lopezi	591	Bradypterus cinnamomeus
572	Melocichla mentalis	637	Sphenoeacus mentalis
573	Schoenicola brevirostris	636	Schoenicola platyura
591	Cisticola chubbi	606	Cisticola hunteri
608	Urolais epichlora	632	Prinia epichlora
609	Spiloptila clamans	631	Prinia clamans
616	Phyllolais pulchella	588	Apalis pulchella
617	Cameroptera brevicaudata	592	Cameroptera brachyura
620	Poliolais lopezi	594	Cameroptera lopezi
647	Melaenornis (Empidornis) pallidus	651	Bradornis pallidus
649	Melaenornis (Fraseria) ocreatus	655	Fraseria ocreata
650	Melaenornis (Fraseria) cinerascens	654	Fraseria cinerascens
653	Muscicapa infuscata	649	Artomyias fuliginosa
654	Muscicapa ussheri	650	Artomyias ussheri
664	Myioparus griseigularis	662	Muscicapa griseigularis
668	Bias flammulatus	672	Megabyas flammulata
672	Batis poensis	668	Batis minima
679	Elminia longicauda	683	Trochocercus longicauda
682	Terpsiphone nitens	685	Trochocercus nitens
685	Illadopsis cleaveri	571	Trichastoma cleaveri
686	Illadopsis puveli	574	Trichastoma puveli
687	Illadopsis rufipennis	575	Trichastoma rufipennis
688	Illadopsis fulvescens	572	Trichastoma fulvescens
690	Kakamega poliothorax	573	Trichastoma poliothorax
693	Kupeornis gilberti	569	Lioptilus gilberti
751	Laniarius erythrogaster	510	Laniarius barbarus erythrogaster
755	Telophorus sulfureopectus	519	Malaconotus sulfureopectus
756	Telophorus multicolor	518	Malaconotus multicolour
757	Telophorus cruentus	516	Malaconotus cruentus
758	Telophorus gladiator	517	Malaconotus gladiator
759	Telophorus blanchoti	515	Malaconotus blanchoti
761	Prionops plumatus	504	Prionops plumata
784	Lamprotornis pulcher	820	Spreo pulcher
818	Anaplectes rubriceps	782	Malimbus rubriceps
836	Nesocharis shelleyi	749	Nesocharis ansorgei
841	Mandingoa nitidula	740	Hypargos nitidulus
846	Euschistospiza dybowskii	729	Clytospiza dybowskii
851	Lagonosticta larvata	735	Estrilda larvata
852	Uraeginthus bengalus	733	Estrilda bengala
882	Emberiza affinis	719	Emberiza forbesi

APPENDIX 6

NEW ENGLISH NAMES USED IN THE SECOND EDITION AND CORRESPONDING NAMES USED IN THE FIRST EDITION

New No.	English name in new Edition	Old No.	English name in First Edition
10	White-breasted Cormorant	10	African Cormorant
20	Black-crowned Night Heron	17	Night Heron
35	Yellow-billed Stork	33	Wood Ibis
45	Olive Ibis	41	Green Ibis
47	Eurasian Spoonbill	45	Spoonbill
76	Bat Hawk	112	Bat-eating Buzzard
91	Smaller Banded Snake Eagle	78	Banded Harrier-Eagle
93	Congo Serpent Eagle	84	Serpent-Eagle
94	African Harrier Hawk	85	Harrier-Hawk
100	African Goshawk	92	West African Goshawk
101	Chestnut-flanked Sparrowhawk	88	Chestnut-flanked Goshawk
105	Black Sparrowhawk	90	Great Sparrow-Hawk
134	Helmeted Guineafowl	138	Guinea-Fowl
139	Latham's Forest Francolin	134	Forest Francolin
147	Little Button-Quail	141	Button-Quail
168	Black Crowned Crane	143	Crowned Crane
174	White-bellied Bustard	163	Senegal Bustard
191	Rock Pratincole	180	White-collared Pratincole
205	White-crowned Plover	193	White-headed Plover
265	Brown Noddy	236	Noddy
269	African Green Pigeon	266	Green Pigeon
276	Western Bronze-naped Pigeon	257	(Gabon) Bronze-naped Pigeon
278	Cameroon Olive Pigeon	255	Olive Pigeon
282	African Mourning Dove	259	Mourning Dove
284	African Collared Dove	261	Pink-headed (or Rosy-grey) Dove
294	Green Turaco	282	Guinea Turaco
295	Yellow-billed Turaco	281	Red-tip Crested Turaco
299	Jacobin Cuckoo	290	Black and White (or Pied) Cuckoo
300	African Striped Cuckoo	291	Levaillant's Cuckoo
306	African Cuckoo	293	Yellow-billed Cuckoo
319	Common Scops Owl	310	Scops Owl
331	Swamp Nightjar	318	White-tailed Nightjar
342	Black Spinetail	325	Ituri Mottled-throated Spinetail
343	Mottled Spinetail	327	Mottle-throated Spinetail
346	African Black Swift	331	Fernando Po Swift
349	Bates's Swift	332	Black Swift
401	African Pied Hornbill	385	Allied Hornbill
407	Yellow-casqued Wattled Hornbill	382	Yellow-casqued Hornbill
428	Greater Honeyguide	406	Black-throated Honey-Guide
434	Rufous-breasted Wryneck	413	Red-breasted Wryneck
441	Speckle-breasted Woodpecker	424	Uganda Spotted Woodpecker
—	[Rusty Bush-Lark]	—	[Dusky Bush-Lark]
456	Greater Short-toed Lark	431	Short-toed Lark
458	Lesser Short-toed Lark	433	Rufous Short-toed Lark
463	Square-tailed Saw-wing	454	Square-tailed Rough-wing Swallow
464	Fanti Saw-wing	455	Fantee Rough-wing Swallow
465	Black Saw-wing	456	Petit's Rough-wing Swallow
466	Mountain Saw-wing	—	[Mountain Rough-wing Swallow]
473	Lesser Striped Swallow	442	Striped Swallow
483	Barn Swallow	449	Swallow
503	Cameroon Montane Greenbul	480	Mountain Little Greenbul
504	Mountain Greenbul	481	Olive-breasted Mountain-Greenbul
523	Grey-headed Greenbul	497	Grey-headed Yellow-bellied Greenbul
524	Red-tailed Bristlebill	486	Bristlebill
527	Western Bearded Greenbul	490	Bearded Greenbul

Appendix 6

529	Red-tailed Greenbul		491	White-bearded Greenbul
530	White-bearded Greenbul		492	Yellow-throated Olive Greenbul
533	Bocage's Akalat		540	Rufous-cheeked Robin-Chat
549	Finsch's Flycatcher-Thrush		566	Finsch's Rufous Flycatcher
550	Rufous Scrub-Robin		537	Rufous Bush-Chat
551	Black Scrub-Robin		538	Black Bush-Robin
555	White-crowned Black Wheatear		560	White-rumped Wheatear
556	Northern Wheatear		561	Wheatear
559	Red-breasted Wheatear		557	Heuglin's Red-breasted Wheatear
562	Northern Ant-eater Chat		552	Ant-eater Chat
565	Mocking Cliff-chat		554	White-crowned Cliff-Chat
566	Mountain Rock-Thrush		550	Rock-Thrush
569	African Thrush		568	Kurrichane Thrush
570	African Bush-Warbler		590	Little Rush-Warbler
571	Cameroon Scrub-Warbler		591	Cinnamon Bracken-Warbler
572	Moustached Grass-Warbler		637	Moustache-Warbler
573	Fan-tailed Grassbird		636	Fan-tailed (Swamp)Warbler
576	Eurasian Reed-Warbler		584	Reed Warbler
580	Greater Swamp Warbler		582	Rufous Swamp Warbler
586	Yellow Flycatcher-Warbler		597	Yellow Flycatcher
591	Chubb's Cisticola		606	Brown-backed Cisticola
602	Black-necked Cisticola		604	Cloud-Scraper
609	Cricket Longtail		631	Scaly-fronted Warbler
613	Yellow-breasted Apalis		586	Yellow-chested Apalis
622	Senegal Eremomela		614	Smaller Green-backed Eremomela
623	Rufous-crowned Eremomela		612	Brown-crowned Eremomela
626	Northern Crombec		646	Crombec
631	Yellow-bellied Hyliota		679	Yellow-bellied Flycatcher
632	Violet-backed Hyliota		—	[Violet-backed Flycatcher]
641	Greater Whitethroat		641	Whitethroat
648	Northern Black Flycatcher		656	Black Flycatcher
649	African Forest Flycatcher		655	Forest Flycatcher
655	Swamp Alseonax		657	Swamp Flycatcher
656	Olivaceous Alseonax		663	Olivaceous Flycatcher
658	Little Grey Alseonax		—	[Little Grey Flycatcher]
659	Yellow-footed Alseonax		664	Yellow-footed Flycatcher
662	Cassin's Alseonax		659	Cassin's Grey Flycatcher
663	Ashy Alseonax		658	Ashy Flycatcher
668	African Shrike Flycatcher		672	Shrike Flycatcher
669	Black-and-White Shrike Flycatcher		671	Black-and-White Flycatcher
670	Senegal Batis		670	Senegal Puff-back Flycatcher
671	Grey-headed Batis		669	Grey-headed Puff-back Flycatcher
672	Fernando Po Batis		668	Fernando Po Puff-back Flycatcher
673	Brown-throated Wattle-eye		676	Wattle-eye
679	African Blue Flycatcher		683	Blue Fairy Flycatcher
683	Black-headed Paradise Flycatcher		680	Red-bellied Paradise Flycatcher
684	African Paradise Flycatcher		681	Paradise Flycatcher
739	Yellow-billed Shrike		524	Long-tailed Shrike
741	Puffback Shrike		505	Puff-back
742	Red-eyed Puffback-Shrike		507	Zanzibar (Red-eyed) Puff-back
744	Sabine's Puffback-Shrike		506	Sabine's Puff-back
839	Melba Finch		759	Green-winged Pytilia
859	Goldbreast		728	Zebra Waxbill
867	Village Indigobird		805	Indigo Birds or Combassous

(NB for most of the final quartile no English names are available from the BoA editors, so many of the First Edition names have continued to be used).

APPENDIX 7

ADDITIONAL SPECIES NOT IN FIRST EDITION

* = sub-species in 1st Edition.

New No.	Scientific Name	English Name
3	Puffinus puffinus	Manx Shearwater
5	Oceanodroma castro	Madeiran Storm-petrel
7	Podiceps nigricollis	Black-necked Grebe
53	Anser albifrons	White-fronted Goose
109	Buteo buteo	Steppe Buzzard
—	[Aquila pomarina]	[Lesser Spotted Eagle]
132	Agelastes niger	Black Guineafowl
157	Porzana parva	Little Crake
166	Grus grus	Common Crane
171	Neotis nuba	Nubian Bustard
186	Cursorius cursor	Cream-coloured Courser
237	Phalaropus lobatus	Red-necked Phalarope
245	Larus cirrocephalus	Grey-headed Gull
277	Columba larvata	Lemon Dove
279	Columba unicincta	Afep Pigeon
328	Glaucidium sjöstedti	Chestnut-backed Owlet
—	[Apus unicolor]	[Plain Swift]
359	Apaloderma aequatoriale	Bare-cheeked Trogon
430*	Indicator conirostris	Thick-billed Honeyguide
450	Smithornis capensis	African Broadbill
462	Eremopterix nigriceps	Black-crowned Sparrow-Lark
482*	Hirundo lucida	Red-chested Swallow
497	Campephaga petiti	Petit's Cuckoo-Shrike
499	Lobotos lobatus	Western Wattled Cuckoo-Shrike
528*	Criniger chloronotus	Eastern Bearded Greenbul
534	Sheppardia cyornithopsis	Lowland Akalat
548*	Neocossyphus fraseri	Rufous Flycatcher-Thrush
560	Oenanthe isabellina	Isabelline Wheatear
581	Acrocephalus gracilirostris	Lesser Swamp Warbler
594	Cisticola dorsti	Dorst's Cisticola
596	Cisticola robustus	Stout Cisticola
607	Drymocichla incana	Red-winged Grey Warbler
610	Apalis pulchra	Black-collared Apalis
612	Apalis jacksoni	Black-throated Apalis
627*	Macrosphenus kempi	Kemp's Longbill
657	Muscicapa adusta	Dusky Alseonax
689	Illadopsis abyssinica	Abyssinian Hill-Babbler
695	Picathartes oreas	Red-headed Rockfowl
730*	Lanius isabellinus	Isabelline Shrike
743	Dryoscopus angolensis	Pink-footed Puffback-Shrike
828	Euplectes hartlaubi	Marsh Whydah
868*	Vidua raricola	Goldbreast Indigobird
869*	Vidua funerea	Variable Indigobird
870*	Vidua wilsoni	Bar-breasted Firefinch Indigobird
873*	Vidua interjecta	Exclamatory Paradise Whydah

APPENDIX 8

CONSERVATION STRATEGY OF THE NIGERIAN GOVERNMENT

1. The establishment of the Nigerian Conservation Foundation (NCF) in 1982 – a Non-Government Organisation representing the Worldwide Fund for Nature (WWF), Birdlife International (ICBP) and other international conservation organisations in Nigeria.

   NCF's practical objectives include: improved protection in defined conservation areas representing a comprehensive spectrum of habitats; creation of buffer-zones for protected areas, with appropriate safeguards and the encouragement of local tourism and eco-tourism; attracting funding from such sources as the EEC, ODA and the national and international development agencies to invest in core-area protection as well as in support-zone work (which includes introduction of more sustainable agricultural methods and assistance to local communities in improving their economies); an increase in general conservation awareness.

   NCF has taken the lead in influencing Government policies on conservation. It has established or collaborated in and with scientific projects designed to act as catalysts for further conservation action in differing ecological zones and, with the support of WWF, it has introduced an effective and fast-expanding conservation education programme for schools.

   Such Non-Government conservation organisations as the Yankari Initiative have expanded work started by NCF and are playing an important role in establishing protection in core areas of existing and proposed National Parks.

   Non-Government Organisations have an important part to play in initiating and supporting conservation action in Nigeria.

2. The acceptance by Government of a National Conservation Strategy for Nigeria. This has led to the establishment of a National Resources Conservation Council (now integrated with the Federal Environment Protection Agency).

3. The adoption by Government of a National Parks policy, the creation, by law, of a National Parks Board and Service and the gazetting of the following Parks with their individual Management Boards:

   Kainji Lake National Park (including the Zugurma Sector).
   Upper Ogun/Old Oyo National Park.
   Cross River National Park (Oban Hills, Ikpan and Oboshi-Okwango Sectors).
   Gashaka-Gumti National Park.
   Yankari National Park.
   Chad Basin National Park.

4. The Accession by Nigeria to the following international Conventions:

   Africa Convention on Conservation of Nature and Natural Resources (OAU).
   Convention concerning the Protection of the World Cultural and Natural Heritage (UNESCO).
   Convention on International Trade in Endangered Species of Wild Fauna and Flora (Berne). Decreed into Nigerian law by Decree No.11 promulgated in 1985.
   Convention on Conservation of Migratory Species of Wild Animals (Bonn).

GAZETTEER

* Rivers, Game Parks etc. that cannot be located exactly
** Places outside Nigeria mentioned in the text

	N	E		N	E
Aba	5°05'	7°24'	**Cameroon Mountain	4°10'	9°12'
Abak	4°46'	7°35'	Chappal Hendu	7°20'	11°44'
Abakaliki	6°18'	8°08'	Chappal Waddi	7°01'	11°41'
Abeokuta	7°09'	3°20'	Cross River Nat. Park	6°20'	8°20'
Aboh	5°30'	6°30'	Damaturu	11°47'	11°50'
Abong	7°30'	11°20'	Dagona Waterfowl		
Abuja	9°15'	7°14'	Sanctuary	12°45'	10°35'
Acha	5°48'	7°17'	Degema	4°45'	6°47'
Achilafia	12°50'	8°30'	Dikwa	12°02'	13°55'
Adirjani Fadama	12°49'	10°25'	*Dodo River	5°30'	5°30'
Ado-Ekiti	7°38'	5°13'	Dumbari	12°37'	10°46'
Afikpo	5°55'	7°56'	Ebe River, Ikpan Block	5°05'	8°40'
Agenebode	7°07'	6°41'	Ede	7°43'	4°26'
Agwarra	10°40'	4°35'	Eggan	8°40'	8°30'
Ajeokuta	7°29'	6°42'	Ekang	5°41'	8°10'
Ajiran (coastal)	Not located		Ekonganaku	5°04'	8°40'
Akure	7°15'	5°11'	Enugu	6°25'	7°28'
Akwanga	9°50'	8°40'	Epe	6°35'	3°59'
Aliya	11°10'	10°55'	Erin-Ijesha	7°36'	4°45'
*Anambara Creek	6°20'	6°50'	Eruwa	7°30'	3°28'
(flows into Niger near			*Escravos River	5°25'	5°25'
Onitsha)			*Falgore G.R.	10°50'	8°40'
*Andoni River	4°40'	7°20'	Felak Farm	10°40'	9°30'
(near Port Harcourt)			Forcados	5°23'	5°26'
Ankpa	7°22'	7°36'	Funtua	11°32'	7°18'
Arege	13°28'	13°20'	Gadau	11°50'	10°10'
Argungu	12°45'	4°30'	Gajebo	12°10'	14°00'
Arochuku	5°22'	7°54'	*Gambari F.R.	7°15'	3°52'
Assop	9°32'	8°37'	Gangirwal	7°02'	11°42'
Atan	5°18'	8°	*Gashaka-Gumti Nat.		
Awgu	6°05'	7°28'	Park	7°20'	11°35'
Azare	11°41'	10°11'	Gashua	12°54'	11°05'
Badam	12°51'	10°26'	Gaya F.R.	11°50'	9°
Bacita	9°10'	4°55'	Gboko	7°20'	8°57'
Badagri	6°22'	2°50'	Geidam	12°47'	11°55'
Bagauda	11°40'	8°30'	*Gongola River	10°00'	12°00'
Bama	11°30'	13°40'	Gorgoram	12°38'	10°40'
**Bambalue	6°00'	10°15'	*Gotel Mountains	7°01'	11°42'
(Cameroon)			Gumti Village	7°38'	11°46'
Baro	8°31'	6°22'	Gwadabawa	13°22'	5°13'
Bashu	6°12'	9°03'	Hadejia	12°27'	10°03'
Bauchi	10°20'	9°50'	Ibadan	7°22'	3°54'
Benin	6°20'	5°35'	Ibi	8°10'	9°45'
Bida	9°04'	5°58'	Idah	7°00'	6°40'
Birnin Gwari	11°00'	6°46'	Ife	7°28'	4°32'
Birnin Kebbi	12°25'	4°10'	Igbetti	8°45'	4°07'
Birnin Kudu	11°27'	9°28'	IITA Ibadan	7°30'	3°55'
Biu	10°40'	12°12'	Ikibiri	4°56'	6°12'
Bokkos	9°17'	9°	Ikom	5°58'	8°43'
Bonny	4°28'	7°10'	Ikoyi (Lagos)	6°25'	3°30'
Bori	4°41'	7°21'	*Ikpan Block (Cross River		
*Boshi F.R.	6°33'	9°16'	N.P.)	5°05'	8°40'
Brass	4°19'	6°14'	Ikwo	6°05'	8°06'
Bukuru	9°48'	8°53'	Ilaro	6°53'	3°01'
Bulatura Oases	13°20'	11°10'	Ilesha	7°38'	4°44'
Burutu	5°19'	5°30'	Ilorin	8°30'	4°33'
Bussa	10°13'	4°33'	Imese-Ile	7°33'	4°38'
Butatong	6°21	9°07'	*Ipake F.R.	6°50'	3°03'
Calabar	4°58'	8°21'	Ipepe	6°14'	4°28'

	N	E		N	E
Iperu	6°52'	3°40'	Mongu	9°30'	9°07'
Iseyin	8°00'	3°35'	Nasarawa	8°30'	7°42'
Itu	5°15'	7°58'	Neghe	5°17'	8°37'
Iwo	7°38'	4°10'	Ngala	12°20'	14°12'
Jagindi	9°20'	8°13'	Ngel Nyaki Forest	7°04'	11°04'
Jakara Dam	12°10'	8°50'	Nguru	12°53'	10°28'
*Jamieson River	6°05'	5°55'	Nibo	6°48'	7°10'
Jebba	9°08'	4°49'	Nikrowa	6°15'	5°20'
Jekko	9°23'	8°40'	Nindam F.R.	9°32'	8°30'
Jeribowl	11°50'	13°15'	Nkpologu	6°45'	7°15'
Jos	9°56'	8°53'	*'Northern Oyo Province'	8°40'	3°40'
Kabba	7°52'	6°03'	Nsukka	6°48'	7°23'
Kaduna	10°32'	7°24'	Numan	9°30'	12°05'
Kafanchan	9°37'	8°18'	Nwajai, Mambilla Plateau	6°55'	11°34'
Kagoro	9°32'	8°30'	Oban	5°20'	8°40'
Kaiama	9°38'	3°57'	*Oban Hills Sector (Cross	5°25'	8°35'
Kainji Lake Nat. Park	10°00'	4°00'	River Nat.Park).		
Kainji Dam	9°50'	4°30'	Obe	6°01'	4°44'
Kamale Pinnacle,			Obubra	6°05'	8°20'
Mandara Mts	11°00'	13°40'	*Obudu Plateau	6°40'	9°20'
Kangiwa	12°35'	3°50'	Odukpani	5°10'	8°20'
Kano	12°00'	8°30'	Ogbomosho	8°08'	4°16'
Kari	11°12'	10°32'	Ogoja	6°40'	8°42'
Katagum	12°16'	10°20'	Okene	7°35'	6°13'
Katsina	13°00'	7°37'	Okigwi	5°50'	7°22'
Kazaure	12°39'	8°23'	Okitipupa	6°29'	4°48'
*Kigom Hills	Near Jos		Okpani (?=Okpai)	5°28'	5°52'
Kirikasama	12°42'	10°15'	*Okomu F.R.	6°25'	5°28'
Kishi	9°05'	3°51'	Okrika	4°40'	7°10'
Kontagora	10°22'	5°28'	*Okwango F.R.	6°14'	9°08'
**Korup (Cameroon)	5°05'	8°45'	*Old Oyo Game Reserve	8°50'	4°20'
Koton Karifi	8°05'	6°48'	*Oli River	9°50'	4°30'
Kotorkoshi	12°08'	6°48'	Olokemeji	7°25'	3°32'
Kuma	6°52'	11°21'	Omanelu	5°12'	6°52'
Kurra	9°25'	8°45'	Omo F.R.	6°50'	4°30'
Kuta	9°50'	6°45'	Ondo	7°05'	4°51'
Kuzu Daguana	12°45'	10°28'	Onitsha	6°10'	6°47'
Kwakwi	9°33'	8°39'	Opobo	4°30'	7°33'
Kwal	9°50'	8°38'	Orlu	5°48'	7°02'
Kwale	5°45'	6°25'	Oron	4°50'	8°15'
Lagos	6°20'	3°25'	Osara	7°37'	6°23'
Lake Alau	11°50'	13°10'	Owai	5°34'	8°15'
Lanlate	7°36'	3°27'	Oyo	7°52'	3°57'
Lau	9°12'	11°17'	Pagalu (Annobon Is.)	2°S	6°00'
Leinde Fadali	6°58'	11°36'	(Gulf of Guinea)		
Lekki Conservation			Pandam Wildlife Park	8°40'	9°03'
Centre	6°20'	3°35'	Panshanu	10°03'	8°58'
Lissam	7°10'	10°03'	Panyam	9°25'	9°12'
Loko	8°00'	7°48'	Papa, near Mayo Ndaga	6°55'	11°24'
Lokoja	7°48'	6°42'	Pategi	8°43'	5°44'
Mada River Bridge	8°55'	8°17'	Port Harcourt	4°51'	7°05'
Maiduguri	11°49'	13°09'	Potiskum	11°45'	11°02'
Makurdi	7°20'	8°33'	Quorra (old name for		
Malamfatori	13°37'	13°23'	Benue River)		
*Mambilla Plateau	7°30'	11°35'	Rano	11°35'	8°40'
*Mamu F.R.	7°10'	3°50'	Rayfield	9°49'	8°54'
Maru	12°15'	6°30'	Ringim	12°10'	9°10'
Mbaakon	7°12'	9°00'	Ririwai	10°45'	8°45'
Mbarakpa	5°10'	8°40'	Rockwater Fish Farm,		
Mberubu	6°14'	7°38'	Rayfield	9°48'	8°54'
Meko (Mekkaw)	7°28'	2°45'	Sambisa G.R.	11°40'	14°20'
Miango	9°51'	8°41'	Sanga River F.R.	9°19'	8°18'
Minna	9°36'	6°33'	Sankwala	6°33'	9°13'
Mongonu	12°40'	13°40'	Sapele	5°55'	5°42'

Gazetteer 281

	N	E		N	E
Sapoba	6°03'	5°52'	Umudim	6°08'	7°00'
Sarakin (Sarkin) Pawa	10°00'	7°10'	Uromi Ishan	6°05'	6°00'
Serti	7°33'	11°20'	Vom	9°42'	8°45'
*Shaffini Swamp Forest	10°30'	4°30'	Wamba	8°55'	8°40'
Shagamu	6°50'	3°39'	Warri	5°31'	5°43'
Shagunu (Lake Kainji)	10°22'	4°27'	Wase Rock	9°04'	9°56'
Shaki	8°41'	3°23'	Wukari	7°50'	9°45'
*Shasha F.R.	7°05'	4°22'	Wulgo	12°29'	14°09'
Shendam	8°54'	9°26'	*Yankari Nat. Park	9°45'	10°30'
*Siluko River (at Siluko)	6°32'	5°10'	Yauri	10°48'	4°42'
Sokoto	13°02'	5°13'	Yelwa, (Mambilla Plateau)	7°04'	11°05'
Taboru	9°53'	8°59'			
Takum	7°13'	10°00'	Yelwa (near Sokoto)	10°52'	4°44'
Tarajim	12°00'	11°00'	Yenagoa	4°55'	6°16'
Tarkwa	6°25'	3°25'	Yo	13°40'	13°13'
Tayu	9°19'	8°36'	Yola	9°12'	12°28'
Ubiaja	6°37'	6°20'	Yusufari	13°05'	11°10'
Ughelli	5°30'	5°59'	Zaria	11°03'	7°42'
Umuagwu	5°20'	6°55'	Zonkwa	9°43'	8°17'

REFERENCES

AGLAND, P. 1985. A list of birds recorded from Korup National Park in Gartland S.(Ed) The Korup Regional Management Plan: Conservation and development of the Ndian Division of Cameroon. WWF Report Publication No. 25-106, Wisconsin Regional Primate Research Centre.

AIDLEY, D. J. & WILKINSON, R. 1987a. Moult of some Palaearctic warblers in northern Nigeria. *Bird Study* 34:219-225.

─────── 1987b. The annual cycle of six *Acrocephalus* warblers in a Nigerian reed-bed. *Bird Study* 34:226-234.

ALEXANDER, BOYD. 1907. From the Niger to the Nile.

ALEXANDER-MARRACK, P. D., AARONSON, M. J., FARMER, R., HOUSTON, W. H. & MILLS, T. R. 1985. Some changes in the bird fauna of Lagos, Nigeria. *Malimbus* 7:121-127.

ASH, J. S. 1987. Surveys of *Picathartes oreas*, *Malimbus ibadanensis* and other species in Nigeria. ICBP and NCF unpublished report.

─────── 1990. Additions to the avifauna of Nigeria, with notes on distributional changes and breeding. *Malimbus* 11:104-116.

─────── 1991. The Grey-necked Picathartes, *Picathartes oreas* and Ibadan Malimbe, *Malimbus ibadanensis* in Nigeria. *Bird Conserv. Int.* 1:93-106.

ASH, J. S., DOWSETT, R. J. & DOWSETT-LEMAIRE, F. 1989. New ornithological distribution records from eastern Nigeria. *Tauraco Res. Rep.* 1:13-27.

ASH, J. S. & SHARLAND, R. E. S. 1987. Nigeria: assessment of bird conservation priorities. ICBP Study Report No 11.

ASHFORD, R. W. 1968. Hirundine records from University of Ibadan campus. *Bull. Niger. Orn. Soc.* 11(40):48.

─────── 1969. Two species new to Ibadan, and associated records. *Bull. Niger. Orn. Soc.* 6(21):30-31.

AYENI, J. S. O. 1983. Home range size, breeding behaviour and activities of Helmet Guineafowl *Numida meleagris* in Nigeria. *Malimbus* 5(1):83.

BANNERMAN, D. A. 1930-51. *The Birds of Tropical West Africa*. 8 Vols. London.

─────── 1953. *The Birds of West and Equatorial Africa*. 2 Vols. London.

BATES, G. L. 1930. *Handbook of the Birds of West Africa*. London.

─────── 1933. Birds of the southern Sahara and adjoining countries in French West Africa. *Ibis* 13:752-780.

BASS, H. G. M. 1967. Notes on birds at Ibadan and elsewhere. *Bull. Niger. Orn. Soc.* 4(13/14):31-35.

BEECROFT, R. & WILKINSON, R. 1983. Additions to local avifaunas: Kano State. *Malimbus* 5:93.

BERTRAM, B. C. R. 1980. Breeding system and strategies of Ostriches. *Proc. 17th Int. Orn. Congr*: 890-894.

BEST, D. 1975. Menetries' Warbler *Sylvia mystacea* new to Nigeria and West Africa. *Bull. Niger. Orn. Soc.* 11(40):85.

BEST, J. R. 1977. Thrush-Nightingale *Luscinia luscinia* new to Nigeria and West Africa. *Bull. Niger. Orn. Soc.* 13(43):81.

BIE, S. DE & MORGAN, N. 1989. Les Oiseaux de la Reserve de la Biosphere 'Boucle du Baoul', Mali. *Malimbus* 11:41-60.

BOUGHTON-LEIGH, P. W. T. 1932. Observations on nesting and breeding habits of birds near Ilorin, Nigeria. *Ibis* Ser. 13(2):457-470.

BOULTER, H. 1964. The Mambilla Plateau. *Bull. Niger. Orn. Soc.* 1(4):17-18.

─────── 1965. The birds of Umudin (Onitsha Province). *Bull. Niger. Orn. Soc* 2(7): 63-65.

BOURDILLON, SIR BERNARD H. 1944. Terns at Lagos Beach, Nigeria. *Ibis* 86:405-407.

BRITTON, P. L. (ed) 1980. *Birds of East Africa*. Nairobi: EANHS.

BROWN, J. F. 1974. Grey Phalaropes near Lagos. *Bull. Niger. Orn. Soc.* 10(38):53.

BROWN, J. L. 1987. *Helping and Communal Breeding in Birds*. Princeton University Press, New Jersey.

BROWN, L. H. 1948. Notes on birds of the Kabba, Ilorin and N. Benin Provinces of Nigeria. *Ibis* 90:525-537.

BROWN, L. H, URBAN, E. K. & NEWMAN, K. 1985. *The Birds of Africa* Vol. I. (Referred to as BoA in the text).
BUTTON, J. A. 1964a. Synopsis of the status of birds at Ilaro. *Bull. Niger. Orn. Soc.* 1(1):5-6.
─────── 1964b. The avifauna of Topo Island, near Lagos. *Bull. Niger. Orn. Soc.* 1(2):5-7.
─────── 1964c. Palaearctic migrants at Ilaro. *Bull. Niger. Orn. Soc.* 1(3):1-2
─────── 1965. Three phases of the Many-coloured Bush-Shrike at Ilaro. *Bull. Niger. Orn. Soc.* 2(8):107-108.
─────── 1966. A second contribution to the avifauna of Topo Island. *Bull. Niger. Orn. Soc.* 3(10):36-41.
─────── 1967-8. The birds of Ilaro. *Bull. Niger. Orn. Soc.* 4(13/14):17-28, 4(15):2-11, 4(16):10-19, 5(17):1-9.
CAWKELL, E. M. & MOREAU, R. E. 1963. Notes on birds in The Gambia. *Ibis* 105:156-178.
CHAPIN, J. P. 1932-53. The birds of the Belgian Congo. Parts 1-3. *Bull. Amer. Mus. Nat. Hist*: 65, 75, 75A.
CHAPPUIS, C. & ERARD, C. 1991. A new cisticola from west-central Africa. *Bull. Brit. Orn. Club* 111:59-70.
CHEKE, R. A. 1982. More bird records from the Republic of Togo. *Malimbus* 4:55-63.
CLARKE, J. D. 1936. The Long-crested Helmet Shrike *Prionops plumata plumata*. *Niger. Field* 5:129-130.
CLIMATIC RESEARCH UNIT, UNIVERSITY OF EAST ANGLIA. 1992. Temperature and Precipitation Data. U.E.A. Norwich.
COLLAR, N. J. & STUART, S. N. (1985) *Threatened Birds of Africa and Related Islands*. International Council for Bird Preservation, Cambridge.
COLLIAS, N. E. & COLLIAS, E. C. 1978. Co-operative breeding in the White-browed Sparrow Weaver. *Auk* 95: 472-484.
COOK, A. W. & MUNDY, P. J. 1980. Ruppell's Griffon Vulture at Kotorkoshi, Nigeria. *Malimbus* 2(2):102-105.
COWPER, S. G. 1977. Dry season birds at Enugu and Nsukka. *Bull. Niger. Orn. Soc.* 13(43):57-63.
CRICK, H. Q. P. 1984. Weight changes, foraging and the role of helpers on Red-throated Bee-eaters. PhD Thesis. University of Aberdeen.
─────── 1987. Intra-specific robbery by Red-throated Bee-eaters, *Ostrich* 58:140-141.
─────── 1992. Load-lightening in co-operatively breeding birds and the cost of reproduction. *Ibis* 134:56-61.
CRICK, H. Q. P. & FRY, C. H. 1986. Effects of helpers on parental condition in Red-throated Bee-eaters (*Merops bullocki*). *J. Anim. Ecol.* 55:893-905.
CRICK, H. Q. P. & MARSHALL, P. J. 1981. The birds of Yankari Game Reserve, Nigeria: their abundance and seasonal occurrence, *Malimbus* 3:103-114.
DEMEY, R. & FISHPOOL, L. D. C. 1991. Additions and annotations to the avifauna of Côte d'Ivoire. *Malimbus* 12:61-86.
DOBBS, K. A. 1959. Some birds of Sokoto, Northern Nigeria, with brief notes on their status. *Niger. Field* 24:103-119.
DOWSETT, R. J. 1968a. Migrants at Malamfatori, Lake Chad, Spring 1968. *Bull. Niger. Orn. Soc.* 5(19):53-56.
─────── 1968b. Broad-billed Sandpiper *Limicola falcinellus* at Lake Chad: a species new to Nigeria. *Bull. Niger. Orn. Soc.* 5(19):61.
─────── 1968c. Greater Sandplover *Charadrius leschenaultii* at Lake Chad: a species new to Nigeria. *Bull. Niger. Orn. Soc.* 5(19):61.
─────── 1968d. Barred Warbler *Sylvia nisoria* at Lake Chad: a species new to Nigeria. *Bull. Niger. Orn. Soc.* 5(20):94.
─────── 1969a. Migrants at Mallam'fatori, Lake Chad, autumn 1968. *Bull. Niger. Orn. Soc.* 6(22):39-45.
─────── 1969b. Breeding biology of the Olivaceous Warbler. *Bull. Niger. Orn. Soc.* 6(23):107-8.
─────── 1993b. A long lived Common Bulbul *Pycnonotus barbatus* in Nigeria. *Malimbus* 15(2):95-96.
DOWSETT, R. J., BACKHURST, G. C. & OATLEY, T. B. 1988. Afrotropical ringing recoveries of Palaearctic migrants. I-Passerines. *Tauraco* 1:29-63.

DOWSETT, R. J. & DOWSETT-LEMAIRE, F. 1993a. A contribution to the distribution and taxonomy of Afrotropical and Malagasy birds; Ch.1. Afrotropical avifaunas: annotated country checklists. *Tauraco Res. Rep.* No.5:1-322.

DOWSETT, R. J. & FORBES-WATSON, A. D. 1993. Checklist of Birds of The Afrotropical and Malagasy Regions Vol.1: Species limits and distribution. *Tauraco Press*, Liège, Belgium.

DOWSETT, R. J. & HOPSON, A. J. 1969. Additions and amendments to the list of birds at Mallam'fatori. *Bull. Niger. Orn. Soc.* 6(22):53-55.

DOWSETT-LEMAIRE, F. & DOWSETT, R. J. 1987. European and African Reed Warblers, *Acrocephalus scirpaceus* and *A. baeticatus*: vocal and other evidence for a single species. *Bull. Brit. Orn. Cl.* 107:74-85.

——————— 1989. Zoogeography and taxonomic relationships of the forest birds of the Cameroon Afromontane region. *Tauraco Res. Rep.* 1:48-56.

DUNGER, G. T. 1965. Wase Rock – its history, geology, fauna and climbs. *Niger. Field.* 30:148-184.

DUPUY, A. R. 1984. Synthèse sur les oiseaux de mer observés au Senegal. *Malimbus* 6:79-84.

DYER, M. 1979. The adaptive significance of co-operative breeding in the Red-throated Bee-eater *Merops bulocki* (Vieillot) and other bee-eaters. PhD Thesis. University of Aberdeen.

——————— 1983. Effects of nest helpers on growth of Red-throated Bee-eaters. *Ostrich* 54: 43-46.

DYER, M. & CRICK, H. Q. P. 1983. Observations on White-throated Bee-eaters breeding in Nigeria. *Ostrich* 54: 52-55.

DYER, M. & FRY, C. H. 1980. The origin and role of helpers in bee-eaters. *Proc. 17th Int. Orn. Congr.* 862-868.

DYER, M., FRY, C. H. & HENDRICK, J. A. 1981. Breeding of Black-headed Bee-eaters in Nigeria. *Malimbus* 4:43-45.

DYER, M. & GARTSHORE, M. E. 1974. Birds of Yankari Game Reserve. *Bull. Niger. Orn. Soc.* 11(40):77-84.

DYER, M., GARTSHORE, M. E. & SHARLAND, R. E. 1986. The birds of Nindam Forest Reserve, Kagoro, Nigeria. *Malimbus* 8:2-20.

EBBUTT, D., HORWOOD, M. T., SHARLAND, R. E. & SMITH, V. W. 1964. Provisional check-list of the birds of Plateau Province over 3000 feet. *Bull. Niger. Orn. Soc.* 1(3):9-14.

ELGOOD, J. H. 1955. On the status of *Centropus epomidis*. *Ibis* 97:586-7.

——————— 1960. Birds of the West African Town and Garden. London.

——————— 1964. Provisional check-list of the birds of Nigeria. *Bull. Niger. Orn. Soc.* 1(1):13-25.

——————— 1965. The birds of the Obudu Plateau. *Niger. Field* 30:60-68.

——————— 1966. African migrants in Nigeria. *Bull. Niger. Orn. Soc.* 3(11):62-69.

——————— 1973. Rufous phase Senegal Coucals in southwest Nigeria: an illustration of Gloger's Rule. *Bull. Brit. Orn. Cl.* 93:173.

——————— 1976. Montane birds of Nigeria. *Bull. Niger. Orn. Soc.* 12(41):31-34.

——————— 1977. Forest birds of southwest Nigeria. *Ibis* 119:462-480.

——————— 1981. The Birds of Nigeria. B.O.U. Check-list No 4. B.O.U. London.

——————— 1982. The case for the retention of Anaplectes as a separate genus. *Bull. Brit. Orn. Cl.* 1982. 102(2):70-75.

——————— 1988. Rediscovery of *Malimbus ibadanensis* Elgood 1958. *Bull. Brit. Orn. Cl.* 1988. 108(4):184-5

ELGOOD, J. H. & DONALD, R. G. 1962. Breeding of the Painted Snipe *Rostratula benghalensis* in southwest Nigeria. *Ibis* 104:253-256.

ELGOOD, J. H., FRY, C. H. & DOWSETT, R. J. 1973. African migrants in Nigeria. *Ibis* 115:1-45, 375-411.

ELGOOD, J. H., SHARLAND, R. E. & WARD, P. 1966. Palaearctic migrants in Nigeria. *Ibis* 108:84-116.

ELGOOD, J. H. & WARD, P. 1960. The nesting of Heuglin's Masked Weaver in Nigeria. *Ibis* 102:472-3.

EMLEN, S. T. 1984. Co-operative breeding in birds and mammals, in Behavioural Ecology : An Evolutionary Approach. 2nd ed. 305-339: (Eds. Krebs, J. R. and N. B. Davies), Blackwell, Oxford.
EYCKERMAN, R. & CUVELIER, D. 1982. The moult of some bird species on Mount Cameroon. *Malimbus* 4:1-4.
FAIRBAIRN, W. A. 1952. *Some Game Birds of West Africa*. London & Edinburgh: Oliver & Boyd.
FARMER, R. 1979. Check-list of the birds of the Ile-Ife area. *Malimbus* 1(1):56-64.
FIELD, G. D. 1993. Breeding of Slender-billed Bulbul *Andropadus gracilirostris* in Sierra Leone. *Malimbus* 15:48-49.
FIELD, G. D. & OWEN, D. F. 1969. Little Gull in Sierra Leone. *Bull. Brit. Orn. Cl.* 89:4.
FORRESTER, M. F. 1971. Birds of Ikoyi, Lagos. *Bull. Niger. Orn. Soc.* 8(30):13-20.
FRIEDMANN, H. 1948. The parasitic cuckoos of Africa. *Wash. Acad. Sci. Monogr.* No.1.
FRY, C. H. 1964a. The Coot: a new Nigerian Bird. *Bull. Niger. Orn. Soc.* 1(2):13.
———— 1964b. Bird notes from north-eastern Sokoto Province. *Bull. Niger. Orn. Soc.* 1(4):2-4.
———— 1965a. The birds of Zaria. *Bull. Niger. Orn. Soc.* 2(5):9-17; 2(6):35-43; 2(7): 68-80; 2(8):91-101.
———— 1965b. Grey-backed Fiscal Shrike in Nigeria. *Bull. Niger. Orn. Soc.* 2(7):83.
———— 1966a. Some aspects of the biology of African bee-eaters. (Meropidae) with particular reference to *Melittophagus bulocki* (Vieillot) Ph.D Thesis, Ahmadu Bello University, Zaria, Nigeria.
———— 1966b. Status of the Bluethroat in Nigeria. *Bull. Niger. Orn. Soc.* 3(12):98.
———— 1966c. An unidentified buzzard in Sokoto. *Bull. Niger. Orn. Soc.* 3(12):95-96.
———— 1967a. A method of identifying Palaearctic buzzards in West Africa. *Bull. Niger. Orn. Soc.* 4(13):37.
———— 1967b. Subspecific identity of the Zaria *Corythornis leucogaster* specimen. *Bull. Niger. Orn. Soc.* 4(15):15.
———— 1967c. Studies of Bee-eaters. *Niger. Field.* 32:4-16.
———— 1972. The social organisation of bee-eaters (Meropidae) and co-operative breeding in hot-climate birds. *Ibis* 114:1-14.
———— 1973. The Biology of African Bee-eaters. *Living Bird* 11: 75-112.
———— 1984. *The Bee-eaters*. Poyser, Carlton.
FRY, C. H. & FERGUSON-LEES, I. J. 1977. Taxonomy of the *Acrocephalus baeticatus* complex of African Marsh Warblers. *Niger. Field* 42:134-137.
FRY, C. H., FRY, K. & HARRIS, A. 1992. *Kingfishers, Bee-eaters and Rollers*. Helm, London.
FRY, C. H. & SMITH, V. W. 1964. The Ortolan Bunting: a new Nigerian bird. *Bull. Niger. Orn. Soc.* 1(2):13.
FRY, C. H., KEITH, S., URBAN, E. K. 1988. *Birds of Africa* Vol III, Academic Press, London. (Referred to as BoA in the text).
FRY, C. H., WILLIAMSON, K. & FERGUSON-LEES, I. J. 1974. A new sub-species of *Acrocephalus baeticatus* from Lake Chad and a taxonomic reappraisal of *Acrocephalus dumetorum*. *Ibis* 116:340-346.
GARTSHORE, M. E. 1975. Some aspects of the breeding biology of the Cinnamon-breasted Rock Bunting *Emberiza tahapisi*. *Bull. Niger. Orn. Soc.* 11(39):27-33.
———— 1982. Additions to Local Avifaunas: Zaria. *Malimbus* 44:46.
GEE, J. P. 1984. Birds of Mauritania. *Malimbus* 6:31-66.
GEE, J. P. & HEIGHAM, J. B. 1971. Red-backed Shrike at Lagos. *Bull. Niger. Orn. Soc.* 8(29):9-10.
———— 1977. Birds of Lagos, Nigeria. *Bull. Niger. Orn. Soc.* 13(43):43-52; 13(44): 103-132.
GEERLING, C. 1978. Birds of Yankari Game Reserve, Nigeria. *Bull. Niger. Orn. Soc.* 14(46):82-83.
GEERLING, C. & AFOLAYAN, T. 1974. Birds on the Kainji lake shore area. *Bull. Niger. Orn. Soc.* 10(38):64-68.
GIBBON, A. K. 1933. Some notes on the birds of North Bornu. *Ibis* Ser (13)3:228-239.
GILL, P. J. 1939. The Long-crested Helmet Shrike *Prionops plumata plumata*. *Niger. Field* 8:110-115.

GINN, P. J. G. 1986. Birds using helpers at the nests. *Honeyguide* 32:45.
GIRAUDOUX, P., DEGAUQUIER, R., JONES, P. J., WEIGEL, J. & ISENMANN, P. 1988. Avifaune du Niger: état des connaissances en 1986. *Malimbus* 10:1-138.
GOLDING, F. D. 1934. A nomad's notes on Nigerian game birds. *Niger. Field* 3:70-72.
GORE, M. E. J., 1981. Birds of the Gambia *BOU Check-list No.3*, British Ornithologists' Union.
GRAY, H. H. 1965a. Some notes on the birds of Tivland. *Bull. Niger. Orn. Soc.* 2(7):66-68.
────── 1965b. New records for Obudu Plateau. *Bull. Niger. Orn. Soc.* 2(7):83.
────── 1968a. Additional notes on the birds of Tiv Division, Benue Province. *Bull. Niger. Orn. Soc.* 5(18):40-42.
────── 1968b. New records for Obudu Plateau. *Bull. Niger. Orn. Soc.* 5(18):49.
────── 1971. Further notes on the birds of the Mambilla Plateau. *Bull. Niger. Orn. Soc.* 8(31/2)):51-54.
────── 1986. Johanna's Sunbird in Nigeria. *Malimbus* 8:44.
GREEN, A .A. 1989. Avifauna of Yankari Reserve, Nigeria: new records and observations. *Malimbus* 11:61-72.
────── 1990. The avifauna of the southern sector of the Gashaka-Gumti Game Reserve, Nigeria. *Malimbus* 12:31-51.
GREEN, A. A. & SAYER, J. A. 1979. The birds of Pendjari and Ark National Parks (Benin and Upper Volta) *Malimbus* 1:14-28.
GREIG-SMITH, P. W. 1977. Mixed species flocking of Nigerian forest birds. *Bull. Niger. Orn. Soc.* 13(43):53-56.
GRIFFITHS, J. F. (Ed) 1972. World Survey of Climatology Vol.10. Climates of Africa. Elsevier Pub.Co., Amsterdam-London-New York.
GRIMES, L. G. 1975. Notes on the breeding of the Kakelaar at Legon, Ghana. *Bull. Niger. Orn. Soc.* 11(40):65-67.
────── 1976a. Co-operative breeding in African birds. *Proc. 16 Int. Orn. Congr., Canberra, 1974* :667-673.
────── 1976b. The occurrence of co-operative breeding behaviour in African Birds. *Ostrich.* 47:1-15.
────── 1980. Observations of group behaviour and breeding biology of the Yellow-billed Shrike *Corvinella corvina*. *Ibis* 122:166-192.
────── 1987. The Birds of Ghana. *B.O.U.Check-list No.9.* B.O.U. London.
GUICHARD, K. M. 1947. Birds of the Inundation Zone of the Niger River. *Ibis* 89:450-489.
HALL, B. P. 1963. The Francolins, a study in speciation. *Bull. Brit. Mus. Nat. Hist. (Zool)* 10:105-204.
HALL, B. P. & MOREAU, R. E. 1962. A study of the rare birds of Africa. *Bull. Brit. Mus. Nat. Hist. (Zool)* 8:315-378.
────── 1970. *An Atlas of Speciation of African Passerine Birds*. London: British Museum (Natural History).
HALL, J.B. 1981. Ecological islands in south-eastern Nigeria. *Afr. J. Ecol.* 19:55-72.
HALL, P. 1976a. Birds of Bulatura Oases, Borno State. *Bull. Niger. Orn. Soc.* 12(41):35-37.
────── 1976b. The birds of Mambilla Plateau. *Bull. Niger. Orn. Soc.* 12(42):67-72.
────── 1977a. The birds of Maiduguri. *Bull. Niger. Orn. Soc.* 13(43):15-36.
────── 1977b. Birds of the Chad Basin boreholes. *Bull. Niger. Orn. Soc.* 13(43):37-42.
────── 1977c. The birds of Serti. *Bull. Niger. Orn. Soc.* 13(43):66-79.
────── 1977d. Black Duck *Anas sparsa* on Mambilla Plateau, first record for Nigeria. *Bull. Niger. Orn. Soc.* 13(43):80.
HAPPOLD, D. C. D. 1970. The Blue Plantain Eater at Abuja. *Bull. Niger. Orn. Soc.* 7(25/6):38.
HARTERT, E. 1915. List of a small collection of birds from Hausaland, Northern Nigeria. *Nov. Zool.* 22:244-266.
HEATON, A. M. & HEATON, A. E. 1980. The birds of Obudu, Cross River State, Nigeria. *Malimbus* 2(1):16-24.
HEDENSTROM, A., BENSCH, S., HASSELQUIST, D. & OTTOSON, U. 1990. Observations of Palaearctic migrants rare to Ghana. *Bull. Brit. Orn. Club* 110:194-197.
HEIGHAM, J. B. 1975. *Comparative Nomenclature of Nigerian Birds for the Amateur*. (Printed privately for Nigerian Ornithologists' Society at Sapele).

―――――― 1976. Birds of mid-west Nigeria. *Bull. Niger. Orn. Soc.* 12(42):76-93.
HOLMES, D. A. 1973-74. Bird notes from the plains south of Lake Chad. *Bull. Niger. Orn. Soc.* 9(35):47-54, 9(36):76-84, 10(37):28-37.
HOLYOAK, D. T. & SEDDON, M. B. 1990. Notes on some birds of Western Cameroon. *Malimbus* 11:123-127.
HOPKINS, B. 1962. A trend towards a longer dry season in south-western Nigeria. *Nature* 194 (4831):861-862.
HOPSON, A. J. 1964a. Preliminary notes on the birds of Malamfatori, Lake Chad. *Bull. Niger. Orn. Soc.* 1(4):7-14.
―――――― 1964b. *Buteo rufinus* (Long-legged Buzzard), a species new to Nigeria. *Bull. Niger. Orn. Soc.* 1(4):15- 16.
HOPSON, J. 1966. Notes on a mixed cormorant and heron breeding colony near Malamfatori, Lake Chad. *Bull. Niger. Orn. Soc.* 3(10):21-33.
HOPSON, J. & HOPSON, A. J. 1965. Additions to local avifaunas: Malamfatori, Lake Chad. *Bull. Niger. Orn. Soc.* 2(5):18-19.
HUFF, J. N. & AUTA, J. 1977. Nests of White-fronted Black Chats. *Bull. Niger. Orn. Soc.* 13(44):148.
HUTSON, H. P. W. & BANNERMAN, D. A. 1930-31. The birds of northern Nigeria. *Ibis* Ser.12(4):600-637, Ser.13(1):18-43.
IRWIN, M. P. S. 1987. What are the affinities of the Black-capped Apalis, *Apalis nigriceps?* - the need for field studies. *Malimbus* 9:130-131.
JARDINE, W. & FRASER, L. 1852. (re *Nectarinia johannae*) *Contr. Orn.*:59.
JOURDAIN, F. C. R & SHUEL, R. 1935. Notes on a collection of eggs and breeding-habits of birds near Lokoja, Nigeria. *Ibis.* Ser.13(5):623-663.
KEAY, R. W. J. 1949. *An Outline of Nigerian Vegetation.* Lagos: Govt. Printer.
KEITH, S., URBAN, E. K. & FRY, C. H. 1992. *The Birds of Africa.* Vol.IV. Academic Press. London. (Referred to as BoA in the text).
KILHAM, H. 1956. Breeding and other habits of Casqued Hornbills (*Bycanistes subcylindricus*). *Smithsonian Misc. coll.* 131(9):1-45.
KOEMAN, J. H., RIJKSEN, H. D. & SMIES, M. 1974. Faunal changes in a swamp habitat in Nigeria sprayed with insecticide to exterminate *Glossina. Neth. J. Zool.* 21:434-463.
LAMARCHE, B. 1981. Liste commentée des oiseaux du Mali; 2eme partie. *Malimbus* 3: 73-102.
LANG, J. R. 1969a. A Spotted Eagle Owl's Nest. *Bull. Niger. Orn. Soc.* 6(23):101-103.
―――――― 1969b. The nest and eggs of the Moho or Oriole Babbler *Hypergerus atriceps. Bull. Niger. Orn. Soc.* 6(24):127-128.
―――――― 1974. Additions to Plateau check-list. *Bull. Niger. Orn. Soc.* 10(38):54-56.
LAWSON, W. J. 1984. The West African mainland forest dwelling population of *Batis*, a new species. *Bull. Brit. Orn. Cl.* 104(4):144-146
LIGON, J. D. & LIGON, S. H. 1978. The communal social system of the Green Woodhoopoe in Kenya. *Living Bird* 17:159-197.
LIPSCOMB, C. G. 1937. Notes from Nigeria. *Ibis* Ser.14(1):673- 4.
LOUETTE, M. 1981. The Birds of Cameroon. An annotated check-list. *Verhandl. Kon. Acad. Wetensh. Lett. Schone Kunst. Belg.* 43:1-163.
LYNES, H. 1930. Review of the genus *Cisticola. Ibis* Ser.12(6). Suppl.
MACDONALD, M. A. & TAYLOR, I. A. 1977. Notes on some uncommon forest birds in Ghana. *Bull. Brit. Orn. Cl.* 97:116-120.
MACGREGOR, D. E. 1964. Seasonal movements of some birds in Northern Nigeria. *Bull. Niger. Orn. Soc.* 1(3):2-6.
MACKENZIE, P. 1979. Birds of the Calabar area. *Malimbus* 1(1): 47-55.
MACKWORTH-PRAED, C. W., & GRANT, C. H. B. 1970-1973. *African Handbook of Birds, Series III. Birds of West Central and Western Africa.* 2 Vols. London.
MACLAREN, P. I. R. 1950a. Sea-bird stations of West Africa. *Ibis* 92:319-20.
―――――― 1950b. Bird-ant nesting associations. *Ibis* 92:564-6.
―――――― 1953. Bird notes from Nigeria. *Niger. Field* 18:165-171.
―――――― 1954. Notes on Palaearctic terns and waders in West Africa. *Ibis* 96:601-605.
MARCHANT, S. 1942. Some birds of the Owerri Province, southern Nigeria. *Ibis* Ser. 14(6):137-196.

―――――― 1953. Notes on the birds of southeastern Nigeria. *Ibis*.95:38-69.
―――――― 1954. The relationship of the southern Nigerian avifauna to those of Upper and Lower Guinea. *Ibis* 96:371-379.
―――――― 1966. Correspondence: *Artomyias ussheri*. *Bull. Niger. Orn. Soc.* 3(11):75.
MARSHALL, SIR HUGO F. 1977. Additional notes on birds in mid-west Nigeria. *Bull. Niger. Orn. Soc.* 13(44):98-102.
MASON, P. F. 1940. A brief faunal survey of north-western Benin. II Birds. *Niger. Field* 9:68-80.
MEININGER, P. L., DUIVEN, P., MARTEIJN & VAN SPANJE, T. M. 1991. Notable Bird Observations from Mauritania. *Malimbus* 12:19-24.
MOREAU, R. E. 1950. The breeding seasons of birds, 1. Land Birds. *Ibis* 92:223-267.
―――――― 1966. *The Bird Faunas of Africa and its Islands*. Academic Press. London.
―――――― 1972. *The Palaearctic-African Bird Migration Systems*. Academic Press. London and New York.
MORONY, J. J., BOCK, W. J. & FARRAND, J. 1975. *Reference List of the Birds of the World*. New York.
MUNDY, P. J. & COOK, A. W. 1971-2. Sokoto Province. *Bull. Niger. Orn. Soc.* 8(30):21-4, 8(31/2):42-5,46-7, 9(34):18-21.
―――――― 1972-3. Birds of Sokoto. *Bull. Niger. Orn. Soc.* 9(35):26-46, 9(36):61-75, 10(37):1-27.
NEWBY, J. E. 1979. The birds of the Ouadi Rim, Chad. *Malimbus* 1:90-109, 2:29-50.
NEWBY, J. E., GRETTENBERGER, J. & WATKINS, J. 1987. The birds of the northern Aïr, Niger. *Malimbus* 9:4-16.
PARKER, R. H. 1970. Check-list of Nigerian birds. Private circulation to members of Nigerian Ornithologists' Society.
―――――― 1971. Fernando Po Black Swift *Apus barbatus sladeniae* (Ogilvie-Grant) recorded from Nigeria. *Bull. Brit. Orn. Cl.* 91:152-153.
―――――― 1972a. A new subspecies of Freckled Nightjar in Nigeria. *Bull. Niger. Orn. Soc.* 9(33):6-8.
―――――― 1972b. African Black Swift: A species new to Nigeria. *Bull. Niger. Orn. Soc.* 9(33):9-10.
PARKER, R. H. & BENSON, C. W. 1971. Variation in *Caprimulgus tristigma* Ruppell, especially in West Africa. *Bull. Brit. Orn. Cl.* 91:113-119.
PAYNE, R. B. 1968a. Mimicry and relationships of the Indigo-birds or Combassous of Nigeria. *Bull. Niger. Orn. Soc.* 5(19):57-60.
―――――― 1968b. A preliminary report of the relationships of the Indigo-birds. *Bull. Brit. Orn. Cl.* 88:32-36.
―――――― 1973. Behavior, mimetic songs and song dialects, and relationships of the parasitic indigobirds (*Vidua*) of Africa. *Ornithol. Monogr.* 11:333 pp.
―――――― 1977a. The ecology of brood parasitism in birds. *Ann. Rev. Ecol. Syst.* 8:1-28.
―――――― 1977b. Clutch size, egg size, and the consequences of single vs. multiple parasitism in parasitic finches. *Ecology* 58:500-513.
―――――― 1982. Species limits in the Indigobirds (*Ploceidae, Vidua*) of West Africa: mouth mimicry, song mimicry, and description of new species. *Misc. Publ. Univ. Mich. Museum of Zoology* 162:96 pp.
―――――― 1985. The Species of Parasitic Finches in West Africa. *Malimbus* 7(2):103-113.
―――――― 1989. Egg size of African honeyguides (Indicatoridae): specialization for brood parasitism? *Tauraco* 1:201- 210.
PAYNE, R. B & PAYNE, L. L. 1994. Song mimicry and species status of the indigobirds *Vidua*: associations with Quail-finch, Goldbreast and Brown Twinspot. *Ibis*, in press.
PETTET, A. 1975a. Road transects for large-scale surveying. *Bull. Niger. Orn. Soc.* 11(39):2-18.
―――――― 1975b. Breeding behaviour of *Clamator glandarius* at Ibadan in southern Nigeria. *Bull. Niger. Orn. Soc.* 11(39):34-40.
―――――― 1968. A Long-legged Buzzard *Buteo rufinus* in southern Nigeria. *Bull. Niger. Orn. Soc.* 5(18):45.
PETTITT, G. 1967. Lighthouse Beach, Tarkwa Bay. *Bull. Niger. Orn. Soc.* 4(16):21-22.
―――――― 1968. Notes from Tarkwa Bay, Lagos. *Bull. Niger. Orn. Soc.* 5(18):38-39.

RAND, A. L. 1951. Birds from Liberia: with a discussion of barriers between Upper and Lower Guinea subspecies. *Fieldiana Zool. (Chicago)* 32(9):561-653.

REYER, H-U. 1980a. Flexible helper structure as an ecological adaptation in the Pied Kingfisher *(Ceryle rudis rudis L)*. *Behav. Ecol. Sociobiol.* 6:219-227.

——— 1980b. Sexual dimorphism and co-operative breeding in the Striped Kingfisher. *Ostrich* 51:117-118.

RICHARDS, P. W. 1952. *The Tropical Rain Forest*, Cambridge University Press.

ROBINSON, D. M. & ROBINSON, N. W. 1966. Birds of Ilesha. *Bull. Niger. Orn. Soc.* 3(9):11-12.

SANDER, F. 1956-1957. A list of birds of Lagos and its environs, with brief notes on their status. *Niger. Field.* 21:147-162; 22:5-17,55-69.

SERLE, W. 1939-40. Field observations on some northern Nigerian birds. *Ibis.* Ser.14(3): 654-699, Ser.14(4):1-47.

——— 1943. Further field observations on northern Nigerian birds. *Ibis* 85:264-300, 413-436.

——— 1950a. Notes on the birds of southwestern Nigeria. *Ibis*.92:84-94.

——— 1950b. A contribution to the ornithology of the British Cameroons. *Ibis* 92:343-376, 602-638.

——— 1954. A second contribution to the ornithology of the British Cameroons. *Ibis.* 96:47-80.

——— 1956. Migrant land-birds at sea off West Africa. *Ibis* 98:307-311.

——— 1957. A contribution to the ornithology of the Eastern Region of Nigeria. *Ibis* 99:371-418, 628-685.

——— 1959. Some breeding records of birds at Calabar. *Niger. Field* 24:45-48.

——— 1981. The breeding seasons of birds in the lowland rain forest and in the mountain forest of West Cameroon. *Ibis* 123:62-74.

SERLE, W., MOREL, G. J. & HARTWIG, W. 1977. *A Field Guide to the Birds of West Africa.* Collins.

SHARLAND, R. E. *Annual Ringing Reports.*

1st-5th. *Nigerian Field* 24:72-75; 25:125-127; 26:65-69; 27:134-137; 28:129-131. (1959-1963)

6th-20th *Bull. Niger. Orn. Soc.* 1(1):11-13; 2(5):2-5; 3(10):18-21; 4(13/14):12-16; 5(17): 28-31; 6(21):26-29; 7(28):94-98; 9(33):1-6; 9(34):13-16; 10(38):69-73; 11(40):50-52; 12(41):38-40; 13(43):64-65; 14(45):24-26.

21st-22nd *Malimbus* (1979-80) 1(1):43-46; 2(1):71-72.

23rd-28th *Malimbus* (1981-86) 3(1):39-40; 4(2):105-106; 5(2):78; 6:90-91; 7(2):140; 8(1): 44-45.

——— 1964a. Two interesting plateau birds: the Red-capped Lark *Calandrella cinerea* and the Three-banded Plover *Afroxyechus tricollaris*. *Bull. Niger. Orn. Soc.* 1(2):4.

——— 1964b. Seasonal movements of birds in Northern Nigeria. *Bull. Niger. Orn. Soc.* 1(4):5-6.

——— 1966. The European Little Bittern in Nigeria. *Bull. Niger. Orn. Soc.* 3(10):45.

——— 1972. Olive Tree Warbler: A species new to West Africa. *Bull. Niger. Orn. Soc.* 9(33):11.

SHARLAND, R. E. & WILKINSON, R. 1981. The birds of Kano State, Nigeria. *Malimbus* 3:7-30.

SHUEL, R. 1938a. Notes on the breeding habits of birds near Zaria, N. Nigeria, with descriptions of their nests and eggs. *Ibis* Ser.14(2):230-244.

——— 1938b. Further notes on the eggs and nesting habits of birds in Northern Nigeria (Kano Province). *Ibis* Ser. 14(2)463-479.

SIBLEY, C. G. & AHLQUIST, J. E. 1990. Phylogeny and Classification of Birds. A study in Molecular Evolution. Yale Univ. Press, New Haven.

SIBLEY, C. G. & MONROE, B. L. Jnr. 1990. Distribution and Taxonomy of Birds of the World, Yale Univ. Press, New Haven.

SKILLITER, M. 1963. Some notes on Kaduna Birds. *Niger. Field.* 28:34-42.

SKINNER, N. J. 1968. Two-stage northerly local migration of the Grey-headed Kingfisher *Halcyon leucocephala*. *Bull. Niger. Orn. Soc.* 5(20):88-90.

——— 1969. Notes on breeding of the Pygmy Long-tailed Sunbird. *Bull. Niger. Orn. Soc.* 6(24):124-126.

SKUTCH, A. F. 1961. Helpers among birds. *Condor* 63: 198-226.
────── 1987. Helpers at Birds' Nests. University of Iowa Press, Iowa.
SMITH, P. A. 1966a. Palaearctic waders in the Niger Delta. *Bull. Niger. Orn. Soc.* 3(9):2-6.
────── 1966b. Ussher's Flycatcher: a new bird for Nigeria. *Bull. Niger. Orn. Soc.* 3(10):48.
SMITH, V. W. 1958. Some birds which breed near Vom. *Niger. Field* 27:4-33.
────── 1964. The Marsh Owl *Asio capensis* on the Jos Plateau. *Bull. Niger. Orn. Soc.* 1(2):2-3.
────── 1965a. A week at Bokkos. *Bull. Niger. Orn. Soc.* 2(5):5-6.
────── 1965b. Palaearctic migrants at Vom, Plateau Province, over five seasons. *Bull. Niger. Orn. Soc.* 2(6):26-34.
────── 1966. Breeding records for the Plateau Province over 3000 feet, 1957-1966. *Bull. Niger. Orn. Soc.* 3(12):78-91.
────── 1971. The breeding of the Algerian Marsh Owl. *Niger. Field* 36:41-44.
SMITHIES, F. 1941. Ten years weather at Ibadan. *Niger Field* 10:103-112.
SODEINDE, O. A. 1993. Breeding of the Laughing Dove in South West Nigeria. *Malimbus* 14:60-62
STICKLEY, J. 1966. Nesting of the Cut-throat Weaver. *Bull. Niger. Orn. Soc.* 3(11):34-36.
STUART, S. N. 1986. Conservation of Cameroon montane forests. ICBP, Cambridge.
SWAINSON, W. 1837. *Birds of Western Africa.* 2 Vols, Edinburgh.
TARBOTON, W. R. 1981. Co-operative breeding and group territoriality in the Black Tit. *Ostrich* 52:216-225.
TAYLOR, P. B. 1981. Bates's Weaver *Ploceus batesi* near Victoria and other observations from Western Cameroon. *Malimbus* 3:49
THANGAMANI, A., PARAMANANDHAM, K. & JOHNSINGH, A. J. T. 1981. Helpers among the Black Drongo (*Dicrurus adsimilis*). *J. Bombay Nat. Hist. Soc.* 78:602-603.
THIOLLAY, J-M. 1985. The birds of Ivory Coast. *Malimbus* 7:1-59.
THOMAS, J. 1991. Birds of the Korup National Park, Cameroon. *Malimbus* 13:11-23.
TUCK, G. & HEINZEL, H. 1978. *A Field Guide to the Seabirds of Britain and the World.* Collins.
TYE, H. 1992. Reversal of breeding season by lowland birds at higher altitudes in western Cameroon. *Ibis* 134:154-161.
URBAN, E. K., FRY, C. H., KEITH, S. 1986. *Birds of Africa* Vol II, Academic Press, (referred to as BoA in the text).
VINE, H. 1949. Nigerian soils in relation to parent materials. *Comm. Bur. of Soil Science, Tech Communication.* No.46.
VUILLEUMIER, F., LECROY, M., & MAYR, E. 1992. New species of birds described from 1981 to 1990. *Bull. Brit. Orn. Cl. Centenary Suppl.* 112A:280(15).
WALKER, R. B. 1965. Two Sudan Savannah birds at Zaria. *Bull. Niger. Orn. Soc.* 2(5):22-23.
WALLACE, D. I. M. 1969a. Palaearctic migrants in west Lagos: November 1968 to May 1969. *Bull. Niger. Orn. Soc.* 6(22):45-49.
────── 1969b. Lesser Yellowlegs at Lagos: A species new to Nigeria. *Bull. Niger. Orn. Soc.* 6(22):58.
────── 1969c. Little Gulls at Tarkwa, Lagos: A species new to Nigeria. *Bull. Niger. Orn. Soc.* 6(22):59.
────── 1969d. Herring Gulls at Tarkwa, Lagos: A species new to Nigeria. *Bull. Niger. Orn. Soc.* 6(22):59.
────── 1973. Sea birds at Lagos and in the Gulf of Guinea. *Ibis* 115:559-571.
WALSH, F. 1966. A nest of the Violet-backed Sunbird. *Bull. Niger. Orn. Soc.* 3(11):70-1.
────── 1968a. Emin's Bush Shrike in Borgu. *Bull. Niger. Orn. Soc.* 5(17):26-27.
────── 1968b. Magpie Mannikin in Niger Province. *Bull. Niger. Orn. Soc.* 5(18):49.
────── 1968c. A Black Stork in Borgu. *Bull. Niger. Orn. Soc.* 5(18):50.
────── 1968d. Palaearctic waders at Kainji and New Bussa. *Bull. Niger. Orn. Soc.* 5(19):64.
────── 1968e. Grey Plovers inland in Nigeria. *Bull. Niger. Orn. Soc.* 5(19):65.
────── 1968f. Inland records of gulls. *Bull. Niger. Orn. Soc.* 5(19):65
────── 1969. Palaearctic terns on the River Niger in July and August. *Bull. Niger. Orn. Soc.* 6(23):105-106.

——— 1971a. Further notes on Borgu birds. *Bull. Niger. Orn. Soc.* 8(30):25-26.
——— 1971b. Early Palaearctic waders at Kainji and New Bussa in 1969. *Bull. Niger. Orn. Soc.* 8(30):32-34.
WALSH, J. F., CHEKE, R. A. & SOWAH, S. A. 1990. Additional species and breeding records of birds in the Republic of Togo. *Malimbus* 12:2-18.
WARD, P. 1965a. Feeding ecology of the Black-faced Dioch *Quelea quelea* in Nigeria. *Ibis* 107:173-214.
——— 1965b. The breeding biology of the Black-faced Dioch *Quelea quelea* in Nigeria. *Ibis* 107:326-349.
WELLS, D. R. 1966a. The Violet-backed Sunbird nesting in Nigeria. *Bull. Niger. Orn. Soc.* 3(11):72-74.
——— 1966b. A Pomarine Skua inland. *Bull. Niger. Orn. Soc.* 3(12):97.
——— 1966c. Sooty Tern recovery. *Bull. Niger. Orn. Soc.* 3(12):98.
WELLS, D. R. & WALSH, F. 1969. Birds of Northern and Central Borgu. *Bull. Niger. Orn. Soc.* 6(21):1-25, 6(22):63-77, 6(23):78-93.
WILKINSON, R. 1978a. Co-operative breeding in the Chestnut-bellied Starling *Spreo pulcher*. *Bull. Nig. Orn. Soc.* 14(46):71-72.
——— 1978b. Behaviour of Grey-headed Bush Shrikes at their nest. *Bull. Nig. Orn. Soc.* 14:87.
——— 1979. Palaearctic Rufous Scrub-Robin new to Nigeria. *Malimbus* 1(1):65.
——— 1982. Social organisation and communal breeding in the Chestnut-bellied Starling *Spreo pulcher*. *Anim. Behav.* 30:1118-1128.
——— 1983. Biannual Breeding and Moult-Breeding Overlap in the Chestnut-bellied Starling *Spreo pulcher*. *Ibis* 125:353-361.
——— 1988. Long-tailed Glossy Starlings in field and aviary with observations on co-operative breeding in captivity. *Avic. Mag.* 94 : 143-154.
WILKINSON, R. & AIDLEY, D. J. 1982. Additions to local avifaunas: Kano State. *Malimbus* 4:107.
——— 1983. African Reed Warblers in northern Nigeria; morphometrics and the taxonomic debate. *Bull. Brit. Orn. Cl.* 103:135-138.
WILKINSON, R. & BEECROFT, R. 1985. Birds in Falgore Game Reserve, Nigeria. *Malimbus* 7:63-72.
WILKINSON, R., BEECROFT, R. & AIDLEY, D. J. 1982. Nigeria, a new wintering area for the Little Crake *Porzana parva*. *Bull. Brit. Orn. Cl.* 102:139-140.
WILKINSON, R., BEECROFT, R., EZEALOR, A. U. & SHARLAND, R. E. 1987. Dybowski's Twinspot in the Kagoro Hills, Nigeria. *Malimbus* 9:134.
WILKINSON, R. & BROWN, A. E. 1984. Effects of helpers on the feeding rates of nestlings in the Chestnut-bellied Starling *Spreo pulcher*. *J. Anim. Ecol.* 53:301-310.
WOOD, B. 1975. The distribution of races of the Yellow Wagtail overwintering in Nigeria. *Bull. Niger. Orn. Soc.* 11(39):19-26.
WOODS, P. J. E. 1967. Some notes on the birds of the Kigom Hills on the western edge of the Jos Plateau (over 3000 ft.) *Bull. Niger. Orn. Soc.* 4(13/14):29-30.
YOUNG, C. G. 1946. Notes on some birds of the Cameroun Mountain District. *Ibis* 88:348-382.
YOUNG, J. D. 1933. Notes on birds of the Bauchi Plateau, supplementary to Vol II of Bannerman's *The Birds of Tropical West Africa*. *Ibis* Ser.13(1):63-644, Ser.13(3):50-54.
ZACK, S. & LIGON, J. D. 1985. Co-operative breeding in *Lanius* Shrikes. I. Habitat and demography of two sympatric species. *Auk* 102:754-765.

INDEX OF SPECIES

(Page numbers in **bold** refer to the Systematic List)

abdimii, Ciconia 44, **79**
aberrans, Cisticola 21, **203**
abyssinica, Coracias **157**
abyssinica, Hirundo **176**
abyssinica, Illadopsis **222**, 277
abyssinicus, Bucorvus **159**
abyssinicus, Turtur **132**
acuta, Anas **85**, 271
adelberti, Nectarinia **229**
adsimilis, Dicrurus 57, **239**, 290
adusta, Muscicapa **216**, 277
aegyptiacus, Alopochen **82**
aegyptius, Caprimulgus **146**
aegyptius, Pluvianus **113**
aequatoriale, Apaloderma **151**, 277
aequatorialis, Tachymarptis 21, **150**, 273
aereus, Ceuthmochares **140**
aeruginosus, Circus **92**
aethiopica, Hirundo **178**
aethiopica, Threskiornis 50, **81**
aethiops, Myrmecocichla **195**
afer, Euplectes 51, **251**
afer, Nilaus **233**
afer, Ptilostomus **239**
afer, Turtur **131**
affinis, Apus **149**
affinis, Emberiza **265**, 274
africana Actophilornis **110**
africana, Mirafra **171**
africana, Sasia **167**, 274
africanus, Bubo **142**
africanus, Buphagus **244**
africanus, Gyps **89**, 273
africanus, Phalacrocorax 50, **73**
africanus, Spizaetus **97**, 273
aguimp, Motacilla **180**, 274
ahantensis, Francolinus **102**
alba, Calidris **119**, 271
alba, Egretta 50, **77**
alba, Motacilla **180**, 271
alba, Platalea 50, **81**
alba, Tyto **142**
albicapilla, Cossypha **192**
albiceps, Vanellus **117**
albicollis, Ficedula **218**, 272
albicollis, Merops 45, **155**
albifrons, Amblyospiza **253**
albifrons, Anser **82**, 277
albifrons, Myrmecocichla **195**
albifrons, Sterna **128**
albigularis, Phyllastrephus 39, **187**
albinucha, Ploceus **248**
albirostris, Bubalornis **245**
albiventris, Parus **224**
albiventris, Trochocercus **221**
albocristatus, Tockus **160**, 273
albogularis, Francolinus **102**
albus, Corvus **239**
alcinus, Machaerhamphus **87**
alexandrinus, Charadrius **116**, 271

alleni, Porphyrio **107**
alopex, Falco 39, **98**
alpina, Calidris **120**
anaethetus, Sterna **128**
angolensis, Dryoscopus **234**, 277
angolensis, Gypohierax 33, **88**
angolensis, Pitta 43, **171**
angulata, Gallinula **107**
angustirostris, Marmaronetta **86**, 273
anonymus, Cisticola **202**
ansorgei, Andropadus **184**
apiaster, Merops **156**
apivorus, Pernis **87**, 268
apricaria, Pluvialis **116**
apus, Apus **148**
aquatica, Muscicapa **215**
arabs, Ardeotis 60, **109**, 273
ardens, Euplectes **253**
ardesiaca, Egretta 50, **76**
ardosiaceus, Falco **98**
argentatus, Larus **126**
aridulus, Cisticola **205**
arquata, Numenius **121**
arundinaceus, Acrocephalus **200**, 269, 272
asiaticus, Charadrius **116**
astrild, Estrilda 55, **259**
aterrimus, Phoeniculus **159**
atra, Fulica **108**
atrata, Ceratogymna **161**
atricapilla, Sylvia **212**, 269, 272
atriceps, Hypergerus 31, **210**, 287
atricollis, Ortygospiza 55, **260**
atripennis, Dicrurus **239**
atripennis, Phyllanthus **223**
atroflavus, Laniarius **236**
atroflavus, Pogoniulus **163**
audeberti, Pachycoccyx **138**
auguralis, Buteo **95**
aurantium, Anthreptes **227**
aurantius, Ploceus 51, **247**
auratus, Oriolus **240**
auritus, Nettapus 38, **83**
australis, Tchagra **235**
avosetta, Recurvirostra 58, **111**
axillaris, Euplectes **252**
azurea, Coracina **183**

baboecala, Bradypterus **197**
badia, Halcyon **151**
badiceps, Eremomela **209**
badius, Accipiter 45, **93**
baeticatus, Acrocephalus **199**, 284, 285
baglafecht, Ploceus **245**
bairdii, Prinia **205**
balaenarum, Sterna **128**
bannermani, Ploceus **245**
barbarus, Laniarius **236**
barbatus, Apus **148**, 288
barbatus, Criniger **188**
barbatus, Pycnonotus 39, **189**, 283

Index of species

bassana, Sula 72
batesi, Apus 149
batesi, Nectarinia 227
baumanni, Phyllastrephus 186
beaudouini, Circaetus 90
bellicosus, Polemaetus 97
bengalus, Uraeginthus 258, 274
benghalensis, Rostratula 111, 284
bergii, Sterna 127
biarmicus, Falco 99
bicalcaratus, Francolinus 103
bicolor, Dendrocygna 82
bicolor, Lonchura 260
bicolor, Nigrita 254
bicolor, Ploceus 249
bidentatus, Lybius 164
bilineatus, Pogoniulus 163
blanchoti, Telophorus 237, 274
blissetti, Platysteira 220
bocagei, Sheppardia 189, 274
boehmi, Sarothrura 105
bollei, Phoeniculus 59, 158
bonelli, Phylloscopus 41, 212, 272
borin, Sylvia 212, 269, 270, 272
bottae, Oenanthe 194
bouvieri, Nectarinia 229
bouvieri, Scotopelia 143
brachydactyla, Calandrella 173
brachypterus, Cisticola 204
brachyrhynchus, Oriolus 240
brachyura, Sylvietta 209
brehmeri, Turtur 131
brevicaudata, Cameroptera 57, 208, 274
brevirostris, Schoenicola 198, 274
breweri, Merops 154, 273
bullocki, Merops 11, 45, 155, 283, 284
burtoni, Serinus 264
buteo, Buteo 94, 277

cabanisi, Emberiza 265
caerulescens, Estrilda 258
caerulescens, Muscicapa 217
caeruleus, Elanus 88
caesia, Coracina 182
caffer, Apus 149
cailliautii, Campethera 168
calurus, Criniger 188
calva, Treron 130, 273
calvus, Gymnobucco 51, 162
camelus, Struthio 71
camerunensis, Vidua 55
campestris, Anthus 180, 271
camurus, Tockus 160
canicapilla, Bleda 39, 43, 188
canicapilla, Nigrita 255
caniceps, Prionops 238
canorus, Cuculus 139
cantans, Cisticola 202
cantillans, Mirafra 171, 274
cantillans, Sylvia 213, 272
canutus, Calidris 119, 268
capensis, Anas 84
capensis, Asio 144, 290
capensis, Burhinus 112
capensis, Euplectes 252

capensis, Microparra 110
capensis, Oena 132
capensis, Smithornis 171, 277
capensis, Sula 72, 268, 273
capistrata, Nesocharis 255
caprius, Chrysococcyx 140
carbo, Phalacrocorax 50, 72
caroli, Campethera 168
caspia, Sterna 126, 268, 273
cassini, Muscicapa 217
cassini, Neafrapus 147, 273
castanea, Platysteira 219
castaneiceps, Phoeniculus 158
castanilius, Accipiter 93
castro, Oceanodroma 44, 71, 277
caudatus, Lamprotornis 243
cervinus, Anthus 181, 271
cetti, Cettia 197
chalcopterus, Cursorius 113
chalcurus, Lamprotornis 242
chalybaeus, Lamprotornis 242
chalybeata, Vidua 54, 55, 262
chelicuti, Halcyon 59, 152
chicquera, Falco 99
chinensis, Coturnix 101
chloris, Nicator 238
chloronota, Camaroptera 39, 208
chloronotus, Criniger 188, 277
chloropus, Gallinula 107
chloropygia, Nectarinia 230
chloropterus, Lamprotornis 242
chrysoconus, Pogoniulus 163
chubbi, Cisticola 202, 274
ciconia, Ciconia 79, 268, 271
cincta, Riparia 45, 175
cinerascens, Circaetus 91
cinerascens, Melaenornis 214, 274
cinerea, Apalis 207
cinerea, Ardea 77, 269
cinerea, Calandrella 173
cinerea, Glareola 114
cinereus, Circaetus 90
cinereus, Xenus 123, 271, 273
cinnamomeiventris, Myrmecocichla 21, 196
cirrocephalus, Larus 38, 125, 277
clamans, Baeopogon 185
clamans, Spiloptila 206, 274
clamosus, Cuculus 138
clappertoni, Francolinus 103
clara, Motacilla 43, 179
cleaveri, Illadopsis 222, 274
climacurus, Caprimulgus 145
clypeata, Anas 86, 271
coccinigaster, Nectarinia 230
collaris, Anthreptes 226
collaris, Lanius 233
collurio, Lanius 231, 272
collybita, Phylloscopus 41, 211, 272
comitata, Muscicapa 216
communis, Sylvia 212, 270, 272
concolor, Macrosphenus 210
concreta, Platysteira 220
conirostris, Indicator 166, 277
coqui, Francolinus 102
coronatus, Stephanoaetus 97

Index of species

corvina, Corvinella 233, 286
coryphaeus, Pogoniulus 162
coturnix, Coturnix 101, 271
crassirostris, Vanellus 45, 118
crecca, Anas 84, 271
crex, Crex 106
cristata, Corythaeola 136
cristata, Corythornis 153, 273
cristata, Galerida 173
croceus, Macronyx 181
crossleyi, Zoothera 196, 274
cruentus, Telophorus 237, 274
crumeniferus, Leptoptilos 80
cucullata, Lonchura 260
cucullatus, Ploceus 39, 45, 50, **247**
cuculoides, Aviceda 87
cuprea, Nectarinia 230
cupreus, Chrysococcyx 140
curruca, Sylvia 213, 272
cursor, Cursorius 113, 277
curvirostris, Andropadus 184
cuvieri, Falco 99
cyanea, Platysteira 31, **219**
cyanocampter, Cossypha 191
cyanogaster, Coracias 157
cyanolaema, Nectarinia 228
cylindricus, Ceratogymna 161, 274
cyornithopsis, Sheppardia 189, 277

daurica, Hirundo 177
decipiens, Streptopelia 133
delegorguei, Coturnix 101
denhami, Neotis 60, **109**
dentata, Petronia 244
denti, Sylvietta 209
deserti, Ammomanes 172
deserti, Oenanthe 194
diademata, Alethe 192
dominica, Pluvialis 116
dorsti, Cisticola 11, **203**, 277
dougallii, Sterna 127, 268
dubius, Charadrius 115, 268, 271
dubius, Hieraaetus 96
dubius, Lybius 164
duchaillui, Buccanodon 163
dumetorum, Acrocephalus 199, 285
dybowskii, Euschistospiza 55, **257**, 274

ecaudatus, Terathopius 58, **91**
edolioides, Melaenornis 214
egregia, Crex 105
elachus, Dendropicos 169
elata, Ceratogymna 162
elegans, Sarothrura 105
elliotii, Dendropicos 170, 274
epichlora, Urolais 206, 274
episcopus, Ciconia 79
epops, Upupa 159, 271
epulata, Muscicapa 216
erithacus, Psittacus 33, **134**
erythrogaster, Laniarius 236, 274
erythrogaster, Malimbus 250
erythrops, Cisticola 201
erythrops, Quelea 251
erythroptera, Prinia 205

erythropus, Accipiter 93
erythropus, Tringa 122, 271
erythropygia, Pinarocorys 172, 274
erythrorhynchus, Tockus 160
erythrothorax, Stiphrornis 39, **189**
europaeus, Caprimulgus 146, 271
excubitor, Lanius 232
excubitorius, Lanius 232
exilis, Indicator 166
eximia, Bleda 187
eximius, Cisticola 205
exustus, Pterocles 130

falcinellus, Limicola 120, 283
falcinellus, Plegadis 80
familiaris, Cercomela 195
fasciata, Amadina 261
fasciatus, Tockus 59, **160**
ferina, Aythya 86
ferruginea, Calidris 119, 268, 271
ferrugineus, Laniarius 235
finschi, Neocossyphus 193, 274
fistulator, Ceratogymna 161, 273
flammeus, Asio 144
flammulatus, Bias 218, 274
flava, Motacilla 18, 41, **179**, 269, 270, 271
flavicans, Macrosphenus 210
flavicollis, Chlorocichla 186
flavida, Apalis 207
flavifrons, Anthoscopus 225
flavigaster, Hyliota 210
flavigularis, Chrysococcyx 140
flavipes, Tringa 122
flavirostris, Amaurornis 106, 273
flavirostris, Rynchops 130
flaviventris, Emberiza 265
forbesi, Charadrius 115
fraseri, Anthreptes 225
fraseri, Neocossyphus 192, 277
fringilloides, Lonchura 261
frontalis, Sporopipes 245
fulgidus, Onychognathus 241
fulicarius, Phalaropus 44, **124**
fuliginosa, Hirundo 177
fuliginosa, Nectarinia 228
fuliginosa, Psalidoprocne 175
fuligula, Aythya 86
fuligula, Hirundo 21, **177**
fulvescens, Illadopsis 39, **222**, 274
funerea, Vidua 55, **262**, 277
fuscata, Sterna 24, **128**, 268
fuscescens, Dendropicos 169
fusconota, Nigrita 254
fuscus, Larus 126, 268

gabar, Micronisus 92, 273
gabonensis, Dendropicos 169
gabonicus, Anthreptes 226
galactotes, Cercotrichas 193, 271
galactotes, Cisticola 203
gallicus, Circaetus 90
gallinago, Gallinago 120, 270, 271
gambagae, Muscicapa 214
gambensis, Dryoscopus 234
gambensis, Plectropterus 83

Index of species

garrulus, Coracias **157**
garzetta, Egretta 50, **76**, 268
genei, Larus **126**
gilberti, Kupeornis **223**, 274
gladiator, Telophorus **237**, 274
glandarius, Clamator **138**, 271, 288
glareola, Tringa **123**, 268, 270, 271
glaucurus, Eurystomus **158**
goertae, Dendropicos **170**, 274
goliath, Ardea **78**
gracilirostris, Acrocephalus **200**, 277
gracilirostris, Andropadus **184**, 285
gracilis, Andropadus **184**
grillii, Centropus **141**, 273
griseigularis, Myioparus **217**, 274
griseopyga, Pseudhirundo **176**
griseus, Passer **244**
griseus, Puffinus 44, **71**, 273
grus, Grus **108**, 277
gubernator, Lanius **232**
guinea, Columba **133**
gularis, Cuculus **139**, 273
gularis, Egretta **76**, 273
gularis, Eurystomus **158**
gularis, Merops **154**
gularis, Serinus **264**
guttatus, Ixonotus **185**

haematina, Spermophaga 39, **256**
haematopus, Himantornis **104**
hagedash, Bostrychia **80**
haliaetus, Pandion **87**, 268
hartlaubi, Euplectes **253**, 277
hartlaubi, Tockus **160**
hartlaubii, Pteronetta 31, **83**
herberti, Phylloscopus **211**
heuglini, Cossypha 59, **191**
heuglini, Ploceus **247**
hiaticula, Charadrius **115**, 270, 271
himantopus, Himantopus **111**, 271
hirsuta, Tricholaema **164**, 274
hirundineus, Merops **155**
hirundo, Sterna **127**, 268, 271
hispanica, Oenanthe **194**, 271
hordeaceus, Euplectes 51, **252**
hortensis, Sylvia **213**, 272
hortulana, Emberiza **264**, 272
horus, Apus **149**
hottentota, Anas **85**
hottentotta, Turnix **104**
hybridus, Chlidonias **129**, 273
hypogrammica, Pytilia 55, **256**
hypoleuca, Ficedula **217**, 270, 272
hypoleucos, Actitis **123**, 268, 271
hypopyrrha, Streptopelia **134**, 273

ibadanensis, Malimbus 5, 17, 60, 65, **250**, 282, 284
ibis, Bubulcus **75**, 273
ibis, Mycteria **78**, 273
icterina, Hippolais **201**, 272
icterinus, Phyllastrephus **187**
icteropygialis, Eremomela **208**
imberbis, Anomalospiza **253**
incana, Drymocichla **206**, 277

indicator, Baeopogon **185**
indicator, Indicator **166**
infuscata, Muscicapa **215**, 274
inornatus, Caprimulgus **145**
insignis, Ploceus **249**
insignis, Prodotiscus **165**
interjecta, Vidua 54, 55, **263**, 277
intermedia, Egretta 50, **77**
interpres, Arenaria **123**
iriditorques, Columba **132**, 273
isabellae, Cossypha **190**
isabellina, Oenanthe **195**, 277
isabellinus, Lanius **231**, 277

jacobinus, Oxylophus **137**, 273
jacksoni, Apalis **207**, 277
johannae, Nectarinia **230**, 287
juncidis, Cisticola **204**

kempi, Macrosphenus 15, **210**, 277
klaas, Chrysococcyx **140**
krameri, Psittacula **135**

lacteus, Bubo **143**
lamelligerus, Anastomus **78**
lapponica, Limosa **121**
larvata, Columba **132**, 277
larvata, Lagonosticta 55, **258**, 274
larvaticola, Vidua 55
lateralis, Cisticola **202**
lathami, Francolinus 43, **102**
latirostris, Andropadus **185**
lecontei, Ceyx **152**
leschenaultii, Charadrius **116**, 283
leucocephala, Halcyon **151**, 289
leucocephalus, Lybius **164**
leucogaster, Centropus **141**
leucogaster, Cinnyricinclus **243**
leucogaster, Corythornis **153**, 273, 285
leucogaster, Sula **72**
leucolophus, Tauraco **136**
leucolophus, Tigriornis **74**
leucomelas, Parus **224**
leuconotus, Gorsachius **75**, 273
leuconotus, Thalassornis **82**
leucophrys, Anthus **181**
leucopleura, Thescelocichla **186**
leucopogon, Prinia **205**
leucopterus, Chlidonias **129**, 271, 273
leucopyga, Oenanthe **194**
leucopygius, Serinus **263**
leucorhynchus, Laniarius **236**
leucorodia, Platalea **81**
leucosoma, Hirundo **178**
leucostictus, Bubo **143**
leucotis, Eremopterix **174**
leucotis, Otus **142**
leucurus, Vanellus **118**
levaillantii, Oxylophus **138**, 273
limosa, Limosa **121**, 271
lobatus, Lobotos **182**, 277
lobatus, Phalaropus 44, **124**, 277
longicauda, Elminia 31, **220**, 274
longicaudus, Stercorarius **124**
longipennis, Macrodipteryx **146**

Index of species

longuemarei, Anthreptes 226
lopezi, Bradypterus **198**, 274
lopezi, Poliolais **208**, 274
lucida, Hirundo **178**, 277
ludwigii, Dicrurus **238**
luehderi, Laniarius **235**
lugens, Sarothrura **104**
lugubris, Poeoptera **241**
lugubris, Vanellus **118**
luscinia, Luscinia **190**, 271, 282
luscinioides, Locustella **198**, 272
luteifrons, Nigrita **254**
luteolus, Ploceus **246**
luteus, Passer 45, **244**

mackinnoni, Lanius **232**
macrorhynchus, Tauraco **136**
macroura, Vidua 55, **262**
macrourus, Circus **92**, 271
macrourus, Euplectes **252**
macrourus, Urocolius **150**, 273
macrourus, Urotriorchis **94**
maculatus, Indicator **166**
malabarica, Lonchura **260**
malimbica, Halcyon 59, **152**
malimbicus, Malimbus 51, **250**
malimbicus, Merops 37, 51, **156**
margaritatus, Trachyphonus **165**
marginalis, Aenigmatolimnas **106**, 273
marginatus, Charadrius **116**
maxima, Megaceryle **153**, 273
maxima, Sterna **127**
mccalli, Erythrocercus **220**
mechowi, Cercococcyx **139**
media, Gallinago **121**, 268, 271
megarhynchos, Luscinia **190**, 269, 271
meiffrenii, Ortyxelos **103**
melanocephala, Ardea **77**
melanocephalus, Ploceus **248**
melanogaster, Anhinga 50, **73**, 273
melanogaster, Eupodotis **110**
melanogaster, Ploceus **247**
melanoleucus, Accipiter **94**
melanopygia, Telacanthura **147**, 273
melanotos, Sarkidiornis **83**
melba, Pytilia 55, **255**
melba, Tachymarptis **150**, 273
meleagris, Numida **100**, 282
melpoda, Estrilda 55, **259**
mentalis, Melocichla **198**, 274
metabates, Melierax 59, **92**
migrans, Milvus **88**, 268
minimus, Lymnocryptes **120**, 271, 273
minor, Indicator **166**
minor, Lanius **232**
minor, Phoeniconaias **81**, 273
minulla, Nectarinia **230**
minuta, Calidris **119**, 271
minuta, Tchagra **234**
minutus, Anous **129**, 273
minutus, Ixobrychus **74**, 271
minutus, Larus **125**
modesta, Galerida **173**
monachus, Centropus **141**
monachus, Necrosyrtes **89**, 273

monogrammicus, Kaupifalco **94**
montanus, Andropadus **183**
monteiri, Clytospiza 55, **257**
morio, Onychognathus **241**
mozambicus, Serinus **264**
muelleri, Merops **154**
multicolor, Telophorus **237**, 274
musicus, Bias **218**
mystacea, Sylvia **213**, 272, 282

naevia, Coracias **157**
naevia, Locustella **198**
narina, Apaloderma **151**
nasutus, Tockus **160**
natalensis, Caprimulgus **145**
natalensis, Chloropeta **201**
natalensis, Cisticola **204**
natalensis, Cossypha **191**
naumanni, Falco **98**
ndussumensis, Criniger **189**, 274
nebularia, Tringa **122**, 268, 271
niger, Agelastes **100**, 277
niger, Chlidonias **129**, 273
nigeriae, Vidua **54**
nigerrimus, Ploceus 45, 50, 57, **248**
nigra, Ciconia **79**
nigra, Myrmecocichla **195**
nigriceps, Apalis **206**, 287
nigriceps, Eremopterix **174**, 277
nigricollis, Ploceus **246**
nigricollis, Podiceps **72**, 277
nigripennis, Oriolus **240**
nigriscapularis, Caprimulgus **145**, 273
nigrita, Hirundo **178**
nigromitratus, Trochocercus **221**
nilotica, Gelochelidon **126**, 273
nisoria, Sylvia **213**, 283
nitens, Malimbus **250**
nitens, Psalidoprocne **174**
nitens, Terpsiphone **221**, 274
nitidula, Mandingoa **256**, 274
niveicapilla, Cossphya **191**
nivosa, Campethera **168**
nonnula, Estrilda **255**
nordmanni, Glareola **114**
novaeseelandiae, Anthus **180**
nuba, Neotis **109**, 277
nubicus, Lanius **233**
nubicus, Merops 37, 51, **156**
nuchalis, Glareola **114**
nycticorax, Nycticorax **75**, 268
nyroca, Aythya **86**

obscura, Psalidoprocne **174**
obsoletus, Picoides **170**, 274
occipitalis, Aegypius **90**, 273
occipitalis, Lophaetus **96**
oceanicus, Oceanites **44**, 71
ochropus, Tringa **123**, 271
ocreatus, Melaenornis **214**, 274
ocularis, Ploceus **246**
oculeus, Canirallus **104**
oedicnemus, Burhinus **112**
oenanthe, Oenanthe **194**, 271
olivacea, Bostrychia **80**

Index of species

olivacea, Nectarinia 227
olivaceus, Linurgus 264
olivascens, Muscicapa 215
olivetorum, Hippolais 201, 272
olivinus, Cercococcyx 139
onocrotalus, Pelecanus 39, 51, 73
oreas, Picathartes 224, 277, 282
orientalis, Batis 218
orientalis, Merops 156
orientalis, Vidua 54, 55, 263
oriolus, Oriolus 240, 272
oritis, Nectarinia 228
orix, Euplectes 51, 252
ostralegus, Haematopus 42, 111
ostrinus, Pyrenestes 256
ovampensis, Accipiter 93

pallida, Hippolais 200, 272
pallidus, Apus 148
pallidus, Melaenornis 213, 274
paludicola, Riparia 175
palustris, Acrocephalus 200
paradisaea, Sterna 128, 268
parasiticus, Stercorarius 124
parva, Porzana 106, 277, 291
parvulus, Anthoscopus 225
parvus, Cypsiurus 148
pavonina, Balearica 60, 108
pectoralis, Coracina 183
pecuarius, Charadrius 115
peli, Gymnobucco 51, 162
peli, Scotopelia 143
pelios, Turdus 197
pelzelni, Ploceus 246
penelope, Anas 84
pennatus, Hieraaetus 96
percnopterus, Neophron 89
peregrinus, Falco 100
perlatum, Glaucidium 144
persa, Tauraco 59, 136
persicus, Merops 156, 273
petiti, Campephaga 182, 277
petrosus, Ptilopachus 21, 101
phaeopus, Numenius 121, 268
phoenicea, Campephaga 182
phoenicoptera, Pytilia 55, 255
phoenicurus, Phoenicurus 193, 270, 271
picta, Ceyx 153
piscator, Crinifer 137
platurus, Anthreptes 226
platyrhynchos, Anas 84, 265
plebejus, Turdoides 223
plumatus, Prionops 238, 274, 283, 285
plumbeus, Myioparus 217
podobe, Cercotrichas 193
poecilolaemus, Dendropicos 169
poensis, Batis 219, 274
poensis, Bubo 143
poensis, Laniarius 236
poensis, Neocossyphus 192
poensis, Phyllastrephus 187
poliocephala, Alethe 192
poliocephalus, Phyllastrephus 187
poliopareia, Estrilda 258
polioptera, Cossypha 59, 190

poliothorax, Kakamega 223, 274
polyglotta, Hippolais 201, 272
pomarina, Aquila 95, 277
pomarinus, Stercorarius 38, 124
porphyrio, Porphyrio 107
porzana, Porzana 106
prasina, Hylia 211
pratincola, Glareola 114
preussi, Hirundo 177, 274
preussi, Nectarinia 229
preussi, Ploceus 249
princei, Zoothera 197, 274
pristoptera, Psalidoprocne 174
pucherani, Guttera 100, 273
puffinus, Puffinus 44, 71, 277
pugnax, Philomachus 120, 268, 270, 271
pulchella, Nectarinia 231
pulchella, Phyllolais 207, 274
pulcher, Lamprotornis 243, 274
pulchra, Apalis 206, 277
pulchra, Sarothrura 105
pullaria, Agapornis 135
punctifrons, Anthoscopus 224
punctuligera, Campethera 168
purpuratus, Trachyphonus 165
purpurea, Ardea 77, 268
purpureiceps, Lamprotornis 242
purpureus, Lamprotornis 242
purpureus, Phoeniculus 159
pusilla, Eremomela 209
pusillus, Merops 155
puveli, Illadopsis 222, 274
pygargus, Circus 92, 268
pyrrhogaster, Dendropicos 59, 169, 274

quadribrachys, Alcedo 153
quadricinctus, Pterocles 21, 130
quelea, Quelea 16, 36, 45, 251, 291
querquedula, Anas 85, 268, 270, 271
quiscalina, Campephaga 182

racheliae, Malimbus 249
ralloides, Ardeola 75, 268, 271
rapax, Aquila 95
rara, Lagonosticta 55, 257
raricola, Vidua 54, 55, 262, 277
rectirostris, Anthreptes 226
regulus, Prodotiscus 165
reichenbachii, Nectarinia 228
reichenovii, Cryptospiza 256
reinwardtii, Turdoides 223
ridibundus, Larus 38, 125
riocourii, Chelictinia 44, 45, 88, 273
riparia, Riparia 37, 175, 268, 270, 271
roberti, Cossyphicula 190, 274
robustus, Cisticola 203, 277
robustus, Melichneutes 165
robustus, Poicephalus 135
roseogrisea, Streptopelia 134
rubetra, Saxicola 193, 270, 271
rubricata, Lagonosticta 55, 258
rubriceps, Anaplectes 251, 274
rubricollis, Malimbus 251
rudis, Ceryle 154, 289
rueppellii, Gyps 39, 51, 89

Index of species

rufa, Mirafra 172
rufa, Sarothrura 105
rufescens, Acrocephalus 200
rufescens, Calandrella 173, 271
rufescens, Pelecanus 73
ruficeps, Cisticola 203
ruficollis, Corvus 240
ruficollis, Jynx 167
ruficollis, Tachybaptus 72, 273
ruficrista, Eupodotis 109
rufigena, Caprimulgus 45, 146
rufinus, Buteo 95, 287, 288
rufipennis, Butastur 94
rufipennis, Illadopsis 222, 274
rufiventer, Terpsiphone 57, 221
rufiventris, Ardeola 75
rufocinnamomea, Mirafra 172
rufogularis, Apalis 207
rufolateralis, Smithornis 171
rufopicta, Lagonosticta 55, 257
rufus, Cisticola 204
rushiae, Pholidornis 261
rustica, Hirundo 179, 269, 270, 271

sabini, Dryoscopus 234
sabini, Larus 125
sabini, Rhaphidura 147, 273
sandvicensis, Sterna 127, 268
saxatilis, Monticola 196, 272
scandens, Pyrrhurus 186
schoenobaenus, Acrocephalus 199, 270, 272
scirpaceus, Acrocephalus 199, 269, 272, 284
scolopaceus, Pogoniulus 162
scops, Otus 142, 271
scutatus, Malimbus 250
seimundi, Nectarinia 227
semirufa, Hirundo 176
semitorquata, Streptopelia 133
senator, Lanius 233, 270, 272
senegala, Lagonosticta 55, 257
senegala, Tchagra 235
senegalensis, Batis 218
senegalensis, Burhinus 112
senegalensis, Centropus 141
senegalensis, Dryoscopus 234
senegalensis, Ephippiorhynchus 80
senegalensis, Eupodotis 110
senegalensis, Halcyon 59, 152
senegalensis, Hirundo 176
senegalensis, Nectarinia 46, 229
senegalensis, Podica 108
senegalensis, Streptopelia 39, 134
senegalensis, Zosterops 225
senegallus, Vanellus 117
senegalus, Poicephalus 34, 135
serina, Calyptocichla 185
serpentarius, Sagittarius 97
sethsmithi, Muscicapa 216
shelleyi, Nesocharis 36, 255, 274
sibilatrix, Phylloscopus 41, 212, 270, 272
similis, Anthus 181
simplex, Chlorocichla 186
sjostedti, Columba 132, 273
sjöstedti, Glaucidium 144, 277
skua, Catharacta 124, 273

smithii, Hirundo 178
solitarius, Cuculus 138
solitarius, Monticola 196, 272
sparsa, Anas 85, 286
spectabilis, Dryotriorchis 91
spilogaster, Hieraaetus 96
spilonotus, Salpornis 225
spinosus, Vanellus 118
splendidus, Lamprotornis 243
squamatus, Francolinus 102
squatarola, Pluvialis 117
stagnatalis, Tringa 122, 271
stellaris, Botaurus 74
stolidus, Anous 129
strepera, Anas 84
striata, Muscicapa 214, 269, 272
striatus, Butorides 31, 76
striatus, Colius 150
sturmii, Ixobrychus 74
subbuteo, Falco 99
subcylindricus, Ceratogymna 161, 274
subflava, Amandava 55, 260
subflava, Prinia 205
subsulphureus, Pogoniulus 163
sulfureopectus, Telophorus 237, 274
superba, Nectarinia 231
superciliaris, Camaroptera 208
superciliosus, Plocepasser 245
superciliosus, Ploceus 249
superciliosus, Vanellus 118
svecica, Luscinia 190, 271
sylvatica, Turnix 103
syndactyla, Bleda 187

tachiro, Accipiter 93, 273
tahapisi, Emberiza 21, 265, 285
tectus, Vanellus 117
temminckii, Calidris 119, 271
temminckii, Cursorius 113
tephrolaemus, Andropadus 183
tessmanni, Muscicapa 216
tinnunculus, Falco 24, 98, 268
tonsa, Platysteira 219
torquata, Saxicola 193
torquilla, Jynx 167, 271
totanus, Tringa 122, 268, 271
tracheliotus, Aegypius 90
tricollaris, Charadrius 45, 115
tricolor, Ploceus 248
tristigma, Caprimulgus 21, 146, 288
trivialis, Anthus 181, 271
trochilus, Phylloscopus 41, 211, 269, 270, 272
troglodytes, Cisticola 204
troglodytes, Estrilda 259
tullbergi, Campethera 168
turtur, Streptopelia 134, 271
tympanistria, Turtur 131
typus, Polyboroides 91, 273

umbretta, Scopus 31, 78
undulata, Anas 85
unicincta, Columba 132, 277
unicolor, Apus 148, 277
urbica, Delichon 179, 269, 271
ussheri, Muscicapa 215, 274
ussheri, Telacanthura 147, 273

Index of species

variegatus, Merops 155
velatus, Ploceus 247
venusta, Nectarinia 229
vermiculatus, Burhinus 112
verticalis, Nectarinia 228
vespertinus, Falco 99
vexillaria, Macrodipteryx 45, 147
viduata, Dendrocygna 82
vieilloti, Lybius 164
vinacea, Streptopelia 133
violacea, Hyliota 211
violacea, Musophaga 137
virens, Andropadus 39, 183
virens, Sylvietta 209

virgo, Anthropoides 108
viridis, Terpsiphone 221
vittatum, Apaloderma 151
vocifer, Haliaeetus 88

waalia, Treron 131
wahlbergi, Aquila 96
walleri, Onychognathus 241
willcocksi, Indicator 167
wilsoni, Vidua 54, 55, **262**, 277
woodfordii, Strix **144**, 273
woodhousei, Parmoptila 254

xantholophus, Dendropicos **170**, 274

INDEX OF GENERA

(Systematic List only)

Accipiter 93–94
Acrocephalus 199–200
Actophilornis 110
Actitis 123
Aegypius 90
Aenigmatolimnas 106
Agelastes 100
Agapornis 135
Alcedo 153
Alethe 192
Alopochen 82
Amadina 261
Amandava 260
Amaurornis 106
Amblyospiza 253
Ammomanes 172
Anaplectes 251
Anas 84–86, 265
Anastomus 78
Andropadus 183–85
Anhinga 73
Anomalospiza 253
Anous 129
Anser 82
Anthoscopus 224–25
Anthreptes 225–27
Anthropoides 108
Anthus 180–81
Apalis 206–07
Apaloderma 151
Apus 148–49
Aquila 95–96
Ardea 77–78
Ardeola 75
Ardeotis 109
Arenaria 123
Asio 144
Aviceda 87
Aythya 86

Baeopogon 185
Balearica 108
Batis 218–19
Bias 218
Bleda 187–88
Bostrychia 80
Botaurus 74
Bradypterus 197–98
Bubalornis 245
Bubo 142–43
Bubulcus 75
Buccanodon 163
Bucorvus 159
Buphagus 244
Burhinus 112
Butastur 94
Buteo 94–95
Butorides 76

Calandrella 173

Calidris 119–20
Calyptocichla 185
Camaroptera 208
Campephaga 182
Campethera 168
Canirallus 104
Caprimulgus 145–46
Catharacta 124
Centropus 141
Ceratogymna 161–62
Cercococcyx 139
Cercomela 195
Cercotrichas 193
Ceryle 154
Cettia 197
Ceuthmochares 140
Ceyx 152–53
Charadrius 115–16
Chelictinia 88
Chlidonias 129
Chlorocichla 186
Chloropeta 201
Chrysococcyx 140
Ciconia 79
Cinnyricinclus 243
Circaetus 90–91
Circus 92
Cisticola 201–05
Clamator 138
Clytospiza 257
Colius 150
Columba 132–33
Coracias 157
Coracina 182–83
Corvinella 233
Corvus 239–40
Corythaeola 136
Corythornis 153
Cossypha 190–92
Cossyphicula 190
Coturnix 101
Crex 105–06
Crinifer 137
Criniger 188–89
Cryptospiza 256
Cuculus 138–39
Cursorius 113
Cypsiurus 148

Delichon 179
Dendrocygna 82
Dendropicos 169–70
Dicrurus 238–39
Drymocichla 206
Dryoscopus 234
Dryotriorchis 91

Egretta 76–77
Elanus 88
Elminia 220

Index of Genera

Emberiza 264–65
Ephippiorhynchus 80
Eremomela 208–09
Eremopterix 174
Erythrocercus 220
Estrilda 258–59
Euplectes 251–53
Eupodotis 109–10
Eurystomus 158
Euschistospiza 257

Falco 98–100
Ficedula 217–18
Francolinus 102–03
Fulica 108

Galerida 173
Gallinago 120–21
Gallinula 107
Gelochelidon 126
Glareola 114
Glaucidium 144
Gorsachius 75
Grus 108
Guttera 100
Gymnobucco 162
Gypohierax 88
Gyps 89

Haematopus 111
Halcyon 151–52
Haliaeetus 88
Hieraaetus 96
Himantopus 111
Himantornis 104
Hippolais 200–01
Hirundo 176–79
Hylia 211
Hyliota 210–11
Hypergerus 210

Illadopsis 222
Indicator 166–67
Ixobrychus 74
Ixonotus 185

Jynx 167

Kakamega 223
Kaupifalco 94
Kupeornis 223

Lagonosticta 257–58
Lamprotornis 242–43
Laniarius 235–36
Lanius 231–33
Larus 125–26
Leptoptilos 80
Limicola 120
Limosa 121
Linurgus 264
Lobotos 182
Locustella 198
Lonchura 260–61
Lophaetus 96

Luscinia 190
Lybius 164
Lymnocryptes 120

Machaerhamphus 87
Macrodipteryx 146–47
Macronyx 181
Macrosphenus 210
Malimbus 249–51
Mandingoa 256
Marmaronetta 86
Megaceryle 153
Melaenornis 213–14
Melichneutes 165
Melierax 92
Melocichla 198
Merops 154–56
Micronisus 92
Microparra 110
Milvus 88
Mirafra 171–72
Monticola 196
Motacilla 179–80
Muscicapa 214–17
Musophaga 137
Myioparus 217
Mycteria 78
Myrmecocichla 195–96

Neafrapus 147
Nectarinia 227–31
Necrosyrtes 89
Neocossyphus 192–93
Neophron 89
Neotis 109
Nesocharis 255
Nettapus 83
Nicator 238
Nigrita 254–55
Nilaus 233
Numenius 121
Numida 100
Nycticorax 75

Oceanites 71
Oceanodroma 71
Oena 132
Oenanthe 194–95
Onychognathus 241
Oriolus 240
Ortygospiza 260
Ortyxelos 103
Otus 142
Oxylophus 137–38

Pachycoccyx 138
Pandion 87
Parmoptila 254
Parus 224
Passer 244
Pelecanus 73
Pernis 87
Petronia 244
Phalacrocorax 72–73
Phalaropus 124

Index of Genera

Philomachus 120
Phoeniconaias 81
Phoeniculus 158–59
Phoenicurus 193
Pholidornis 261
Phyllanthus 223
Phyllastrephus 186–87
Phyllolais 207
Phylloscopus 211–12
Picathartes 224
Picoides 170
Pinarocorys 172
Pitta 171
Platalea 81
Platysteira 219–20
Plectropterus 83
Plegadis 80
Plocepasser 245
Ploceus 245–49
Pluvialis 116–17
Pluvianus 113
Podica 108
Podiceps 72
Poeoptera 241
Pogoniulus 162–63
Poicephalus 135
Polemaetus 97
Poliolais 208
Polyboroides 91
Porphyrio 107
Porzana 106
Prinia 205
Prionops 238
Prodotiscus 165
Psalidoprocne 174–75
Pseudhirundo 176
Psittacula 135
Psittacus 134
Pterocles 130
Pteronetta 83
Ptilopachus 101
Ptilostomus 239
Puffinus 71
Pycnonotus 189
Pyrenestes 256
Pyrrhurus 186
Pytilia 255–56

Quelea 251

Recurvirostra 111
Rhaphidura 147
Riparia 175
Rostratula 111
Rynchops 130

Sagittarius 97
Salpornis 225
Sarkidiornis 83
Sarothrura 105

Sasia 167
Saxicola 193
Schoenicola 198
Scopus 78
Scotopelia 143
Serinus 263–64
Sheppardia 189
Smithornis 171
Spermophaga 256
Spiloptila 206
Spizaetus 97
Sporopipes 245
Stephanoaetus 97
Stercorarius 124
Sterna 126–28
Stiphrornis 189
Streptopelia 133–34
Strix 144
Struthio 71
Sula 72
Sylvia 212–13
Sylvietta 209

Tachybaptus 72
Tachymarptis 150
Tauraco 136
Tchagra 234–35
Telacanthura 147
Telophorus 237
Terathopius 91
Terpsiphone 221
Thalassornis 82
Thescelocichla 186
Threskiornis 81
Tigrionis 74
Tockus 160
Trachyphonus 165
Treron 130–31
Tricholaema 164
Tringa 122–23
Trochocercus 221
Turdoides 223
Turdus 197
Turnix 103–04
Turtur 131–32
Tyto 142

Upupa 159
Uraeginthus 258
Urocolius 150
Urolais 206
Urotriorchis 94

Vanellus 117–18
Vidua 261–63

Xenus 123

Zoothera 196–97
Zosterops 225

INDEX OF ENGLISH NAMES

(Systematic List only)

Akalats 189
Alethes 192
Alseonaxes 215–17
Anaplectes 251
Ant-Thrush 192
Apalises 206–07
Avocet 111

Babblers 223
Barbets 162–65
Bateleur 91
Batises 218–19
Bee-eaters 154–56
Bishops 251–52
Bitterns 74
Blackcap 212
Blue-bill 256
Bluethroat 190
Booby 72
Boubous 235–36
Bristlebills 187–88
Broadbills 171
Brubru 233
Buffalo-weaver 245
Bulbul 189
Buntings 265
Bush-Larks 171–72
Bush-Shrikes 234–35, 237
Bush-Warbler 197
Bustards 109–10
Button-Quails 103–04
Buzzards 87, 94–95

Camaropteras 208
Canary 264
Chats 195
Chiffchaff 211
Cisticolas 201–05
Cliff-Chat 196
Coot 108
Cordon-bleu 258
Cormorants 72–73
Corncrake 106
Coucals 141
Coursers 113
Crakes 104–06
Cranes 108
Creeper 225
Crimson-wing 256
Crocodile Bird 113
Crombecs 209
Crow 239
Cuckoos 137–40
Cuckoo Falcon 87
Cuckoo-Shrikes 182–83
Curlews 112, 121
Cut-Throat 261

Darter 73
Doves 131–34

Drongos 238–39
Ducks 82–83, 85–86
Dunlin 120

Eagles 88, 90–91, 95–97
Eagle-Owls 142–43
Egrets 75–77
Eremomelas 208–09

Falcons 99–100
Finfoot 108
Fire-Finches 257–58
Fishing-Owls 143
Flamingo 81
Flufftails 104–05
Flycatchers 213–18, 220–21
Flycatcher-Thrushes 192–93
Flycatcher-Warbler 201
Francolins 102–03

Gadwall 84
Gallinules 107
Gannet 72
Garganey 85
Geese 82–83
Godwits 121
Goldbreast 260
Gonoleks 236
Goshawks 92
Grassbird 198
Grass-Warblers 198
Grebes 72
Greenbuls 183–89
Greenshank 122
Griffon 89
Ground-Thrushes 196–97
Guineafowl 100
Gulls 125–26

Hadada 80
Hamerkop 78
Harriers 92
Harrier Hawk 91
Hawks 87, 94
Hawk-Eagles 96–97
Helmet-Shrike 238
Herons 74–78
Hill-Babbler 222
Hobbies 99
Honeybirds 165
Honeyguides 165–67
Hoopoe 159
Hornbills 159–62
Hylia 211
Hyliotas 210–11

Ibises 80–81
Illadopses 222–23
Indigobirds 262

Index of English names

Kestrels 98
Kingfishers 151–54
Kites 88
Knot 119

Lapwings 118
Larks 171–73
Leaf-Loves 186
Lily-trotters 110
Longbills 210
Longclaw 181
Longtail 206
Lovebird 135

Magpie 239
Malimbes 249–51
Mallard 84, 265
Mannikins 260–61
Martins 175, 177, 179
Melba Finch 255
Moorhens 107
Mountain-Babbler 223
Mousebirds 150

Negro-Finches 254–55
Nicator 238
Nightingale 190
Nightjars 145–47
Noddies 129

Olive-backs 255
Orioles 240
Oriole-Finch 264
Ortolan 264
Osprey 87
Ostrich 71
Owlets 144
Owls 142, 144
Oxpecker 244
Oyster-catcher 111

Painted-Snipe 111
Parakeet 135
Parrots 134–35
Partridge 101
Pelicans 73
Penduline Tits 224–25
Petronia 244
Phalaropes 124
Piapiac 239
Piculet 167
Pigeons 130–33
Pintail 85
Pipits 180–81
Pitta 171
Plantain-eater 137
Plovers 113, 115–18
Pochards 86
Pratincoles 114
Prinias 205
Puff-back Shrikes 234
Pytilias 255–56

Quails 101
Quail-Finch 260

Quail-Plover 103
Queleas 251

Rails 104
Raven 240
Redshanks 122
Redstart 193
Robin 189
Robin-Chats 190–92
Rockfowl 224
Rock Thrushes 196
Rollers 157–58
Ruff 120

Sanderling 119
Sandgrouse 130
Sand-Martins 175
Sandpipers 119–20, 122–23
Sand-Plover 115–16
Saw-wings 174–75
Scops Owls 142
Scrub-Robins 193
Scrub-Warbler 198
Secretary Bird 97
Seed-cracker 256
Seed-eaters 263–64
Serpent-Eagle 91
Shearwaters 71
Shikra 93
Shoveler 86
Shrikes 231–33, 238
Silver-bill 260
Skimmer 130
Skuas 124
Snipe 120–21
Sparrows 244
Sparrowhawks 93–94
Sparrow-Larks 174
Sparrow-Weaver 245
Spinetails 147
Spoonbills 81
Sprosser 190
Starlings 241–43
Stilt 111
Stints 119
Stonechat 193
Storks 78–80
Storm-petrels 71
Sunbirds 225–31
Swallows 176–79
Swifts 148–50

Teal 84–86
Terns 126–29
Thicknees 112
Thrushes 197
Tinkerbirds 162–63
Tits 224
Tit-Flycatcher 217
Tit-Weaver 261
Trogons 151
Turacos 136–37
Turnstone 123
Twin-spots 256–57

Index of English names

Vultures 88–90

Wagtails 179–80
Warblers 197–201, 206–08, 210–13
Wattle-eyes 219–20
Waxbills 258–59
Weavers 245–50, 253
Weaver-Finch 254
Wheatears 194–95
Whimbrel 121
Whinchat 193
White-Eye 225

Whitethroats 212–13
Whydahs 253, 262–63
Widow-birds 252
Wigeons 84
Wood-Doves 131–132
Wood-Hoopoes 158–59
Woodpeckers 168–70
Wrynecks 167

Yellow-bill 140
Yellowlegs 122